Points of Departure

A Collection of Contemporary Essays

THIRD EDITION

Michelle J. Brazier

Are experiences shape who we are and our voice. Our voices are unique and should be expressed. Jay-Z and Zadie Smith explain in their work how we are limited, structed, are freed by that experience. Jay-Z experienced hardships on the grungy streets of Brooklyn, NY. While Zadie Smith coming from a multicultural background struggled to find her voices. Thee experiences in life shapes who they are.

Limited

Shifted

Freed

Conclusion

CENGAGE Learning

Australia • Brazil • Japan • Korea • Mexico • Singapore • Spain • United Kingdom • United States

Points of Departure: A Collection of Contemporary Essays, Third Edition
Michelle J. Brazier

Executive Editors:
Maureen Staudt
Michael Stranz

Senior Project Development Manager:
Linda deStefano

Marketing Specialist:
Courtney Sheldon

Senior Production/Manufacturing Manager:
Donna M. Brown

PreMedia Manager:
Joel Brennecke

Sr. Rights Acquisition Account Manager:
Todd Osborne

Cover Image:
Getty Images*

*Unless otherwise noted, all cover images used by Custom Solutions, a part of Cengage Learning, have been supplied courtesy of Getty Images with the exception of the Earthview cover image, which has been supplied by the National Aeronautics and Space Administration (NASA).

ISBN-13: 978-1-133-06802-0

ISBN-10: 1-133-06802-2

Cengage Learning
5191 Natorp Boulevard
Mason, Ohio 45040
USA

Cengage Learning is a leading provider of customized learning solutions with office locations around the globe, including Singapore, the United Kingdom, Australia, Mexico, Brazil, and Japan. Locate your local office at:
international.cengage.com/region.
Cengage Learning products are represented in Canada by Nelson Education, Ltd.
For your lifelong learning solutions, visit **custom.cengage.com.**
Visit our corporate website at **cengage.com.**

Printed in the United States of America

Contents

Introduction v

Lisa Belkin, *The Made-to-Order Savior* 1

Wendell Berry, *God, Science, and Imagination* 21

Susan Blackmore, *Strange Creatures* 31

Ian Bremmer, *Democracy in Cyberspace: What Technology Can and Cannot Do for Us* 41

Amy Chua, *Why Chinese Mothers are Superior* 51

Alain de Botton, *On Habit* 59

Diana L. Eck, *Preface: After September 11 & Introduction to a New America* 67

James Fallows, *Win in China!* 101

Janet A. Flammang, *The Taste for Civilization: Food, Politics, and Civil Society* 111

Malcolm Gladwell, *Small Change: Why the Revolution Will Not Be Tweeted* 133

Jane Goodall, *In the Forests of Gombe* 145

Adam Gopnik, *Bumping into Mr. Ravioli* 153

Alison Gopnik, *Possible Worlds: Why Do Children Pretend?* 163

Arlie Russell Hochschild, *From the Frying Pan into the Fire* 183

Naomi Klein, *Fences of Enclosure, Windows of Possibility* 195

Nicholas D. Kristof and Sheryl WuDunn, *The Girl Effect* 203

Gregory Orr, *Return to Hayneville* 217

Lauren Slater, *Who Holds the Clicker?* 233

Zadie Smith, *Speaking in Tongues* **247**

Sherry Turkle, *Alone Together* **263**

Jeanette Winterson, *The World and Other Places* **283**

Kenji Yoshino, *Covering: The Hidden Assault on Our Civil Rights* **293**

Contributors **319**

Introduction

Contemporary "Composition as Explanation" and Our Time-Sense

Consider the subtitle of this book you are holding, *Points of Departure: A Collection of Contemporary Essays*. What is a "contemporary essay"? We could say a number of things: an essay of the moment, current, of the same period as something else, modern. But in these days of immediacy via technology, instant communication and information, should our idea of what "contemporary" means be reconsidered? Is something written a day ago, a year ago, five years ago, still "contemporary"? What does "contemporary" mean in a world where a click of the finger brings us immediately across space and time? In order to answer that question, I'd like to start with what may seem to be, well, very anti-contemporary: I'd like to turn first to the past and introduce you to a somewhat difficult thought-experiment by an admittedly difficult writer.

In her essay from 1926, "Composition as Explanation," Gertrude Stein works through what it means to be a contemporary artist. She proposes a connection between what she calls "composition" and "time-sense," that is, the time that passes between an artist creating a composition or work of art, the public experiencing that composition, and then remembering it later. For Stein, being "contemporary" actually meant being unaccepted and misunderstood, because the rest of the world had not yet caught up to her vision as a modern artist. The common expression for this phenomenon is that "an artist is ahead of his or her time." But Stein would say that an artist is absolutely of her time; the problem is that nobody, none of her "contemporaries," can recognize this until later. She put it this way: "Those who are creating the modern composition authentically are naturally only of importance when they are dead because by that time the modern composition having become past is classified and the description of it is classical. That is the reason why the creator of the new composition in the arts is an outlaw until he is a classic..." In other words, the works of real value are only recognized as such long after the artist created them, and no doubt, long after that artist has moved on to something else that the general public now regards as unacceptable or unworthy in that new time-sense. In this understanding of "contemporaneity" it is nearly impossible for the average person to figure out what will be of lasting value in the moments we live through. We will only learn after time has passed. So what does this all mean for our Collection of Contemporary Essays? Are they "contemporary" if we consider them like Stein would? Let's come back to the present to push our thought experiment a bit further, and hopefully begin connecting it to you and this book.

This book you are holding, by nature of being in print, will be out of date before it is even in your hands. That is the reality of print communication today. So what is the point of calling this a contemporary collection? Do I have an argument to stand on for your having to purchase, read, reflect on, and write about these essays that are already dated? Can we even call them "contemporary"? In short, I believe I do and I believe that they are, and here is why: we have the same problem today that Gertrude Stein recognized in 1926. It is nearly impossible to tell what will be really and truly lasting. But those ideas, those issues, those problems for humanity, the truly lasting ones, they are the ones we want you to learn about, to become smarter and more knowledgeable about than we, your instructors, are. In fact, we are counting on you for this.

What we need more than anything in higher education today is a renewed relationship between writing, reading, and reflection. What does this mean? For a quick example, what was the last thing you read that you thought about deeply for more than 10 uninterrupted minutes? Can you remember what it was? If so, I applaud you for sustained thought about one thing in an era of deliberate distractions. If not, I must admit I am not surprised. Contemporary culture, such as it is, does not reward sustained, uninterrupted, thought. It takes work and it takes commitment to concentrate on one thing. I would like to propose that by being forced (assuming you're reading these essays for a required class), you have an opportunity to experience, perhaps for the first time, a serious relationship between writing, reading, reflection, and contemporary thought. Some of this opportunity comes because of when you are reading these essays, our time-sense.

It seems to me that in 2011, the second decade of the 21st century, we have become settled in this new millennium, knowing that we will probably not live to see the next, and so are wondering what will happen in the 90 years until we celebrate a new beginning? Part of that wondering, not being able to see the future, has us reflecting back on our origins: the origins of humankind, the origins of civil rights, the origins of economic crises, of religious tolerance and intolerance, of sexual discrimination, of the risks and benefits of public and private lives, and the effects of technology. What does it mean when our "contemporary" thoughts and concerns are consumed with the past? When we are trying as a society, as a nation, as a culture, as a people, as a race, to figure out where to go from here mostly by finally reflecting on where we've been?

This cultural reflection is especially strange given how consumed we also are with what Stein called the "continuous present." Think Twitter and you have a real idea of what she meant. Here is her explanation: "Continuous present is a continuous present. [In my book The Making of Americans] I made a thousand pages of a continuous present. Continuous present is one thing and beginning again and again is another thing. These are both things. And then there is using everything... in [these books] there was an elaboration of the complexities of using everything and of a continuous present and of beginning again and again and again." The main difference between Stein's continuous present in her writing, and ours with our continual status updates of "What's on your mind?" is that we are not conscious about "making" anything as we begin again and again. There is no "elaboration of the complexities" as Stein described. Our concurrent looking back to the past may be, in part, a symptom of the daily whitenoise of the continuous present, a need for grounding, not unlike what we experience when we read Gertrude Stein.

We are on a cusp, not sure whether the future will get better or worse, but it seems, also, that we are starting to believe that we have an active role to play in which direction we go. Not just governments, but individuals, can influence the direction of our attention, if only for a few moments. Indeed, moments are frequently all we have. So much of our current existence seems caught up with documenting our own lives, via Twitter, Facebook, or YouTube, or the next social media tool that renders these obsolete. A single video gone viral may capture everyone (who has access to it) for a day, and disappear, and we simply move on to the next one. Will these be the stories we remember? The anxiety is whether what we remember will have any meaningful consequence at all. When we look back on this period, what will we see? What will these "compositions" mean to us? How will we feel? How are our individual and collective memories being shaped by the massive amount of information we take in, and let loose, every day? The real question is whether and how our current stories will hold up over time.

The manner of recording these stories will change, but I believe that we are in a period now—the period during your college lives—where this idea of the "contemporary," the idea of this time-sense we are living in now, needs to become more than an accumulation of cultural references that imprint randomly on our collective consciousness. If we want to play an active role in shaping the future, we need to connect the speed at which we can post an update with the reflection that thinking on the past provides. We to elaborate on the complexities of our lives.

In this reader, we consider the tension between the stories that persist, that have held our attention for decades, and those we are writing now on a daily basis – the stories of your textual lives – those texts that seem so ephemeral but can get you in trouble, the video that seems like a lark, but can cause great damage to your career. These are the risks and challenges of our contemporary lives. How different they seem from the challenge Gertrude Stein had in being understood as a difficult writer! And yet, we are all still caught in a "time-sense" that produces disconnection, both for the creator and the audience. How do these examples relate to the stories of the 1950s, 60s, and 70s which some of our authors in this reader remember and tell? Or to the events of the 2000s that would have seemed impossible even a few years before?

One of my goals for you with this reader is to begin thinking about your own reading and writing within these larger time-space contexts. To understand that the words you read and produce are part of a history of reading and writing, that the stories you tell are documenting a period that is worth remembering. The other goal is for you to believe that we can, in this age of disposable everything, create lasting ideas, and for you to want what you read and write to be substantial enough to be worth remembering in ten years. That requires something I also believe we are ready for and desperately need: reflection. After a whirlwind decade of everything new and change coming fast, we need a breather. We need to slow down a moment, consider how far we've come, how we've gotten here, and ponder where we want to go next.

So to return to the idea of "contemporary" that began this introduction. I'm not sure what Gertrude Stein would say about texting, or Twitter, or Facebook, or whether they would change the way she wrote, but I am fairly certain that she would have thoughts on how they change us, what we see, what we value, how we think, and what we will ultimately contribute to the world around us. I think she would want us to think beyond the text message to contemplate what we want the lasting message of the text to be.

Beyond the Text Message

Reading practices have changed dramatically in the past twenty years. Just imagine, when your instructors were undergraduates, college students rarely carried cell phones, many didn't know what email was, let alone how to use it, instant messaging was only used by techies, and smartphones and texting did not exist. Students got most of their news from the papers and network TV. Now, you're more likely to check your phone to see what is going on in the world. Advances in technology have changed our way of reading, and not just *where* we read or *what* we read, but *how* we read. Technological innovation is nothing new, of course. It began with the printing press over five hundred years ago, and continually offers up new media for communicating across space and time. As we adapt to the quicker pace of life, we are all perfecting the text-message, a shorthand written form of speech that serves efficiency and direct communication, but almost never complexity or nuance.

But the world is a complex place, becoming more-so every day, and the power and prevalence of the text-message has not replaced our need to communicate and understand this complexity through reading and writing. You may have done this kind of reading and writing only in school, unless you are an avid reader or writer. But even if you don't consider yourself an active reader, the truth is that you're reading all the time. You're just not reading extended pieces of prose, the kind of writing that invites you to process complex ideas, develop your own, and fashion a response of equal complexity and depth. Learning to read and write with complexity are two privileges and responsibilities of being a college student, and the need for these skills doesn't end when you receive your diploma. In your professional lives, regardless of your career, future employers and employees will expect you, as a college graduate, to be capable of this kind of reading and writing.

With this collection of essays, you'll be reading beyond the text message, beyond the text bites of daily life. It's our great hope that in the process of simply reading these essays, you'll find that reading beyond the text message, finding your own position, and articulating your own response in writing can be a rewarding experience, an enjoyable initiation into the reading practices of a literate public. This collection is designed for you as a way to begin that initiation. It's also designed for your instructors, as a way to connect with you through reading and writing about contemporary issues that affect us all. Each essay in this collection is for you a point of access into higher education and the world beyond, and a point departure as you write your way into the on-going conversation.

Reading in the University, Reading in the World

In the university, you will observe, and soon participate in, two kinds of conversations: first, conversations in which members of specific departments, or disciplines, communicate with one another using their professional vocabularies, and share the unique insights that their own discipline has laid claim to; and second, conversations in which individuals across the university use a common vocabulary to discuss issues that mutually affect their disciplines. The first kind of conversation privileges those who have already adopted the vocabulary, or learned the discourse, of a discipline; for example, two physicians can talk to one another about a disease in great depth because their shared vocabulary can accommodate details that a typical patient's vocabulary cannot. Because of a shared vocabulary, those physicians may be able to communicate some of that knowledge to a biologist, or chemist, or even engineer. But the depth of a doctor's knowledge is useless to a patient who has not learned that vocabulary, unless the doctor can translate it into a language that is understandable and clear.

That is why the second kind of conversation is of interest to me when teaching reading and writing. If we want to introduce you to the scholarship of the university, and you enter college needing to practice or improve your reading skills, enhance your vocabulary, and become more confident with your writing skills, then it's in your best interest and that of your instructors to begin communicating with each other through essays that use a common language. You will learn a specialized vocabulary, the discourse of your discipline, upon choosing your major or entering a professional school. This anthology will not teach you the technical language of the biochemist, the political scientist, the theologian, the physician, or the literary critic. But in designing this book, we were interested in initiating conversations about issues of importance to these specialists. We believe that composition courses at their best can teach you to read and write at the college level using essays that open up topics of importance to the entire university community, and using language that invites you in, rather than language that makes you feel excluded at the outset. We see these cross-curricular conversations within the university as the jumping-off place for conversations in and about the world around us.

As a result, this collection is not a typical composition rhetoric or introduction to writing within an English department. You will notice that the table of contents is not organized in units by topic, or style of writing, as is common in composition readers. Instead, it is purposely cross-disciplinary, without announcing at the outset the differences between these disciplines. We hope you will discover in college where and how these disciplines overlap, to find those points of access where inter-disciplinary conversations emerge, and we believe that the writing composition classroom is an ideal place to begin. We encourage you and your instructors to create the cross-curricular connections between these essays that are most compelling to you. For example, you might begin the course reading about the civil rights movement, and wind your way through a consideration of reality TV in China; Twitter and political revolution; globalization, women's health, and economic expansion; religious diversity in the U.S.; and end reading about our romance with technology. We invite you to read and write across these essays, and across the categories in which we could place them, and we've selected essays that allow you specifically to do this kind of work, to introduce you to the possibilities of thinking "connectively" within and beyond your composition classroom.

To help you begin making these kinds of connections, most of the essays in this collection, even those by recognized scholars and experts in traditionally academic fields, are written for popular or mainstream publications. Included are essays by anthropologist Jane Goodall, sociologist Arlie Russell Hochschild, law professors Amy Chua and Kenji Yoshino, political scientists Ian Bremmer and Janet Flammang, psychologists Alison Gopnik and Lauren Slater, and philosopher Alain de Botton, among many from other fields. I've brought these authors together in one table of contents to create the kinds of cross-curricular conversations that have potential to thrive in a university setting, but are easily lost in the translation between departments or professional schools. Many of these authors move seamlessly in their careers between university communities or research centers and the general public. We might even call some of them public intellectuals. For example, for more than fifty years, Jane Goodall has communicated her deep knowledge of anthropology, through her study of the chimpanzees of Gombe in Africa, to people all over the world. In her essay, "In the Forests of Gombe," she considers her scientific work in the context of a personal loss, and explores the connections between anthropology, religion, and spirituality in nature. In her chapter on capitalism and the family, Arlie Russell Hochschild shows us how an individual decision to go to a shopping mall may be part of a much larger economic and social structure. In addition to being scholars, these two authors, and many others in this collection, are experienced in writing to communicate with a broad audience; that is, they have written essays, opinion pieces, and articles for newspapers and popular journals in the course of their academic careers.

All of these essays are written for an audience of readers who want to learn about an issue, figure out their own position, and join the discussion. That's one reason they are so readable, and so enjoyable. They are written for the literate public. That is what you are becoming a part of as a college student, regardless of your major or your intended career. And your semesters in college composition classes are the first steps toward joining this literate public. We would like you to regard your time spent using this collection as practice in the art and skill of reading; to learn that, with discipline and commitment, reading well can be valuable to your overall education and pleasurable along the way; and that even at college age – as adults – you can shape the way you think and learn by regarding reading as less of a burden or a challenge, and more as a useful project in and of itself. We want to give you practice with reading, make you excited about reading, and we have done our best to choose essays that you will find interesting and relevant.

Working with This Collection

You may have heard the expression, "Practice makes perfect." Most people accept this as true with activities that take visible effort, like sports or music. Most people also understand that practice alone really isn't enough; it also takes a good coach and the resources to back you up. You will only become a great basketball player by practicing consistently over the years, and finding the right coach for motivation and technique. Having a good pair of shoes also helps. You will only become a concert violinist by practicing several hours a day for many years, and finding the right violin teacher for guidance and support. You don't need a Stradivarius to be a fine violinist, but with enough practice you can certainly appreciate one. The same goes with reading and writing. The more time and effort you invest in both, with the right resources, and the right guidance, the better you will become at both – and the more enjoyable reading and writing will become for you. Your instructor will provide the guidance; this collection and a good dictionary are your current set of resources. It's up to you to put in the time and effort, to practice.

Prepare yourself for this kind of practice, and try to think of it as an opportunity. You will be reading a great deal over the course of your semester. We do not expect you to absorb in a few months what you might have been absorbing over ten years of consistent, dedicated reading. But we can expect that within one semester, your reading skills will improve dramatically when focused on longer essays that demand reading concentration over time. Unlike many composition readers in which some essays may be as short as two or three pages, the essays in this collection range from 8 to 34 pages, every one a complete book chapter or article. We have included only one excerpt in this collection (a section of Naomi Klein's preface), in part because of our commitment to longer texts, and in part because we want to give you examples of complete works, in content and structure. We ask nothing less from you than to produce papers that are complete, thoughtful, well-constructed responses to the essays in this collection.

We have chosen essays that are examples of what we want you to produce in writing, and what we hope you will learn to value – in their vocabulary and clear sentences, assertion of a position and project, paragraph structure and development, and investment in contemporary issues. Every essay presents a critical, and often creative, assessment of a contemporary issue that will be familiar to some of you, unfamiliar to others, but of relevance to all. The essays are accessible because they use language you have probably been practicing in speech throughout your education, but have not explored deeply in reading, or yet managed to translate into writing of your own. On the surface, these essays are no more difficult than the reading we would hope accessible to all high school graduates. In order to produce an equally critical and creative response in writing, however, you will have to learn to read actively, to think "connectively," and to develop your own position, not unlike what the authors themselves have done. Consider Ian Bremmer's essay, "Democracy in Cyberspace," in which he discusses the potential for Internet technologies to bring democracy to repressive regimes. Bremmer makes his position clear: he is not convinced that democracy will follow inevitably from innovations in modern communication, an optimistic and commonly held view with some evidence to support it. Instead, he advises caution in what we believe technology can do to increase political freedom in authoritarian states. In his essay, Bremmer presents the optimistic point of view – a position Bremmer does not accept—with integrity, demonstrating one productive way to disagree with a theory or person in writing, especially with a viewpoint that is reasonable and based on evidence.

Many essays in this collection, like Bremmer's, highlight the kinds of positions we are asking you to take in response to our assignment questions. They also present the kinds of overall projects you can aspire to in your own writing. You'll notice that many are written from the first person. They demonstrate individuals working through information they've gathered, in an effort to come to some understanding regarding a complex issue or problem: for example, Lisa Belkin and Lauren Slater tackle the controversial topics of genetic engineering and psychosurgery by working through multiple conflicting positions; Wendell Berry and Jane Goodall embrace the unknown at the crossroads of religion and science; Diana Eck, Gregory Orr, Malcolm Gladwell, and Janet Flammang share historical contexts that expand our thinking about religion, civil rights, democracy, and civility in the U.S.; James Fallows, Nicholas Kristof and Sheryl WuDunn, Naomi Klein describe the challenges, opportunities, tragedies, and victories of globalism; and Zadie Smith,and Kenji Yoshino offer slice-of-life experiences that enrich our understanding of our many-voiced contemporary culture. These authors explore a small part of the world's complexity. This is the kind of writing we are asking you to do, and that we believe will help you to become more intuitive about articulating your own position in response to anything you might read. We want you to begin recognizing how writers can address many sides of a complicated problem, carve out their own positions, assert their own project, and still keep the complexity alive, rather than closing it down a simple, but inadequate, solution.

How can we encourage these kinds of reading and writing practices in a world of text messaging? Not simply by helping you read. But by helping you want to read. That's my main goal with this collection, and one of the primary drivers in the selection of these essays. I hope you sense that as you read them. I hope they open up your interests in the contemporary issues, problems and opportunities that you are inheriting even today. I hope that, with practice, you begin to experience the value of reading beyond the text message. Finally, I hope you can imagine these essays as useful points of departure in your own writing: from discovering within them a reason to want to read, to discovering within yourself a host of reasons to want to write.

Thanks to:

The Rutgers instructors of Basic Composition courses for your interest in—and patience waiting for—this 3rd edition of Points of Departure. I hope the new table of contents and questions are worthy of your expertise in the classroom. My sincere gratitude—and the promise of more tangible thanks someday—to Deborah Allen, Tracy Budd, Donna Cantor, Lynda Dexheimer, Donald Dow, Karen Kalteissen, Heather Robinson, and George Schroepfer, for your direct contributions to the content in this reader. You will see your work everywhere.

Michael Goeller, Associate Director of the Rutgers Writing Program, and Course Coordinator of Basic Composition Courses, for your dedication to Points of Departure and your vision for greater things to come. I look forward to working with you on new and exciting projects.

Debby Seme, for being a constant enthusiast and supportive presence at the Rutgers Writing Program, and for faith that a reader without "Dr. Daedalus" will still fly.

Liza Rudneva-Salters, Joshua Wells, Todd Osborne, and Tracy Smith of Cengage Learning, for tenacious assistance with the 3rd edition, and Sheryl Nelson, for expert editing.

The authors of these *wonderful* essays, for permission to share them with our college students.

Finally, thanks to the Rutgers students in Basic Composition courses, for your hard work at connective thinking, and for continually making the possibilities in this collection of essays come alive in your papers.

This collection is dedicated lovingly to Heather Robinson who has been here from the start.

Michelle

The Made-to-Order Savior

Lisa Belkin

Points of Access—Pre-Reading

1. Imagine how you would feel if you learned that you had been conceived and born so that someone in your family could be treated for a life-threatening disease. Would it change your feeling of being valued in your family? How? Freewrite for 15 minutes.
2. How might you feel if you learned that one of your siblings had been conceived in order to save your life? Would it change how you thought of your sibling? How?
3. What kind of sacrifice is too great to save one person's life? Is there such a thing? Can you think of a situation where medical technology should *not* be used to save someone's life?

Henry Strongin Goldberg was the first to arrive in Minneapolis. His parents decorated his room on the fourth floor of the Fairview-University Medical Center with his inflatable Batman chair, two Michael Jordan posters, a Fisher-Price basketball hoop and a punching bag hanging from the curtain rod over the bed. They took turns sleeping (or not) in his room for more than a month. It was too risky for his little brother to visit, but there was a playground across the courtyard, and if Henry, who was 4, stood at the window and Jack, who was 3, climbed to the top of the slide, the boys could wave to each other.

Henry had lost his hair by the time 6-year-old Molly Nash moved in down the hall on the bone-marrow transplant unit. Soon she, too, was bald. The two children had always looked alike, just as all children with this type of Fanconi anemia look alike, with their small faces and small eyes and bodies that are tiny for their age. The "Fanconi face" is one more reminder of the claim of the disease. Over time, Fanconi children also come to sound alike, with a deep, mechanical note in their voices, the result of the androgens they take to keep the illness at bay. Once their scalps were bare, Henry and Molly looked nearly identical. But there was one invisible difference between them—a difference that could mean everything.

These two families, the Strongin-Goldbergs and the Nashes, had raced time, death, threats of government intervention and (although they cringe to admit it) each other, to make medical history. The best chance to save a Fanconi child is a bone-marrow transplant from a perfectly matched sibling donor. Many Fanconi parents have conceived second children to save their first, hoping that luck would bring them a match. These two couples became the first in the world not to count on luck. Using in-vitro fertilization, then using even newer technology to pick and choose from the resulting embryos, they each spent years trying to have a baby whose marrow was guaranteed to be an ideal genetic fit.

One family would succeed and one would fail. One child would receive a transplant from a perfectly matched newborn brother and the other from a less well-matched stranger. One would have an excellent chance of survival; the fate of the other was not as clear. Their parents, now friends, would find themselves together in the tiny lounge at the end of the transplant hall, waiting for the new cells to take root, sharing pizza and a pain that only they could understand.

When the rest of the world learned about the baby born to be a donor, there were questions. Is it wrong to breed a child for "spare parts"? ethicists asked. If we can screen an embryo for tissue type, won't we one day screen for eye color or intelligence? There was talk in the news media of "Frankenstein medicine" and threats by Congress to ban embryo research, which had made this technique possible.

It is the kind of talk heard with every scientific breakthrough, from the first heart transplant to the first cloned sheep. We talk like this because we are both exhilarated and terrified by what we can do, and we wonder, with each step, whether we have gone too far. But though society may ask, "How could you?" the only question patients and families ask is, "How could we not?"

Which is why there is virtually no medical technology yet invented that has not been used. It is human nature to do everything to save a life and just as human to agonize over everything we do. The story of Molly and Henry is the story of groundbreaking science. It is also the story of last-ditch gambles on unproven theories, of laboratory technique cobbled from instinct and desperation, of a determined researcher who sacrificed his job and more trying to help and of a frantic drive through a hurricane to deliver cells on time. In other words, it is simply the story of what it now takes, in the 21st century, to save one child.

* * *

Back at the beginning, it was Molly who arrived first. She was born on July 4, 1994, at Rose Medical Center in Denver, and from the start it was clear that something was terribly wrong. She was missing both thumbs, and her right arm was 30 percent shorter than her left. Her parents, Lisa and Jack, saw her, but could not hold her, before she was whisked off to the ICU, where doctors would eventually find two separate malformations of her heart. (She was also deaf in one ear, but that would not be known until later.) Lisa, wide awake and distraught at 4 a.m. in the maternity ward, made a phone call to the nearby university hospital where she worked as a neonatal ICU nurse caring for babies just like this one, and asked a friend to bring her the book of malformations. Flipping from page to page, she landed on a photo of a Fanconi face and saw in it the face of her newborn daughter.

Named for the Swiss physician who first identified it in 1927, Fanconi anemia causes bone marrow failure, eventually resulting in leukemia and other forms of cancer. Until very recently, children with Molly's form of FA rarely lived past the age of 6, the age Molly is right now. Fanconi is a recessive disorder, which means both parents must pass along one copy of the mutated gene in order for a child to develop the disease. Among the general population, one of every 200 people has a Fanconi mutation. Every ethnic group carries its own genetic baggage, however, and among Ashkenazi Jews like the Nashes and Strongin-Goldbergs, the incidence is 1 in 89, meaning that if both parents are Ashkenazi Jews the chance of having an affected baby is 1 in 32,000. But Lisa, with all her medical training, had never heard of the disease, and Jack, a Denver hotel manager, certainly had not, either.

The holes in Molly's heart closed by themselves, but her other problems remained. She failed to eat, she failed to grow and she was always sick. She had already been through three major surgeries by Oct. 25, 1995, when Henry Strongin Goldberg entered the world at the George Washington University Hospital in Washington. Doctors had warned his parents that he would be quite small, but Laurie Strongin and Allen Goldberg were not worriers, because life had never given them anything to worry about. "Our family history," Laurie says wistfully, "was blue, sunny skies."

Henry was born with an extra thumb on his right hand and a serious heart defect that would require surgery to fix. His parents were devastated, but within days the prognosis worsened. "Fanconi anemia," Laurie wrote in her journal. "If only it was just the heart and thumb. Please take me back a minute ago and make me feel lucky that is it only the heart and the thumb. Fanconi anemia. Rare. Fatal. Henry."

Laurie had spent her career working for nonprofit organizations; Allen had spent his in the computer industry. Both in their early 30's, they were new to parenting and to Fanconi anemia, but they both knew how to navigate a medical database, and within days they found Arleen Auerbach, a researcher at Rockefeller University in New York and the keeper of the Fanconi patient registry in the United States and Canada, a list that contains about 800 names. Although Molly's parents and Henry's parents still knew nothing of each other, the Nashes had found Auerbach, too, because all Fanconi children eventually find their way to her cluttered Manhattan office.

The rarer the disease, the more it needs a single champion, someone to keep the lists, track the trends, follow the research of others while relentlessly pursuing his or her own. Arleen Auerbach is that person for Fanconi anemia—a sweet, grandmotherly type at the core but with sharp outer edges, armor born of years spent delivering bad news.

She had little but bad news for the Nashes and the Strongin-Goldbergs when they first called. Of the eight separate genes that can mutate and cause Fanconi anemia, Molly and Henry both had Type C, which bares its teeth early and kills often. Had these children been born as recently as 1982, Auerbach explained, there would have been no possible treatment. Bone-marrow transplants—obliterating the faulty immune system and then replacing it with a donated one—used to be fatal for Fanconi patients, because their cells were fragile and crumbled during the chemotherapy and radiation that cleared the way for the actual transplant.

Then, in 1982, doctors in France found that if Fanconi patients were given a significantly lower dose of the chemotherapy drug Cytoxan they could survive. The chances of their survival were increased even further if the donor was a sibling who was a perfect match. The reason for this is found in a web of six proteins that together are known as human leukocyte antigen, or HLA, which is the radar by which bodies recognize what is "self" and what is "intruder." HLA is key to the immune system, and since a bone-marrow transplant is a replacement of the immune system, the HLA of the donor must be as close as possible to that of the recipient, or the new immune system can reject its new container, a life-threatening condition known as graft-versus-host disease.

Over the years it was discovered that the rate of success for sibling transplants was even higher if the sibling was a newborn, because then the transplanted cells could come from "cord blood" taken from the umbilical cord and placenta at birth. These are purer, concentrated, undifferentiated cells, meaning that they are less likely to reject their new body. Back in 1995, when Auerbach first spoke to the Nashes and the Strongin-Goldbergs, the survival odds of a sibling cord-blood transplant were 85 percent, while the odds of a nonrelated bone-marrow transplant were 30 percent and the odds of a nonrelated transplant for patients with Henry and Molly's particular mutation were close to zero.

If there was one thing working in their favor, Auerbach told them, it was that their children's disease was diagnosed so early in life. Fanconi anemia is rare, and few doctors have ever seen a case, which means the condition is often missed or mistaken for something else. Auerbach has seen too many children with this same Fanconi mutation whose blood fails, with little prior warning, at age 5. Those parents don't have time to do the only thing there is to do, the one thing the Nashes and Strongin-Goldbergs could do—have a baby.

Ten weeks into a pregnancy, Auerbach explained, a chorionic villus sampling test can determine whether the fetus is healthy and if it is a compatible donor. Couples regularly abort when they learn that the unborn child has Fanconi, Auerbach says; having seen the devastation wrought by the disease on one of their children, they refuse to allow it to claim another. Few couples abort, however, when they learn that the baby is healthy but not a donor. "Only three that I know of terminated for that reason," she says. "They were getting older, their child was getting sicker and they were running out of time." Far more common, she says, is for couples to keep having children, as many as time will allow, praying that one will be a match.

Timing a child's transplant means playing a stomach-churning game of chicken with leukemia. The younger a patient is when undergoing a transplant, the better the outcome, because the body is stronger and has suffered fewer infections. On the other hand, the longer the transplant can be delayed, the greater the odds of conceiving a sibling donor, and the better the chance that transplant technology will have improved. The risk of waiting is that every Fanconi patient will develop leukemia, and once that happens a transplant is all but impossible. "You want to wait as long as you can," Auerbach says, "but not so long that it's too late."

* * *

Good doctors learn from their patients, and so it was when Dr. John Wagner answered his telephone one afternoon seven years ago. A lanky, easygoing man, Wagner is scientific director of clinical research in the Marrow Transplant Program at the University of Minnesota, and he says he believes he has performed more bone-marrow transplants on Fanconi children than any other doctor in the country. The caller who set him thinking, however, was not the parent of a Fanconi patient, but rather the father of a toddler with thalassemia, another rare blood disease. The man was calling to inquire about a sibling cord-blood transplant. "You have another child who is a match?" Wagner asked. "No," came the reply. "But we will."

The father went on to explain that he and his wife were using a relatively new technique known as pre-implantation genetic diagnosis, or PGD, to guarantee that their next child would be free of thalassemia. PGD is an outgrowth of in-vitro fertilization; sperm and egg are united in a petri dish, and when the blastocyst (it is still technically too small to be called an embryo) reaches the eight-cell stage, it is biopsied (meaning one of those cells is removed and screened). Only blastocysts found to be healthy are returned to the womb. Then the waiting game begins—more than two months until it is possible to know if the fetus is a transplant match, then an agonizing choice if it is not. Why, the caller wondered, can't the donor-compatibility tests be done before the embryos are implanted?

Wagner was intrigued by the possibility. Why use PGD just as prevention, he wondered, when it could be used as treatment? Why not, in effect, write a prescription that says "one healthy baby who is going to be a perfect donor"?

Wagner called Mark Hughes, who pioneered the technique and who was working with this family. Hughes is known as a brilliant researcher, simultaneously passionate and wary, a scientist and physician who chose the field of genetics because it combined the intellectual rigor of the lab with the emotional connection to flesh-and-blood patients. In 1994, at about the time he first spoke to Wagner, Hughes was recruited to work at the National Institutes of Health and also as director of Georgetown University's Institute for Molecular and Human Genetics, where his salary was paid in part by the NIH In other words, much of his research was supported by the government. At that time he was also a member of a federal advisory committee that developed guidelines for the type of single-cell embryo analysis that was central to PGD. But no sooner had those guidelines been developed than Congress banned all federal financing of embryo research, and Hughes was forced to continue his research with private funds only.

Under the current Bush administration there is talk of banning all embryo research, even work supported by private funds. For that reason—and for reasons that will become clearer as this tale unfolds—Hughes has developed a healthy distrust of the limelight and refused to be interviewed for this story. As Wagner and Auerbach tell it, Hughes had certainly thought of the possibility of using PGD to determine HLA type long before Wagner called, but he had several concerns.

The ones that weighed heaviest were ethical. It could be argued that using PGD to eliminate embryos with disease helps the patient—in this case, the embryo, the biopsied organism—by insuring that it is not born into a life of thalassemia or cystic fibrosis or Duchenne muscular dystrophy or any of the other agonizing illnesses for which Hughes was screening. Using the same technique to select for a compatible donor, however, does not help the "patient" whose cells are being tested. "It helps the family," says Arleen Auerbach, "and it helps the sibling with Fanconi, but it does not help the embryo."

What Wagner proposed, therefore, would be stepping into new territory. If society gives its blessing to the use of one child to save another, then what would prevent couples from someday going through with the process but aborting when the pregnancy was far enough along that the cord blood could be retrieved? Or what would prevent couples whose child needed a new kidney from waiting until the fetal kidney was large enough, then terminating the pregnancy and salvaging the organs? What would stop those same couples from waiting until the child was born and subjecting it to surgery to remove one kidney? Once the technology exists, who decides how to use it?

Ethicists think in terms of a slippery slope. But is the potential for abuse in some circumstances reason not to pursue research that can be lifesaving under the right circumstances? Unlike donating a kidney, or even donating bone marrow, donating cord blood involves negligible harm to the newborn donor. The stem cells are collected at birth, directly from the placenta, not from the baby. That is one reason why Wagner argued that HLA testing is ethically defensible. A second reason, he said, was that it is indefensible not to try.

"I'm here as the patient's advocate," he says, meaning Molly and Henry and all the other children in need of transplants. "It's my obligation to push the envelope because I see how bad the other side can be. I see the results of a sibling transplant; they're the easiest transplant to do. And then I walk into the room of the patient who had an unrelated donor, I see that their skin is sloughing off, the mucous membranes are peeling off and they have blood pouring out of their mouths. You cannot imagine anything so horrible in your entire life, and you're thinking, I did this—because there was nothing else available for me to do."

That was apparently what Hughes's gut told him, too, and he agreed to try to develop a lab procedure to screen HLA at the single-cell level. His participation came with certain conditions. First, that the mother must be younger than 35, because younger women produce more eggs, increasing the odds of a healthy match. Second, that he would work only with families who carried a specific subset of the Type C mutation, known as IVS4, because it is the most common. And, last of all, the child being created must be wanted. Only families who had expressed a wish for more children would be approached for this procedure. Hughes did not want to create a baby who was nothing but a donor.

Arleen Auerbach immediately thought of two couples who were the right age, fit the specific genetic profile and who had always planned to have a houseful of children. Her first phone call was to Lisa and Jack Nash in Denver. Without a moment's hesitation, they said yes. Her second call was to Laurie Strongin and Allen Goldberg in Washington.

"If I told you that you could potentially go into a pregnancy knowing that your baby was healthy and a genetic match for Henry, would you be interested?" she asked.

Two hours earlier, Laurie had taken a home pregnancy test. It was positive. If early test results were negative for Fanconi she would carry to term, she answered, even if the baby were not the right HLA type to save Henry's life.

Henry was only 5 months old. His heart surgery had gone smoothly, he was happy and looked deceptively healthy. Fate seemed to be on his side. "If this baby's not a match, we'll try it your way in nine months," Laurie remembers telling Auerbach. "We still thought," she says, "that we had a lot of time."

* * *

Henry became a big brother in December 1995. Jack Strongin-Goldberg was free of Fanconi and was not even a carrier of the disease, so there was no chance that he might pass it on to his own children. His HLA, however, was as unlike Henry's as a biological brother's could possibly be. Laurie and Allen admit that they were briefly disappointed when they heard this last piece of news, three months into the pregnancy. Then they brushed off their psyches and called Mark Hughes, telling him they would be ready to try PGD at the start of the following year.

As baby Jack was being born, Lisa Nash was undergoing the shots and monitoring that are part of in-vitro fertilization. Theirs would be a very difficult case, Hughes had told them. Of the cluster of genes that together determine HLA type, science, at the time, could look at only three. As it happened, Lisa and Jack's patterns were almost identical on those three genes, making it nearly impossible to sort hers from his. That genetic quirk, he warned, could lead to the wrong results. The science to fix this didn't exist yet, he said, and he was figuring it all out as they spoke.

Hughes was also struggling with other problems, ones that had nothing to do with the Nashes' DNA. On the day that Lisa's eggs were retrieved by laparoscopy and fertilized in a dish, the headline in *The Washington Post* read: "NIH Severs Ties With Researcher Who Experimented on Embryos." Hughes had been accused of using federal funds for embryo research, in violation of the Congressional ban. Hughes denied that government money was used for that portion of his work and argued that in any case his research was not even on embryos since all that ever arrived in his lab was DNA extracted from a biopsied cell.

Lisa Nash did not become pregnant.

Mark Hughes resigned from his positions with N.I.H. and Georgetown University rather than agree to stop his research.

The turn of events was devastating for Hughes. He was out of a job and forced to uproot his two young sons and his wife, who was fighting a battle of her own, against breast cancer. Those close to him say he talked of quitting medicine entirely, so frustrated and angry was he that the rug had been pulled out from under him.

The turn of events was also devastating for the Nashes. "We called him two, three times a week," Jack Nash remembers, and as he speaks a frantic note creeps into his voice. "But he wouldn't return our calls. Months went by, then a year." Over those months they learned that Hughes was moving halfway across the country to a new, privately financed lab where he could continue his work. Then they learned that Hughes's wife was critically ill, that her cancer had spread, that the prognosis was grim. The one thing they did not learn was when and if their quest to save Molly might begin again.

They now understand that science solves the simplest equation first, then moves on to the more difficult ones; their complicated genetic makeup meant their case had to wait. Added to that was the fact that the initial decoding of their DNA had been done at Hughes's former lab in Washington, and he no longer had access to the data. They now also understand that Hughes was in this to save lives, and that having to come to the phone and say that he couldn't, that he didn't know how to match an HLA type for Molly, was more than he could bear. But at the time they didn't understand. At the time they were angry.

"When we manage to speak to him he says we have to give him a few more months to get the lab set up," Jack says. "Meanwhile Molly's counts are dropping and he's the only one who can do this, and he won't help."

* * *

Life for a chronically ill child is a jumble of numbers. The average platelet count in a healthy child: 150,000 to 450,000. The lowest that platelets are allowed to drop before Dr. Wagner urges a transplant: 40,000. Where Henry's platelets hovered when Jack was born: 100,000. The cost of each in-vitro cycle: $11,000. The amount paid by insurance: officially, $0, because the in-vitro fertilization was not being done to treat infertility, nor was it being done to directly treat Henry. The amount the Strongin-Goldbergs raised for Fanconi anemia research at the fundraiser they held on Henry's first birthday: $67,500. The odds of a blastocyst being healthy: 3 in 4. The odds of a blastocyst being a match: 1 in 4. The odds of a blastocyst being a match and also being healthy, and of Laurie becoming pregnant and delivering before Henry had to have a transplant: God only knows.

Since the day Henry's FA was diagnosed, life for Laurie and Allen was filtered through these numbers, through the lens of Fanconi anemia. "Every ensuing pregnancy," she wrote in her journal after baby Jack was born, "will be marred by the fact that the little baby in my belly could have a fatal disease. Every job that Allen and I consider has to offer medical insurance without excluding pre-existing conditions and with compassion and flexibility. Every relationship has to offer quiet understanding of our travails accompanied by the capacity to give without expecting too much in return."

While Mark Hughes worked to set up his new lab at Wayne State University School of Medicine, near Detroit, the Nashes and the Strongin-Goldbergs were at home, waiting in two very different ways. A crisis can strip a family down to its skeleton of strengths and faults, peeling the niceties away and revealing the bare core of who they are. Henry's parents, for instance, effervescent, embracing and fiercely optimistic from the start, became more so as the clock ran out. They took on Hughes's problems as their own, bonding with him deeply, knowing that they needed him to bond back if they were to save Henry. Molly's parents, in turn, are determined and intense, and they did not waste emotional energy that might be spent protecting their daughter. They were demanding of Hughes, but no more demanding than they were of themselves or of anyone else who could help Molly.

Until the spring of 1997, the two families had still not met. In May of that year, when Hughes was promising both of them that he would be able to resume work soon, a retreat for Fanconi families was held near Portland, Me. The Strongin-Goldbergs went there determined to meet the anonymous couple Arleen Auerbach had mentioned—the couple who had already tried HLA screening with Hughes. Armed with two facts—that the couple had a daughter, and that they lived in Colorado—the Strongin-Goldbergs skimmed the directory and found a family who fit that description.

When Laurie Strongin shook Lisa Nash's hand for the first time she felt an instant bond with the only other mother in the world whose life paralleled her own. Lisa was more reserved. Up to that moment she hadn't realized that the elusive Hughes was working with a second family. Six months later, however, by the time of Laurie's initial in-vitro attempt, the women had paddled past their opening awkwardness and were close telephone friends. When Henry, now 2, talked about his future, he spoke in gradations: first he would be "better," then "super better," then "super-duper better." When all this was over, Lisa and Laurie promised each other, when their children were both "super-duper better," the two families would travel to Disneyworld to celebrate.

In January 1998, when Hughes was finally ready for them, Laurie took the train up to New York City for her appointment with Dr. Zev Rosenwaks, the baby-making guru at the in-vitro fertilization clinic at New York Weill Cornell Medical Center. Henry's platelet count was 71,000 that morning. Eighteen days later, after 18 shots of Lupron, a brutal migraine, hot sweats and cold chills, Laurie's body refused to cooperate, and the in-vitro fertilization process for that cycle had to be abandoned. That week Henry's platelet count dropped to 31,000, its lowest level up to that point.

Doctors often suggest that in-vitro fertilization patients wait a month or more between attempts, but Laurie didn't have a month, and in early February she was in New York again. This time the numbers were on her side. She produced 24 eggs, and 21 of them were mature enough to be fertilized. Statistically that meant six should be perfect matches for Henry, and three or four of those six should also be disease free.

Sixteen blastocysts survived the biopsy. Allen refused to entrust the cells to anyone, so he flew them to Detroit himself. At the airport he handed his Styrofoam hope chest to a waiting Mark Hughes, then got on the next plane back to New York. The following evening, Laurie was at the Rosenwaks clinic ready for the re-implantation when word came from Hughes. Of the 16 blastocysts tested, 2 were absolutely perfect matches to Henry. Both those matches had Fanconi anemia.

"I'm struggling to come to terms with how much pain I can withstand," Laurie wrote in her journal. She and Allen shared that pain long-distance with the Nashes, who still had not heard when and if Hughes would begin to work with them again. Jack and Lisa were supportive, but also envious and confused. "Were they the family of choice because he liked them better?" Jack remembers wondering. "Is this personal? Does he have something against us, and he's taking that out on Molly? Things like that definitely go through your mind."

The Nashes sent frantic e-mail messages to Hughes, telling him what he already knew—that Molly's counts were dropping and that they were running out of time. In August 1998, when Molly's platelet count had fallen to 30,000, they received his answer. He couldn't help them, he wrote in an e-mail message. Their case was too complicated, both genetically and politically. The genetic analysis he'd so painstakingly done on them belonged to the NIH. "We tried to get the lab at Georgetown to help us, since they were key in our being able to do this for you the first time around," Hughes wrote. The lab has been ordered by the "Catholic administration" of the university "not to get involved 'in any way."'

Hughes continued: "Go ahead without us. You are anxious, and we understand that very well. But I cannot make this work today and I don't know when I will be able to do so. I am sorry. Science sucks sometimes."

Reeling, Lisa and Jack called Laurie and Allen, who were about to begin their third in-vitro cycle—one that would produce 26 eggs, 24 of which were mature and 21 of which would fertilize. Of those, three would be perfect, healthy matches for Henry. The

Strongin-Goldbergs would not share these details with the Nashes because they had come to understand that other people's good news is sometimes too difficult to hear.

* * *

Taking Mark Hughes's advice, the Nashes did go on without him. They'd decided to jump into a cross-your-fingers pregnancy when they learned, almost by accident, of a private clinic in Chicago that had been quietly doing PGD for nearly 10 years, though never for Fanconi anemia. This news was "like opening a door," say the Nashes, who had not realized that other labs in the country besides Hughes's were providing PGD. If this Chicago lab could test for cystic fibrosis and Tay-Sachs, they wondered, why not Fanconi? And if it had the equipment to screen DNA for disease, why not also screen for HLA?

Lisa and Jack brought Molly along on their trip to the Reproductive Genetics Institute, on the theory that doctors couldn't say no with their adorable but ashen-cheeked child in the room. Her platelets were half what they had been a month earlier. She was weak and tired. They could not have walked into a more receptive office. A year earlier, Charles Strom, then the head of the institute's genetics lab, had heard Mark Hughes speak at a genetics meeting about his attempts to screen DNA for an anonymous couple who were trying to have a child who would be a cord-blood match. "It was like a revelation to me," says Strom, a broad, genial bear of a man now at Quest Diagnostics in California, who could, at that time, perform PGD for 35 diseases but had never thought of HLA screening. "This is what pre-implantation genetics should be about."

A few in the audience expressed their disapproval, he remembers, fearing that this was a step on the road to eugenics. Strom, on the other hand, was enthusiastic. "I stood up and said I thought this was great," he says. "I'm trained not just as a geneticist, but as a pediatrician, and I was tired of watching kids die. I thought this would be the future, and from then on, I was basically waiting for someone to ask me to do it." So when the very same "anonymous" couple arrived and asked, Strom said yes.

He immediately discovered what Hughes had struggled with for years—the "nightmare" caused by the near-identical patterns in the HLA portion of Jack and Lisa's DNA. But he and his team tried something new—they looked farther down the strand, beyond the three known genes, to a spot where it was easier to differentiate one parent from the other. This increased the risk of being wrong, but Molly's blood counts were dropping, and they did not have time to waste. "This isn't what we want to do, but it will probably work," Strom told the Nashes two months after they first met.

It is one thing to screen embryos; it is another to become pregnant, and adding HLA screening to Fanconi anemia screening lowers the odds even more. Only 1 in 6 blastocysts is likely to be both healthy and a matched donor, and that one might not be the quality that the reproductive endocrinologist would have chosen under ideal circumstances. Lisa spent all of 1999 trying to defy those odds. In January she produced 12 eggs, 2 of which were healthy matches; she became pregnant, then miscarried. In June she produced only four eggs, one of which was a match but did not result in a pregnancy. In September she produced eight eggs, six of which had Fanconi anemia; the single healthy match was implanted, but again, her pregnancy test was negative.

In October the Nash family traveled to Minneapolis for Molly's twice-yearly checkup with Dr. Wagner. Her platelets were down to 10,000. In every measurable way she was failing, and she needed a bone-marrow transplant. "You have to stop," Wagner told her parents. It was time to proceed with a transplant from a nonrelated donor. "There comes a point where I have to say: 'It's over. You've done it. You've done the best you could."'

He began to search for a donor. Lisa and Jack went ahead with the in-vitro that had been scheduled for December. "I couldn't hear the word no," Lisa says. "No' meant Molly could die."

Because they knew it was the last try, and because they needed to feel certain that they had done the best they could, the Nashes insisted on one change of procedure for this final try. It troubled them that Lisa was producing so few eggs per cycle, and they wondered if a different in-vitro fertilization clinic might do better. They approached Dr. William Schoolcraft, an infertility doctor in Colorado known for pushing the envelope. He changed Lisa's hormone regimen and in December 1999 retrieved 24 eggs from her ovaries. For two days the Nashes fantasized about twins and even triplets. Then Strom called to say that there was only one match.

It all came down to one embryo that, statistically, had less than a 30 percent chance of taking hold and staying put. "All it takes is one, all it takes is one," Lisa reminded herself as she drove to Dr. Schoolcraft's office nine days later for a pregnancy test. Minutes after she left, her cell phone rang.

"You're pregnant," said the nurse on the other end.

It was too soon, however, for a happy ending. And indeed, seven weeks into the pregnancy Lisa had just gotten out of the shower when deep red blood began flowing down her legs. The drive to Schoolcraft's office was a blur, but the memory of the picture on the ultrasound screen is vividly clear: a large gap where the placenta had separated from the uterine wall, and the flub-dub pulses of a tiny, living, beating heart.

Lisa went home and went to bed. She was permitted to get up three or four times a day to use the bathroom and once a week for an appointment with Schoolcraft, nothing more. Every time she stood up she began to bleed. Molly, too weak to really play, was on her own manner of bed rest, and mother and daughter spent entire days lying upstairs together.

In March, Molly's blood tests showed signs of pre-leukemia. Wagner sent more data to the national bone-marrow bank, escalating his search for an unrelated donor. In April, Molly's platelets fell to 3,000. She began to need blood transfusions but fought whoever tried to insert the needle; one particularly rocky weekend Strom flew to Denver from a business meeting in Los Angeles, because he was the only one Molly would permit to start the IV. April became May; May turned to June. Along the way, Lisa asked her doctors what could be done should she spontaneously lose the baby. They began to discuss whether stem cells could be harvested from a fetal liver. And all the while, Lisa was still bleeding—clawing her way through the pregnancy, trying to hold onto her baby while holding off her daughter's transplant.

* * *

Back when the Nashes were deciding whether to go ahead with Molly's transplant or try somehow to wait until summer, the Strongin-Goldbergs were making their own impossible choice: whether or not to give up. Their optimism back in August 1998, when they had three healthy embryos, had long since faded. That in-vitro attempt did not result in a pregnancy. Neither did attempt No. 4, in November, when 30 eggs failed to provide a single healthy match.

Attempt No. 5, in February 1999, was almost more than they could bear. Laurie produced 17 eggs and was waiting to be summoned to the clinic when she received another call instead. Allen had taken to scanning the Detroit newspapers online, knowing that Mark Hughes's wife was dying, but not wanting to pester his friend. The morning of Laurie's retrieval, Allen found the news he'd been dreading in the obituary section. Laurie's ovaries were past the point of no return, so Rosenwaks went ahead with the retrieval and fertilization without any idea who would screen the blastocysts. "I couldn't imagine doing this without our friend on the other end and didn't even know if it was possible," Laurie wrote.

But saving Henry had come to mean as much to Hughes as to Laurie and Allen. The researcher had watched his own life nearly destroyed in defense of this work, and he promised he would be there. Fourteen blastocysts survived the biopsy, and on the morning of Feb. 11,1999, just a few days after Hughes's wife's death, Allen loaded his

Styrofoam box with vials and dry ice and boarded the 11:10 a.m. flight to Detroit. He took the container to the lab, where he was moved to tears to find a large picture of his own son hanging on the wall. Underneath it was the question, "Can we help save Henry's life?"

Allen was certain that this attempt would work. There was bittersweet poetry in the timing: death preceding life and preventing death. But when Hughes called the Strongin-Goldbergs in New York, his news was not the stuff of poetry. There was only one match. It did not result in a pregnancy.

Attempt No. 6 took place in June 1999. Twenty-eight eggs, two healthy matches. No pregnancy. Attempt No .7 came in the middle of Hurricane Floyd. Allen drove his Styrofoam box through the eye of the storm—1,200 miles in 26 hours—and delivered the cells, alive, at 2 a.m. Laurie became pregnant, then miscarried.

Their eighth try took place in February 2000. Laurie was in New York, at the clinic, the morning that Allen raced Henry to the hospital with pneumonia so serious doctors warned it could kill him. Laurie agonized over whether to come home (canceling the in-vitro cycle) or stay where she was. If she left, she was certain Henry would die, because he would have lost this chance for a sibling donor. If she stayed, then she was equally certain that Henry would die—of pneumonia, in a Georgetown hospital, without his mother.

She stayed. Henry received two blood transfusions and was pumped full of three intravenous antibiotics. Laurie produced 21 eggs and only one implantable match. "I did not get pregnant," she says, "and I still haven't recovered from the experience."

As the Strongin-Goldbergs dragged themselves from one attempt to the next, the technology of bone-marrow transplants was changing. Specifically, Wagner was testing a new method of removing T-cells from donor blood. T-cells are the ones that recognize the host as foreign, leading to graft-versus-host disease. Simultaneously, Wagner was using fludarabine, an immunosuppressant that appears to encourage the new cells to engraft, or take root. Based on a tiny sample of patients, Wagner's best guess was that these adjustments to the protocol showed promise, apparently increasing the odds of surviving an unrelated bone-marrow transplant from 30 percent to 50 percent in a Fan- coni anemia patient. This was still far lower than the 85 percent odds of a sibling cord- blood transplant, but better than it had been before.

Laurie went through one last, disappointing in-vitro cycle, then she and Allen grabbed those new 50-50 odds. Wagner warned that it was time to stop, and they knew, from looking at Henry, that he was probably right. Henry had had two platelet and two red-cell transfusions in the past two months, and he had been on Anadrol, a steriod to boost his blood counts, for two and a half years. There comes a point at which a child is too sick for a transplant, and Henry, like Molly, was all but there. In two and a half years of desperate trying, Laurie had 353 injections, produced 198 eggs and had no successful pregnancy. During the same time period, Henry's platelets fell from a high of 103,000 to a low of 10,000.

"We gave it all we had," Laurie wrote when her last pregnancy test was negative and the family was leaving for Minneapolis, for Henry's transplant. "We worked with the world's best doctors. We hoped. We believed. We were brave. We persevered. And despite all that it didn't work. I am left with my belief system intact. I believe in love and science. Nothing more, nothing less."

* * *

A bone-marrow transplant is a medical resurrection. First doctors all but kill a patient; then they bring him back to life. Treacherous and risky, in the end it all comes down to one squishy plastic bag of pale brown liquid which could easily be mistaken for rusty water from a tap. Henry's bag of marrow was collected from an anonymous donor somewhere in the United States on the morning of July 6, 2000, and was flown to the Fairview-University Medical Center, arriving in Room 5 of the bone-marrow transplant floor around dinnertime. A nurse came in with a Polaroid, snapped a few pictures, then added the bag to Henry's leafy IV tree. There was no blaring of trumpets, no rolling of drums. From 8:15 to 8:30 Central Daylight Time, the fluid dripped soundlessly.

Molly Nash's bag was collected with more drama. Lisa's pregnancy had managed to hold. For months Molly's baby brother had been trying to arrive prematurely, and now that he was due, he didn't seem eager to arrive at all. By the evening of Aug. 29, Lisa had been in labor for 52 hours, insisting she be allowed to continue because she knew that more cord blood could be collected during a vaginal birth. Finally, when it looked as if the baby was in distress, he was delivered by C-section. Dr. Strom—his godfather—collected the cord blood. Lisa cradled both the newborn Adam and the warm intravenous bag in her arms.

"God created Adam in his image," Lisa says, explaining how she chose her son's name. "Adam was the first. And from Adam—from his rib, which is full of marrow—God created woman, which is fitting because God used our Adam to give Molly a second chance at life."

When he was 9 days old, Adam flew with his parents and his sister to Minneapolis. Molly settled into the room down from Henry's for the standard four-month stay—a surreal time when it seems as if every child in the world is having a bone-marrow transplant, because every child that you see is. Molly went through all that Henry had gone through a month before her, and yet everything was different. She had a higher chance of engraftment and a far lower chance of rejection. Her parents were rubbed emotionally raw watching her suffer in order to live. But then they looked at Henry, whose parents feared he was showing early signs of graft-versus- host disease—something Molly would almost certainly never get. They looked beyond Henry, too, at the eight patients who died in the bone-marrow transplant unit during Molly's endless summer.

In the end, Molly's life was saved. That is the Nashes' answer to people who question their right to manipulate nature. Their right springs from the difference between 30 percent and 85 percent; the difference between Molly and Henry. That is also their answer to those who would urge the government to ban all embryo research because it harms unborn children. The research, they say, saves children like Molly.

"We did what we needed to do to keep our daughter from dying," Lisa Nash says. "That is what any parent would do. Isn't this what parents are supposed to do? How can anything be wrong with that?"

Yes, ethicists say, it is exactly what any parent would do, and that is why it is troubling. Parents are being asked to make a choice not only on behalf of their living child, but also on behalf of their unborn child, and that can be an impossible position when the choices get hard. If Molly were closer to death, for instance, would her parents have terminated the pregnancy and used stem cells from Adam's fetal liver to save her?

"We know people will do anything to save their child," says Jeffrey Kahn, an ethicist at the University of Minnesota, where there was much debate about the decisions of the transplant team at the hospital next door. "Now we are learning what 'anything' really means."

Susan M. Wolf, a professor of law and medicine at the University of Minnesota, says she believes that this case is emblematic of the whole of reproductive technology, which she describes as "a multibillion dollar industry based solely on consumer demand." While it might seem logical in each isolated case to let the parents decide, all those single choices add up to a hodgepodge of technology scattered throughout private clinics and laboratories, with no one authorized to say no.

Wagner and Strom agree. They say they do not believe that they, or any other individual doctor, should have the responsibility of sorting through this thicket alone. "As the technology progresses," Strom says, "I see the possibility that someone will come to us and say: 'While you're screening for Tay-Sachs, how about making sure he's not going to have heart disease, too? And while you're at it, why not check for the gene that predisposes him to lupus or makes him immune to HIV?"

"It has the potential to be abused," agrees Wagner. But the response to that potential, he warns, should not be to ban the research or suspend federal financing of the procedure. "It's not going to go away," he says. "We can't put our heads in the sand and say it doesn't exist. I have a stack of requests this high from all over the world, couples asking if they can come use this technology."

Compounding the problems caused by the current ban on federal financing, he says, is the accompanying lack of federal rules. "It's all been forced into the private sector," he says, "where there are no controls. There should be controls. There should be limits. It is up to us, as a society, to decide what they are."

* * *

Since her transplant, Molly Nash has gone back to school. More accurately, school has started to come to her, but her visiting teacher has to wear a mask during lessons. Her ballet teacher comes for in-home classes, too, and Molly twirls and plies and giggles. Her hair is beginning to grow back. Instead of taking 44 pills every day she only takes 10. She is still fed through a stomach tube that her mother hooks up four times a day, and she doesn't have much of an appetite, which is characteristic of Fanconi anemia. The transplant did not cure her of that disease; it merely erased her risk of developing imminent leukemia. She is still likely to suffer Fanconi's other complications, particularly cancers of the mouth and neck. But those will not show themselves for many years, and, her mother says, "maybe they will have a cure by then."

Henry Strongin Goldberg has been ill almost since the day he left the hospital in Minnesota. While Molly's platelet count is 381,000, Henry's is 15,000. He spent months looking yellow and feeling miserable, moaning instead of talking, the result of a near fatal liver infection that is common in transplant patients because of the drugs they are given to suppress their immune system.

In January, for the first time in his tortured life, his parents were struck full force by the thought that he was dying. "All I can think about," Allen said then, "is how much I'll miss him."

Since then, things have gotten even worse. Allen lost his job at an Internet start-up in January, and although he is now working again, the family has burned through its savings. Laurie, who takes home $600 every other week, has spent months sleepwalking through work, hanging on partly out of a need to have one foot tenuously in the real world but also because Henry needed health insurance. Henry's liver slowly improved, but he then began to lose weight at an alarming rate—20 percent of his body weight within weeks—and his skin began to disintegrate, turning red, scaly and raw. Several painful skin biopsies were inconclusive, suggesting that this was either an allergy to a medication or a sign of graft-versus-host disease.

While Henry was at the clinic having his skin examined, one doctor noticed that he was dragging his left leg when he walked. Two weeks later his left side became so weak that he could not lift himself to a sitting position in bed. He was rushed back to Minneapolis, where a scan showed a mass of unknown origin in his brain. Doctors operated but were unable to determine the cause. Whatever it was, it may have spread to his chest. Just last week, Henry was rushed to the hospital again—his sixth hospitalization in the past 12 weeks—where doctors found lesions in his lungs.

Of the 21 Fanconi patients who have received transplants within the past two years at Fairview under the new drug protocol that gave the Strongin-Goldbergs so much hope, 13 have survived so far. Of those, Henry is in the greatest danger. The first anniversary of his transplant is this coming Friday, a milestone that no longer seems like a victory.

What might have been another red-letter day will come in October, when the Nashes and the Strongin-Goldbergs had planned to meet in Disneyworld. The Strongin-Goldbergs will not be there. After years of technology and intervention, Laurie became pregnant the old-fashioned way, and her baby is due this fall. Tests show him to be a healthy boy who is not an HLA match for Henry.

Points of Engagement—Reading Comprehension

1. Look up the word "ethics" in your dictionary or online. Using your understanding of that definition, explain in your own words the ethical dilemma Belkin outlines in her essay. Who or what is at stake? Refer to two passages in the text to show how you know.
2. According to Belkin, the doctors she interviewed agree that the technology used to create a viable donor for a child with Fanconi anemia could be abused, but that the related research should not be banned. Name two potentials for abuse mentioned in the essay. Do you think the research should be banned? Why or why not?
3. At the end of the essay the two children profiled—Molly and Henry—end up with very different prognoses. Do an online search for both of them to find out what has happened since Belkin's essay was published. What factors were involved in their respective fates? Do those factors suggest how society might approach questions of medical ethics?

Points of Departure—Assignment Questions

1. In "Made-to-Order Savior" Lisa Belkin describes controversial medical technology that enables parents to conceive a child genetically configured to be a bone marrow donor for another child. She cites critics who question the right of these parents to "manipulate nature." Use Belkin's discussion to consider another text that also addresses the use of technology to alter what is natural, such as Lauren Slater's "Who Holds the Clicker," or Sherry Turkle's Introduction to *Alone Together.* What would these authors have to say about Belkin's question on page 7: "Once the technology exists, who decides how to use it?" Write a paper in which you engage with the controversies the authors present concerning technological intervention, and suggest an answer of your own to that difficult question.

2. On page 7 Belkin refers to the slippery slope argument, or the "potential for abuse in some circumstances" of medical technology. Read another text in which the slippery slope argument figures in the discussion, such as Kristof and WuDunn's "Introduction: The Girl Effect," Naomi Klein's "Preface: Fences of Enclosure, Windows of Possibility," or Lauren Slater's "Who Holds the Clicker." Use the two texts together to explore the slippery slope idea and the challenges of creating social policy to balance the potential for good against the potential for misuse.

3. On page 16 Belkin quotes parent Laurie Strongin who says, "I believe in love and science. Nothing more, nothing less," while Lisa Nash says, "God used our Adam to give Molly [her daughter] a second chance at life." How are these two parental responses to adversity different? Now consider another text such as Wendell Berry's "God, Science, and Imagination," Susan Blackmore's "Strange Creatures," or Jane Goodall's "In the Forests of Gombe," that specifically addresses the idea of scientific versus spiritual, or religious, thinking. How might these different belief systems, and the potential conflicts that arise between them, influence the discussion of medical ethics? Your project for this paper is to reconsider the dilemmas and decisions made by the Strongin and Nash families by using your insight on religious and scientific thinking from one of these other essays.

God, Science, and Imagination

Wendell Berry

Points of Access—Pre-Reading

1. What is faith? Is it inherently religious? Why or why not?
2. What is the difference between faith and imagination? How are they similar?
3. What kinds of ideas come to your mind when you think of a "fundamentalist"?
4. When you think about your basic human rights, what kinds of rights come to your mind? Where do those rights come from?

Among the oddest bedevillers of our time are the eminent scientists who use their heaped up credentials, achievements, and awards as pedestals from which to foretell the future and pronounce upon the ultimate questions of life and religion. One of the most recent of these is Steven Weinberg's essay "Without God" in the *New York Review of Books* for September 25, 2008.

The oddity of these ventures, of which Professor Weinberg's is fairly typical, is in their ready—and, it seems to me, their thoughtless—abandonment of scientific rigor and methodology. For example, despite his protest that he does not want "to try to talk anyone out of their religion," Prof. Weinberg sets forth an elaborate argument for the nonexistence of God, an argument obviously meant to be persuasive but based entirely on opinion.

As a fundamentalist of science, like the fundamentalists of religion, he is clearly evangelizing, hoping to convert or at least to disturb those who disagree with him. And, like the religious fundamentalists, he uses a language that presents belief as knowledge. But more troubling than the authority he grants to his own opinions is his claim to know what cannot be known. "As religious belief weakens," he writes, "more and more of us know that after death there is nothing." The only fact available here is that Prof. Weinberg and more and more of us do not, and will never, know any such thing. There is no proof of this "nothing," and there is no scientific or other procedure by which to attempt such a proof.

Prof. Weinberg is a physicist, and he says that he is "professionally concerned with finding out what is true." But as a mere person, evidently, he is concerned, like too many others, merely with investing his opinions with power. This is the concern of fundamentalists of all kinds: religious, atheistical, scientific, technological, economic, and political. They all seek power— they seek victory, in fact—by abandoning the proprieties that permit us to seek and to honor what is true while acknowledging the limits of our ability to know.

Not far into his essay Prof. Weinberg says, with proper humility: "Of course, not everything has been explained, nor will it ever be." But, two paragraphs later, speaking of "religious conservatives," he abandons the careful and exacting speech of humility, and prognosticates with the absolute confidence and gleeful vengefulness of a religious conservative: "I can imagine how disturbed they will feel in the future, when at last scientists learn how to understand human behavior in terms of the chemistry and physics of the brain, and nothing is left that needs to be explained by our having an immaterial soul." This is something else that he does not know. Nor does he hesitate over the apparent difficulty of a material proof of the nonexistence of something immaterial.

The argument about the existence of God necessarily must be conducted in the absence of evidence that would stand as proof either in a laboratory or a court of law. There is no objective or empirical or experimental evidence on either side. The argument, as such, is by definition hopeless—a piece of foolishness and a waste of time. Even so it has long existed and no doubt it will long continue, but only for the paltry reason that it cannot be won. Chaucer defined the problem about six hundred years ago in the Prologue to the *Legend of Good Women,* and I doubt that it can be more clearly defined:

> A thousand tymes have I herd men telle
> That ther ys joy in hevene and peyne in helle,
> And I acorde wel that it ys so;
> But, natheles, yet wot I wel also
> That ther nis noon dwellyng in this contree,
> That eyther hath in hevene or helle ybe,
> Ne may of hit noon other weyes witen,
> But as he hath herd seyd, or founde it writen;
> For by assay ther may no man it preve.

People of religion, and not just fundamentalists, can speak with tiresome confidence of knowing what in fact they don't know but believe. None of us is immune to the temptation to do this. Modern science itself, ignoring its famous devotion to empirical proof and factuality, has pampered and marketed itself by beliefs that have proved to be empirically flimsy and unimaginably damaging. Chemistry, while helping us to "live better," has poisoned the whole world; the "elegant" science of nuclear physics, while making us "safe" from our enemies and offering us "cheap" and "peaceful" power, has littered the world with lethal messes that are apparently irremediable; and so on, to genetic engineering and other giddy "miracles." These developments, at least in their origin, are scientific. But the science involved has not been comprehensive or humble or self-critical or neighborly or publicly responsible. Mere self-interest obliges us to doubt the scientific faith that facts alone can assure the proper or safe use of facts. Modern science, as we have known it and as it has represented itself to us, has encouraged a healthy skepticism of everything but itself. But surely it implies no disrespect for science if we regard it with the skepticism upon which it prides itself.

We human beings, because we are short-lived creatures of limited intelligence, are going to remain under the necessity of talking about things that we don't provably know. But respect for "what is true," for what we don't know, and for our neighbors and fellow creatures requires us to know and to say when we *don't* know.

Prof. Weinberg understands religious belief as "the belief in facts about God or the afterlife." This is a mistake. If *fact* means what we have agreed that it means and if we respect the word, then we have to say with Chaucer that none of us knows any facts about God or the afterlife. If we did, there would be no issue of "belief." We know for sure that it is possible to speak of beliefs and opinions as facts, but that does not make the beliefs and opinions factual; it only makes them lies.

Most writers about religion, however, have not been scientists, or consciously subject to the methodological strictures of science. If they speak of knowledge, they may mean the things one knows from tradition or from unreplicable experience or "from the heart." Even so, in the Bible the language of belief often falls far short of the confidence of factual knowledge. It is most moving—and, to me, it seems most authentic—when it is honestly confronting its own inadequacy or the inadequacy or failure of knowledge. Far from the cocksureness of fundamentalism, the starting place of authentic belief or faith is not-knowing.

One of the primary characteristics of the biblical God is his irreducibility: He cannot be confined in any structure of human comprehension. And so in I Kings, having completed his temple, Solomon cries out, not with confident religiosity, but with despair; his mighty work has contradicted what apparently was its purpose: "But will God indeed dwell on the earth? behold, the heaven and heaven of heavens cannot contain thee; how much less this house that I have builded" (8:27)? The supplication of Mark 9:24 is likewise authenticated by its honest unknowing, unconfidence, and sense of struggle: "Lord, I believe; help thou my unbelief." And Paul's letter to the Romans is precise and unrelenting in his definition of hope: "For we are saved by hope: but hope that is seen is not hope: for what a man seeth, why doth he yet hope for? But if we hope for that we see not, *then* do we with patience wait for it" (8:24-25). *Faith,* at root, is related to *bide* and *abide.* It has certainly the sense of belief, but also of difficult belief, of waiting, of patience, of endurance, of hanging on and holding together.

And so Prof. Weinberg's definition of belief involves not only a misuse of the word *facts,* but also an implicit misunderstanding of the word *faith.*

I dislike very much the disciplinary provincialisms of the universities; therefore, as a literary person, I ought to be delighted that Prof. Weinberg finds literature as irresistible as religion. But I am obliged instead to regret that he speaks of it with complacent oversimplification and ineptitude. When he says, for example, that "nothing prevents those of us who have no religious belief from enjoying religious poetry," does he mean that such enjoyment is the same for believers and unbelievers? If so, how does he know this? Does he have a way of comparing objectively the degrees and kinds of enjoyment? I would gladly agree that enjoyment is a desirable, maybe even a necessary, result of any art; but is enjoyment the only or the highest effect of religious art? What is it about religious art that unbelievers enjoy? The underlying question here, and an important one, is this: how do you authenticate, and make credible to somebody else, your response to a work of art? Prof. Weinberg seems not to have suspected that this question exists, or that it implies a careful difficult job of work.

He likewise suspects no danger in his assertion that "we see already that little English language poetry written in the past few decades owes anything to belief in God." But who is "we"? How many decades does he have in mind? What is signified by "little"? The existence of God is not a statistical issue to be proved or disproved by quantities of belief or numbers of believers. If God exists, then, like Prof. Weinberg, He exists independently of anybody's knowledge or anybody's belief or disbelief in His existence. If *nobody* believed in God, Prof. Weinberg would still have his case to make, and evidence would be required of him that he cannot produce.

He says further that "very great poetry can be written without religion," using Shakespeare as his example, apparently unaware that Shakespeare's religion is still a controversial issue among Shakespearean scholars. But you don't have to be an expert— you only have to read the Bible and the plays— to know of Shakespeare's frequent allusions to scripture and his concern with scriptural themes such as mercy and forgiveness and scriptural characters such as the good and faithful servant. But, if great poetry can be written without religion, what does that prove about religion? It proves only that great poetry can be written without it.

In the boring, pointless, and destructive quarrel between fundamentalist science and fundamentalist religion, it seems to me that both sides are wrong. The religious fundamentalists are wrong because their disrespect for the materiality of the world involves, as a matter of course, disrespect for material evidence. They are like a jury that sees no significance in a smoking gun because its members don't believe in guns or smoke. The fundamentalist scientists are wrong because they counter one absolutism with another. Against their own history and tradition they assume the posture of absolute certainty and unquestionability. Both sides assume that they are right now and forever. Neither can say "I don't know" or "I wonder." Both are bigoted, unforgiving, and humorless.

In his troubled and consoling last book of poems, *Second Space,* Czeslaw Milosz includes a poem of exemplary generosity:

> If there is no God,
> Not everything is permitted to man.
> He is still his brother's keeper
> And he is not permitted to sadden his brother,
> By saying there is no God.

This instruction, as Milosz undoubtedly knew, is perfectly reversible: if there is a God, that does not justify condescension or insult to your atheist neighbor. Such differences, so far as I can see, become issues of justice only when one side attempts to abridge or deny the freedom of the other.

If in fact the fundamentalist scientists were as smart as they think they are, and if the religious fundamentalists were as secure in their belief as they claim to be, then they would (except for issues of justice) leave one another in peace. These camps keep pestering each other because they need each other. The sort of mind that is inclined to fundamentalism is not content within itself or within its own convictions or principles. It needs to humiliate its opponents. It needs the sustenance of converts. It is fundamentally insecure and ungenerous.

Worst of all, the fundamentalists of both science and religion do not adequately understand or respect imagination. Is imagination merely a talent, such as a good singing voice, the ability to "make things up" or "think things up" or "get ideas"? Or is it, like science, a way of knowing things that can be known in no other way? We have much reason to think that it is a way of knowing things not otherwise knowable. As the word *imagination* itself suggests, it is the power to make us *see,* and to see, moreover, things that without it would be unseeable. In one of its aspects it is the power by which we sympathize. By its means we may see what it was to be Odysseus or Penelope, or David or Ruth, or what it is to be one's neighbor or one's enemy. By it we may "see ourselves as others see us." It is also the power by which we see the place, the predicament, or the story we are in.

To use what is by now the most notorious example, the creation story in Genesis is neither science nor pseudo-science, neither history nor pseudo-history. Like other traditional creation stories, it welled up out of the oldest, deepest human imagination to help us, even now, to see what it is to have a wondrous world that had a beginning in time. It is not true by the corroboration of contemporary documents or of physical evidence. It is the imagination, in the high sense given to it by the greatest poets, that assents to its truth, just as it assents to the story of King Lear or Blake's rendering of Jacob's vision. The following lines by Hayden Carruth, rightly ignoring the unwinnable contest of science versus religion, were written with a proper deference to mystery and a proper respect for imagination:

> The *Iliad*, the *Odyssey*, the book of Genesis,
> These were acts of love, I mean deeply felt gestures, which
> continuously bestow upon us
> What we are.
>
> —*Toward the Distant Islands*

As for the afterlife, it has been imagined by Homer, Virgil, the biblical writers, Dante, and others, with the result that at least some of us, their willing heirs, have imagined it also.

I don't see that scientists would suffer the loss of any skin from their noses by acknowledging the validity and the power of imaginative truths, which are harmless to the truths of science, even though imagination in the highest sense seems allied less to science than to religion. The first chapters of Genesis are imagined and imaginable, whereas the big bang theory is the result of calculation. If you have read Dante, you can imagine Hell, Purgatory, and Heaven, but reading Prof. Weinberg cannot help you to imagine "nothing."

Perhaps the most interesting thing that Prof. Weinberg says in his essay is this: "There are plenty of people without religious faith who live exemplary moral lives (as for example, me)." This of course is a joke, modeled on the shameless self-commendation of politicians; but it is a joke without a context sufficient to reveal how large and sad a joke it is. The large sad fact that gives the joke its magnitude and its cutting edge is that there is probably not one person now living in the United States who, by a strict accounting, could be said to be living an exemplary moral life.

We are still somewhere in the course of the most destructive centuries of human history. And, though I believe I know some pretty good people whom I love and admire, I don't know one who is not implicated, by direct participation and by proxies given to suppliers, in an economy, recently national and now global, that is the most destructive, predatory, and wasteful the world has ever seen. Our own country in only a few hundred years has suffered the loss of maybe half its arable topsoil, most of its original forest and prairie, much too much of its mineral wealth and underground water. Most of its surface water and all of its air are polluted. Its rural cultures—the cultures, at their best, of husbandry—have been almost annihilated. Many of its plants and animals, both wild and domestic, are extinct or in danger. It is littered with wastelands, landfills, and, most shameful and fearful of all, dumps, industrial sites, and whole landscapes made dangerous virtually forever by radioactive waste. An immense part of this damage has been done in the years since World War II, when the machinery and chemicals of industrial warfare have been turned upon the land—to make production "efficient" by the most doubtful standards and to replace the people-of-the-land economies. I have no doubt that the dualisms of body and soul, heaven and earth, too prominent among the religious, have been damaging both to people and to the world, for that division has made it easy to withhold the necessary protections from material things. But the materialists of the science-technology-industry complex, whose minds are not so divided, and who might have been expected to value highly the material world, have instead held it in contempt and damaged it more than anybody.

Scientists and scholars in the knowledge industry—corporate or academic, if there is a difference—are probably in the greatest moral jeopardy of anybody except political, military, and corporate leaders. All knowledge now is potentially a commodity, and there is no way for its originators to control, or even foresee, the uses to which it may be put.

I would like, in conclusion, to bring up a question of religion and politics that I think needs more attention from everybody, but maybe especially from atheists. Before going on, I had better say that I adhere absolutely to the First Amendment. Any form of religious coercion by religious organizations or by governments would be intolerable to me. The idea of the separation of church and state seems to me fairly clear when it is a matter simply of limiting the powers of institutions. But the world is not so simple as to allow a neat clear separation of politics and religion or of politics and irreligion.

My question is about the origin and existence of human rights. How did we get them? How are they authenticated? In ancient traditional cultures such as those of surviving peasant or hunter-gatherer communities, the people may be said to possess certain rights by tradition and inheritance; because they have possessed them immemorially, they possess them still. No modern government, younger and of shallower origin, could rightfully revoke or ignore them. A younger nation of recent immigrants such as the United States possesses no rights by immemorial tradition and inheritance. The founders understood this, and so they stated in our Declaration of Independence the principle that "all men" (which we now construe as "all people") "are endowed by their Creator with certain inalienable Rights."

I don't think it is adequately appreciated how essential, and what a stroke of political brilliance, that statement is. The purport of it is that, as humans, we have rights that precede the existence of any government. We therefore were not on our knees to the government of Great Britain then, and we are not kneeling to our own government now, beseeching a grant of rights. As a would-be free people we were, and we are, requiring any government whatever to recognize and honor the rights we have always possessed by divine gift. The difference between rights granted by a government and rights given by "our Creator" is critical, for it is the difference between rights that are absolute and rights that are contingent upon the will or the whim of those in power.

The possession of rights by divine endowment obviously is an article of faith, for it has no objective or empirical standing. It would have no standing at all with a government in principle atheistic. (We had better hope, I think, that the separation of church and state implies the separation of institutional atheism and the state.) But, vulnerable as this principle may be, as an article merely of faith, I know of no other authorization of human rights that can adequately replace it.

It is easy to anticipate that some who will not allow any validity to divine rights will bring forward "natural rights" as an alternative. But this too would be an article of faith, and it forces upon us the probably unanswerable question of what, in the nature of nature, might bring forth and confer upon us rights specifically human.

I am not able to settle such questions even to my own satisfaction. And so I am obliged to conclude by offering the possibility that we humans are by definition, and perhaps by nature, creatures of faith (which we are as likely to place in luck or science or the free market or our own intelligence as in some version of God) and that we are further defined by principles and cultural properties, not objectively verifiable, that we inherit.

Points of Engagement—Reading Comprehension

1. How does Berry define fundamentalism? What are the roles of "power" and "victory" in fundamentalism? Cite places in the text to support your answer.
2. What is the basis of Berry's objection to Weinberg's argument?

3. According to Berry, what is the value of imagination? What is its relationship to science? What is its relationship to God?
4. Why does Berry believe that arguments between religious fundamentalists and scientific fundamentalists are "boring, pointless, and destructive"(25)? What would such arguments destroy?
5. What does Berry mean that "the starting place of faith is not-knowing" (23)? Why is this important to his argument regarding fundamentalism in religion and science?
6. What is Berry's primary argument regarding science, god and imagination? Try to write it in 2 sentences using all 3 terms.

Points of Departure—Assignment Questions

1. For Berry, any kind of fundamentalism, whether "religious, atheistical, scientific, technological, economic, and political," will be dangerous because fundamentalist thinking insists on claiming to know the one and only truth. It oversimplifies by insisting it must win the either/or battle against a more complex both/and kind of thinking. Zadie Smith is also concerned about being forced to oversimplify complex relationships. Smith points out that each of us is made up of a complicated back-story and multiple histories. When and how can disparate ideas exist side by side? What makes it possible to "speak simultaneous truths" as Smith describes? How might Smith's idea of the "double voice" help us understand Berry's dispute with science and religion? Consider, too, how each author thinks of "inheritance." You may also answer this question by using Goodall, Eck, or Orr.
2. Wendell Berry criticizes Steven Weinberg for writing the following: "I can imagine how disturbed they [religious conservatives] will feel in the future, when at last scientists learn how to understand human behavior in terms of the chemistry and physics of the brain and nothing is left that needs to be explained by our having an immaterial soul" (22). In other words, when there are no more "gaps" in scientific knowledge to be "filled in" by God or the soul, then God will not be needed. What do you think about this idea? Does belief in science make God unnecessary? Or is there a place for God in the world of science? Write a paper in which you answer these questions referencing Wendell Berry's essay, and one of the following authors, who are all social or physical scientists: Susan Blackmore, Jane Goodall, Alison Gopnik, or Lauren Slater. Be sure to explain their positions in response to these questions as you frame your own.

3. Wendell Berry believes that fundamentalists of both religion and science do not adequately understand or respect imagination, which, when properly defined, is a "way of knowing" as much as science or religion is. Moreover, imagination is a window into things that are "not otherwise knowable." Imagination "is the power to make us see…things that without it would be unseeable" (25). Both Alison Gopnik and Adam Gopnik also write about our irrepressible imaginations. Your project for this paper is to work with Berry and either Alison or Adam Gopnik to form your position on this question: What contributions can imagination make to our "knowing the world" that cannot or would not be made in any other way? You might also work with Alain de Botton or Jeanette Winterson.
4. Wendell Berry studies the language and meaning of human rights that are "endowed by the Creator." These rights, Berry argues, are articles of faith and he believes that humans are creatures of faith (28). Yet where do these rights derive their authority when faith is not shared? Kristof and WuDunn study the example of girl trafficking which may be among the most heinous violations of human rights; however, is the principle that identifies these rights "vulnerable," as Berry suggests, if no Creator has endowed them? Berry admits himself that an article of faith about human rights "would have no standing at all with a government in principle atheistic" (28). Even if we claim "'natural rights' as an alternative … what, in the nature of nature, might bring forth and confer upon us rights specifically human"? (28) Use Berry and Kristof and WuDunn to develop your own position on the origin and enforcement of human rights. Is it possible for them to be universal? If so, how? If not, why not?

Strange Creatures

Susan Blackmore

Points of Access—Pre-Reading

1. What have you learned about genetics from your biology classes? How do genes replicate? Why do some genetic traits survive, while others die off?
2. Think about something—an idea, a fashion, or an object—that you used to think was really cool, but no longer is. Why did you think that something was 'cool' in the first place? How did you find out about it? Why do you think it's not cool any more? Did someone tell you, or did you decide gradually on your own?
3. What do you think it is that makes humans different from other animals? What ideas have you heard? What do *you* believe?

We humans are strange creatures. There is no doubt that our bodies evolved by natural selection just as other animals' did. Yet we differ from all other creatures in many ways. For a start we speak. We believe ourselves to be the most intelligent species on the planet. We are extraordinarily widespread and extremely versatile in our ways of making a living. We wage wars, believe in religions, bury our dead and get embarrassed about sex. We watch television, drive cars and eat ice cream. We have had such a devastating impact upon the ecosystems of our planet that we appear to be in danger of destroying everything on which our lives depend. One of the problems of being a human is that it is rather hard to look at humans with an unprejudiced eye.

On the one hand, we are obviously animals comparable with any others. We have lungs, hearts and brains made of living cells; we eat and breathe and reproduce. Darwin's theory of evolution by natural selection can successfully explain how we, along with the rest of life on this planet, came to be here, and why we all share so many characteristics. On the other hand, we behave quite differently from other animals. Now that biology has so successfully explained much of our similarity with other creatures we need to ask the opposite question. What makes us so different? Could it be our superior intelligence, our consciousness, our language, or what?

A common answer is that we are simply more intelligent than any other species. Yet the notion of intelligence is extremely slippery, with interminable arguments about how to define it, how to measure it, and to what extent it is inherited. Research in artificial intelligence (AI) has provided some nice surprises for those who thought they knew what makes human intelligence so special.

In the early days of AI, researchers thought that if they could teach a computer to play chess they would have reproduced one of the highest forms of human intelligence. In those days the idea that a computer could ever play well, let alone beat a Grand Master, was unthinkable. Yet now most home computers come with passable chess programmes already installed, and in 1997 the program *Deep Blue* beat World Champion Garry Kasparov, ending unquestioned human supremacy at the game. Computers may not play chess in the same way as humans, but their success shows how wrong we can be about intelligence. Clearly, what we thought were human beings' most special capabilities may not be.

Quite the opposite goes for some apparently quite unintelligent things like cleaning the house, digging the garden or making a cup of tea. Time and again AI researchers have tried to build robots to carry out such tasks and been defeated. The first problem is that the tasks all require vision. There is a popular (though possibly apocryphal) story about Marvin Minsky at MIT (the Massachusetts Institute of Technology) that he once gave his graduate students the problem of vision as a summer project. Decades later the problem of computer vision is still just that—a problem. We humans can see so effortlessly that we cannot begin to imagine how complex the process has to be. And in any case, this kind of intelligence cannot distinguish us from other animals because they can see too.

If intelligence does not provide simple answers perhaps consciousness might. Many people believe that human consciousness is unique and is responsible for making us human. Yet scientists cannot even define the term 'consciousness'. Everyone knows what their own consciousness is like but they cannot share that knowledge with anyone else. This troublesome fact—the subjectivity of consciousness—may explain why for most of this century the whole topic of consciousness was more or less banned from scientific discussion. Now at last it has become fashionable again, but scientists and philosophers cannot even agree on what an explanation of consciousness would look like. Some say that the 'Hard Problem' of subjectivity is quite different from any other scientific problem and needs a totally new kind of solution, while others are sure that when we fully understand brain function and behaviour the problem of consciousness will have disappeared.

Some people believe in the existence of a human soul or spirit that transcends the physical brain and explains human uniqueness. With the decline in religious belief fewer and fewer people intellectually accept that view, yet most of us continue to think of ourselves as a little conscious 'me' inside our brain; a 'me' who sees the world, makes the decisions, directs the actions and has responsibility for them.

As we shall see later, this view has to be wrong. Whatever the brain is doing it does not seem to need help from an extra, magical self. Various parts of the brain carry on their tasks independently of each other and countless different things are always going on at once. We may feel as though there is a central place inside our heads into which the sensations come and from which we consciously make the decisions. Yet this place simply does not exist. Clearly, something is very wrong with our ordinary view of our conscious selves. From this confused viewpoint we cannot say with certainty that other animals are not conscious, nor that consciousness is what makes us unique. So what does?

What Makes Us Different?

The thesis of this book is that what makes us different is our ability to imitate.

Imitation comes naturally to us humans. Have you ever sat and blinked, or waved, or 'goo gooed', or even just smiled, at a baby? What happens? Very often they blink too, or wave, or smile back at you. We do it so easily, even as an infant. We copy each other all the time. Like seeing, it comes so effortlessly that we hardly think about it. We certainly do not think of it as being something very clever. Yet, as we shall see, it is fantastically clever.

Certainly, other animals do not take naturally to it. Blink, or wave, or smile at your dog or cat and what happens? She might purr, wag her tail, twitch, or walk away, but you can be pretty sure she will not imitate you. You can teach a cat, or rat, to beg neatly for its food by progressively rewarding it, but you cannot teach it by demonstrating the trick yourself—nor can another cat or rat. Years of detailed research on animal imitation has led to the conclusion that it is extremely rare. Though we may think of mother cats as teaching their kittens to hunt, or groom, or use the cat door, they do not do it by demonstration or imitation. Parent birds 'teach' their babies to fly more by pushing them out of the nest and giving them the chance to try it than by demonstrating the required skills for them to copy.

There is a special appeal to stories of animals copying human behaviour, and pet owners are fond of such tales. I read on the Internet about a cat who learned to flush the toilet and soon taught a second cat the same trick. Now the two of them sit together on the cistern flushing away. A more reliable anecdote was told by Diana Reiss, a psychologist at Rutgers University. She works with bottlenose dolphins, who are known to be able to copy vocal sounds and artificial whistles, as well as simple actions (Bauer and Johnson 1994; Reiss and McCowan 1993). She trained the dolphins by giving them fish as a reward and also by a 'time out' procedure for punishment. If they did the wrong thing she would walk away from the water's edge and wait for one minute before returning to the pool. One day she threw a fish to one of the dolphins but had accidentally left on some spiky bits of fin. Immediately the dolphin turned, swam away, and waited for a minute at the other side of the pool.

That story touched me because I could not help thinking of the dolphins as *understanding* the action, as having intelligence and consciousness and intentionality like ours. But we cannot even define these things, let alone be sure that the dolphin was using them in this apparent act of reciprocation. What we can see is that it imitated Dr. Reiss in an appropriate way. We are so oblivious to the cleverness of imitation that we do not even notice how rare it is in other animals and how often we do it ourselves.

Perhaps more telling is that we do not have separate words for radically different kinds of learning. We use the same word 'learning' for simple association or 'classical conditioning' (which almost all animals can do), for learning by trial and error or 'operant conditioning' (which many animals can do), and for learning by imitation (which almost none can do). I want to argue that the supreme ease with which we are capable of imitation, has blinded us to this simple fact—that *imitation* is what makes us special.

Imitation and the Meme

When you imitate someone else, something is passed on. This 'something' can then be passed on again, and again, and so take on a life of its own. We might call this thing an idea, an instruction, a behaviour, a piece of information . . . but if we are going to study it we shall need to give it a name.

Fortunately, there is a name. It is the 'meme'.

The term 'meme' first appeared in 1976, in Richard Dawkins's best-selling book *The Selfish Gene*. In that book Dawkins, an Oxford zoologist, popularised the increasingly influential view that evolution is best understood in terms of the competition between genes. Earlier in the twentieth century, biologists had blithely talked about evolution occurring for the 'good of the species' without worrying about the exact mechanisms involved, but in the 1960s serious problems with this view began to be recognised (Williams 1966). For example, if a group of organisms all act for the good of the group then one individual who does not can easily exploit the rest. He will then leave more descendants who in turn do not act for the group, and the group benefit will be lost. On the more modern 'gene's eye view', evolution may *appear* to proceed in the interests of the individual, or for the good of the species, but in fact it is all driven by the competition between genes. This new viewpoint provided a much more powerful understanding of evolution and has come to be known as 'selfish-gene theory'.

We must be absolutely clear about what 'selfish' means in this context. It does not mean genes *for* selfishness. Such genes would incline their carriers to act selfishly and that is something quite different. The term 'selfish' here means that the genes act only for themselves; their only interest is their own replication; all they want is to be passed on to the next generation. Of course, genes do not 'want' or have aims or intentions in the same way as people do; they are only chemical instructions that can be copied. So when I say they 'want', or are 'selfish' I am using a shorthand, but this shorthand is necessary to avoid lengthy explanations. It will not lead us astray if we remember that genes either *are* or *are not* successful at getting passed on into the next generation. So the shorthand 'genes want x' can always be spelled out as 'genes that do *x* are more likely to be passed on'. This is the only power they have—replicator power. And it is in this sense that they are selfish.

Dawkins also introduced the important distinction between 'replicators' and their 'vehicles'. A replicator is anything of which copies are made, including 'active replicators' whose nature affects the chances of their being copied again. A vehicle is the entity that interacts with the environment, which is why Hull (1988a) prefers the term 'interactors' for a similar idea. Vehicles or interactors carry the replicators around inside them and protect them. The original replicator was presumably a simple self-copying molecule in the primeval soup, but our most familiar replicator now is DNA. Its vehicles are organisms and groups of organisms that interact with each other as they live out their lives in the seas or the air, the forests or fields. Genes are the selfish replicators that drive the evolution of the biological world here on earth but Dawkins believes there is a more fundamental principle at work. He suggested that wherever it arises, anywhere in the universe, 'all life evolves by the differential survival of replicating entities' (1976, p. 192). This is the foundation for the idea of Universal Darwinism; the application of Darwinian thinking way beyond the confines of biological evolution.

At the very end of the book he asked an obvious, if provocative, question. Are there any other replicators on our planet? The answer, he claimed, is 'Yes'. Staring us in the face, although still drifting clumsily about in its primeval soup of culture, is another replicator—a unit of imitation.

> We need a name for the new replicator, a noun that conveys the idea of a unit of cultural transmission, or a unit of *imitation*. 'Mimeme' comes from a suitable Greek root, but I want a monosyllable that sounds a bit like 'gene'. I hope my classicist friends will forgive me if I abbreviate mimeme to meme.

As examples, he suggested tunes, ideas, catch-phrases, clothes fashions, ways of making pots or of building arches'. He mentioned scientific ideas that catch on and propagate themselves around the world by jumping from brain to brain. He wrote about religions as groups of memes with a high survival value, infecting whole societies with belief in a God or an afterlife. He talked about fashions in dress or diet, and about ceremonies, customs and technologies—all of which are spread by one person copying another. Memes are stored in human brains (or books or inventions) and passed on by imitation.

In a few pages, Dawkins laid the foundations for understanding the evolution of memes. He discussed their propagation by jumping from brain to brain, likened them to parasites infecting a host, treated them as physically realised living structures, and showed how mutually assisting memes will gang together in groups just as genes do. Most importantly, he treated the meme as a replicator in its own right. He complained that many of his colleagues seemed unable to accept the idea that memes would spread for their own benefit, independently of any benefit to the genes. 'In the last analysis they wish always to go back to "biological advantage"' to answer questions about human behaviour. Yes, he agreed, we got our brains for biological (genetic) reasons but now we have them a new replicator has been unleashed. 'Once this new evolution begins, it will in no necessary sense be subservient to the old' (Dawkins 1976, pp. 193-4). In other words, memetic evolution can now take off without regard to its effects on the genes.

If Dawkins is right then human life is permeated through and through with memes and their consequences. Everything you have learned by imitation from someone else is a meme. But we must be clear what is meant by the word 'imitation', because our whole understanding of memetics depends on it. Dawkins said that memes jump from 'brain to brain via a process which, in the broad sense, can be called imitation' (1976, p. 192). I will also use the term 'imitation' in the broad sense. So if, for example, a friend tells you a story and you remember the gist and pass it on to someone else then that counts as imitation. You have not precisely imitated your friend's every action and word, but something (the gist of the story) has been copied from her to you and then on to someone else. This is the 'broad sense' in which we must understand the term 'imitation'. If in doubt, remember that something must have been copied.

Everything that is passed from person to person in this way is a meme. This includes all the words in your vocabulary, the stories you know, the skills and habits you have picked up from others and the games you like to play. It includes the songs you sing and the rules you obey. So, for example, whenever you drive on the left (or the right), eat curry with lager or pizza and coke, whistle the theme tune from *Neighbours* or even shake hands, you are dealing in memes. Each of these memes has evolved in its own unique way with its own history, but each of them is using your behaviour to get itself copied.

Take the song 'Happy Birthday to You'. Millions of people—probably thousands of millions of people the world over—know this tune. Indeed, I only have to write down those four words to have a pretty good idea that you may soon start humming it to yourself. Those words affect you, probably quite without any conscious intention on your part, by stirring up a memory you already possess. And where did that come from? Like millions of other people you have acquired it by imitation. Something, some kind of information, some kind of instruction, has become lodged in all those brains so that now we all do the same thing at birthday parties. That something is what we call the meme.

Memes spread themselves around indiscriminately without regard to whether they are useful, neutral, or positively harmful to us. A brilliant new scientific idea, or a technological invention, may spread because of its usefulness. A song like Jingle Bells may spread because it sounds OK, though it is not seriously useful and can definitely get on your nerves. But some memes are positively harmful—like chain letters and pyramid selling, new methods of fraud and false doctrines, ineffective slimming diets and dangerous medical 'cures'. Of course, the memes do not care; they are selfish like genes and will simply spread if they can.

Remember that the same shorthand applies to memes as to genes. We can say that memes are 'selfish', that they 'do not care', that they 'want' to propagate themselves, and so on, when all we mean is that successful memes are the ones that get copied and spread, while unsuccessful ones do not. This is the sense in which memes 'want' to get copied, 'want' you to pass them on and 'do not care' what that means to you or your genes.

This is the power behind the idea of memes. To start to think memetically we have to make a giant flip in our minds just as biologists had to do when taking on the idea of the selfish gene. Instead of thinking of our ideas as our own creations, and as working for us, we have to think of them as autonomous selfish memes, working only to get themselves copied. We humans, because of our powers of imitation, have become just the physical 'hosts' needed for the memes to get around. This is how the world looks from a 'meme's eye view'.

Meme Fear

This is a scary idea indeed. And perhaps that is why the word 'meme' is so often written with inverted commas around it, as though to apologise for using it. I have even seen eminent lecturers raise both hands and tweak them above their ears when forced to say 'meme' out loud. Gradually, the word has become more generally known, and has even been added to the *Oxford English Dictionary.* There are discussion groups and a *Journal of Memetics* on the Internet, and the idea almost seems to have acquired a cult following in cyberspace. But in academia it has not yet been so successful. A perusal of some of the best recent books on human origins, the evolution of language and evolutionary psychology shows that the word does not appear at all in most of them ('meme' is not in the indexes of Barkow *et al.* 1992; Diamond 1997; Dunbar 1996; Mithen 1996; Pinker 1994; Mark Ridley 1996; Tudge 1995; Wills 1993; Wright 1994). The idea of memes seems extremely relevant to these disciplines, and I want to argue that it is time for us to take on board the notion of a second replicator at work in human life and evolution.

One of the problems with the idea of memes is that it strikes at our deepest assumptions about who we are and why we are here. This is always happening in science. Before Copernicus and Galileo, people believed they lived at the centre of the universe in a world created especially for them by God. Gradually, we had to accept not only that the sun does not revolve around the earth, but that we live on some minor little planet in an ordinary galaxy in a vast universe of other galaxies.

A hundred and forty years ago Darwin's theory of evolution by natural selection provided the first plausible mechanism for evolution without a designer. People's view of their own origin changed from the biblical story of special creation in the image of God, to an animal descended from an apelike ancestor—a vast leap indeed, and one that led to much ridicule and fanatical opposition to Darwin. Still—we have all coped with that leap and come to accept that we are animals created by evolution. However, if memetics is valid, we will have to make another vast leap in accepting a similar evolutionary mechanism for the origin of our minds and our selves.

* * *

What will determine whether the theory of memes is worth having or not? Although philosophers of science argue over what makes a scientific theory valid, there are at least two commonly agreed criteria, and I will use these in judging memetics. First, a theory must be able to explain things better than its rival theories; more economically or more comprehensively. And second, it must lead to testable predictions that turn out to be correct. Ideally, those predictions should be unexpected ones—things that no one would have looked for if they were not starting from a theory of memetics.

My aim in this book is to show that many aspects of human nature are explained far better by a theory of memetics than by any rival theory yet available. The theory starts only with one simple mechanism—the competition between memes to get into human brains and be passed on again. From this, it gives rise to explanations for such diverse phenomena as the evolution of the enormous human brain, the origins of language, our tendency to talk and think too much, human altruism, and the evolution of the Internet. Looked at through the new lens of the memes, human beings look quite different.

Is the new way better? It seems obviously so to me, but I expect that many people will disagree. This is where the predictions come in. I shall try to be as clear as I can in deriving predictions and showing how they follow from mimetic theory. I may speculate and even, at times, leap wildly beyond the evidence, but as long as the speculations can be tested then they can be helpful. In the end, the success or failure of these predictions will decide whether memes are just a meaningless metaphor or the grand new unifying theory we need to understand human nature.

Points of Engagement—Reading Comprehension

1. What is a meme? Point to two passages in Blackmore's essay to support your answer.
2. What relationship do memes have with genes?
3. How do memes replicate? Be specific. Give two examples: one from Blackmore's essay, and one of your own.

Points of Departure—Assignment Questions

1. In "Strange Creatures," Susan Blackmore offers a theory of what differentiates humans from other animals: the meme. She proposes that "what makes us different is our ability to imitate" (33). Other animals may not be able to imitate, but Sherry Turkle presents a compelling case that robots already can, and will only get better. What do we make of advances in imitative and responsive technologies, which, of course, have been invented by humans? Are we making our own uniqueness obsolete by creating robots more and more like ourselves? Write a paper in which you explore this dilemma using the ideas of Blackmore and Turkle, and proposing a clear answer of your own.

2. In this chapter of her book, *The Meme Machine*, Blackmore claims that human beings are "merely physical 'hosts' needed for the memes to get around" (37). But what about our human abilities to entertain "counterfactuals," or "possible worlds," as Alison Gopnik calls them, those "coulda-woulda-shouldas of life" that are not part of past, present or future reality? Gopnik's "science of the imagination" (164) seems to contradict directly Blackmore's theory of memes as somehow "controlling" what and how we think. Whose explanation for the origin and transmission of human thought do you find more compelling? Why? Can they both be right?
3. Is there a God in the Meme Machine? Can we understand everything using scientific reasoning, the logic of the finite mind, or is there a superordinate power? If so, what is it? Your project is to answer those questions while engaging with the ideas of Susan Blackmore and Wendell Berry and/or Jane Goodall. Do you agree more with Blackmore or the other author/s you've chosen? Do you think that God might be a parable for understanding memes, that memes might be a scientific explanation for understanding God, or do you think the two must be kept separate? Why?
4. In her essay, "Who Holds the Clicker," Lauren Slater discusses the history, arguments for and against, and implications of "psycho-surgery" or "neurosurgery for psychiatric disorders." She suggests that "psychosurgery, by its very nature, brings with it a thicket of ethical twisters. Whose head is it?" (234). Given Blackmore's argument about genetics, memetics, and the "meme's eye view," we might ask the same question of all human beings. Do we have control of our own minds at all? What do you think? Your project in this paper is to answer these questions using relevant claims and examples from both Slater and Blackmore's essays.
5. *Religion as meme?* Consider the following quote from Susan Blackmore's essay: "One of the problems with the idea of memes is that it strikes at our deepest assumptions about who we are and why we are here" (38). Religion is one way that many human beings aim to understand this very question of "who we are." What, then, if religion is simply a meme? What does it mean that we have so many different religions, and that they can cause such havoc and also such comfort? If religion is a meme, how would that understanding affect the way we read Diana Eck's history of religious diversity and pluralism in America? If religion is a meme, how would that affect our understanding of Wendell Berry's argument in "God, Science, and Imagination"? Write a paper in which you answer one of these questions using Blackmore and either Eck or Berry.

Democracy in Cyberspace: What Technology Can and Cannot Do for Us

Ian Bremmer

Points of Access—Pre-Reading

1. Do you think the U.S. government should be allowed to read your text messages? Why or why not? What is gained and lost depending on how you answer?
2. Is it ever appropriate for a government to censor information on the Internet? If so, what kind of information? For what reasons?
3. When you post something online (on Twitter or Facebook or the latest form of social media) do you think about who is reading it? If you do, do you think twice about what you post?
4. Do you think of the Internet as something free and open? If you knew it were being censored or your activities followed, would you feel differently about using it? Change your behavior? How?

"Information technology has demolished time and distance," Walter Wriston, the former CEO of what is now Citigroup wrote in 1997. "Instead of validating Orwell's vision of Big Brother watching the citizen, [it] enables the citizen to watch Big Brother. And so the virus of freedom, for which there is no antidote, is spread by electronic networks to the four corners of the earth." Former Presidents Ronald Reagan, Bill Clinton, and George W. Bush have articulated a similar vision, and with similarly grandiose rhetoric. All have argued that the long-term survival of authoritarian states depends on their ability to control the flow of ideas and information within and across their borders. As advances in communications technology—cellular telephones, text messaging, the Internet, social networking—allow an ever-widening circle of people to easily and inexpensively share ideas and aspirations, technology will break down barriers between peoples and nations. In this view, the spread of the "freedom virus" makes it harder and costlier for autocrats to isolate their people from the rest of the world and gives ordinary citizens tools to build alternative sources of power. The democratization of communications, the theory goes, will bring about the democratization of the world.

There seems to be plenty of evidence to support these ideas. In the Philippines in 2001, protesters sent text messages to organize the demonstrations that forced President Joseph Estrada from office. In the lead-up to the 2004 presidential election in Ukraine, supporters of Viktor Yushchenko, then the leader of the opposition, used text messaging to organize the massive protests that became the Orange Revolution. In Lebanon in 2005, activists coordinated via e-mail and text messaging to bring one million demonstrators into the streets to demand that the Syrian government end nearly three decades of military presence in Lebanon by withdrawing its 14,000 troops. (Syria complied a month later, under considerable international pressure.) Over the past few years, in Colombia, Myanmar (also known as Burma), and Zimbabwe, demonstrators have used cell phones and Facebook to coordinate protests and transmit photographs and videos of government crackdowns. The flood of words and images circulated by protesters following Iran's bitterly disputed 2009 presidential election—quickly dubbed the "Twitter revolution" —seemed to reinforce the view that Tehran has more to fear from "citizen media" than from the U.S. ships patrolling the Persian Gulf.

But a closer look at these examples suggests a more complicated reality. Only in democracies—the Philippines, Ukraine, Lebanon, and Colombia—did these communications weapons accomplish an immediate objective. In Myanmar, Zimbabwe, and Iran, they managed to embarrass the government but not to remove it from power. As Wriston acknowledged, the information revolution is a long-term process, cyberspace is a complex place, and technological advances are no substitute for human wisdom. Innovations in modern communications may help erode authoritarian power over time. But for the moment, their impact on international politics is not so easy to predict.

There are many reasons why the optimistic view of the relationship among communications, information, and democracy has taken root in the United States. First, these communications tools embody twenty-first-century innovation, and Americans have long believed in the power of invention to promote peace and create prosperity. And with good reason. Admirers of Reagan argue that the United States' ability to invest in strategic missile defense sent the Soviet leadership into a crisis of confidence from which it never recovered. The light bulb, the automobile, and the airplane have changed the world, bringing greater personal autonomy to many Americans. Similarly, Americans believe that the millions of people around the world who use the Internet, an American invention, will eventually adopt American political beliefs, much like many of those who wear American jeans, watch American movies, and dance to American music have. Champions of the Internet's power to promote pluralism and human rights point to bloggers in China, Russia, and the Arab world who are calling for democracy and the rule of law for their countries, sometimes in English.

But of the hundreds of millions who blog in their own languages—there are more than 75 million in China alone—the vast majority have other priorities. Many more of them focus on pop culture rather than on political philosophy, on pocketbook issues rather than political power, and on national pride rather than cosmopolitan pretensions. In other words, the tools of modern communications satisfy as wide a range of ambitions and appetites as their twentieth-century ancestors did, and many of these ambitions and appetites do not have anything to do with democracy.

Net Neutrality

A careful look at the current impact of modern communications on the political development of authoritarian states should give pause to those who hail these technologies as instruments of democratization. Techno-optimists appear to ignore the fact that these tools are value neutral; there is nothing inherently pro-democratic about them. To use them is to exercise a form of freedom, but it is not necessarily a freedom that promotes the freedom of others.

In enabling choice, the introduction of the Internet into an authoritarian country shares something fundamental with the advent of elections. Some have argued that promoting elections in one country in the Middle East will generate demand for elections elsewhere there. "A free Iraq is going to help inspire others to demand what I believe is a universal right of men and women," Bush said in July 2006; elections in Iraq would prompt the citizens of Iraq's neighbors to ask why Iraqis were now free to choose their leaders whereas they were not. Similarly, some have argued that the freedom that comes with the Internet will inevitably democratize China. Once Chinese people read about the freedoms of others, the thinking goes, they will want the same for themselves. The tools of modern communications will reveal to Chinese citizens the political freedoms they do not yet have and provide the means to demand them.

But the limited history of elections in the Middle East shows that people do not always vote for pluralism. Sometimes, they vote for security or absolutism, sometimes to express outrage or defend local interests. The same pattern holds true for the Internet and other forms of modern communications. These technologies provide access to information of all kinds, information that entertains the full range of human appetites—from titillation to rationalization, from hope to anger. They provide the user with an audience but do not determine what he will say. They are a megaphone, and have a multiplier effect, but they serve both those who want to speed up the cross-border flow of information and those who want to divert or manipulate it.

Cyberspace can be a very dark place. In *You Are Not a Gadget,* Jaron Lanier argues that the anonymity provided by the Internet can promote a "culture of sadism," feeding an appetite for drive-by attacks and mob justice. In China, the Internet has given voice to wounded national pride, anti-Western and anti-Japanese resentment over injuries both real and imagined, and hostility toward Tibetans, Muslim Uighurs, and other minority groups. It has also become a kind of public square for improvised violence. In an article for *The New York Times Magazine* earlier this year, Tom Downey described the "human-flesh search" phenomenon in China, "a form of online vigilante justice in which Internet users hunt down and punish people who have attracted their wrath." The targets of these searches, a kind of "crowd-sourced detective work," as Downey put it, can be corrupt officials or enemies of the state, or simply people who have made other people angry.

These problems are hardly unique to China. In Russia, skinheads have filmed murderous attacks on dark-skinned immigrants from the Caucasus and Central Asia and posted the footage online. Also in Russia—and in the United States and Europe—hate groups and militants of various kinds use the Internet to recruit new members and disseminate propaganda. Of course, beyond all this fear and loathing, many more people around the world use the Internet as a global shopping mall and a source of entertainment. The Internet makes it easier for users with political interests to find and engage with others who believe what they believe, but there is little reliable evidence that it also opens their minds to ideas and information that challenge their worldviews. The medium fuels many passions—consumerism and conspiracy theories, resentment and fanaticism—but it promotes calls for democracy only where there is already a demand for democracy. If technology has helped citizens pressure authoritarian governments in several countries, it is not because the technology created a demand for change. That demand must come from public anger at authoritarianism itself.

Stateside

Citizens are not the only ones active in cyberspace. The state is online, too, promoting its own ideas and limiting what an average user can see and do. Innovations in communications technology provide people with new sources of information and new opportunities to share ideas, but they also empower governments to manipulate the conversation and to monitor what people are saying.

The collapse of Soviet communism a generation ago taught authoritarian leaders around the world that they could not simply mandate lasting economic growth and that they would have to embrace capitalism if they hoped to create the jobs and the higher standards of living that would ensure their long-term political survival. But to embrace capitalism is to allow for dangerous new freedoms. And so in order to generate strong growth while maintaining political control, some autocrats have turned to state capitalism, a system that helps them dominate market activity through the use of national oil companies, other state-owned enterprises, privately owned but politically loyal national champions, state-run banks, and sovereign wealth funds.

Following precisely the same logic, authoritarian governments are now trying to ensure that the increasingly free flow of ideas and information through cyberspace fuels their economies without threatening their political power. In June, the Chinese government released its first formal statement on the rights and responsibilities of Internet users. The document "guarantee[d] the citizens' freedom of speech on the Internet as well as the public's right to know, to participate, to be heard, and to oversee [the government] in accordance with the law." But it also stipulated that "within Chinese territory, the Internet is under the jurisdiction of Chinese sovereignty." That caveat legitimates China's "great firewall," a system of filters and re-routers, detours and dead ends designed to keep Chinese Internet users on the state-approved online path.

The Chinese leadership also uses more low-tech means to safeguard its interests online. The average Chinese Web surfer cannot be sure that every idea or opinion he encounters in cyberspace genuinely reflects the views of its author. The government has created the 50 Cent Party, an army of online commentators that it pays for each blog entry or message-board post promoting the Chinese Communist Party's line on sensitive subjects. This is a simple, inexpensive way for governments to disseminate and disguise official views. Authoritarian states do not use technology simply to block the free flow of unwelcome ideas. They also use it to promote ideas of their own.

Nonaligned Movement

The techno-optimists who hope that modern communications tools will democratize authoritarian states are also hoping that they will help align the interests of nondemocracies with those of democracies. But the opposite is happening. Efforts by police states to control or co-opt these tools are inevitably creating commercial conflicts that then create political conflicts between governments.

In January, Google publicly complained that private Gmail accounts had been breached in attacks originating in China—attacks that Chinese officials appeared to tolerate or even to have launched themselves. In protest, Google announced that it would no longer censor the results of users' searches in mainland China, which it had reluctantly agreed to do when it entered the Chinese market in 2006. Beijing refused to back down, and Google automatically redirected searches by Chinese users to the uncensored Hong

Kong version of the site. But much to the relief of mainland users, mostly students and researchers who prefer Google's capabilities to its main domestic rival, Baidu, Chinese officials eventually announced the renewal of Google's operating license. (It is possible that they backtracked because they believed that they could control Google or use it to monitor the online activities of political dissidents.)

As Chinese technology companies begin to compete on a par with Western ones and the Chinese government uses legal and financial means to more actively promote domestic firms that see censorship as a routine cost of doing business, there will be less demand for Google's products in China. In August 2010, the state-run Xinhua News Agency and China Mobile, the country's largest cell-phone carrier, announced plans to jointly build a state-owned search-engine and media company. In response to these developments, U.S. technology companies will undoubtedly turn to U.S. lawmakers for help in creating and maintaining a level commercial playing field in China. Far from aligning American and Chinese political values and bringing the citizens of the two countries closer together, conflicts over the flow of information through cyberspace will further complicate the already troubled U.S.-Chinese relationship.

Signs of strife are already visible. When Google first went public with its complaints about cyberattacks and censorship, Beijing looked past the company, which it sees as a high-tech arm of the U.S. government, and addressed its response directly to Washington. A Chinese Communist Party tabloid ran an editorial under the headline "The World Does Not Welcome the White House's Google"; it argued, "Whenever the U.S. government demands it, Google can easily become a convenient tool for promoting the U.S. government's political will and values abroad." In response, U.S. Secretary of State Hillary Clinton urged companies such as Google not to cooperate with "politically motivated censorship," further emphasizing the difference, not the convergence, of political values in the United States and China.

Revealing similar fears about the future of its political control, the United Arab Emirates and Saudi Arabia took action earlier this year against Research in Motion (RIM), the Canadian company that makes the BlackBerry, for equipping its devices with encryption technology that authorities cannot decode. Arguing that terrorists and spies could use BlackBerries to communicate within the UAE without fear of being detected, Emirati officials announced in August that they would soon suspend BlackBerry service unless RIM provided state officials with some means of monitoring BlackBerry messaging. Within two days, Saudi Arabia announced a similar shutdown, although Riyadh and RIM have since reached a compromise that requires RIM to install a relay server on Saudi territory, which allows Saudi officials to monitor messages sent from and within the country. The UAE will probably also make a deal with RIM: there are half a million BlackBerry users in the UAE (about ten percent of the population), and the country wants to remain the Arab world's primary commercial and tourist hub. Yet far from promoting Western values in non-Western police states, the BlackBerry has sparked a new round of debate over the willingness of Western technology companies to protect their market shares by making concessions that help authoritarian governments spy on their citizens.

In fairness to these governments, the world's leading democracies are no less concerned about potential terrorist threats posed by unmonitored messaging. The Indian government has also threatened to ban BlackBerries unless RIM gives it access to certain data, and counterterrorism officials in the United States and Europe are considering the option as well. Via efforts to amend the Electronic Communications Privacy Act, the Obama administration has already taken steps to help the FBI gain access to "electronic communication transactional records"—recipients' addresses, logs of users' online activities, browser histories—without a court order if investigators suspect terrorism or espionage. Politicians and technology companies such as Google and RIM will be fighting these battles for years to come.

Of course, authoritarian governments, unlike democracies, also worry that individuals who are neither terrorists nor spies will use new communications tools to challenge their political legitimacy. China, Iran, Myanmar, North Korea, Saudi Arabia, and other authoritarian states cannot halt the proliferation of weapons of modern communications, but they can try to monitor and manipulate them for their own purposes. That struggle will continue as well, limiting the ability of new technologies to empower the political opposition within these countries and creating more conflicts over political values between democratic and authoritarian states.

Feedback Loops

The Internet may have changed the world, but now the world is changing the Internet. For 30 years, new communications technologies have driven globalization, the defining trend of the times. The companies that created these products made long-term plans based on the wants and needs of consumers, not governments. Their profits rose as they connected billions of customers with one another; borders became increasingly less important.

But now, the pace of technological change and the threat of terrorism are forcing policymakers to expand their definitions of national security and to rethink their definitions of "critical infrastructure." As a result, governments are turning to high-tech communications firms to help shore up emerging security vulnerabilities, and high-tech communications firms have begun to think more like defense contractors—companies whose success depends on secrecy, exclusivity, political contacts, and security clearances.

As a result, political borders, which the rise of information technology once seemed set to dissolve, are taking on a new importance: if greater openness creates new opportunities, it also creates new worries. Unable to match U.S. defense spending, China and Russia have become adept at information warfare. The Pentagon reported last August that China continues to develop its ability to steal U.S. military secrets electronically and to deny its adversaries "access to information essential to conduct combat operations." In 2007, a massive cyberattack launched from inside Russia damaged digital infrastructure in neighboring Estonia. The United States' vulnerabilities range from its nuclear power plants and electrical grids to the information systems of government agencies and major U.S. companies. Despite their political and commercial rivalries, the United States, China, Russia, India, and many other states also share a vulnerability to cyberattacks, and they have pledged to work together to build a joint cybersecurity strategy. But when it comes to espionage, governments can never fully trust one another. And of course the Obama administration does not want to share technologies that would make it easier for security officials in Beijing or Moscow to track the online activities of political dissidents.

Other problems will exacerbate international tensions. Technology firms in the United States and Europe, mindful of Google's recent troubles in China, will increasingly turn to their governments for help with their own security needs. As cyberthreats become ever more sophisticated, these companies will collaborate more actively with national security agencies on developing new technologies. This will pull more technology companies into the orbit of the military-industrial complex. That, in turn, will make them even more suspect to authoritarian regimes and likelier targets for hackers and spies of all kinds. Borders are about to become much more important.

The result will be a world that has not one Internet but a set of interlinked intranets closely monitored by various governments. The Internet is not about to disappear, but the prediction that a single Internet could accommodate both the West and the evolving demands of authoritarian states was never realistic. American and European users will access the same Internet as before, but the Chinese government has already made clear its intention to declare sovereignty over an Internet of its own. Other authoritarian states have every incentive to follow its lead.

There are far too many variables at work to predict with confidence the full, long-term impact of modern tools of communications on the political development of authoritarian states. But it seems safe to expect that their effects will vary as widely as the motives of the people and the states that use them.

Points of Engagement—Reading Comprehension

1. What is the "freedom virus" (41)? What does it produce? Using correct punctuation, quote or paraphrase relevant passages from the essay in your response. What is Bremmer's position on this idea of the "freedom virus"? How do you know?
2. According to Ian Bremmer, what factors need to be present in a country for the Internet and social media to promote democracy and political freedoms? What happens with the Internet in countries with authoritarian political regimes if those factors are not present? What is the relationship that Bremmer sees between democracy and social media like Twitter and Facebook?
3. What is Bremmer arguing against? What points of view or positions on political freedoms and the Internet is he trying to change? Cite passages from the text to support your answer.
4. What is "Net Neutrality" (43)? How might Twitter, Facebook, and other forms of social media help groups promoting democratic freedoms? How might these media be used against these groups? What is Bremmer's position on the future of Internet use by citizens and their governments?

Points of Departure—Assignment Questions

1. While Ian Bremmer and Malcolm Gladwell, author of "Small Change," are both skeptical of the capacity of Twitter and Facebook to effect profound social change, they each point out advantages social media provide groups of like-minded people. Write a paper exploring the role of social media in promoting a cause and making real changes in people's thinking, discussing both the advantages and disadvantages social media bring to achieving that goal. Take the following steps in order to produce your draft:
   - Consider first how each writer depicts the successful use of social media by groups advocating for change. Where do you see similarities between the two essays? Where do you see differences in emphasis?
   - Then consider where the two writers see social media fall short in support of social change. You should continue to identify and respect differences in emphasis and

position between the two writers.

- Finally, reflect on what you think would need to happen for one group of people to change everyone else's mind about something. Can social media help to accomplish this?

2. James Fallows in "Win in China!" looks at another medium and its potential for social change: reality television. While reality-TV in America might reflect certain values and beliefs about business and free markets, those values may not be as common in a country that has come to capitalism only lately. Fallows writes about the use of a reality-TV show in China to educate the Chinese, who have been raised on communism for several generations, in those Western values necessary to capitalism. In your own view, how successfully does Fallows think the show promotes some of capitalism's basic values? Consider what advice Bremmer might give the show's producers on how to promote these values, and what predictions he might make about the show's success. Where might he see promise? Where might he see difficulty? Your project for your paper should be to explain how successful you think the show will be in achieving its goals based on what you have gathered from the essays by Bremmer and Fallows, and to reflect on how beneficial you think might it be for the Chinese should it prove to be successful.
3. The potential for the exportation of Western values and culture across the world to promote political freedoms is controversial, to say the least. Naomi Klein in "Fences of Enclosure, Windows of Possibility" looks at some of the promises and realities of bringing capitalism, free markets, and democracy to other countries, what we call globalization, and finds a complex and at times frightening relationship between liberalization and new restrictions. She uses the metaphor of fences to describe new restrictions on political freedom that sometimes accompany economic freedoms, and windows for new and unexpected areas of freedom that open up. Bremmer talks about how borders are changing as Internet technologies advance and shift. How might the Internet and social media be like windows in Klein's sense? How might they be used to create fences? What borders are being affected? In what ways do Bremmer and Klein share a point of view about democracy and social change? In what ways might they disagree about globalization? Write an essay in which you make your own argument about the connections between social media, globalization, and democratic freedoms, using the similarities and differences between Klein and Bremmer to fix your own position. Be sure also to use their terms—fences, windows, and borders—to help you.

Why Chinese Mothers are Superior

Amy Chua

Points of Access—Pre-Reading

1. Think about the most important caretakers in your life: parents, grandparents, godparents, family friends. How would you describe the way they raised you? Strict? Lenient? Permissive? Controlling? What effect did their parenting approach have on you and the way you think about yourself? Did you find their parenting approach effective? Why or why not?
2. Where are your grandparents from? Where are your parents from? Where were you born? How have these places of origin influenced the way they raised you, and the way you grew up? Do you think there is a connection between where people are from and how they approach parenting, child-rearing, and family?
3. Consider the title of this essay, "Why Chinese Mothers Are Superior." How do you feel about this statement? How does it make you feel about the author? Now consider this: the author of this article, Amy Chua, did not provide the title; the title was chosen and printed by the editors of the *Wall Street Journal,* where the article appeared. Does that change your gut reaction? Will knowing this change the way you read this essay? How? Why or why not?

A lot of people wonder how Chinese parents raise such stereotypically successful kids. They wonder what these parents do to produce so many math whizzes and music prodigies, what it's like inside the family, and whether they could do it too. Well, I can tell them, because I've done it. Here are some things my daughters, Sophia and Louisa, were never allowed to do:

- attend a sleepover
- have a playdate
- be in a school play
- complain about not being in a school play
- watch TV or play computer games
- choose their own extracurricular activities

- get any grade less than an A
- not be the No. 1 student in every subject except gym and drama
- play any instrument other than the piano or violin
- not play the piano or violin.

I'm using the term "Chinese mother" loosely. I know some Korean, Indian, Jamaican, Irish and Ghanaian parents who qualify too. Conversely, I know some mothers of Chinese heritage, almost always born in the West, who are not Chinese mothers, by choice or otherwise. I'm also using the term "Western parents" loosely. Western parents come in all varieties.

All the same, even when Western parents think they're being strict, they usually don't come close to being Chinese mothers. For example, my Western friends who consider themselves strict make their children practice their instruments 30 minutes every day. An hour at most. For a Chinese mother, the first hour is the easy part. It's hours two and three that get tough.

Despite our squeamishness about cultural stereotypes, there are tons of studies out there showing marked and quantifiable differences between Chinese and Westerners when it comes to parenting. In one study of 50 Western American mothers and 48 Chinese immigrant mothers, almost 70% of the Western mothers said either that "stressing academic success is not good for children" or that "parents need to foster the idea that learning is fun." By contrast, roughly 0% of the Chinese mothers felt the same way. Instead, the vast majority of the Chinese mothers said that they believe their children can be "the best" students, that "academic achievement reflects successful parenting," and that if children did not excel at school then there was "a problem" and parents "were not doing their job." Other studies indicate that compared to Western parents, Chinese parents spend approximately 10 times as long every day drilling academic activities with their children. By contrast, Western kids are more likely to participate in sports teams.

What Chinese parents understand is that nothing is fun until you're good at it. To get good at anything you have to work, and children on their own never want to work, which is why it is crucial to override their preferences. This often requires fortitude on the part of the parents because the child will resist; things are always hardest at the beginning, which is where Western parents tend to give up. But if done properly, the Chinese strategy produces a virtuous circle. Tenacious practice, practice, practice is crucial for excellence; rote repetition is underrated in America. Once a child starts to excel at something —whether it's math, piano, pitching or ballet—he or she gets praise, admiration and satisfaction. This builds confidence and makes the once not-fun activity fun. This in turn makes it easier for the parent to get the child to work even more.

Chinese parents can get away with things that Western parents can't. Once when I was young—maybe more than once—when I was extremely disrespectful to my mother, my father angrily called me "garbage" in our native Hokkien dialect. It worked really well. I felt terrible and deeply ashamed of what I had done. But it didn't damage my self-esteem or anything like that. I knew exactly how highly he thought of me. I didn't actually think I was worthless or feel like a piece of garbage.

As an adult, I once did the same thing to Sophia, calling her garbage in English when she acted extremely disrespectfully toward me. When I mentioned that I had done this at a dinner party, I was immediately ostracized. One guest named Marcy got so upset she broke down in tears and had to leave early. My friend Susan, the host, tried to rehabilitate me with the remaining guests.

The fact is that Chinese parents can do things that would seem unimaginable—even legally actionable—to Westerners. Chinese mothers can say to their daughters, "Hey fatty—lose some weight." By contrast, Western parents have to tiptoe around the issue, talking in terms of "health" and never ever mentioning the f-word, and their kids still end up in therapy for eating disorders and negative self-image. (I also once heard a Western father toast his adult daughter by calling her "beautiful and incredibly competent." She later told me that made her feel like garbage.)

Chinese parents can order their kids to get straight As. Western parents can only ask their kids to try their best. Chinese parents can say, "You're lazy. All your classmates are getting ahead of you." By contrast, Western parents have to struggle with their own conflicted feelings about achievement, and try to persuade themselves that they're not disappointed about how their kids turned out.

I've thought long and hard about how Chinese parents can get away with what they do. I think there are three big differences between the Chinese and Western parental mind-sets.

First, I've noticed that Western parents are extremely anxious about their children's self-esteem. They worry about how their children will feel if they fail at something, and they constantly try to reassure their children about how good they are notwithstanding a mediocre performance on a test or at a recital. In other words, Western parents are concerned about their children's psyches. Chinese parents aren't. They assume strength, not fragility, and as a result they behave very differently.

For example, if a child comes home with an A-minus on a test, a Western parent will most likely praise the child. The Chinese mother will gasp in horror and ask what went wrong. If the child comes home with a B on the test, some Western parents will still praise the child. Other Western parents will sit their child down and express disapproval, but they will be careful not to make their child feel inadequate or insecure, and they will not call their child "stupid," "worthless" or "a disgrace." Privately, the Western parents may worry that their child does not test well or have aptitude in the subject or that there is something wrong with the curriculum and possibly the whole school. If the child's grades do not improve, they may eventually schedule a meeting with the school principal to challenge the way the subject is being taught or to call into question the teacher's credentials.

If a Chinese child gets a B—which would never happen—there would first be a screaming, hair-tearing explosion. The devastated Chinese mother would then get dozens, maybe hundreds of practice tests and work through them with her child for as long as it takes to get the grade up to an A.

Chinese parents demand perfect grades because they believe that their child can get them. If their child doesn't get them, the Chinese parent assumes it's because the child didn't work hard enough. That's why the solution to substandard performance is always to excoriate, punish and shame the child. The Chinese parent believes that their child will be strong enough to take the shaming and to improve from it. (And when Chinese kids do excel, there is plenty of ego-inflating parental praise lavished in the privacy of the home.)

Second, Chinese parents believe that their kids owe them everything. The reason for this is a little unclear, but it's probably a combination of Confucian filial piety and the fact that the parents have sacrificed and done so much for their children. (And it's true that Chinese mothers get in the trenches, putting in long grueling hours personally tutoring, training, interrogating and spying on their kids.) Anyway, the understanding is that Chinese children must spend their lives repaying their parents by obeying them and making them proud.

By contrast, I don't think most Westerners have the same view of children being permanently indebted to their parents. My husband, Jed, actually has the opposite view. "Children don't choose their parents," he once said to me. "They don't even choose to be born. It's parents who foist life on their kids, so it's the parents' responsibility to provide for them. Kids don't owe their parents anything. Their duty will be to their own kids." This strikes me as a terrible deal for the Western parent.

Third, Chinese parents believe that they know what is best for their children and therefore override all of their children's own desires and preferences. That's why Chinese daughters can't have boyfriends in high school and why Chinese kids can't go to sleepaway camp. It's also why no Chinese kid would ever dare say to their mother, "I got a part in the school play! I'm Villager Number Six. I'll have to stay after school for rehearsal every day from 3:00 to 7:00, and I'll also need a ride on weekends." God help any Chinese kid who tried that one.

Don't get me wrong: It's not that Chinese parents don't care about their children. Just the opposite. They would give up anything for their children. It's just an entirely different parenting model.

Here's a story in favor of coercion, Chinesestyle. Lulu was about 7, still playing two instruments, and working on a piano piece called "The Little White Donkey" by the French composer Jacques Ibert. The piece is really cute—you can just imagine a little donkey ambling along a country road with its master—but it's also incredibly difficult for young players because the two hands have to keep schizophrenically different rhythms.

Lulu couldn't do it. We worked on it nonstop for a week, drilling each of her hands separately, over and over. But whenever we tried putting the hands together, one always morphed into the other, and everything fell apart. Finally, the day before her lesson, Lulu announced in exasperation that she was giving up and stomped off.

"Get back to the piano now," I ordered.

"You can't make me."

"Oh yes, I can."

Back at the piano, Lulu made me pay. She punched, thrashed and kicked. She grabbed the music score and tore it to shreds. I taped the score back together and encased it in a plastic shield so that it could never be destroyed again. Then I hauled Lulu's dollhouse to the car and told her I'd donate it to the Salvation Army piece by piece if she didn't have "The Little White Donkey" perfect by the next day. When Lulu said, "I thought you were going to the Salvation Army, why are you still here?" I threatened her with no lunch, no dinner, no Christmas or Hanukkah presents, no birthday parties for two, three, four years. When she still kept playing it wrong, I told her she was purposely working herself into a frenzy because she was secretly afraid she couldn't do it. I told her to stop being lazy, cowardly, self-indulgent and pathetic.

Jed took me aside. He told me to stop insulting Lulu—which I wasn't even doing, I was just motivating her—and that he didn't think threatening Lulu was helpful. Also, he said, maybe Lulu really just couldn't do the technique—perhaps she didn't have the coordination yet—had I considered that possibility?

"You just don't believe in her," I accused.

"That's ridiculous," Jed said scornfully. "Of course I do."

"Sophia could play the piece when she was this age."

"But Lulu and Sophia are different people," Jed pointed out.

"Oh no, not this," I said, rolling my eyes. "Everyone is special in their special own way," I mimicked sarcastically. "Even losers are special in their own special way. Well don't worry, you don't have to lift a finger. I'm willing to put in as long as it takes, and I'm happy to be the one hated. And you can be the one they adore because you make them pancakes and take them to Yankees games."

I rolled up my sleeves and went back to Lulu. I used every weapon and tactic I could think of. We worked right through dinner into the night, and I wouldn't let Lulu get up, not for water, not even to go to the bathroom. The house became a war zone, and I lost my voice yelling, but still there seemed to be only negative progress, and even I began to have doubts.

Then, out of the blue, Lulu did it. Her hands suddenly came together—her right and left hands each doing their own imperturbable thing—just like that.

Lulu realized it the same time I did. I held my breath. She tried it tentatively again. Then she played it more confidently and faster, and still the rhythm held. A moment later, she was beaming.

"Mommy, look—it's easy!" After that, she wanted to play the piece over and over and wouldn't leave the piano. That night, she came to sleep in my bed, and we snuggled and hugged, cracking each other up. When she performed "The Little White Donkey" at a recital a few weeks later, parents came up to me and said, "What a perfect piece for Lulu—it's so spunky and so *her.*"

Even Jed gave me credit for that one. Western parents worry a lot about their children's self-esteem. But as a parent, one of the worst things you can do for your child's self-esteem is to let them give up. On the flip side, there's nothing better for building confidence than learning you can do something you thought you couldn't.

There are all these new books out there portraying Asian mothers as scheming, callous, overdriven people indifferent to their kids' true interests. For their part, many Chinese secretly believe that they care more about their children and are willing to sacrifice much more for them than Westerners, who seem perfectly content to let their children turn out badly. I think it's a misunderstanding on both sides. All decent parents want to do what's best for their children. The Chinese just have a totally different idea of how to do that.

Western parents try to respect their children's individuality, encouraging them to pursue their true passions, supporting their choices, and providing positive reinforcement and a nurturing environment. By contrast, the Chinese believe that the best way to protect their children is by preparing them for the future, letting them see what they're capable of, and arming them with skills, work habits and inner confidence that no one can ever take away.

Points of Engagement—Reading Comprehension

1. What are some of the characteristics that Chua attributes to Chinese parenting? How do "Chinese mothers" view their children and their own role in raising them? What are some of the characteristics she attributes to Western parenting? According to Chua, how do "Western parents" see their children and their own responsibilities in raising them? Cite specific passages that support your answers.
2. Amy Chua articulates three main differences between the Chinese and Western parental mind-sets. What are they? Quote or paraphrase each difference, using correct punctuation, and provide a short example from Chua's text for each. Do you agree with Chua on the differences between "Chinese" and Western parenting? Why or why not?
3. Chua claims that "Chinese parents can get away with things that Western parents can't" (53). What is she referring to in this quotation? Why do you think she makes this claim? What point is she trying to make? Do you agree with her? Why or why not?
4. Consider the last sentence of Chua's article: "Western parents try to respect their children's individuality, encouraging them to pursue their true passions, supporting their choices, and providing positive reinforcement and a nurturing environment. By contrast, the Chinese believe that the best way to protect their children is by preparing them for the future, letting them see what they're capable of, and arming them with skills, work habits and inner confidence that no one can ever take away" (56). She presents a very black and white view of these two models of parenting. Based on your experience as a child being raised, where does she hit the mark? Where is she off? How would you revise her claims about "Chinese" and "Western" parents based on your own experience?

Points of Departure—Assignment Questions

1. How much is too much to give up in order to provide a better life for someone else? Consider the parent-child relationships in essays by Amy Chua, Lisa Belkin, and Arlie Russell Hochschild. What have the parents in these essays sacrificed for the children? What have they lost or gained themselves by doing what they have done? Do these authors think that the children and families are better off for the sacrifices? In what ways? Why or why not?
2. Think about the dual identities many Americans claim: Chinese-American, Japanese-American, African-American. What does the hyphen do to the sense of identity

for people who claim it? For people who do not? What are the *risks* and *realities* of stereotyping groups of people based on their ethnicity, heritage, place of origin, or any other marker of identity? Write a paper in which you discuss the ideas and experiences of Amy Chua and one of the following: Diana Eck, Zadie Smith, or Kenji Yoshino. Use their terms to help you.

3. Amy Chua, James Fallows, and Kenji Yoshino all depict the intersection of Western and East Asian cultures as a clash and absorption of behaviors, beliefs, and values. However, the authors present different evaluations of what happens when people and ideas from Chinese, Japanese and Western cultures meet, and mingle. What do we learn about "America" translated through another culture, such as Chua's critique of Western parenting, Yoshino's parents' Japanese view of American education, or as we see reality TV—a quintessentially American creation—through Chinese TV? Consider the reverse: what do we learn about Chinese or Japanese culture translated through American experience, such as the Tiger Mother raising her children in the U.S., or Kenji Yoshino's experience of being raised both in the U.S. and Japan?
4. Alison Gopnik and Amy Chua present very different pictures of children, their potential, their behavior, and the adults around them. Think about the parenting strategies describe by Amy Chua, both Chinese and Western. How does Gopnik's chapter on the brains of babies influence our understanding of Chua's claims? Where is the balance between discipline, choosing for your children, and freedom, letting their imaginations determine what they do? What would Gopnik say to the title of Chua's essay? *Are* Chinese mothers superior? Or does Western parenting better respond to Gopnik's findings about the way children learn?

Brainstorm
Trump is President
for new experiences
to get away
more culture
diff. language

On Habit

Alain de Botton

Points of Access—Pre-Reading

1. Why do you think people go away on vacation? Write down five reasons that you can think of. What are you able to do, and to see, on vacation that it is impossible to do at home?
2. What can cause you to act differently from the way you normally act? Do you think that your physical environment causes you to act in certain ways? Can changing your physical environment cause changes in your behavior? Can you change your behavior without changing your physical environment, or is it often too difficult to do so?
3. Look at some familiar object in your room. Try to write half a page describing it. Think of this description as trying to paint the object with words. Do you notice things about it that you had not before? What makes this experience different from the way you usually experience this object? Has your attitude towards the object changed after looking at it in so much detail?

1.

I returned to London from Barbados to find that the city had stubbornly refused to change. I had seen azure skies and giant sea anemones, I had slept in a raffia bungalow and eaten a kingfish, I had swum beside baby turtles and read in the shade of coconut trees. But the home town was unimpressed. It was still raining. The park was still a pond, and the skies funereal. When we are in a good mood and it is sunny, it is tempting to impute a connection between what happens inside and outside of us, but the appearance of London on my return was a reminder of the indifference of the world to any of the events unfolding in the lives of its inhabitants. I felt despair to be home. I felt there could be few worse places on earth than the one I had been fated to spend my existence in.

2.

> The sole cause of man's unhappiness is that he does not know how to stay quietly in his room.
>
> Pascal, *Pensées,* 136

3.

From 1799 to 1804, Alexander von Humboldt undertook a journey around South America, later entitling the account of what he had seen *Journey to the Equinoctial Regions of the New Continent.*

Nine years earlier, in the spring of 1790, a twenty-seven-year-old Frenchman, Xavier de Maistre, undertook a journey around his bedroom, later entitling the account of what he had seen *Journey around My Bedroom.* Gratified by his experiences, in 1798, De Maistre undertook a second journey. This time, he travelled by night and ventured out as far as the window-ledge, later entitling his account *Nocturnal Expedition around My Bedroom.*

Two approaches to travel: *Journey to the Equinoctial Regions of the New Continent, Journey around My Bedroom.* The first required ten mules, thirty pieces of luggage, four interpreters, a chronometer, a sextant, two telescopes, a Borda theodolite, a barometer, a compass, a hygrometer, letters of introduction from the King of Spain and a gun. The second, a pair of pink and blue cotton pyjamas.

Xavier de Maistre was born in 1763 in the picturesque town of Chambéry at the foot of the French Alps. He was of an intense, romantic nature, was fond of reading, especially Montaigne, Pascal and Rousseau, and of paintings, especially Dutch and French domestic scenes. At the age of twenty-three, De Maistre became fascinated by aeronautics. Etienne Montgolfier had, three years before, achieved international renown by constructing a balloon that flew for eight minutes above the royal palace at Versailles, bearing as passengers a sheep called Montauciel (Climb-to-the-sky), a duck and a rooster. De Maistre and a friend fashioned a pair of giant wings out of paper and wire and planned to fly to America. They did not succeed. Two years later De Maistre secured himself a place in a hot air balloon and spent a few moments floating above Chambéry before the machine crashed into a pine forest.

Then in 1790, while he was living in a modest room at the top of an apartment building in Turin, De Maistre pioneered a mode of travel that was to make his name: room-travel.

Introducing *Journey around My Bedroom,* Xavier's brother, the political theorist Joseph de Maistre, emphasized that it was not Xavier's intention to cast aspersions on the heroic deeds of the great travellers of the past: 'Magellan, Drake, Anson and Cook'. Magellan had discovered a western route to the Spice Islands around the southern tip of South America, Drake had circumnavigated the globe, Anson had produced accurate sea charts of the Philippines, and Cook had confirmed the existence of a southern continent. 'They were no doubt remarkable men,' wrote Joseph; it was just that his brother had discovered a way of travelling that might be infinitely more practical for those neither as brave nor as wealthy as they.

'Millions of people who, before me, had never dared to travel, others who had not been able to travel and still more who had not even thought of travelling will now be able to follow my example,' explained Xavier as he prepared for his journey. 'The most indolent beings won't have any more reason to hesitate before setting off to find pleasures that will cost them neither money nor effort.' He particularly recommended room-travel to the poor and to those afraid of storms, robberies and high cliffs.

4.

Unfortunately, De Maistre's own pioneering journey, rather like his flying machine, did not fly very far.

The story begins well. De Maistre locks his door and changes into his pink and blue pyjamas. Without the need for luggage, he travels to the sofa, the largest piece of furniture in the room. His journey having shaken him from his usual lethargy, he looks at it through fresh eyes and rediscovers some of its qualities. He admires the elegance of its feet and remembers the pleasant hours he has spent cradled in its cushions, dreaming of love and advancement in his career. From his sofa, De Maistre spies his bed. Once again, from a traveller's vantage point, he learns to appreciate this complex piece of furniture. He feels grateful for the nights he has spent in it and takes pride that his sheets almost match his pyjamas. 'I advise every man who can to get himself pink and white bedlinen,' he writes, for these are colours to induce calm and pleasant reveries in the fragile sleeper.

But thereafter De Maistre may be accused of losing sight of the overall purpose of his endeavour. He becomes mired in long and wearing digressions about his dog, Rosinne, his sweetheart, Jenny, and his faithful servant, Joannetti. Travellers in search of a specific report on room-travel risk closing *Journey around My Bedroom* feeling a little betrayed.

And yet De Maistre's work springs from a profound and suggestive insight that the pleasure we derive from journeys is perhaps dependent more on the mindset with which we travel than on the destination we travel to. If only we could apply a travelling mindset to our own locales, we might find these places becoming no less interesting than the high mountain passes and butterfly-filled jungles of Humboldt's South America.

What, then, is a travelling mindset? Receptivity might be said to be its chief characteristic. We approach new places with humility. We carry with us no rigid ideas about what is interesting. We irritate locals because we stand on traffic islands and in narrow streets and admire what they take to be strange small details. We risk getting run over because we are intrigued by the roof of a government building or an inscription on a wall. We find a supermarket or hairdresser's unusually fascinating. We dwell at length on the layout of a menu or the clothes of the presenters on the evening news. We are alive to the layers of history beneath the present and take notes and photographs.

Home, on the other hand, finds us more settled in our expectations. We feel assured that we have discovered everything interesting about a neighbourhood, primarily by virtue of having lived there a long time. It seems inconceivable that there could be anything new to find in a place which we have been living in for a decade or more. We have become habituated and therefore blind.

De Maistre tried to shake us from our passivity. In his second volume of room-travel, *Nocturnal Expedition around My Bedroom,* he went to his window and looked up at the night sky. Its beauty made him frustrated that such ordinary scenes were not more generally appreciated: 'How few people are right now taking delight in this sublime spectacle which the sky lays on uselessly for dozing humanity! What would it cost those who are out for a walk or crowding out of the theatre, to look up for a moment and admire the brilliant constellations which gleam above their heads?' The reason they weren't looking was that they had never done so before. They had fallen into the habit of considering their universe to be boring—and it had duly fallen into line with their expectations.

5.

I attempted to travel around my bedroom, but it was so small, with barely enough space for a bed, that I concluded that the De Maistrean message might prove more rewarding if it was applied to the neighbourhood as a whole.

So on a clear March day, at around three in the afternoon, several weeks after my return home from Barbados, I set out on a De Maistrean journey around Hammersmith.

It felt peculiar to be outside in the middle of the day with no particular goal in mind. A woman and two small blond children were walking along the main road, which was lined with a variety of shops and restaurants. A double-decker bus had stopped to pick up passengers opposite a small park. A giant billboard was advertising gravy. I walked along this particular road almost every day to reach my Underground station and was unused to considering it as anything other than a means to my end. Information that assisted me in my goal attracted my attention, what did not was judged irrelevant. I was therefore sensitive to the number of people on the pavement, for they might interrupt my path, whereas their faces and expressions were invisible to me, as invisible as the shapes of the buildings or the activity in the shops.

It had not always been thus. When I had first moved to the area, my attention had been less jealously focused. I had at that time not settled so firmly on the goal of reaching the Underground quickly.

On entering a new space, our sensitivity is directed towards a number of elements, which we gradually reduce in line with the function we find for the space. Of the 4,000 things there might be to see and reflect on in a street, we end up actively aware of only a few: the number of humans in our path, the amount of traffic and the likelihood of rain. A bus, which we might at first have viewed aesthetically or mechanically or as a springboard to thoughts about communities within cities, becomes simply a box to move us as rapidly as possible across an area which might as well not exist, so unconnected is it to our primary goal, outside of which all is darkness, all is invisible.

I had imposed a grid of interests on the street, which left no space for blond children and gravy adverts and paving stones and the colours of shop fronts and the expressions of businesspeople and pensioners. The power of my primary goal had drained me of the will to reflect on the layout of the park or on the unusual mixture of Georgian, Victorian and Edwardian architecture along a single block. My walks along the street had been excised of any attentiveness to beauty, of any associative thoughts, any sense of wonder or gratitude, any philosophical digressions sparked by visual elements. And in its place, there was simply an insistent call to reach the Underground posthaste.

However, following De Maistre, I tried to reverse the process of habituation, to disassociate my surroundings from the uses I had found for them until then. I forced myself to obey a peculiar kind of mental command: to look around me as though I had never been in this place before. And slowly, my travels began to bear fruit.

Under the command to consider everything as of potential interest, objects released latent layers of value. A row of shops which I had known as one large, undifferentiated reddish block acquired an architectural identity. There were Georgian pillars around one flower shop, and late Victorian Gothic-style gargoyles on top of the butcher's. A restaurant became filled with diners rather than shapes. In a glass-fronted office block, I noticed some people gesticulating in a boardroom on the first floor. Someone was drawing a pie chart on an overhead projector. At the same time, just across the road from the office, a man was pouring out new slabs of concrete for the pavement and carefully shaping their corners. I got on a bus and, rather than slipping at once into private concerns, tried to connect imaginatively with other passengers. I could hear a conversation in the row ahead of me. Someone in an office somewhere, a person quite high up in the hierarchy apparently, didn't understand. They complained of how inefficient others were, but never reflected on what they might have been doing to increase that inefficiency. I thought of the multiplicity of lives going on at the same time at different levels in a city. I thought of the similarities of complaints—always selfishness, always blindness—and the old psychological truth that what we complain of in others, others will complain of in us.

The neighbourhood did not just acquire people and defined buildings, it also began to collect ideas. I reflected on the new wealth that was spreading into the areas. I tried to think why I liked railway arches so much, and why the motorway that cut across the skyline.

It seemed an advantage to be travelling alone. Our responses to the world are crucially moulded by whom we are with, we temper our curiosity to fit in with the expectations of others. They may have a particular vision of who we are and hence subtly prevent certain sides of us from emerging: 'I hadn't thought of you as someone who was interested in flyovers,' they might intimidatingly suggest. Being closely observed by a companion can inhibit us from observing others, we become taken up with adjusting ourselves to the companion's questions and remarks, we have to make ourselves seem more normal than is good for our curiosity. But I had no such concerns, alone in Hammersmith in mid-afternoon. I had the freedom to act a little weirdly. I sketched the window of a hardware shop and word-painted the flyover.

6.

De Maistre was not only a room-traveller. He was also a great traveller in the classic sense. He journeyed to Italy and Russia, he spent a winter with the royalist armies in the Alps and fought a Russian campaign in the Caucasus.

In an autobiographical note written in 1801 in South America, Alexander von Humboldt had written of his motives for travelling: 'I was spurred on by an uncertain longing to be transported from a boring daily life to a marvellous world.' It was this dichotomy, 'boring daily life' pitted against 'marvellous world', that De Maistre had tried to redraw with greater subtlety. He would not have told Humboldt that South America was dull, he would merely have urged him to consider that his native Berlin might have something to offer too.

Eight decades later, Nietzsche, who had read and admired De Maistre (and spent much time in his room), picked up on the thought:

> When we observe how some people know how to manage their experiences—their insignificant, everyday experiences—so that they become an arable soil that bears fruit three times a year, while others—and how many there are!—are driven through surging waves of destiny, the most multifarious currents of the times and the nations, and yet always remain on top, bobbing like a cork, then we are in the end tempted to divide mankind into a minority (a minimality) of those who know how to make much of little, and a majority of those who know how to make little of much.

We meet people who have crossed deserts, floated on icecaps and cut their way through jungles—and yet in whose souls we would search in vain for evidence of what they have witnessed. Dressed in pink and blue pyjamas, satisfied within the confines of his own bedroom, Xavier de Maistre was gently nudging us to try, before taking off for distant hemispheres, to notice what we have already seen.

Points of Engagement—Reading Comprehension

1. On page 63 de Botton claims that he had imposed a "grid of interests" on the suburb, Hammersmith, where he lives. Explain, in your own words, what it means to impose a grid of interests on something. Is it possible that such a view of the world could be positive, or is it only ever negative way, as de Botton sees it?
2. In the first paragraph of his essay, de Botton expresses a feeling of discontent, of malaise (if you don't know what this word means, look it up). By the end of the essay, he says something quite different: he seems to be cured of his restlessness, and viewing his world in quite a different way. How do you think he cured himself? Give two quotations from the essay, and explain what you think they show.
3. Give two reasons from de Botton as to why traveling around your bedroom, or around your town, is a good idea. Why is it better than embarking on a von Humboldt-style journey? Why is it not the same? Provide evidence from the text.

Points of Departure—Assignment Questions

1. While de Botton discusses our reactions to physical spaces, the same thinking can be applied to our interactions with people and with ideas. Think about what may

help people, or cause people, to change their perspectives or the way they interact with the world. Is being confronted with new places, objects, or people the only way we can cause a change in our attitudes, or are there other ways? Answer this question using de Botton and one other essay by Jane Goodall, Malcom Gladwell, Zadie Smith, or Jeanette Winterson.

2. Like Alain de Botton and Xavier de Maistre in "On Habit," the little girl Olivia in Adam Gopnik's "Bumping into Mr. Ravioli" pays a lot of attention to, and is deeply affected by, aspects of her environment. Is it ever possible to notice too much? To be too sensitive and reactive to the world around us? What are the consequences if we are? Can stimulation from your environment influence your behavior and your character in negative or distressing ways, or is it all, ultimately, to the good? Propose your own answers to these questions in conversation with the essays by de Botton and one of the following authors: Adam Gopnik, Arlie Russell Hochschild, Gregory Orr, Jeanette Winterson, or Kenji Yoshino.
3. How does Alain de Botton's idea of what can be achieved by someone who adopts a "travelling mindset" apply either to Gregory Orr's memoir or Zadie Smith's ideas about the unique nature of those from what she calls "Dream City"? Does de Botton's essay complicate, contradict or complement the ideas in the other text? In what ways?
4. Alison Gopnik claims that "human beings don't live in the real world" (163). With his interests in observation and perception, Alain de Botton's essay provides vivid examples of how this statement is true. Think about other authors in this reader whose experiences move between the "real" world of here and now, and a future or past world that doesn't exist in the present. In these essays, what is the relationship between imagining these other "possible worlds," and creating new, or re-creating, real worlds in which they live? Is there a difference, in the end? If so, what is it? Use the ideas and terms in Alison Gopnik and Alain de Botton to shed light on the life experiences described by Gregory Orr or Zadie Smith.

Preface: After September 11 & Introduction to a New America

Diana L. Eck

Points of Access—Pre-Reading

1. You were probably very young on September 11, 2001. From whom or what did you learn what happened? Did anybody try to explain to you why it happened? Do you think your sources were objective?
2. What do you think of when you think of "hate crimes"? Who do you think are usually the targets of hate crimes?
3. About which of these religious groups could you form a simple sentence explaining their basic beliefs: Buddhists? Christians? Muslims? Jews? Sikhs? Hindus? Mormons?
4. Look up the word "xenophobia." Have you ever witnessed examples of xenophobia?
5. Is religion "visible" around you? Do you see religious groups gathering to study, worship, or converse among themselves or with other groups? Do you notice any religious discrimination?
6. Is religion as important to you as to your parents? Less? More? Why do you think?

Preface: After September 11

The September 11, 2001, catastrophe brought to the United States a new consciousness of the transformation of American society that is the subject of this book. During the lazy summer months of 2001, as I spoke about *A New Religious America* to audiences across the country I found many people still surprised to learn about Americas new religious diversity and reluctantly challenged to think about what this diversity means for America. Muslim voter registration drives? Hindu temples being built in the suburbs? Turbaned Sikhs going to court over job discrimination?. These were relatively new considerations for most of us. But on a brilliant blue September morning when hijacked planes exploded into the towers of the World Trade Center and the Pentagon, a new era began for us all. Within hours an unprecedented rash of xenophobic incidents began—from low-level harassment, ethnic slurs, broken windows, and threatening calls to arson, beatings, and murders. While the roster of hate crimes was growing, so were prodigious efforts at local and national outreach across religious boundaries—interfaith services, civic education programs, and escorts for Muslim women afraid to leave home wearing a head scarf. It is too soon to gauge the climate of the new religious America in which we all now live. One thing is certain: the challenge of relations between and among people of different religious and cultural traditions, both here in the United States and around the world, is moving to the top of the agenda.

In the early afternoon of September 11, I received an e-mail from the Muslim Public Affairs Council. Members of the council were taking an immediate initiative, as Muslims, to denounce the violence and to express solidarity as Americans. Within a few hours eleven national Muslim organizations had joined in a statement condemning "vicious and cowardly acts of terrorism" and calling for "the swift apprehension and punishment of the perpetrators." It signaled a relatively well developed American Muslim infrastructure that these organizations could and did respond so swiftly and publicly. Individual Muslim scholars and leaders also raised their voices in countless public forums, yet their voices could not compete with searing coverage of the devastation at what came to be called Ground Zero and the distant devastation in what came to be called America's New War. Months later, people were still asking, "Why don't Muslim leaders say something?" It was clear that Muslim voices could not easily be heard in the storm.

Although Muslim groups condemned terrorist violence, there was an unprecedented wave of attacks on Muslims and Muslim communities. As I document in chapter 7, America's newest, smallest, and most vulnerable religious communities—whether Vietnamese Buddhists, Gujarati Hindus, or Pakistani Muslims—have experienced all along some of the recurring xenophobia that has haunted American history. But the shock and anger palpable in America after September 11 amplified, for a time, the voices hostile to Muslims, to Sikhs, to South Asian immigrants, to anyone who had the look and feel of "different." In the days following the attack, a furious man smashed his car through the plate-glass door of the mosque in Cleveland. A crowd approached the Bridgeview mosque in Chicago shouting anti-Arab slogans. As Muslims gathered at their mosque in Sterling, Virginia, to take a chartered bus to a blood drive, they found a message inscribed on the building in big black letters: "Die Pigs" and "Muslims Burn Forever!" In Alexandria, Virginia, someone hurled bricks wrapped with hate messages through the windows of an Islamic bookstore, shattering the glass. A firebomb landed in the mosque in Denton, Texas, on the outskirts of Dallas, and rifle fire pierced the stained-glass dome of the mosque in Perrysburg, a suburb of Toledo, Ohio. The rash of scattershot incidents across the country also included Hindu temples attacked in Medinah, Illinois, and in Matawan, New Jersey; a Gujarati-owned convenience store fire-bombed in Somerset, Massachusetts; and an Iraqi pizzeria burned down in Plymouth, home of the Pilgrims.

Sikhs were also attacked, as we know, for the beards and turbans that marked them, in the eyes of the uninformed, as cousins of Osama bin Laden. Sikh organizations tracking the attacks received reports of over two hundred incidents: a Sikh attacked with a baseball bat in Queens, beaten unconscious in Seattle, assaulted at a stoplight in San Diego. On September 12, a New England Sikh who was traveling by train from Boston to Washington was pulled off the train in Providence, Rhode Island, questioned, handcuffed, and detained by the police. While they found no evidence he was anyone other than a Sikh traveling by train, he was arrested and charged with carrying a concealed weapon—his *kirpan,* the ceremonial knife to which he himself called the officer's attention. Only weeks later and after a deluge of letters to the governor of Rhode Island and the mayor of Providence were the charges dropped.

There were also shootings and murders. The clearest instance of a hate crime was in Mesa, Arizona, where a Sikh was shot and killed as he was planting flowers around his Chevron station and convenience store. In Pleasant Grove, Texas, a Pakistani Muslim was shot in his grocery store. In San Gabriel, California, a Coptic Christian who had fled religious persecution in Egypt twenty years ago was shot and killed in his store. Whether all these and other killings are successfully prosecuted as hate crimes remains to be seen, but it is clear that they were part of a much larger nationwide wave of xenophobia.

On the whole, however, we would have to say that these incidents of backlash unleashed by the terrorist attacks ultimately revealed something more complex, and more heartening, about American society. The response evoked by each ugly incident made clear that the multireligious and multicultural fabric of the U.S. was already too strong to rend by random violence. Despite new fears of "sleeper cells" of Muslim terrorists and "assimilated terrorists" lounging by the condominium pool, Americans would not condone indiscriminate violence against neighbors of any faith or culture. The Palestinian bookstore owner in Alexandria, Virginia, stunned by the shattered glass and its message of hatred, soon discovered hundreds of supportive neighbors he did not know who sent him bouquets of flowers and cards expressing their sorrow at what had happened. In Toledo, Cherrefe Kadri, the woman president of the Islamic community, reflected on the September 11 rifle fire: "That small hole in the dome created such a huge outpouring of support for our Islamic community," she said. "A Christian radio station contacted me wanting to do something. They called out on the airwaves for people to come together at our center to hold hands, to ring our mosque, to pray for our protection. We expected three hundred people and thought that would be enough to circle the mosque, but two thousand people showed up to hold hands around the mosque. I was amazed!" In Plymouth, the Iraqi pizzeria owner whose shop had been burned out was inundated with flowers, trays of brownies, and offers of financial support. In Mesa, Arizona, where one man shot and killed a Sikh, hundreds of people left flowers at the gas station where he had died, and thousands of people who had never met him or any other Sikh came to the civic center for a public memorial service. By early 2002 his family had received more than ten thousand letters and messages of condolence. Statistically, one would have to say that benevolence outweighed the backlash.

The impetus toward education and outreach was nationwide. As American bombers were preparing to fly nonstop to Afghanistan, mosques all over the country were preparing outreach programs and holding open houses, inviting neighbors in to learn more about Islam. The Islamic Society of Boston in Cambridge published an open letter to its neighbors, saying, "We utterly condemn the use of terror to further any political or religious cause. As Muslims, we abhor the killing of innocent civilians. Our holy book, the Qur'an, teaches: 'If anyone kills an innocent person, it is as if he has killed all of humanity. And if anyone saves a life, it is as if he has saved all of humanity' (chap. 5, verse 32)." The· letter announced an Islamic Society blood drive and a community open house to be held the following Sunday. It closed, "God willing, we can lend one another strength to find hope in these uncertain times." More than seven hundred people came to the open house, many of them visiting a mosque for the first time. The story was the same across the country In Austin, Texas, for example, hundreds showed up for the Sunday afternoon open house. A woman interviewed by the *Austin American-Statesman* put the matter plainly and succinctly for many Americans when she said, "The time of not getting to know each other is over."

Getting to know each other is often difficult and filled with tension, misunderstanding, and real disagreement. Yet as the months pass, Americans have displayed a consistent new level eagerness, even urgency, to learn more about Islam, to hear from Muslims, to know something about the Sikhs. We have seen a very practical, very American "get busy and learn" response to tragedy. Translations of the Qur'an and books about Islam were among the best-sellers on the Internet and in bookstores. Seminars and programs on Islam took place in colleges, universities, churches, and civic organizations all over the country. Oprah hosted a version of "Islam 101" on her daytime television program, while talk show host Larry King invited Muslim guests into his late-night dialogues.

At the annual meeting of the American Academy of Religion in late November, a prominent journalist compared the two months prior to September 11 and the two months after the tragedy News and feature articles on Islam had multiplied sevenfold.[1]

1 Jeff Sheler, *U.S. News and World Report*, participating in a panel on "A New Religious America," November 23, 2001.

During these months Americans probably saw and heard more Muslim Americans on television, radio, and in the print media than in the entire thirty-five years since the new wave of immigration began in 1965. Public awareness of a new religious America has never been higher.

Local newspapers seemed to create a counterpoint to the images of Muslim hijackers. Muslims were the subjects of hundreds of human interest stories, like the piece on Muslim Girl Scouts in the *Charlotte Observer* on October, 2, 2001. It featured color photographs of three green-uniformed Girls Scouts with head scarves and sashes of merit badges, holding their hands to their eyes in a gesture of prayer. The back of one head scarf bore the words "I Love Being a Muslim Girl Scout;" Aside from the scarf, these were typical ten- to fourteen-year-olds, but recently they had been taunted by fellow students who associated their Islamic dress with terrorism. "Go back to where you came from!" said one classmate. "I came from Connecticut," responded a ten-year-old scout. "We don't believe in blowing up stuff. Islam is not terrorist," said her thirteen-year-old sister. Even so, as the scout troop met at the Islamic Society of Greater Charlotte, three squad cars sat outside in response to threatening phone calls. Rose Hamid, whom the girls call Auntie Rose, is their troop leader, and we will meet her again in chapter 7, for she is the flight attendant trainer for U.S. Air who had lost her job as a frontline flight attendant when she began wearing *hijab.*

As the month of Ramadan began in November, local papers all across the country carried human interest stories about the Muslim families in their communities. The word *ifiar,* the fast-breaking meal at the end of a day of Ramadan, became part of the American lexicon, as community leaders responded to the Muslim invitations to share the *ifiar* meal with them. While recent years have seen *ifiars* on Capitol Hill and at the State Department, Ramadan in 2002 saw the first-ever *ifiar* in the White House, a banquet hosted for Muslim leaders by President George W. Bush.

The iconography of inclusion took a quantum leap in the weeks after September 11. As we explore in the final chapter of this book, the gradual civic recognition of the multiplicity of American religious traditions had grown through the past decade, with Muslim and Hindu prayers in Congress and Sikh Day parades through the city streets. But the fall of 2001 gave America new and powerful images that made the "we" much clearer. President Bush stood with Muslim leaders at the mosque on Massachusetts Avenue in Washington, D.C., and the National Day of Mourning Service at the National Cathedral in Washington included the prayers of a Muslim imam. Two weeks later the multifaith service in Yankee Stadium gave Americans who had never before heard Muslim, Sikh, or Hindu prayers a chance to see and to listen in. As part of its response to September

11, a national Sikh organization published a widely distributed informational brochure with plenty of red, white, and blue and the "United We Stand" motto on the cover. It featured photographs of Sikhs holding American flags and a photograph of Sikh leaders meeting with President George W. Bush in the White House on September 26.

Most of us do not yet have an overall view of how Americans of many faiths have responded to this tragedy in cities and towns across the country. For many weeks we watched a national story focused on Ground Zero and a faraway international story focused on Afghanistan. What has not yet come into view is the cumulative picture of thousands of local stories from cities and towns all over America, struggling in new ways with religious and cultural differences. People of every religious tradition and none died on September 11. People of every religious tradition mourned, held services in their respective places of worship, and participated in volunteer activities in record numbers. We heard little of Hindu communities in these months, but Hindu temples held special prayers and posted the American flag on their flagpoles and on their Web sites. We heard very little of the Buddhists during these months, but we should know that there were also Buddhist services across the country. On September 11 the huge Hsi Lai Buddhist temple in Los Angeles echoed with the prayer of Master Hsing Yun:

> Great and Compassionate Buddha!
> There, buildings collapsed and devastation abounds amidst the wreckage and rubble.
> There, buildings tumbled over and people died, anguish and shock everywhere.
> So many were trapped in the wreckage, filled with fear.
> So many were bound in danger, unable to escape.
> So many lost their family in just one morning, with loved ones forever separated.
> So many lost their lives in a flash.
> They are desperate for the relief of the rescue crew!
> Buddha, they are in dire need of your blessing and protection!
> For they are like lost travelers looking for a secure home,
> Fearful lambs seeking a safe shelter.
> Great and compassionate Buddha!
> For the many that-lost their lives,
> And for the many that were injured.
> Buddha, we pray for you to please bless them.

The burgeoning interfaith movement in the United States made great advances in these months. Interfaith networks from Washington, D.C., to Milwaukee to Seattle sprang into action with immediate civic leadership. Cities like Portland, Oregon, that had never had an interfaith council formed one. These organized instruments of relationship between people of many faiths became more important than ever, for the easy, tolerant goodwill· of civic life is truly tested in times of tension and suspicion. At an interfaith-service in the San Francisco Bay Area, the governor of California, Gray Davis, put it clearly: "Our enemies have failed to divide us. We are one people. We are Americans. We don't care if you were born in the Mission District or the Middle East." And in Washington, D.C., at the National Cathedral, Bishop Jane Holmes Dixon said, "Those of us who are gathered here—Muslim, Jew, Christian, Sikh, Buddhist, Hindu—say to this nation and to the world that love is stronger than hate."

There were many frayed edges in the common fabric, to be sure. The Missouri Synod Lutheran Church battled over whether its religious leaders should have participated in an interfaith service. Some charged that by participating they were acknowledging that other faiths were somehow valid. And there were some very conservative Christian leaders like Franklin Graham, Jerry Falwell, and Pat Robertson who gave public expression to their Islamophobia and made intemperate remarks, fueling monolithic stereotypes about Islam. In every case, however, they were criticized, immediately and decisively, by fellow Christians.. The days when Christian church leaders could ignorantly assail Islam with impunity were over.

Muslim-Jewish relations suffered most in these months. Some American Jews were critical of American Muslims for what they believed was a long silence on Islamist terrorism, especially the Palestinian suicide attacks in Israel. Jews' criticism of what they saw as extremist Islamic organizations, such as the American Muslim Council and the Council on American Islamic Relations, was relentless. American Muslims, who consider these organizations to be moderate and mainstream, bristled at the allegations. The oft-quoted quip, "Now all Americans are Israelis," because now we had experienced firsthand the random civilian violence that Israelis had known for years, offended and affronted many Muslims, who felt that there was little or no U.S. critique of Israeli violence in the West Bank and Gaza. Hard talk went back and forth, and Americans of every faith found it difficult to sustain any public discussion of the Israeli-Palestinian conflict and America's role in it. Perhaps the most honest conclusion was that the mistrust between the Jews and Muslims was amplified by the lack of authentic knowledge of each other on both sides. As James Rudin of the American Jewish Committee put it, "Muslims know practically nothing about authentic Judaism. . . . So, too, most Jews know little about the Muslim faith and community"[2] While the term *Abrahamic faiths* has become an increasingly common designation in conversations among Jews, Christians, and Muslims, it is clear that there is still a long way to go in establishing relationships of trust and respect, even among moderate, open-minded people of the three traditions.

Most important in the wake of September 11 is the widening realization that all three religious communities and many more are now a permanent part of American religious life. All of America's religious communities are also part of worldwide networks of coreligionists, and global interdependence is a reality of religious life in the twenty-first century. There are tiny Christian communities in Pakistan and Palestine, Muslim communities in Columbus, Ohio, and Cairo, and American Jewish communities whose life is inextricably involved with the well- being of the state of Israel. Awakening, as we have, to a new religious America, we face a world of understanding and relationships from which there is no retreat.

2 James Rudin, "Can American Jews and Muslims Get Along?" *Reform Judaism*, Winter 2001.

Introduction to a New America

The huge white dome of a mosque with its minarets rises from the cornfields just outside Toledo, Ohio. You can see it as you drive by on the interstate highway. A great Hindu temple with elephants carved in relief at the doorway stands on a hillside in the western suburbs of Nashville, Tennessee. A Cambodian Buddhist temple and monastery with a hint-of a Southeast Asian roofline is set in the farmlands south of Minneapolis, Minnesota. In suburban Fremont, California, flags fly from the golden domes of a new Sikh gurdwara on Hillside Terrace, now renamed Gurdwara Road. The religious landscape of America has changed radically in the past thirty years, but most of us have not yet begun to see the dimensions and scope of that change, so gradual has it been and yet so colossal. It began with the "new immigration," spurred by the Immigration and Nationality Act of 1965, as people from all over the world came to America and have become citizens. With them have come the religious traditions of the world—Islamic, Hindu, Buddhist, Jain, Sikh, Zoroastrian, African, and Afro-Caribbean. The people of these living traditions of faith have moved into American neighborhoods, tentatively at first, their altars and prayer rooms in storefronts and office buildings, basements and garages, recreation rooms and coat closets, nearly invisible to the rest of us. But in the past decade, we have begun to see their visible presence. Not all of us have seen the Toledo mosque or the Nashville temple, but we will see places like them, if we keep our eyes open, even in our own communities. They are the architectural signs of a new religious America.

For ten years I have gone out looking for the religious neighbors of a new America. As a scholar, I have done the social equivalent of calling up and inviting myself, a stranger, to dinner. I have celebrated the Sikh New Year's festival of Baisakhi with a community in Fairfax County, Virginia. I have feasted at the Vietnamese Buddhist "Mother's Day" in a temple in Olympia, Washington, and I have delivered an impromptu speech on the occasion of Lord Ram's Birthday at a new Hindu temple in Troy, Michigan. I have been received with hospitality, invited to dinner, welcomed into homes, shown scrapbooks of family weddings', and asked to return for a sacred thread ceremony or a feast day. In the early 1990s I mapped out an ambitious plan of research that I called the Pluralism Project, enlisting my students as hometown researchers in an effort to document these remarkable changes, to investigate the striking new religious landscape of our cities, and to think about what this change will mean for all of us, now faced with the challenge of creating a cohesive society out of all this diversity.

Our first challenge in America today is simply to open our eyes to these changes, to discover America anew, and to explore the many ways in which the new immigration has changed the religious landscape of our cities and towns, our neighborhoods and schools. For many of us, this is real news. We know, of course, that immigration has been a contentious issue in the past few decades. Today the percentage of foreign-born Americans is 10.4 percent, more than doubling in the thirty years since 1970, when it was 4.7 percent. The fastest growing groups are Hispanics and Asians. Between 1990 and 1999 the Asian population grew 43 percent nationwide to some 10.8 million, and the Hispanic population grew 38.8 percent to 31.3 million, making it almost as large as the black population. The questions posed by immigration are now on the front burner of virtually every civic institution from schools and zoning boards to hospitals and the workplace. How many customs and languages can we accommodate? How much diversity is simply too much? And for whom? We know that the term *multiculturalism* has crept into our vocabulary and that this term has created such a blaze of controversy that some people mistake it for a political platform rather than a social reality But for all this discussion about immigration, language, and culture, we Americans have not yet really thought about it in terms of religion. We are surprised to discover the religious changes America has been undergoing.

We are surprised to find that there are more Muslim Americans than Episcopalians, more Muslims than members of the Presbyterian Church USA, and as many Muslims as there are Jews—that is, about six million. We are astonished to learn that Los Angeles is the most complex Buddhist city in the world, with a Buddhist population' spanning the whole range of the Asian Buddhist world from Sri Lanka to Korea, along with a multitude of native-born American Buddhists. Nationwide, this whole spectrum of Buddhists may number about four million. We know that many of our internists, surgeons, and nurses are of Indian origin, but we have not stopped to consider that they too have a religious life, that they might pause in the morning for few minutes' prayer at an altar in the family room of their home, that they might bring fruits and flowers to the local Shiva-Vishnu temple on the weekend and be part of a diverse Hindu population of more than a million. We are well aware of Latino immigration from Mexico and Central America and of the large Spanish-speaking population of our cites, and yet we may not recognize what a profound impact this is having on American Christianity, both Catholic and Protestant, from hymnody to festivals.

Historians tell us that America has always been a land of many religions, and this is true. A vast, textured pluralism was already present in the lifeways of the Native peoples—even before the European settlers' came to these shores. The wide diversity of Native religious practices continues today, from ,the Piscataway of Maryland to the Blackfeet of Montana. The people who came across the Atlantic from Europe also had diverse religious traditions—Spanish and French Catholics, British Anglicans and Quakers, Sephardic Jews and Dutch Reform Christians. As we shall see, this diversity broadened over the course of three hundred years of settlement. Many of the Africans brought to these shores with the slave trade were Muslims. The Chinese and Japanese who came to seek their fortune in the mines and fields of the West brought with them a mixture of Buddhist, Taoist, and Confucian traditions. Eastern European Jews and Irish and Italian Catholics also arrived in force in the nineteenth century. Both Christian and Muslim immigrants came from the Middle East. Punjabis from northwest India came in the first decade of the twentieth century. Most of them were Sikhs who settled in the Central and Imperial Valleys of California, built America's first gurdwaras, and intermarried with Mexican women, creating a rich Sikh-Spanish subculture. The stories of all these peoples are an important part of America's immigration history

The immigrants of the last three decades, however, have expanded the diversity of our religious life dramatically, exponentially. Buddhists have come from Thailand, Vietnam, Cambodia, China, and Korea; Hindus from India, East Africa, and Trinidad; Muslims from Indonesia, Bangladesh, Pakistan, the Middle East, and Nigeria; Sikhs and Jains from India; and Zoroastrians from both India and Iran. Immigrants from Haiti and Cuba have brought Afro-Caribbean traditions, blending both African and Catholic symbols and images. New Jewish immigrants have come from Russia and the Ukraine, and the internal diversity of American Judaism is greater than ever before. The face of American Christianity has also changed with large Latino, Filipino, and Vietnamese Catholic communities; Chinese, Haitian, and Brazilian Pentecostal communities; Korean Presbyterians, Indian Mar Thomas, and Egyptian Copts. In every city in the land church signboards display the meeting times of Korean or Latino congregations that nest within the walls of old urban Protestant and Catholic churches. While the central chapters of this book focus on the Hindu, Buddhist, and Muslim streams of America's religious life, old and new, it is important to hold in mind that these are but part of a far more complex religious reality of encyclopedic dimensions.

Through these same decades since the liberalization of immigration policy in 1965, the Moral Majority and the Christian Coalition have raised the public profile of fundamentalist Christianity. The language of a "Christian America" has been voluminously invoked in the public square. However, I sense in some of the most strident Christian communities little awareness of this new religious America, the one Christians now share with Muslims, Buddhists, and Zoroastrians. They display a confident, unselfconscious assumption that *religion* basically means Christianity, with traditional space made for the Jews. But make no mistake: in the past thirty years, as Christianity has become more publicly vocal, something else of enormous importance has happened. The United States has become the most religiously diverse nation on earth. In the past thirty years massive movements of people both as migrants ' and refugees have reshaped the demography of our world. Immigrants around the world number over 130 million, with about 30 million in the United States, a million arriving each year. The dynamic global image of our times is not the so-called clash of civilizations but the marbling of civilizations and peoples. Just as the end of the Cold War brought about a new geopolitical situation, the global movements of people have brought about a new georeligious reality Hindus, Sikhs, and Muslims are now part of the religious landscape of Britain, mosques appear in Paris and Lyons, Buddhist temples in Toronto, and Sikh gurdwaras in Vancouver. But nowhere, even in today's world of mass migrations, is the sheer range of religious faith as wide as it is today in the United States. Add to India's wide range of religions those of China,[1] Latin America, and Africa. Take the diversity of Britain or Canada, and add to it the crescendo of Latino immigration along with the Vietnamese, Cambodians, and Filipinos. This-is an astonishing new reality. We have never been here before.

The new era of immigration is different, from previous eras not only in magnitude and complexity but also in its very dynamics. Many of the migrants who come to the United States today maintain strong ties with their homelands, linked by travel and transnational communications networks, e-mails and faxes, satellite phone lines, and cable television news. They manage to live both here and there in all the ways that modern communications and telecommunications have made possible. When my own grandparents and great-grandparents left Sweden, they did not return every few years and never again heard the voices of those they had left behind. Indeed, only my paternal grandmother ever returned at all. But today's globalization enables an immigrant from India to read the *Times of India* every morning on the Internet, to subscribe to Indian cable news on the satellite dish, to bring artisans from rural India to work on Hindu temples in suburban America, and to return home for a family wedding. As our own identities become increasingly multilocal, the formation of complex national identities becomes increasingly challenging.

What will the idea and vision of America become as citizens, new and old, embrace all this diversity? The questions that emerge today from the encounter of people of so many religious and cultural traditions go to the very heart of who we see ourselves to be as a people. They are not trivial questions, for they force us to ask in one way or another: Who do we mean when we invoke the first words of our Constitution, "We the people of the United States of America"? Who do we mean when we say "we"? This is a challenge of citizenship, to be sure, for it has to do with the imagined community of which we consider ourselves a part. It is also a challenge of faith,, for people of every religious tradition live today with communities of faith other than their own, not only around the world but also across the street.

"We the people of the United States" now form the most profusely religious nation on earth. But many, if not most, Christian, Jewish, or secular Americans have never visited a mosque or a Hindu or Buddhist temple. Many Americans are not so sure what Sikhs or Muslims believe, let alone Jains and Zoroastrians. Similarly, Muslim or Hindu Americans may have sketchy and stereotypical views of Christians and Jews. So where do we go from here? It's one thing to be unconcerned about or ignorant of Muslim or Buddhist neighbors on the other side of the world, but when Buddhists are our next-door neighbors, when our children are best friends with Muslim classmates, when a Hindu is running for a seat on the school committee, all of us have a new vested interest in our neighbors, both as citizens and as people of faith.

As the new century dawns, we Americans are challenged to make good on the promise of religious freedom so basic to the very idea and· image of America. Religious freedom has always given rise to religious diversity, and never has our diversity been more dramatic than it is today. This will require us to reclaim the deepest meaning of the very principles we cherish and to create a truly pluralist American society in which this great diversity is not simply tolerated but becomes the very source of our strength. But to do this, we will all need to know more than we do about one another and to listen for the new ways in which new Americans articulate the "we" and contribute to the sound and spirit of America.

Envisioning the New America

President Lyndon Baines Johnson signed the new immigration act into law on July 4, 1965, at the base of the Statue of Liberty. America's doors were opened once again to immigrants from all over the world. Since 1924 an extremely restrictive quota system had virtually cut off all immigration. Entry from Asia had always been extremely limited, beginning with the 1882 Chinese Exclusion Act. The scope of Asian exclusion expanded decade after decade to exclude Japanese, Koreans, and other "Asiatics" as well. Asian-born immigrants could not become citizens, argued the Supreme Court in the case of Bhagat Singh Thind. Thind was a Sikh, a naturalized citizen, who had served in World War I. Drawing on a 1790 statute, the court declared Asians to be outside the range of "free White men" who could become citizens. In 1923 he was stripped of his citizenship. The 1924 immigration law then barred from immigration anyone ineligible for citizenship, and that meant all Asians.

The Immigration and Nationality Act of 1965 was linked in spirit to the Civil Rights Act passed just a year earlier. As Americans became critically aware of our nation's deep structures of racism, we also saw that race discrimination continued to shape immigration law, excluding people from what was then called the Asia-Pacific triangle. Early in his term President John F. Kennedy prepared legislation to "eliminate discrimination between peoples and nations on a basis that is unrelated to any contribution immigrants can make and is inconsistent with our traditions of welcome.'" Robert Kennedy, the attorney general, observed, "As we are working to remove the vestiges of racism from our public life, we cannot maintain racism as the cornerstone of our immigration laws." And so began a new era of immigration and a new, complex, and vivid chapter in America's religious life.

The framers of the Constitution and the Bill of Rights could not possibly have envisioned the scope of religious diversity in America at the beginning of the twenty-first century. When they wrote the sixteen words of the First Amendment, "Congress shall make no law respecting an establishment of religion or prohibiting the free exercise thereof," they unquestionably did not have Buddhism or the Santeria tradition in mind. But the "principles they articulated—the "nonestablishment" of religion and the "free exercise" of religion—have provided a sturdy rudder through the past two centuries as our religious diversity has expanded. After all, religious freedom is the fountainhead of religious diversity. The two go inextricably together. Step by step, we are beginning to claim and affirm what the framers of the Constitution did not imagine but equipped us to embrace. Even so, the road is rocky.

In November of 1998, President Clinton sent a letter to the Sikh communities of America on the occasion of the 529th birthday of the teacher who launched the Sikh movement in the sixteenth century, Guru Nanak. The president wrote "We are grateful for the teachings of Guru Nanak, which celebrate the equality of all in the eyes of God, a message that strengthens our efforts to build one America. Religious pluralism in our nation is bringing us together in new and powerful ways."[3] I am certainly among those who agree with him, for I believe that our society becomes stronger as each group's religious freedom is exercised and as people like the Sikhs articulate principles like equality and freedom in their own voice and in their own key.

For many Americans, however, religious pluralism is not a vision that brings us together but one that tears us apart. The controversies of the public square are just

---

3 *San Diego Union-Tribune,* November 13,1998.

beginning. "Screw the Buddhists and kill the Muslims" was the response of one public official to the issue of religious diversity in May of 1997. The context was a discussion in South Carolina on whether the Ten Commandments should be posted in the public schools. The official, a member of the state board of education, was also quoted as having spoken of Islam as a "cult," worshipers of "Lucifer." The Council on American Islamic Relations (CAIR), an Islamic advocacy group, called for his resignation from the state board of education, saying,

> American Muslims, and particularly Muslim parents in South Carolina, view these remarks with great alarm. The remarks demonstrate a level of bigotry and intolerance that is entirely inappropriate for a person charged with formulating public policy. As you may recall, when a South Carolina mosque was the target of an arson attack in October of 1995, the suspect in the case was quoted as saying he set the fire to "rid the world of evil." [His] comments can only serve to incite further acts of violence.[4]

No doubt this is an extreme case. It was widely publicized and widely repudiated, although the official did not lose his job on the state board of education. Most incidents of bigotry and hatred are not so widely publicized, from the 1990 arson attack on the old Islamic center here in Quincy, Massachusetts, to the destruction of a Minneapolis mosque by arson in 1999. The final decade of the twentieth century saw dozens of attacks on Muslims and their places of worship. In June of 2000, a Memphis man opened fire with his shotgun as worshipers approached the mosque next door for prayers. A few weeks later in Boston, vandals vaulted a fence into a Vietnamese temple compound and smashed to smithereens the white image of the bodhisattva of compassion. Difference can all too easily become a license for violence, and watchdog groups have been formed by Muslims, Sikhs, and Hindus to monitor and record assaults on the rights and dignity of their members. There are also more muted controversies, like the new issues that have landed on the agenda of the armed services, the public schools, the zoning board, and the workplace. Can a Sikh wear his turban on a hard-hat job or as part of his uniform in the U.S. Army? Can a practitioner of Wicca exercise his or her religion on a Texas army base? Can a Sikh high school student carry the symbolic dagger of Sikh religious initiation to school? Will the Whirlpool Corporation in Nashville find a way for Muslim employees to meet their obligations for prayer? Does a Hindu temple have to look more "Spanish" to meet the planning board standards of Norwalk, California?

---

4 Council on American Islamic Relations press release, "CAIR Calls for Removal of South Carolina Office Who Said 'Kill the Muslims"' (Washington, DC, May 19,1997).

Will a young Jain, an observant vegetarian, find the contents of the meals in her school cafeteria clearly marked?

As we think through the challenges of a new multireligious America, we will need to take stock of the many difficult questions "we the people" encounter today, questions not fully anticipated by the framers of our Constitution. And we will need to face squarely the fact that many of our newest immigrants have experienced some of the same kinds of prejudice and hatred that greeted Irish and Italian Catholics and Russian and Polish Jews,a century ago. They have been attacked for wearing a red dot on the forehead, for observing Islamic dress with a head scarf, or for wearing a turban.

Religion is never a finished product, packaged, delivered, and passed intact from generation to generation. There are some in every religious tradition who think of their religion that way, insisting it is all contained in the sacred texts, doctrines, and rituals they themselves know and cherish. But even the most modest journey through history proves them wrong. Our religious traditions are dynamic not static, changing not fixed, more like rivers than monuments. The history of religion is an ongoing process. America today is an exciting place to study the dynamic history of living faiths, as Buddhism becomes a distinctively American religion and as Christians and Jews encounter Buddhists and articulate their faith anew in the light of that encounter or perhaps come to understand themselves part of both traditions. Even humanists, even secularists, even atheists have to rethink their worldviews in the context of a more complex religious reality. With multitheistic Hindus and nontheistic Buddhists in the picture, atheists may have to be more specific about what kind of "god" they do not believe in.

Just as our religious traditions are dynamic, so is the very idea of America. The motto of the republic, *E Pluribus Unum,* "From Many, One," is not an accomplished fact but an ideal that Americans must continue to claim. The story of America's many peoples and the creation of one nation is an unfinished story in which the ideals articulated in the Declaration of Independence and the Constitution are continually brought into being. Our *pluribus* is more striking than ever—our races and faces, our jazz and *qawwali* music, our Haitian drums and Bengali tablas, our hip-hop and *bhangra* dances, our mariachis and gamelans, our Islamic minarets and Hindu temple towers, our Mormon temple spires and golden gurdwara domes. Amid this plurality, the expression of our *unum,* our oneness, will require many new voices, each contributing in its own way—like the voices of Sikhs who will stand up for the "self-evident truth" of human equality not only because it is written in the Declaration of Independence but also because it is part of the teachings of Guru Nanak and a principle of their faith as Sikhs. Hearing new ways of giving expression to the idea of America is the challenge we face today

As we enter a new millennium, Americans are in the process of discovering who "we" are anew. Each part of the composite picture of a new religious America may seem small, but each contributes to a new self-portrait of America. One word may signal a shift in consciousness. For example, as Muslims become more numerous and visible in American society, public officials have begun to shift from speaking of "churches and synagogues" to "churches, synagogues, and mosques." The annual observance of the Ramadan month of Muslim fasting now receives public notice and becomes the occasion for portraits of the Muslims next door in the *Dallas Morning News* or the *Minneapolis Star Tribune. The* fast-breaking meals called *iftar* at the close of each day have become moments of recognition. In the late 1990s there were *iftar* observances by Muslim staffers on Capitol Hill, in the Pentagon, and in the State Department. In 1996 the White House hosted the first observance of the celebration of Eid al-Fitr at the end of the month of Ramadan, a practice that has continued. The same year also saw the U.S. Navy commission its first Muslim chaplain, Lieutenant M. Malak Abd al-Muta Ali Noel, and in 1998 the U.S. Navy's first mosque was opened on Norfolk Naval Base in Virginia, where Lieutenant Noel was stationed. When fifty sailors attend Friday prayers at this facility, they signal to all of us a new era of American religious life.

Hindus have begun to signal their American presence as well. For instance, on September 14, 2000, Shri Venkatachalapathi Samudrala, a priest of the Shiva Vishnu Temple of Greater Cleveland in Parma, Ohio, opened a session of the U.S. House of Representatives with the chaplain's prayer of the day. He prayed in Hindi and English and closed with a Sanskrit hymn, all recorded on the temple's Web site. The occasion was the visit of the prime minister of India to the United States, but the wider message was clearly that Ohio too has its Hindus, as does every state in the union. As Americans, we need to see these signs of a new religious America and begin to think about ourselves anew in terms of them.

As we shall see at the very end of the book, America's burgeoning interfaith movement gives us another set of signals about what is happening in America today as people of different faith traditions begin to cooperate in concrete ways. One example is of interest because it was led by Buddhists. In the spring of 1998, from the dazzling white Peace Pagoda, which sits on a hilltop of maples in the rural countryside of Leverett, Massachusetts, a community of Buddhist pilgrims launched the Interfaith Pilgrimage of the Middle Passage. Bringing together American "pilgrims" of all races and religions, they walked fifteen to twenty miles a day for seven months, visiting sites associated with slavery all along the coast from Boston to New Orleans. From there, some of them continued the journey by sea to the west coast of Africa. The Buddhist community sponsoring the walk, a group called the Nipponzan Myohoji, was small in size, but, like the Quakers, this group extends leadership far beyond its numbers. It was not the first time this group had walked for racial and religious harmony. It had also journeyed from Auschwitz to Hiroshima to remind the world of the atrocities of the concentration camps and the atomic bomb. On a local level, every year this group walks for three days from its hilltop pagoda to downtown Springfield, Massachusetts, to observe Juneteenth, the annual celebration of black liberation from slavery. In each case, members walk to remind the rest of us of our deepest commitments.

Envisioning the new America in the twenty-first century requires an imaginative leap. It means seeing the religious landscape of America, from sea to shining sea, in all its beautiful complexity. Between the white New England churches and the Crystal Cathedral of southern California, we see the sacred mountains and the homelands of the Native peoples, the Peace Pagoda amid maples in Massachusetts, the mosque in the cornfields outside Toledo, the Hindu temples pitched atop the hills of Pittsburgh and Chicago, the old and new Buddhist temples of Minneapolis. Most of us have seen too little of this new religious America. But having seen what I have seen, with my own eyes and through the eyes of my students and colleagues, this is the landscape I now call home. This is the America I find rich and full of promise precisely because of all it embraces.

"Let's go for the gold!" said a city councilwoman in San Diego in the fall of 1998. The issue before them was whether the Sikhs could build a temple with three gold domes along the West Valley Parkway in Escondido. The planning commission wanted the new building to have a red tile roof in order to fit in with the Mediterranean style of the area, but the city council overturned their recommendations, allowing the Sikhs to proceed with their traditional design—and the gold domes. Here, in the language of architecture, is the issue we Americans face. Do we, whoever "we" are, demand conformity, or do we "go for the gold" and open our eyes and hearts to the new differences that are ours?

Passage to America

Let me tell the story of the new religious America another way, beginning here at Harvard University, where I have taught for more than twenty years. I first came to Harvard as a graduate student at the end of the 1960s. I studied comparative religion, focusing on India, where the texture of religious life is so complex that a comparative approach is essential. I had already spent a year in India as a college student, in the days before satellite telecommunications and e-mail, when it took a whole afternoon to place a phone call and more than a month to send a letter home and receive a response. I was fascinated by India's many religious communities and their interrelations, tensions, and movements over many centuries. India became a kind of second home for me as I moved back and forth between Boston and Banaras, doing my fieldwork on the other side of the world and then returning to Harvard Square, which seemed by comparison a quiet village, moving at a leisurely pace.

When I began teaching comparative religion at Harvard in the mid-1970s, the challenge was to get my students to take seriously what we then called the "other," to begin to glimpse what the world might look like from the perspective of a Hindu, Muslim, or Sikh, those people whose lives and families I had come to know on the other side of the world. My students held all the usual preconceptions and misconceptions afloat in mainstream American culture; these religions were seen as exotic, deeply spiritual, perhaps seductive, even dangerous. In any case, they were far away, at least until the gurus of the "new age" brought them to America. But never did I imagine as I started teaching at Harvard in the 1970s that by the 1990s there would be scores of Hindu, Muslim, and Sikh students in my classes—not just international students from India but second-generation Americans, the children of what we have come to call the new immigration. Never did I imagine that by the 1990s I would be taking my students to Hindu temples, Islamic centers, and Sikh gurdwaras right here in Boston. Or that by the 1990s the very interest that had drawn me to India—the study of a complex, multireligious society—would lead me to study the world's religions in my own country.

My return passage from India to America started right here at Harvard. I remember the moment it began in the spring of 1990. A bright young freshman named Mukesh showed up at my office door. He had enrolled in my class called Hindu Myth and Image and had a thousand questions for me, trying to relate what he was learning in class to what the swami had taught him at a Hindu summer camp in Pennsylvania. I had no idea there was a Hindu summer camp in the Poconos, and I had never had a Hindu student engaged in the tumultuous searching I had known so often among Christian or Jewish students, trying to relate the critical study of religion to their own faith. In fact, it had never occurred to me that one of my roles is a professor would be to teach American-born Hindus about their own religious tradition.

I had always had a few students from India in my classes, but that year marked the beginning of a new era of students like Mukesh. They were Indian Americans, born and raised in San Antonio, Baltimore, or Cleveland. They were the children of the first generation of immigrants who had settled in America after 1965. From the perspective of India, I knew all about the effects of the new immigration. We called it the "brain drain," as thousands of Indian engineers, doctors, and scientists left India for the United

States. But I had never stopped to think what the new immigration would mean for the United States, at least not until Mukesh and his classmates reached college age and enrolled in my classes. Some of them came from secular families and had learned little of their Indian heritage; their parents were professionals who had gained their own cultural and religious knowledge by osmosis in India or Pakistan but could pass it on in only a very diluted form to their children. Others had grown up in the new Hindu or Muslim institutions their parents had begun to create here in the U.S. Some had been to a Muslim youth leadership camp organized by the Islamic Society of North America or to a Hindu family camp at Arsha Vidya Gurukulam in Saylorsberg, Pennsylvania. There were young Jains who had been founding members of the Jain Youth of North America. Straddling two worlds, critically appropriating two cultures, they lived in perpetual tension between the distinctive cultures of their parents and grandparents and the forceful assimilative currents of American culture. In their own struggles with identity lay the very issues that were beginning to torment the soul of a newly multicultural America.

The questions that emerged in my classes were not only those that underlay the foreign cultures requirement of Harvard's core curriculum, such as, How might we understand some "other" civilization so different from our own? New questions pushed themselves to the front of the agenda: What does it mean to speak of "our own" culture? What does it mean to find different streams of culture within ourselves? How are *difference* and *otherness* defined, and by whom? The word *multicultural* found a new place in our vocabulary, signaling the fact that every dimension of American culture had become more complex as a result of immigration and increasing globalization. Racial issues took on many sides, with Hispanic and Latino, Korean and Filipino, Chinese and Indian perspectives. Religious diversity was greater than ever before. In the 1950s the sociologist Will Herberg had confidently described America as a "three religion country"—Protestant, Catholic, and Jewish. By the 1990s it was Protestant, Catholic, Jewish, Muslim, Buddhist, Hindu, and Sikh, and our collective consciousness of the wide and deep presence of America's Native peoples was greater than ever before.

During the first few years of the 1990s, the sons and daughters of the first generation from South Asia alone grew in numbers to become about 5 percent of the Harvard undergraduate population. In the spring of 1993, during the graduation ceremonies for Mukesh's class, I happily discovered in the balcony of The Memorial Church the families of both Mukesh and his classmate Moitri. Mukesh's family had immigrated to the U.S. from Bihar and Moitri's family from the neighboring state of Bengal. Mukesh and Moitri were the first marshals of the Harvard and Radcliffe graduating classes that year, meaning their classmates had elected them to lead in the commencement activities. Both were Hindus. In the baccalaureate ceremonies Moitri recited a hymn from the Rig Veda in ancient Sanskrit, while Mukesh told a devotional story from his family tradition. Other members of the graduating class read from the sources of their own traditions—the Quran, the Hebrew Bible, and the New Testament. A year or two earlier, the ceremonies enacted beneath the white steeple were carefully constructed in the Catholic-Protestant-Jewish framework, but this was a new Harvard. It had happened in four years, and it had changed the university forever.

Harvard is hardly a bellwether of American culture. Having myself come east from the Rocky Mountains in Montana with an eye trained in the vastness of the West, I know how easy it is to lose perspective among the bricks, maples, and hills of New England. Nonetheless, Harvard *is* old, and its history as a place of higher education spans the history of our nation, from the time of the first European settlement to today. Like many of America's private colleges, Harvard College began as a religious school with a normative, Christian vision of itself. In 1636 the Puritans of New England founded it to educate Christian clergy. In their own words, so often quoted from *New England's First Fruits,* published in 1643, "After God had carried us safe to New England, and we had builded our houses, provided necessaries for our livelihood, reared convenient places for God's worship, and settled the civil government, one of the next things we longed for and looked after was to advance learning and perpetuate it to posterity; dreading to leave an illiterate ministry to the churches, when our present ministers shall lie in the dust."

Harvard was a Christian college, as exclusively and unapologetically as Massachusetts was a Christian commonwealth. In 1649 a Sephardic Jewish merchant named Solomon Franco was "warned out" of the town of Boston, which is to say he was invited to leave. In 1720, however, another Sephardic Jew, an Italian named Judah Monis, managed to get an M.A. from Harvard and eventually published *A Grammar of the Hebrew Tongue,* a text for the young would-be clerics who were then required to learn Hebrew, Greek, and Latin. But before Monis was hired to teach Hebrew in 1722, he publicly converted to Christianity. Over three and a half centuries, the small homogeneous college of young men faced the struggles of our wider culture: In the late nineteenth century, as the numbers of Catholics grew, so did prejudice against them. As the numbers of Jews mushroomed in the first two decades of the twentieth century, from 7 percent in 1900 to 21.5 percent in 1922, some voiced concern, including President Abbott Lawrence Lowell, who suggested a quota for Jewish students. The faculty wisely rejected the idea but began to cast a new and wider net for admissions in urban centers beyond the East Coast.[5]

---

5 The complexity of these proceedings is recorded in Nitza Rosovsky, *The Jewish Experience at Harvard and Radcliffe* (Cambridge: Harvard University Press, 1986), 8–25.

Both the Puritan founders of Harvard and our first Jewish instructor, Judah Monis, would be astounded at the Harvard of today. Harvard's Christians now flock to a vibrant Catholic student center, to ecumenical, evangelical, and mainline Christian groups, and to energetic Chinese and Korean Christian fellowships. The new Rosovsky Center for the Jewish community is named after a beloved dean, Henry Rosovsky, often referred to as the "rabbi" of the Faculty of Arts and Sciences. It is already bursting at the seams with Reform, Conservative, and Orthodox congregations. The building has a glass exterior, making its busy life of study, mealtime fellowship, and prayer completely transparent to the passing motorist or pedestrian, signaling the visible presence Jews now have at the university.

The Harvard Islamic Society, launched in the 1950s, has moved time and again to larger, but still temporary, quarters as the numbers of Islamic students in the university has grown. While the organization has a designated prayer room in the basement of one of the freshman dormitories, Friday prayers need a larger space and are held in the Lowell Lecture Hall. Symbolically, the Islamic presence gained public recognition when, in June of 1997, Imam Tajal Eid stood on the platform of The Memorial Church before twenty-five thousand people assembled for commencement and opened the ceremonies with prayer. This was the first time in Harvard's history that the preacher of the day had been Muslim. One Friday in the fall of 1998, I climbed the steps of Widener Library to hear a young African American from the Harvard Islamic Society recite the call to noontime prayer. It was the conclusion of the annual Islam Awareness Week, and those who heard the lilting Arabic broadcast across Harvard Yard were hearing a call sounded for the first time in this space at the heart of America's oldest university.

In December of 1994, I attended the ceremony of the Buddha's Enlightenment Day It was the first public event of the newly founded Harvard Buddhist Community. In a stately, wood-paneled room at the Divinity School, beneath august portraits of a long lineage of Divinity deans, some fifty Harvard students from a dozen Buddhist lineages sat on rows of square *zabutons,* listening to Pali, Tibetan, and Vietnamese chanting. One by one, they rose to bow to the Buddha and to make offerings of incense. The Divinity School eventually purchased a dozen *zafus* and *zabutons* for sitting meditation, and by the Buddha's Enlightenment Day of 1998 there were six Buddhist sitting groups. The fixed pews of the Divinity School chapel had been removed in favor of chairs to accommodate Buddhist meditators.

For most of the 1990s, there was no specifically Hindu organization at Harvard. Swami Sarvagatananda of Boston's old Ramakrishna Vedanta Society in the Back Bay had a place on Harvard's United Ministry, but Harvard Hindus did not gravitate to the downtown center or to Vedanta. In 1997 they organized a Hindu student group called Dharma—the first in Harvard's 360 years. One Sunday afternoon a month, they now gather in a common room to sing devotional songs called *bhajans* and study the Bhagavad Gita together. They also organize observances of Hindu festivals. That first year the Festival of Lights, or Diwali, a domestic celebration of the goddess Lakshmi, took place in the suite of a Harvard senior named Kavita and her roommates. There was a makeshift altar to which everyone contributed the images of the gods they had brought from home; there were strings of electric lights, flowers, fruits, sweets, incense, and candles. "When I came to college," said Kavita, "I didn't realize how much I would miss Diwali. At home, Diwali was our favorite holiday, but I never had to *do* anything for Diwali to happen at home. It just happened. But here at Harvard I realized that Diwali would not just happen. There would be no Diwali celebration unless I made one. So I called home and found out what to do."

In the fall of 1998 my partner, Dorothy Austin, and I moved onto campus to be house masters in one of the student houses. It had not been an easy decision. On the plus side, it meant having the opportunity to help create a pluralist community in a living context. On the downside, it meant giving up my planned sabbatical leave in India and missing the festival of the Goddess, called Navaratri, which I had not been able to attend for over twenty years. But the first week in October, I received an invitation to a Navaratri festival organized by Dharma. The group had booked the common room in the house for a worship service, called a *puja,* to be followed by a *rasgarbha* dance, the traditional stick dance now all the rage in the South Asian American subculture, across the way in the dining hall.

That night, I put on my black-mirrored *selvarkamiz* and went to the common room. There at the far end of the room, under the stern portraits of Harvard dignitaries, they had arranged an altar. Students were swirling about the room in their holiday best—the young women in a rainbow of silk saris and *selvarkamizes* and the young men in pressed *kurtas.* They had brought a range of deities for the altar, the ones they ordinarily kept on their dorm room bureaus or bookshelves in the makeshift altars of college life. Manish and Monica, the chief organizers, sat at the altar and began the ceremonies. Manish led the *puja,* reciting Sanskrit verses and explaining the steps of worship as he performed them. Monica encouraged the assembled students to share in singing their favorite *bhajans,* and they did, occasionally apologizing for the parts they could not remember. Finally, they stood for the lamp offering called *arati* and sang the traditional Hindi verses, which many of the students knew by heart. It was a simple celebration, but in the life of an American institution like Harvard, even such a simple celebration is truly a revolution. With a happy heart, I stayed for the *rasgarbha* and danced till I dropped.

What has happened here has also happened at colleges and universities throughout the country. Our campuses have became the laboratories of a new multicultural and multireligious America. The interreligious issues we face here are not just Harvard's issues or America's issues. They have become our own distinctive recasting of the world's issues—the issues of India and South Africa, Bosnia and Sierra Leone, China and Indonesia. Will· all these differences of race, culture, ethnicity, and religion fracture our communities, or will they lead us toward the common purpose of an informed, energetic, and even joyous pluralism?

The Pluralism Project

When I first met these new students—Muslims from Providence, Hindus from Baltimore, Sikhs from Chicago, Jains from New Jersey—they signaled to me the emergence in America of a new cultural and religious reality about which I knew next to nothing. At that point I had not been to an American mosque, I had never visited a Sikh community in my own country, and I could imagine a Hindu summer camp only by analogy with my Methodist camp experience. I felt the very ground under my feet as a teacher and scholar begin to shift. My researcher's eye began to refocus—from Banaras to Detroit, from Delhi to Boston.

It became clear to me that the very shape of our traditional fields of study was inadequate to this new world. In the field of religious studies, those of us who study Buddhism, Islam, or Hinduism traditionally earn our academic stripes by intensive study in Japan, Egypt, or India, doing language studies, textual editions and translations, and fieldwork. Now it became clear that to teach a course on Hinduism, I would also have to know something about Hinduism in America. Something similar was happening to my colleagues in the field of American religion. For decades they had focused largely on the Protestant mainstream, or perhaps on American Catholicism or Judaism. But what about the many submerged histories—the old Islamic traditions of the African slaves, the old Chinese temple communities in Montana and Idaho, or the early Sikh communities in California's Imperial Valley? And what about the immigrant religious histories just now unfolding—the Korean Buddhists and Christians, the Tamil Hindus, the Indian and Pakistani Muslims? Didn't these also belong in a course on American religion? Other colleagues were on the front lines of the developing fields of multicultural studies or ethnic studies. Reading their works, I was astonished to find a strong normative, ideological secularism that seemed studiously to avoid thinking about religion at all. For them, the religious traditions of America's ethnic minorities were simply not on the screen. Their lively discussions of Asian immigrants, for example, proceeded as if Asian Americans had no religious lives, built no religious institutions, gathered in no religious communities.

I scarcely had time to undertake new research, so I decided on a makeshift strategy: teaching a class on a subject I knew nothing about. I announced a research seminar called World Religions in New England. In the company of twenty-five students, I set out to study multireligious America, beginning here in Boston. I had lived in the city for twenty-five years, and I was amazed. Yes, the imagined New England landscape of white steeples and colonial town greens was still here, almost picture perfect, but what a range of other communities had settled right next door!

We visited the spectacular new Sri Lakshmi temple in Ashland, not far from the starting point of the Boston marathon, a temple designed by Hindu ritual architects, its ornate tall towers decorated with images of Hindu deities and consecrated with the waters of the Ganges mingled with the waters of the Mississippi, Colorado, and Merrimac Rivers. We joined weekend worshipers for the weekly Saturday ,morning liturgies as the tall granite image of Lord Vishnu was bathed in gallons of milk and royally dressed to receive the offerings of the faithful and dispense his gifts of grace—sanctified fruits and water. The next week we split into teams to visit half a dozen other Hindu communities in the Boston area—from the older Vedanta Society and the Hare Krishna temple to the Swaminarayan temples of Lowell and Stow.

One Friday we took the subway down to Quincy, where New England's first mosque was built in the 1950s in the shadow of the great cranes of the Quincy shipyards. Back then, the community consisted of Lebanese who immigrated early in the century, but the hundreds of Muslims who come today for Friday prayers are from all over the world. We discovered that some twenty other mosques and Islamic centers are members of the Islamic Council of New England. On a quiet residential street in Norwood, we visited the Jain community gathered in what was formerly a Swedish Lutheran church. The Jains of New England are heirs of an ancient religious tradition going back to the beginning of the first millennium B.C.E. in India. Now halfway around the world, they were celebrating the end of their yearly season of fasting with songs, dancing, and feasting. We found Boston's Sikhs, also from India, gathered in what was formerly a Kingdom Hall of the Jehovah's Witnesses in the town of Milford, and in nearby Millis was a community of American-born Sikhs of the Sikh Dharma movement.

There were more Buddhist communities than we could readily visit, even in teams. Down the street from the university we all spent an hour sitting in silence at the Cambridge Insight Meditation Center. Then we heard about the history of Insight meditation in the West from the resident teacher, Larry Rosenberg, who had taught psychology before heading for Southeast Asia to study Buddhist meditation practice. The next week we fanned out to see the, Korean Kwan Um Zen Center and the old Cambridge Zen Center, the Dharmadhatu Tibetan center, and the Korean Zen Martial Arts Center. North of Boston, in the old industrial city of Lynn, one of our seminar members attended the monastic ordination of a young Cambodian man who had come to the U.S. as a refugee. He kneeled, his head shaved, to receive his robes, amid a Cambodian community that by then had three temples in the northern outskirts of Boston. Some of us visited the Vietnamese temple in Roslindale, the Chinese Buddhist temple in Lexington, and the new Thousand Buddha Temple built by Chinese nuns in Quincy. The variety was breathtaking. While some, like the Insight Meditation Center, were exclusively devoted to meditation practice, others, like those in the Chinese communities, practiced the chanting and recitations of Pure Land Buddhism. One fine day, the Thousand Buddha Temple community chartered a harbor cruise boat and took hundreds of live lobsters out into Boston Harbor to release them into the sea as an act of compassion.

This is Boston today, a city that would astonish its Puritan founders—as it astonished us. That semester the reading list took a backseat to our citywide forays, which resulted in animated and serious discussion like I had never before experienced in a seminar. Eventually we published *World Religions in Boston*, a documentary guide to a city whose Asian population had doubled in ten years, a city that gave us our first glimpse of the new religious America.

This was the genesis of the Pluralism Project. I was sure that what had happened here in Boston was happening also in many other American cities. What about Houston, Denver, Detroit? With foundation funding, I hired students to spend the summer in their own hometowns and find out what changes were under way there. For three summers students fanned out across the United States, staying with parents, grandparents, and roommates, visiting mosques, Sikh gurdwaras, and Hindu, Buddhist, and Jain temples. It was a fascinating summer job and not always easy. All these students—no matter what race or religion—had to become strangers in their own homes. As Jonathan, a religion major from Minneapolis, put it, "I grew up in the Twin Cities, so I have lived here all my life. But the city I discovered this summer was something I had never imagined." Minneapolis and St. Paul, traditionally 34 percent Lutheran, are now home to more than 80,000 Asians and Pacific Islanders, approximately half of whom are refugees, including

14,000 Hmong, 10,000 Vietnamese, 8,000 Lao Buddhists, and 7,000 Cambodians. Their temples are an important part of the religious texture of the cities today—along with Islamic Centers, Baha'i communities, and the temples of Minnesota Hindus and Jains.

Like Jonathan, all of our Pluralism Project researchers found a religious landscape they had not known before. Of course, this new religious reality is most visible in the sprawling cosmopolitan cities of America, in world cities like Los Angeles, New York, and Houston. But even in the heartland of America, the new multireligious reality is becoming a Main Street phenomenon. Muslims, Hindus, and Buddhists live in the heavily Mormon neighborhoods of Salt Lake City and in the Bible Belt of Dallas. One of America's most spectacular new mosques is in the suburbs of Cleveland. One of the most beautiful Hindu temples sits on a hilltop south of Chicago. There are Cambodian and Vietnamese Buddhist communities in Iowa and Oklahoma, Tibetan Buddhist retreat centers in the mountains of Vermont and Colorado, and Sikh gurdwaras in the wooded suburban countryside of Fairfax County, Virginia.

These changes to the American landscape have only recently become visible at least architecturally The first generation of American mosques could be found in places like a former watch factory in Queens, a U-Haul dealership in Pawtucket, Rhode Island, a gymnasium in Oklahoma City, and a former mattress showroom in Northridge, California. You could easily drive right on by the warehouse, the storefront, or gymnasium and not notice anything new at all. Because the meeting places were invisible, many Americans, understandably, remained unaware of the new communities. The 1980s and 1990s, however, saw a crescendo of construction. Dozens of new mosques were built, such as the mosque on 96th Street and Third Avenue in New York, the Bridgeview and Villa Park mosques in Chicago, or the Southwest Zone mosque in Houston, to name but a few. There are now multimillion-dollar Hindu temples, like the Bharatiya Temple in the wealthy northern suburbs of Detroit and the spectacular Sri Meenakshi Temple rising from the flats south of Houston. The Buddhists have also made a striking architectural imprint, with the huge Hsi Lai temple in Hacienda Heights, California, a construction project resisted at every step by the community and now so beautiful that "temple view" real estate is coveted—and expensive. In the western Chicago suburb of Bartlett, the Jains have built a large new temple, and to the north in Palatine lies the visually striking hexagonal gurdwara of the Sikhs.

Driving out New Hampshire Avenue, one of the great spokes of the nation's capital, just beyond the Beltway is a stretch of road only a few miles long where one can glimpse in brief compass the new landscape of religious America. Set back from the road on a grassy slope is a new Cambodian Buddhist temple with its graceful, sloping tiled roof.

Then one sees the new copper-domed mosque of the Muslim Community Center, set between an onion-domed Ukrainian Orthodox Church and a Disciples of Christ church. Farther along is a new brick Gujarati Hindu temple called Mangal Mandir, and just off New Hampshire Avenue is a Jain temple. The many churches along the way also reveal the new dimensions of America's Christian landscape, with Hispanic Pentecostal, Vietnamese Catholic, and Korean evangelical congregations sharing facilities with more traditional English-speaking mainline churches.

We must be clear about the fact that this diversity alone does not constitute pluralism. It is plain evidence of the new religious America, but whether we are able to work together across the lines of religious difference to create a society in which we actually know one another remains to be seen. On New Hampshire Avenue, that process is just beginning. Schoolchildren come for visits to the mosque and the Cambodian temple; the two churches that flank the Islamic center lend their parking lots for the two large Eid prayers; and all these communities have a growing awareness of the InterFaith Conference of Metropolitan Washington.

Beyond the changing landscape of our cities, the Pluralism Project is interested in how these religious traditions are changing as they take root in American soil. When Tristan, one of our summer researchers, interviewed a Vietnamese monk in Phoenix, the monk said, "We have to take the plant of Buddhism out of its Asian pot and plant it in the soil of Arizona." The monk's observation could apply to any of the new religious communities. What does Buddhism look like as it begins to grow in its new soil? What will Islam become as it spreads into the suburban life of Houston? What will Hinduism look like as it takes root in central Minneapolis, where Hindu young people take ski trips together and celebrate their high school graduation at the temple with a *puja?* Religions are not like stones passed from hand to hand through the ages. They are dynamic movements, more like rivers—flowing, raging, creative, splitting, converging. The history of religions is unfolding before our eyes. Perhaps nowhere in the world is it more interesting to study the process of dynamic religious change in this new century than in America.

Not only is America changing these religions, but these religions are also changing America. This too is an important question for ongoing study. What does this new religious diversity mean for American electoral politics, for the continuing interpretation of church-state issues by the Supreme Court? What does it mean for American public education and the controversies of school boards? What will it mean for colleges and universities with an increasingly multireligious student body? What about hospitals and health care programs with an increasingly diverse patient population? While many people are just beginning to become aware of the changing religious landscape, the issues it has begun to raise for the American pluralist experiment are already on the agenda of virtually every public institution.

Our new questions are hot only civic, however, but also spiritual and theological. How will Christians and Jews, long dominant in America, respond to this new diversity? Churches, synagogues, and theological school have barely begun to take notice of this new religious reality. Yet, with the changing landscape, the entire context of ministry has begun to change. Adherents of other faiths are no longer distant metaphorical neighbors in some other part of the world but next-door neighbors. A block down the street from a United Church of Christ congregation in Garden Grove, California, is the Lien Hoa Buddhist temple, the home of several Vietnamese Buddhist monks. Next door to the Atonement Lutheran Church in San Diego is San Diego's largest Islamic Center. In Flushing, New York, a synagogue stands next door to a storefront Sikh gurdwara, across the street from Swaminarayan Hindu temple, and down the street from the Ganesha Hindu Temple. And yet few theological schools are able to equip Christian or Jewish clergy for their changing educational roles in this new ministerial context. The issue of living in a pluralist society and thinking theologically about the questions it poses is important today for every community of faith. How do we think about our own faith as we come into deeper relationship with people of other faiths and as we gain a clearer understanding of their religious lives?

As a Christian, a Montana-born, lifelong Methodist who has lived and studied in India, I too have asked this question. How do I articulate my faith in a world in which neighbors, colleagues, and students live deeply religious lives in other communities of faith?'When I began my studies of the Hindu tradition, living in the sacred city of Banaras, I tried to articulate, in *Banaras, City of Light,* what this holy city and all it represents means for Hindus. Further along life's journey, I wrote *Encountering God: A Spiritual Journey from Bozeman to Banaras,* which tackled another equally difficult question: What does Banaras and all it represents mean for me, as a Christian? Through the years I have found my own faith not threatened, but broadened and deepened by the study of Hindu, Buddhist, Muslim, and Sikh traditions of faith. And I have found that only as a Christian pluralist could I be faithful to the mystery and the presence of the one I call God. Being a Christian pluralist means daring to encounter people of very different faith traditions and defining my faith not by its borders, but by its roots.

Many Christians would not agree with me. In the fall of 1999 the Southern Baptist Convention published a prayer guide to enable Christians to pray for Hindus during Diwali, their fall festival of lights. It spoke of the 900 million Hindus who are "lost in the hopeless darkness of Hinduism . . . who worship gods which are not God."[6] Many Christians have no trouble at all speaking of "our God" in exclusivist terms as if God had no dealings with Hindus. The problem with such a response, however, is that it misunderstands both Hindu worship and Hindu experience of God. The American Hindus who carried placards protesting the Southern Baptist prayer guide before Second Baptist Church in Houston did so not because they were averse to being the focus of Christian prayers, but because the characterization of their religious tradition was so ill-informed and ignorant. As I would put it in the language of my own tradition, it is fine for Baptists to witness to their faith; indeed, it is incumbent upon Christians to do so. But it is not fine for us to bear false witness against neighbors of other faiths.

Articulating one's own faith anew in a world of many faiths is a task for people of every religious tradition today, and in every tradition there are thinkers and movements taking up this task. We cannot live in a world in which our economies and markets are global, our political awareness is global, our business relationships take us to every continent, and the Internet connects us with colleagues half a world away and yet live on Friday, or Saturday, or Sunday with ideas of God that are essentially provincial, imagining that somehow the one we call God has been primarily concerned with us and our tribe. No one would dream of operating in the business or political world with ideas about Russia, India, or China that were formed fifty, a hundred, or five hundred years ago. I might sing "Give me that old-time religion! It's good enough for me!" with as much gusto as anyone, but in my heart I know that the old-time religion is not "good enough" unless those of us who claim it are able to grapple honestly and faithfully with the new questions, challenges, and knowledge posed to us by the vibrant world of many living faiths. To be good enough, the old-time religion has to be up to the challenges of an intricately interdependent world.

Theological questions and civic questions are different, however. And it is important that we understand the difference. No matter how we evaluate religions that are different from our own, no matter how we think about religion if we are atheists or secularists, the covenants of citizenship to which we adhere place us on common ground. The Southern Baptists who pray for Hindus who are "lost" are perfectly free to do so. Their theological ideas are not governed by our Constitution, but their commitment to the

6 *Divali: Festival of Lights Prayer for Hindus* (Richmond, VA: International Mission Board of the Southern Baptist Convention, 1999); see www.imb.org.

free exercise of religion, even for Hindus, is. For a moment in September of 2000, the conservative Family Research Council became confused about this distinction. When the first-ever Hindu invocation was given at the U.S. House of Representatives, the council denounced in as a move toward "ethical chaos," saying it was "one more indication that our nationals drifting from its Judeo-Christian roots. . . ." On second thought, the council issued a much-needed clarification: "We affirm the truth of Christianity, but it is not our position that America's Constitution forbids representatives of religions other than Christianity from praying before Congress."[7]

Today all of us are challenged to claim for a new age the very principles of religious freedom that shaped our nation. We must find ways to articulate them anew, whether we are Christian, Jewish, Muslim, Buddhist, or secular Americans. We must embrace the religious diversity that comes with our commitment to religious freedom, and as we move into the new millennium we must find ways to make the differences that have divided people the world over the very source of our strength here in the U.S. It will require moving beyond laissez-faire inattention to religion to a vigorous attempt to understand the religions of our neighbors. And it will require the engagement of our religious traditions in the common tasks of our civil society. Today, right here in the U.S., we have an opportunity to create a vibrant and hopeful pluralism, in a world of increasing fragmentation where there are few models for a truly pluralistic, multireligious society.

Points of Engagement—Reading Comprehension

1. According to Eck, what is pluralism? How is it different from diversity? Look on page 76, 80, and 90 for help. Why is this difference important to Eck?
2. Eck describes some of her students at Harvard this way: "…straddling two worlds, critically appropriating two cultures, they live in perpetual tension between the distinctive cultures of their parents and grandparents and the forceful assimilative currents of American culture. In their own struggles with identity lay the very issues that were beginning to torment the soul of a newly multicultural America" (86). What does this quote mean? Is "perpetual tension" a positive or negative thing? Explain your answer. Why did Eck choose the word "torment"? Support your answer by referring to other passages in the text.
3. Eck believes "benevolence outweighed the backlash" (70) after terrorist attacks. Cite three examples of the evidence she offers for this position. How does this belief help form her vision of "A New Religious America"?

7 Stephen Koff, "Criticism of Hindu Plucked from the Web," *Cleveland Plain Dealer*, September 23, 2000.

4. How does Eck articulate her own faith? Explain what she means by the label she gives herself. Why does she find her belief the best way for her to be faithful?
5. What do you think of the Pluralism Project? Look it up online. Is it possible to be a believer of one religion and to be tolerant of others? Why or why not? What are the benefits of both? The risks?

Points of Departure—Assignment Questions

1. *Strong ties, weak ties.* Diana Eck claims that the immigrant experience today is different from the immigrant experiences of the past. Modern communications technologies enable the immigrant to "live both here and there" (78) and maintain ties with religious communities in their homelands. On the other hand, Malcolm Gladwell, in "Small Change: Why the Revolution Will Not Be Tweeted," does not believe technology can do much to create or sustain "strong tie relationships." Using Eck and Gladwell, explore how modern technology will influence the new religious landscape of America. You might also consider Sherry Turkle and Ian Bremmer's essays in your discussion of the effects of technology on communities and relationships.
2. Diana Eck envisions a desirable religious pluralism that is beyond tolerance and beyond diversity, enriched not by a "so-called clash of civilizations but the marbling of civilizations and peoples" (78). While she acknowledges the potential divisive dangers of diversity, she also points out that difference may "lead us toward the common purpose of an informed, energetic, and even joyous pluralism" (90). For Eck, difference may weaken or strengthen us. Zadie Smith, in "Speaking in Tongues," considers the "doleful conclusion" that may await the African American person who integrates many voices (258), but Smith also looks at a possible "Dream City" that begins with splitting one's voice in two, proceeds to flexibility, moves forward to expanded vision, and ends in an inclusive conviction that "the claims that are particular to [the voice] are no stronger than anyone else's" (258). Do you find Eck's and Smith's fears or their hopes about the direction "difference" will take us more compelling? Why? You may also use the work of Naomi Klein or Kenji Yoshino.
3. Diana Eck is concerned that the emergence of a "New Religious America" has been hurt by ignorance and fear, particularly about Islam. How might Alison Gopnik's insight into counterfactual and causal thinking (gone wrong) help us understand the errors that have fed Islamophobia? How might those same abilities help us reconsider misjudgments and imagine different solutions to the challenge of living in the most religiously diverse country in the world?

4. Diana Eck believes that "not only is America changing these religions [of new immigrant groups], but these religions are changing America" (94). Eck claims that religious values help sculpt the national agenda in everything from politics to education to health care. James Fallows, in "Win in China," writes that "there is no religion in China" (108) but "traditional Chinese values" inform Chinese society. While Eck describes America as a place of many religions, James Fallows describes China as a place of none. Both nations have the issue, then, of determining where their values come from. Where do you think national values come from? Where should they come from? Write a paper in which you answer these questions using Eck and Fallows. Decide if you believe values rooted in religion have a different kind or degree of influence on a society than values based on non-religious ideas.

Win in China!

James Fallows

Points of Access—Pre-Reading

1. When you hear the phrase "reality TV" what do you think of? Does it have a positive or negative connotation? Explain.
2. Given the chance, would you want to be a participant in a reality TV show? Why or why not?
3. What is an entrepreneur? What do you think about the idea of entrepreneurs as "heros" or "role models"? Do you think this is mostly an American idea? Why or why not?
4. How "real" is reality TV? Does it reflect reality? Distort reality? Have no connection to reality? Look up the word "oxymoron." Is "reality TV" an oxymoron? Why or why not?

You think TV is bad in America, and then you watch it someplace else. For all of its defects, American TV generally has high production values—attractive people to look at, sets and staging that don't seem homemade—and it is often the place where new ideas get their start, just before they become worldwide clichés.

Right now the curse of Chinese TV, apart from its being state-controlled and de facto censored, is the proliferation of stupid low-budget "reality" shows. The oddest reality show I've come across while channel surfing was a "World's Strongest Man-type contest between teams of midgets. The cruelest, put on by the state-owned China Central Television (CCTV), pitted young families against each other in elimination events. Each family team had three members—father, mother, elementary-school-aged child—and did coordinated stunts. Three families survived each show to appear in future rounds, and three were sent home, the children inconsolable and the husbands and wives looking daggers at each other.

Fortunately there is also a best Chinese reality show, or at least one that my wife and I followed avidly through its increasingly suspenseful Tuesday-night episodes last year. We first heard of *Ying Zai Zhongguo,* or *Win in China,* from a Chinese-American friend, Baifang Schell, who was involved in the production. We became so interested that in

December we traveled to Beijing to be in the audience at CCTV's cavernous main studio for the live, final episode, in which one grand champion was chosen from five remaining contestants. Like many other Chinese reality shows, this one featured a segment known by the English letters "PK." This means nothing to most English speakers (penalty kick?), but it is widely recognized in China as meaning "Player Kill" in online games.

The PK stage of *Win* served the function of the Tribal Council in *Survivor* or the Boardroom in *The Apprentice:* After a contest or judges' assessment each week, two of that episode's competitors ended up pitted against each other in a three-minute lightning elimination. This is PK, in which one opponent issues a question, challenge, or taunt, and the other tries to answer, outwit, and provoke the first. Once done speaking, a competitor slams a hand down on a big button, stopping his or her own clock (as with a chess-match timer) and starting the opponent's. Faster and faster, each contestant tries to manage the time so as to get the very last word. The audience gasps, cheers, and roars with laughter at the gibes—and at the end, one contestant is "killed," as determined by audience vote or a panel of judges. Even if you can barely follow the language, it's exciting.

But something else distinguishes *Win in China*—not just from the slew of other reality shows but also from its American model, *The Apprentice*, with Donald Trump. "The purpose of *The Apprentice* was very functional," Wang Lifen, the producer and on-camera host of the show, told me (in English) shortly after the final episode. "There's some job that already exists, and Donald Trump is just looking for somebody to fill it, while providing entertainment." Wang said that she had higher ambitions for her show: "We want to teach values. Our dream for the show is to enlighten Chinese people and help them realize their own dreams." Having seen the program and talked with contestants and compared it with some superficially similar Chinese reality shows, I don't scoff at what she said.

The didactic and uplifting ambitions of the show could be considered classically Chinese, the latest expression of a value-imprinting impulse that stretches from the Analects of Confucius to the sayings of Chairman Mao. Or they could be considered, like the Horatio Alger novels of young, muscular America, signs of an economy at an expansive moment when many people want to understand how to seize new opportunities. Either way, the particular message delivered by the show seems appropriate to China at this stage of its growth. Reduced to a moral, *Win in China* instructs Chinese people that they have chances never open to their compatriots before—but also that, as one contestant told me at the end of the show, "The only one I can rely on is myself."

Wang Lifen moved from Beijing to Washington, D.C., in the fall of 2004, for a one-year fellowship at the Brookings Institution. She was then in her late 30s and was an influential figure in CCTV's news division, where she had created and produced documentaries and talk shows. By the time she returned to CCTV, a year later, she was ready to act on a question she'd asked while watching American TV: What would an improved, Sinified version of *The Apprentice* look like?

It would be Chinese in being huge. There would be thousands of initial candidates, with entry open to any adult "of Chinese origin" anywhere in the world. More than 100 (versus *The Apprentice*'s 18) would have a serious chance to compete on-camera for the prize. The nature of that prize indicated why *Win in China* could seem more American than its American model. Instead of a job and a paycheck within a Trump-style empire, Wang offered seed money for new entrepreneurial ventures—and for more than just one contestant. By Chinese standards, the sums were enormous. The ultimate victor would receive 10 million yuan, or nearly $1.3 million. The runner-up would get 7 million yuan, and the three other finalists would get 5 million yuan apiece. With other prizes and incentives, the money the show was offering came to nearly $4 million.

This would be large even for a U.S. show, but the source of the prizes was even more unusual. Wang raised the money not from sponsors or the network but from individual investors in China—for instance, Andrew Yan, of Softbank Asia Infrastructure Fund, who had recently been named "Venture Capitalist of the Year" by the Chinese Venture Capital Association. Yan and a few other investors, including Kathy Xu, of Capital Today, and Hugo Shong, of the U.S.-based company IDG, put up the pool of prize money—in return for a 50 percent share in the real-world businesses the winning contestants would use it to create or expand. Twenty percent would belong to the contestants, and 15 percent to the show's production company. The remaining 15 percent would go by "lucky draw" to viewers who had voted for candidates, via mobile-phone text messages, during the show's run. In effect, the many weeks of the program (33 episodes were shown in all, some live) amounted to a drawn-out, public version of a pitch to venture capitalists (the investors) from entrepreneurs seeking their backing (the contestants). Every week, contestants would be put through some kind of quiz or business-oriented team challenge that would whittle their numbers down. Wang had an additional hope for this process: that it would give viewers practical tips on starting businesses of their own.

Within a few months of her return, Wang had rounded up the financial backing, gotten the show on CCTV's schedule, and begun the hunt for candidates. (China is a timeless civilization and so on, but today's business deals can happen very fast.) Her team posted Web notices and placed ads in 20 newspapers around the country, asking potential entrepreneurs to send in résumés and business plans. In March 2006, the top 3,000 (!) files were sent to screening teams, which reduced the pool to about 500.

Interviews of at least 15 minutes apiece then produced 108 semifinalists—an auspicious number, because of the "108 heroes" (also known variously as the "108 bandits" and "108 generals") of a famed uprising in the Shandong mountains a thousand years ago.

All of the 108 came to Beijing at their own expense and made a mass climb of the Great Wall, along with the investors, producers, and judges, to build team spirit for the challenges ahead. Then, in one televised debut episode, the 108 were divided into two big teams and winnowed down to a field of 36, based on their performance in a computerized simulation of business decisions. Meanwhile, all 108 were given off-camera seminars on finance, personnel management, and other skills each would need as an entrepreneur.

Through the next stage, the 36 survivors appeared in groups of four before panels of judges that included prominent Chinese business and academic figures. The best known was Jack Ma, co-founder and CEO of China's dominant e-commerce site, Alibaba. Each contestant had two minutes to present his or her business plan (three women were among the 36), after which the judges would begin the interrogation. What about holes in the plan? What was Plan B, if the sales projections didn't pan out? Why was this plan better than other candidates'? Often the questions came from investors whose own money was at stake.

On September 5, the producers held a reception at CCTV's Beijing headquarters for 6,000 guests: contestants, friends and family, press, and business dignitaries. The 12 finalists were announced—and then taken away to the Huang Yuan hotel in Beijing, where they would spend the next four weeks being filmed competing.

The seven further weeks of the show, which took the 12 contestants down to the five who would compete in the finale we went to, drew an audience that grew to 5 million (considered large for this "serious" a show), were discussed avidly in numerous blogs, and had a structure more or less familiar from American reality shows. The competitive pattern was essentially like that of *The Apprentice:* The 12 contestants were divided into two teams, which then competed against each other in some real-world business task—selling life insurance, raising money for charity, improvising a solution to some other business problem. Members of the winning team got to come back for the next episode. Members of the losing team went through various other assessments that included a final PK. Based on how the pair sounded when debating, a panel of judges would send one or the other home.

All the contestants were interesting, but we found ourselves rooting for four. Zhou Jin, one of two women among the final 12, was general manager of an advertising agency, and her project was to develop new labor-training services. She had been seven months pregnant when the competition began, and was granted permission for a brief absence from the competition, but then fought her way back into consideration with strong performances. Ms. Zhou had a sassy air and, as best I could judge from others' reactions, a sharp tongue. She had a lot of backing in blogs because of the way she handled her pregnancy.

We came to think of Song Wenming as the social-conscience candidate. He was a mild-looking, baby-faced man in his early 30s from Anhui province, an impoverished area many of whose people end up as illegal migrant workers in the big coastal cities. Song himself had earned an M.B.A. and held a job with a big international accounting firm. He resigned and, with two friends, started an employment firm to match Anhui people with jobs. His business plan was to expand these operations with new capital.

Zhou Yu was jokingly called by his competitors "Wolf' or "Wild Wolf," but we thought of him as Country Boy. He was a tall, rangy 35-year-old with a buzz cut who had worked for years in the clothing business, and his business plan was to expand factories for lingerie and other ladies' apparel. In manner, he was much earthier than most of the other contestants—barking out remarks, grimacing, predictably losing his temper at some point in each show. Among the final 12, he was the only one not to have gone past high school, and during PKs he talked about the limits of book learning and the value of the school of hard knocks. He was a favorite in mobile-phone voting.

Then there was Zhao Yao, who struck us as the smoothest of the candidates. He grew up in Beijing but now lives in Los Angeles, having been based in America since 1995. He'd left China to get an M.B.A. at the University of Wyoming, and then tried to set up what he later described to me as his "Wyoming-based selfservice tour-planning company." After work-permit problems, he'd moved to California, where he was a computer programmer, an accountant, and a business consultant. He dreamed of bringing the "direct-response marketing" business to China. Direct-response marketing is the polite name for the infomercial business, and Zhao planned to set up the infrastructure—call centers, payment systems, customer service—that would allow the George Foreman Grill, for example, to be sold on TV in China (except here it would be the Jackie Chan Grill).

Week by week, our candidates survived, until the last episode before the live finale. Zhou Jin, the woman, and Zhao Yao, the Californian, were both on the team that lost that week's competition, and they were pitted against each other in the final PK. One or the other would go down! Their debate was relatively high-road, each pointing out his or her own strengths rather than the other's weaknesses. Ms. Zhou looked shocked when the judges' result was announced: She would go on to the finals, and Zhao was out. This seemed shocking because Zhao had seemed, probably even to her, such a golden-boy candidate. When the series was over, I asked him, in English, how he interpreted his elimination. "If I had just spoken my mind, here is what I would have said before the verdict," he told me. "I would have told the judges, 'I don't think I've given you any reason to eliminate me. But the lady hasn't given you any reason to eliminate her. Under the circumstances—her being pregnant, the struggles of a young mom, the public support—you should just take me out.'" As they did.

Everything about the live final show was meant to be spectacular. Most episodes had three judges; this time there were 11. In addition to famous investors, like Jack Ma and Hugo Shong, there were other prominent business figures, like Niu Gensheng, head of one of China's leading dairy companies. Introduced separately, and given the right to make the final selection, were the heads of the two most respected firms in all of China:

Lenovo, the leading computer company, and Haier, which has a high reputation for quality and which absolutely dominates the domestic "white goods" market for refrigerators, washing machines, and so on. *Win* publicists said this was the first time the two CEOs, Yang Yuanqing of Lenovo and Zhang Ruimin of Haier, had made a joint appearance.

The two finalists who were not among our candidates were the first two eliminated in PKs. Then things got serious. Ms. Zhou, Song "Social Conscience" Wenming, and Zhou "Wild Wolf" Yu answered questions from the judges—and mobile-phone votes showed that Song had done best of the three. Thus the two Zhous had to face off in a PK, whose drama was apparent even if you didn't understand what they were saying. In an earlier round of questions, all five candidates had had to explain their greatest weakness. Mr. Zhou said that he had a bad temper—but that passion was a good thing in a leader! And so, he helpfully pointed out, was the kind of education you couldn't get from books. For her part, Ms. Zhou said that her attention was always flitting from subject to subject; on the other hand, that kind of alert eye could help in running a business.

During the PK, it was as if Ms. Zhou was trying to make Mr. Zhou explode. "You are avoiding my questions, maybe you don't have enough learning to answer." "They call you the Wolf, it would be better for the Wolf to stay in the wilderness." After Mr. Zhou (unwisely) mentioned that he was thinking of going back to school, she dug in: "Even if you get the diploma, it won't mean real skills." After inserting each of her barbs, Ms. Zhou would slap her PK button with a smile at the audience and a little rise of her eyebrows. Wild Wolf would splutter and yell, slamming his fist onto his button, and finally getting a near-ovation from the crowd when he said, "You question my skills, but I am standing here tonight! That should be proof enough for anyone!" He also had the last words, which were: "I'll talk to you later!"

As it turned out, in trying to provoke the Wolf, Ms. Zhou ended up mortally wounding them both. The judges declared him the victor over her in this PK—one said later that he was "like China itself, from a poor background, still crude, but proud of its rise"—and so she had to sit down. But in the anticlimactic final choice between Mr. Zhou and Song Wenming, the M.B.A., Zhou's fiery and uncontrolled outbursts during his PK with Ms. Zhou proved his undoing. All 11 judges spoke, many saying that passion was great, but you needed a steady hand to build an enterprise. Song Wenming was nothing if not steady. The Haier and Lenovo CEOs glanced at each other and gave the winner's name: Song Wenming.

What had it all meant? I got in touch with our four contestants later on, Zhao Yao in person when he visited Shanghai and the others by e-mail through a translator. Each made veiled and provocative comments about the contest itself. When I asked Ms. Zhou about differences between the contest as she experienced it and what viewers saw on TV, she said she could not give any details, "because of traditional Chinese values" of discretion. "All I can say is that the exposure of the most repulsive side of human nature by us—if there was any, because of the award—did not, fortunately, appear in front of the audience." (She added that some altruistic moments had also escaped capture.) She said that she had often felt "condescension and suspicion" toward her talents from others on the show because of her gender, but hoped that her success would be encouraging for Chinese women in general. ("And after all, the United States only now has its first woman speaker of the House.")

When I asked Zhao Yao whether his life was different now, he began in stentorian tones—"The impact of my involvement in the show has been profound"—and then started laughing and said, "I am taking the tone promoted by the show, enthusiastic and assertive!" He said that becoming famous enough to be recognized on the street had been of great practical benefit, since a real venture capitalist had now offered him funding. "I do wonder if the actors in U.S. reality shows would be expected to iron our own shirts and wash our own socks while encamped in a hotel room for a month," he added. "Maybe they do— I only know that's what we did."

Zhou Yu, the Wolf, said he was glad to have been the people's champion. He had also learned that his wife was now referred to as "Wolf's Wife." Song Wenming, the winner, said that he had grown exasperated at times but had been confident he'd do well as long as he could just be himself before the judges. In indirect or open ways, all of them made clear that what was shown onscreen had been trimmed, rearranged, and highlighted to seem more dramatic. "Maybe this is the 'reality' that reality TV is introducing us to!" Zhao Yao said.

About one point all of them sounded utterly sincere: their hope that the program would encourage more people in China to start their own businesses. Song Wenming put it in historic terms: Its age-old ethic of stability was part of the reason China had fallen so far behind Western countries, and even now, "Chinese culture does not facilitate creativity very much." He hoped the show would introduce the "positive power" of entrepreneurship. Ms. Zhou said she hoped potential entrepreneurs would learn the importance of both perseverance and passion.

There was much more in the same vein.

"I have a close friend on the staff of a state-owned company," Wang Lifen, the show's producer, told me. "After the final episode, she called and said: 'I have to quit my work unit and my company! I have to be an entrepreneur, because I want a new life.'" Women must retire from state-owned companies in China by 55; men, by 60. "No one can provide for the next stage of life but me," Wang's friend told her. According to Wang, a "minister-level" official in the Chinese government called the head of CCTV when the series was over and asked, "How can we make everyone watch this show?" (In China, this might not be a purely rhetorical question.) As a start, CCTV has renewed the show for two more seasons.

"There is no religion in China, so it is very important to promote the right kind of values," Wang said. "Today for our society, the entrepreneur can be our hero."

"Hero" might be going too far, but the participants on *Win* seem to have been received in the press and blogs as modern Chinese role models. Having listened to their dreams and followed their onscreen contests, I cannot help wishing all of them well. Even more, I hope China's development is such that their show is eventually looked back on the way Horatio Alger's *Luck and Pluck* is: as an unsubtle and perhaps over-sincere effort to teach people the rules of peaceful prosperity. I hope it doesn't eventually become another bit of evidence about the Chinese bubble: the way people behaved when they thought the good times would always go on.

Points of Engagement—Reading Comprehension

1. On page 102, Wang Lifen, the producer of *Win in China* describes the purpose of the show. Find the passage. Do you think a TV show can achieve these goals? Why or why not?
2. Fallows explains the concept of "PK" on page 102. If the intent of *Win in China* is to instill values and enlighten people, what values does "PK" impart?

3. In the final paragraph, Fallows hopes that *Win in China* will be viewed the way Horatio Alger's *Luck and Pluck* is, in the United States. Do an Internet search on Horatio Alger and his book/s. What similarities do you see? Can you spot any differences?
4. Consider the following claim: "*Win in China* could seem more American than its American model" (103). Look at the context. What, specifically, does this mean?

Points of Departure—Assignment Questions

1. In "Win in China!" James Fallows describes a TV show that the Chinese government hopes will encourage its citizens to dream of a better future. In "Small Change: Why The Revolution Will Not Be Tweeted," Malcolm Gladwell writes about Facebook and Twitter, stating that these social media tools make it "easier for the powerless to collaborate, coordinate, and give voice to their concerns:" (134). Yet, Gladwell also realizes the limitations of these tools. How do traditional media, such as TV, differ from social media as an influence on values, behaviors, and social change? Your project is to engage with the views in both texts and come up with an answer of your own, in light of these views. You could also pair this question with Ian Bremmer's essay, "Democracy in Cyberspace."
2. In their essays, Naomi Klein and Kristof and WuDunn write about many of the serious problems associated with globalism. James Fallows gives us a much more positive view of America's influence abroad. Which "America" do you think is more powerful in the world? The America that other nations imitate? Or the America that they fear as a threat? Why?
3. Is there such a thing as "American values"? "Chinese values"? Are values something personal, individual, or can a nation have a set of "values"? If so, where do they come from? Who decides what they are? Write a paper in which you explore these questions, and provide answers using essays by James Fallows and one or two of the following authors: Ian Bremmer, Amy Chua, Diana Eck, Janet Flammang, or Arlie Russell Hochschild. Keep in mind that you are addressing two *specific* nations in all of these essays: China and the U.S.
4. How can money bring people together? How can it drive them apart? Do communities always benefit from increased wealth? What is the price that they pay, if they pay one at all? In James Fallows' essay, the winner of the competition, Song Wemming, hopes the TV show will introduce the "positive power of entrepreneurship" to fellow Chinese. Back in America, Arlie Russell Hochschild and Janet Flammang observe the negative effects of capitalism and the pursuit of wealth on American family life

and civil society. As China moves from a state-controlled Communistic economy to a capitalistic entrepreneurial economy like we have in the US, what effect might we anticipate on the way people relate to one another in China? In other words, what influences—positive or negative—does an economic system like capitalism, which values money so highly, have on civil society?

5. #winning. In his essay, James Fallows documents the human desire to WIN, but there has recently been more research on the counterbalancing desires to cooperate and collaborate. These two inclination—to win and to work together—may exist within individuals or within cultures in extremes or in various combinations on a continuum. Look for specific examples of the competitive and cooperative spirits in the contestants on *Win in China* and in essays by Amy Chua, Arlie Russell Hochschild, Gregory Orr, or Naomi Klein. Then ask yourself these questions: Why do we care so much winning? What does the drive to win do for us and to us? What are we willing to do in order to win? When and why do we cooperate? If someone wins, does it always mean that someone else loses? Are there some struggles or competitions that simply *cannot* be won? What happens then? Use the experiences described by these authors to help you formulate your own position about what makes individuals more competitive, more cooperative, or a mix of the two.

The Taste for Civilization: Food, Politics, and Civil Society

Janet A. Flammang

Points of Access—Pre-Reading

1. When you were growing up, did you eat regularly as a family at the kitchen or dining table? Which meals? How do you think eating with your family, or not eating with them regularly, has affected your relationships with your family members?
2. Now that you're at college, where do you eat? Who do you eat with? Do you watch TV during meals? Do you talk about your day? How would you characterize the conversations? Are mealtimes now different from when you were growing up? How?
3. What do you think you can learn from eating with other people? Is conversation you have at a table (with food) different from conversation elsewhere? Why or why not?

American women have historically been responsible for the civilizing functions of food—meal planning, table courtesy, the art of conversation, family and group rituals—and in this capacity modeling the virtues of thoughtfulness and generosity. The rise of fast food and the decline of leisurely meals mean fewer opportunities for everyday civility in speech and practice. Civil society and democracy would benefit from a social change where foodwork, conversation, and food rituals were seen as everyone's responsibility, and from an economic change of a shorter workday to allow time for meals. This book focuses on the importance of civility to American democracy and how civility is related to everyday food practices, both at the table and in the wider arenas of public gardens and markets.

In recent years, political writers have focused increased attention on the study of civil society. This book makes an original contribution by examining in detail how food, meals, rituals, and sociability are integral building blocks of civil society, and how this has been forgotten and ignored because of the devalued nature of food and foodwork The concept of civility remains implicit and underdeveloped in most writings about civil society in America. Here it will be made explicit and tied to the civic virtues of thoughtfulness and generosity practiced in everyday life in foodwork and mealtime conversations and rituals. Democratic speech and behavior can be practiced at the table, and as we spend less time in common meals, we are losing an opportunity to learn and teach the art of conversation so essential for civil society and democratic practice.

How can we find time for food rituals in Americas fast-paced, consumer, workaholic culture? Compete with the screen culture? Resuscitate the dying art of conversation? If foodwork and table conversation are be seen as everyone's responsibility and as integral to civil society and democracy, we need to confront major obstacles: the unconscious association of food with women; the mind-body dualism that privileges transcending the body, women, and foodwork; and the devaluation of taste in the hierarchy of senses. This book was inspired by Alice Waters's delicious revolution, which links a sensual approach to food with food's transformative power, not only at the table but also in forging civic ties at farmers' markets and at neighborhood, school, and jail gardens. Food and meals can give people something to talk about across ethnic, race, and class lines. This book calls for an expanded understanding of civil society and democracy by shedding light on the civility that has heretofore been confined to the shadows of women's domestic work with no public ramifications.

Civility, Civil Society, and Democracy

Most Americans think about democracy in terms of electoral politics, lawmaking, and civil rights and liberties. But these aspects of democracy rest on a foundation of civil society. Civil society is a hotly contested concept that has been dubbed *the* big idea for the twenty-first century, figuring prominently in the politics and concerns of disparate groups. Around the world, it has been a rallying call for prodemocracy advocates in former Soviet republics and in Latin America. In the United States, civil society is important for libertarians who want to reduce the scale of the federal government; for communitarians who want stronger family, neighborhood, and religious associations; and for civic-minded pundits and scholars troubled by a disengaged citizenry.[1]

These disparate groups share a common assumption that civil society is a realm of human association separate from the state and the market. Contemporary interest in civil society is in part a corrective to an exaggerated emphasis on the state and the market as optimal forms of human association. Across the globe, the state-based model loomed large between 1945 and the mid-1970s, with capitalist welfare states and socialist centralized planning. Then from the mid-1970s until the early 1990s, the market was ascendant with Reaganomics and Thatcherism, codified in Margaret Thatcher's famous dicta: "There is no alternative to the market" and "There is no such thing as society." The 1990s saw renewed interest in the relationship between the state, the economy, and civil society. Civil society is a complex puzzle, but it has three essential components: associational life, the good society, and the public sphere.[2] Writers differ in the respective weights they give to these three elements. But a common thread is the notion of civility. Civil society is not just society—it is civil.

Political writers—both empiricists and theorists—have danced around the concept of civility rather than embrace it. This is in part because they have focused on the state and the economy, and in part because of the historical baggage of civility as quaint, old-fashioned, and stifling. Michael Walzer observes that political theorists have been so focused on the state and the economy that they "have not thought enough about solidarity and trust nor planned for their future" and "have neglected the networks through which civility is produced and reproduced." He correctly points out that "most men and women have been trapped in one or another subordinate relationship, where the civility' they learned was deferential rather than independent and active." So it is important to reconstruct the dense associational life of civil society and its attendant norms of civility under new conditions of freedom and equality.[3]

Civility in a democracy is not the superficial glossing over of differences. Indeed, it is a virtue that is called into play precisely *when* there are differences, especially among strangers. In Stephen Carter's view, civility is "a virtue that equips us for everyday life with strangers, our daily democratic train ride with people we do not like or do not even know." It entails a generosity of spirit that assumes the best, not the worst, of the stranger. "Civility has two parts: generosity, even when it is costly, and trust, even when there is risk."[4]

The adjectives *civil* and *civilizing* are frequently used to describe activities at the table: taking turns talking, listening attentively, learning from different age groups, eating no more than one's fair share, meeting the needs of the group, showing respect for different tastes, breaking bread with companions, celebrating birthdays and anniversaries, honoring religious and ethnic traditions, meeting for coffee or tea, entertaining friends at dinner, sharing weekly meals with an extended family, experimenting with unfamiliar cuisines, and addressing differences with diplomacy. In spite of these daily experiences with the civil and the civilizing, and the universal value placed on diplomacy, table activities are usually invisible in both philosophical and empirical studies of civil society. Table activities should receive more attention in contemporary understandings of civil society insofar as they provide opportunities to practice the art of conversation and the virtues of thoughtfulness and generosity.

Political Theory: Where's the Household in Civil Society?

Most political theorists have neglected table activities because of their association with the household, a domain typically excluded from civil society. Indeed, it is the household's nonvoluntary and parochial relations that citizens must jettison to form the voluntary and general-good associations of civil society. In his *Politics,* Aristotle divided the associational world into two: the domestic community (*oikos*) and the political community *(koinonia politike* or *polls).* To the ancient Romans, *civis* meant citizen, *civitas* referred to sovereign political units, and civil was distinguished from military. In medieval times civil was contrasted with ecclesiastical. By the late Middle Ages, *civil* referred to the association of citizens in distinction from the institutions of household, government, military, and church. *Civil* also became associated with *civilization,* the acquisition of manners and habits of civil persons. Its antonym was *barbarous* (i.e., foreign), whose Greek root meant "stammering," unable to speak our language. *Civil* acquired its dual usage: it applies to the status of citizen or civil society and to the manners of the civilized.[5] In spite of this dual usage in everyday life, political theorists have paid more attention to citizenship than they have to the manners and habits of civil persons.

The term *civil society* entered Western political discourse in the fifteenth century, when Leonardo Bruni, a Florentine civic humanist, used *societas civilis* to translate Aristotle's *koinonia politike.* Florentines at that time were hearkening back to the Roman Republic and the Athenian *polis* as models for the small, self-governing republics of Renaissance Europe. In the seventeenth century, social-contract theorists began to carve out new territory for civil society to reflect a new social order. The town's independence from the legal scrutiny of the manorial lord was the precondition for a public realm of equal members. As formerly household economic activities moved into town life, civil society became a commercial realm. Rousseau's entry on "Political Economy" in Diderot's *Encyclopedia* contrasted civil or political society with the household. In the *Second Treatise,* Locke said it was possible to dissolve government while leaving civil society intact. Civil society was synonymous with political society. In his 1821 *Philosophy of Right,* Hegel replaced the Aristotelian dichotomy of household and polity with the trichotomy of family, civil society, and the political state. Civil society denoted the sphere of market exchanges and the legal and social frameworks that sustained them. Karl Marx regarded civil society as a vehicle for furthering the economic interests of the capitalist class, removing its moral and pedagogical meaning as preparation for citizenship.[6]

Some political theorists have advanced conceptions of civil society that included aspects amenable to incorporating table activities and their attendant conversation, thoughtfulness, and generosity. Eighteenth-century Scottish Enlightenment theorists of moral sentiments characterized civil society as a realm of social mutuality. In his *Theory of Moral Sentiments,* Adam Smith presumed "natural affections and sociability," and Adam Ferguson's *Essay on the History of Civil Society* posited shared mutuality and trust between citizens, who acted in society "from affections of kindness and friendship." These theorists underscored the social and ethical nature of civil society and the importance of mutuality and recognition.[7]

In *Democracy in America,* Alexis de Tocqueville made a distinction between political society (relations between federal and state governments and between citizens and the state[s]) and civil society (relations of the citizens among themselves). "Political associations" were formed in part to oppose actions of the state and to preserve the independence of the citizens. "Civil associations" addressed the needs of "daily life," aimed at the preservation of civilization itself. Without such associations, citizens in a democracy would descend into "barbarism." Tocqueville expanded civil society to include associations that were not necessarily voluntary, that addressed the needs of daily life, and that were civilized.[8]

Philosophical pragmatists expanded the way we think about civil society by emphasizing political learning by doing, and in the case of John Dewey, learning through everyday food activities. Dewey saw civil society as a realm of shared political life and public improvement through debate, discussion, and persuasion. Face-to-face interactions in the family and the neighborhood were "the means by which dispositions [were] stably formed and ideas acquired which laid hold on the roots of character." The "winged words of conversation in immediate intercourse have a vital import lacking in the fixed and frozen words of written speech. . . . Vision is a spectator; hearing is a participator."[9] Dewey has been described as the philosophical traditions only stomach-friendly thinker. In acknowledgment of humans' food-dependent condition, he established an experimental school in which the stomach took a central place. One of his obsessions was cooking.[10]

Jürgen Habermas sees in civil society both the Marxist notion of class domination and the liberal protection of individual autonomy through communicative actions and structures. Habermas has underscored the centrality of conversation to civic life, and he praises coffeehouses for the free discussions they encouraged. He and other theorists in the deliberative democracy school have elucidated a "talk-centric" democratic theory.[11]

The concept of civil society has been used by political dissidents around the world to connote a desirable social order, characterized by tolerance, nondiscrimination, nonviolence, trust and cooperation, freedom and democracy, so long as these qualities are not defined exclusively in Western terms. Examples are Poland's Solidarity, post-Franco Spain, and opposition movements in Kenya and Zambia.[12] In Latin America, dissidents' focus on civil society has reflected both a struggle against military dictatorships and a conviction that conventional political parties have failed.[13] In many repressive regimes, civil society consists of underground meetings over coffee or tea or at meals in private homes.

Social-capital theorists Pierre Bourdieu, James Coleman, and Robert Putnam have added to our understanding of civil society the importance of resources derived from durable group networks or memberships. Bourdieu emphasizes unequal access to these resources. Coleman focuses on an instrumental investment in social capital. And Putnam is interested in how trust and norms of reciprocity enhance capacity for civic engagement. According to this understanding, "bonding" social capital is within the group, while "bridging" links to outside groups.[14]

Some political theorists have included the household in civil society. Antonio Gramsci agreed with Marx that civil society was the arena of cultural and ideological hegemony, but he thought that it could also be a locus of rebellion. The family was included in civil society because it shaped the political views of citizens.[15] Michael Edwards agrees with Gramsci that we must include family life in our understanding of civil society because it plays a major role in building a society that is civil by influencing "both social norms and the political settlements that translate them into public policy." Edwards concurs with Stephen Carter that families are or should be the first civil societies, marked by sacrifice and caring for others.[16]

Jodi Dean argues that feminist theorists have been "oddly silent" on the subject of civil society.[17] In part this silence has been due to historical depictions of civil society as an arena where women were absent: "civil" was typically contrasted with "natural" (the state of nature for contract theorists) or "familial" (domestic households for most theorists). An important exception is Carole Pateman, who describes social-contract theorists' account of the origins of civil society as a story of "masculine political birth."[18] She includes the family in civil society: "The sphere of domestic life is at the heart of civil society rather than apart or separate from it. A widespread conviction that this is so is revealed by contemporary concern about the crisis, the decline, the disintegration of the nuclear family that is seen as the bulwark of civilized moral life."[19] Anne Phillips notes that while civil society has historically been "gender loaded" as masculine, to the extent that the term has come to mean intermediate associations between the individual and the state, women could be said to have an edge. Historically denied top government posts, women have practiced their politics disproportionately in voluntary and neighborhood associations.[20]

Most communitarians see the family as foundational to civil society. For example, Jean Bethke Elshtain defines civil society as "the many forms of community and association that dot the landscape of democratic culture, from families to churches to neighborhood groups to trade unions to self-help movements to voluntary assistance to the needy."[21] Alan Wolfe contends that the contemporary Left and Right rely on the state and the market to "organize their codes of moral obligation, but what they really need is civil society—families, communities, friendship networks, solidaristic workplace ties, voluntarism, spontaneous groups and movements—not to reject, but to complete the project of modernity."[22]

Empirical Studies: It's Hard to Measure the Table

If many theorists have neglected table activities because of their association with households and families, many empiricists have avoided them because they are so difficult to measure. Most empirical studies shedding light on civil society fall under the rubrics of social capital and civic engagement.[23] These studies typically focus on participation in voluntary groups and employ either survey research methodology, historical accounts of voluntary group membership, or some combination of these methods. But none of them looks at table activities. Some historical accounts of American civic life emphasize citizenship, but not the manners and habits of civil persons.[24] While the historical method lends itself to an understanding of table activities, only a few authors have linked table activities to civil society. For example, Markman Ellis's cultural history of the coffeehouse traces its association with conviviality, sociability, politeness, public opinion, and conversation.[25] More commonly, historians have studied the history of manners in general in Europe and in the United States.[26] A few political scientists, sociologists, and linguists have studied table activities, conversation, and politics. All of them have used qualitative research methods such as discourse analysis, participant observation, and personal interviews.

Political scientist Lyn Kathlene has studied legislative tables and floors. She found significant gender differences in the conversational dynamics of legislative committee hearings in a state legislature. Women chairs spoke less, took fewer turns, and interrupted less frequently. Men used their positions to control hearings, women to facilitate discussion among committee members, sponsors, and witnesses. Male witnesses interrupted female chairs, and female witnesses opposed to a bill had significantly less opportunity to participate compared to male witnesses. Female committee members waited longer before speaking in hearings, spoke less, and were interrupted more frequently.[27] When women sat next to each other and/or could see each other by sitting at a V-shaped table, they participated more actively in the committee hearings.[28]

Linguist Deborah Tannen's analysis of a dinner conversation led her to conclude that interruptions were not necessarily displays of dominance. Some cultural groups used a "high involvement style" with "cooperative overlap": a listener talks along with a speaker not to interrupt but to show enthusiastic listening and participation. This style could be off-putting to speakers who used a "high considerateness" style. This insight made her reluctant to embrace the notion that men dominate women by interrupting them. Tannen described her hermeneutic (interpretive) methodological approach as anthropologically oriented, involving a close examination of individual cases of interaction, in many of which she was a participant, and a consideration of cultural context.[29]

Dinner conversations of thirty-four families were analyzed by linguist Shoshana Blum-Kulka. She was particularly interested in politeness and power in dinner talk and the pragmatic aspects of language use. To become competent conversationalists, children had to learn how to choose and introduce topics for talk, respond appropriately, tell a story, or develop an argument. Cultural variations in providing opportunities for children to participate in dinner talk, and in monitoring their participation, resulted in differential access to adult discourse, reflected variation in perceptions of the relations between power and language, and resulted in different socialization agendas for children.[30]

Sociologist Marjorie L. DeVault conducted interviews in thirty households to understand women's invisible work caring for and feeding their families, including the "interaction work" that women do in conversations. Talk was considered an important part of family meals, and people had to work at it. In all households, children's behavior was monitored and controlled. Many parents were frustrated that they could not arrange for the kind of family meals that they remembered from their childhood, where there were real discussions. The table was also the locus of pleasure and sociability: interviewees looked forward to having people over and a pleasant dinner conversation.[31]

Group conversations in people's homes were studied by sociologist William A. Gamson to determine how people made meaning and developed a political consciousness. Participants used a combination of the media, experiential knowledge, and popular wisdom to understand political issues. Their "legendary conversational style" blended facts and interpretation. The "cynical chic" capitalized on their own ignorance and powerlessness. Gamson saw his book as an antidote to the conventional wisdom that most political issues and events do not make much sense to most working people. He was struck by the deliberative quality of his subjects' construction of meaning about complex issues and the considerable coherence of their views. People were quite capable of conducting informed and well-reasoned discussions about issues. Although most interviewees were not inclined to become politically active, the seeds of political action were present in the minds of many of them—a latent political consciousness that could be activated in the continual creation of social movements.[32]

Sociologist Nina Eliasoph used participant observation of several groups to study how citizens created contexts for political conversation in everyday life. She observed that many people had curious and open-minded private conversations but avoided political talk in wider circles. A cycle of "political evaporation" set in when citizens assumed that talking politics in a publicly minded way was out of place. The further backstage the context, the more public-spirited conversation was possible. People thought that in public they had to couch their motivations in a politics of self-interest, even though this was not necessarily true, as in the case of volunteers. Many women felt that they had to speak "for the children," engage in mandatory "public Momism," and wax nostalgic about community. The silencing of public-spirited conversations was the volunteers' way of looking out for the public good: they did not want to ruin positive feelings or alienate the common person. Each group created and enforced rules for political conversations, political manners, and etiquette. "Cultures of talk" told citizens when they needed to hide their fears and when talking helped work through fears. The democratic norms that really mattered were the unspoken norms for conversation—manners, civility, and tact—that made citizens comfortable engaging in freewheeling political conversation in an everyday-life context. Political etiquette or a sense of civility referred to citizens' companionable ways of creating and maintaining a comfortable context for talk in the public sphere.[33]

In a similar study, political scientist Katherine Cramer Walsh conducted participant observation of two groups: elderly, middle-class white men at a corner store and women in a church craft guild. The women evaded political topics for fear of disrupting the air of politeness. The men were much more likely to talk politics for several reasons: they had more shared experiences and acquaintances, interacted daily as opposed to weekly, met for social rather than instrumental purposes, and convened in the same room as "others" (blacks, women, and youth), enforcing a group solidarity of "us" versus "them." Conversation was the unit of analysis to determine how groups developed a collective perspective based on group identification, and how groups made sense of politics using their shared perspective. Walsh found that the frames did matter, but through conversations people transformed and circumvented these frames by applying their identity-based perspectives to supplement news stories. Socially rooted perspectives were often more important than partisanship. She said that her approach showed the limits of both liberal individualism and civic republicanism. People relied on social attachments and did not act on behalf of a predetermined public good. Ideas about the common good were worked out in interaction. Public discussion was consequential for citizen action insofar as it fostered trust, clarified social identities, and reinforced exclusion of nonmembers. Walsh concluded that more interaction by itself was not the answer to a decline in civic life. Since there were tradeoffs between community and exclusion, she advocated community-wide intergroup dialogue programs.[34]

The Art of Conversation and the Civic Virtues of Thoughtfulness and Generosity

Some empiricists implicitly recognize the importance of household and table activities for civil society. Theda Skocpol recommends revitalizing American civic democracy "by mixing politics and civic activity with family life and socializing."[35] Robert Putnam has noted with concern that Americans are spending much less time breaking bread with family and friends than they did some twenty or thirty years ago. He observes that with fast-food outlets replacing conventional eating places, there are fewer conversational opportunities, but adds that this trend has to some extent been offset by the proliferation of coffee bars.[36]

Theorists have continued to grapple with the chicken-egg relationship between norms of reciprocity and trust, on the one side, and civil society, on the other. Some wonder whether voluntary associations are really so important for civil society since they account for only a few hours a week or month for a small minority of citizens. Perhaps family, school, and work have stronger effects on civil society because people spend so much more time in those settings.[37]

Wherever one draws the definitional line for civil society, table activities can be beneficial for it. They can help to form both bonding and bridging social capital. Family tables typically bring together intimates, kin, and friends. But other tables are bridges to the unfamiliar, to the strangers for whom a minimal comfort level is required for society to be civil: tables in school and workplace cafeterias, in coffeehouses, and at religious celebrations, weddings, holiday parties, picnics in the park, summer camps, and senior centers. Table activities foster the art of conversation. When people gather together for food and drink, it is customary to talk in such a way that a reservoir of goodwill is replenished, to be drawn down in times of tension and conflict. A case in point was the dry reservoir in the U.S. House of Representatives after the 1994 Republican Revolution.

Congressional correspondent Juliet Eilperin attributes a decline in civility to Speaker Newt Gingrich's strategy of encouraging newly elected representatives not to move their families to Washington. Members returned to their home districts on weekends rather than continuing past practices of dining with members of the other political party after hours. This contributed to partisan gridlock: it had been easier for representatives to compromise when they had reservoirs of goodwill replenished at dinner parties.[38]

Thoughtfulness and generosity—toward intimates, strangers, and adversaries—are two virtues given high priority during table activities. It is good to think about the food and beverage preferences of the group, about fair shares, about the common good. Selfish and rude behavior is frowned upon and makes for unpleasantness and indigestion. Conflict cannot be avoided at the table, anymore than it can be avoided in partisan politics. Critics of civility mischaracterize it as the avoidance of conflict. To the contrary, civility is necessary precisely *because* there is conflict—an expected difference between one's wants, needs, desires, impulses, views, and those of others. Civility is not needed when one is by oneself.

As classicist Margaret Visser reminds us, the words *civilized* and *civil* come from the Latin *civis,* which means a dweller in cities. Civil people are found where many people live, in an urban environment, where they become urbane. Unlike homogeneous villagers, in order to prosper city-dwellers need to learn how to deal with people from varied backgrounds: merchants, traders, travelers, borrowers and lenders, employers and employees. Civil behavior is polite: a ritual performed to please and reassure other people, especially where a rough or conflictual time is possible. Roughness needs to be smoothed by rubbing up against one another, becoming polished, to become better able to handle other people. *Polished* derives from the French *poli.* Both *politeness* and *politics* come from the Greek word for a city *(polis).* We are not naturally polite—we teach and learn the rules that grease the wheels of civilizations. Of course, if these rules become overbearing, they can stifle genuine interaction between people. "Politeness forces us to pause, to take extra time, to behave in preset, pre-structured ways, to 'fall in with society's expectations. It is therefore the object of education . . . But nothing about being polite is simple: the 'polish' intended to help people interact with one another can be used to prevent real contact from occurring at all. It can also become itself a barrier, keeping the 'unpolished' beyond the pale."[39]

The dynamics of civilized behavior in cities are the same as those at the table: polishing roughness, performing reassuring rituals, teaching and learning rules of proper behavior, and pausing to take the time to behave in preset ways. When they are not overbearing, civil rules and table manners create conditions for conversation, the respectful, mutual sharing of thoughts for a whole host of reasons: political, economic, social, cultural, religious, familial, and interpersonal. Learning the art of conversation at the table is good practice for the interchange of ideas in other realms.

It is one thing to be trusting and forthcoming at a table with family and friends, but how transferable is this practice to other realms? How can meaningful conversations possibly be expected to occur among strangers or self-interested political adversaries? Politics, after all, is the terrain of intrigue, deception, smooth talking, lies, self-interest, and expedient deals, to say nothing of fights to the death. In talking about politics, isn't a focus on conversation naive and overly reliant on reason to temper strong feelings? And wouldn't a conversation be distorted by whoever had the most dazzling verbal skills, leaving the less verbally aggressive party out in the cold?

The centrality of civil and persuasive speech to politics was noted centuries ago, most famously in Aristotle's *Rhetoric.* Aristotle argued that the politics of persuasion required a certain amount of dissimulation on the part of all speakers. The more one tread farther afield of trusted family and friends, the more one expected less than full candor in conversations. Persuasive and civil speech was also important in the American colonies. At the time of the Revolution, the voting qualifications in the colony of Connecticut included—in addition to being male, aged twenty-one, and a property owner—the ability to be civil in conversation.[40]

Conversations require courtesy, a respect and willingness to consider things from another conversants position. Table manners are one form of courtesy; they are the conventions that make conversation possible. Courtesy predates liberal democracy's emphasis on freedom and equality. Courtesy, like persuasive speech, involves some holding back of what one really wants to do and say, for a larger common purpose: an enjoyable meal or a good law. Being less than forthcoming is justified for larger purposes. Thinking of a circumspect, if not entirely candid, answer to a host's question about the quality of a dish served at a dinner party is the same skill as crafting a respectful, if opposing, response to a legislative colleague.

In both cases, reason is not relied on in place of, or in opposition to, strong feelings or self-interest; rather, reason is used to deliberate about alternative courses of action, in settings with emotional import (hosts wanting to please guests) and strongly held views (political opponents having major differences of opinion). Civil relations create reservoirs of goodwill that can help people get through rough patches. Democratic human associations cannot last long without such reservoirs, given the inevitability of conflict, cruelty, and cycles of hard times.

Conversations do run the risk of leaving less verbally skilled conversants stranded. However, true conversations are democratic insofar as conversants are tuned into differences in extroversion, sophistication of vocabularies, self-confidence, and the like, and make adjustments accordingly. What better place to take such differences into account than the temporary democracy of the table, where people have the motivation and the time to hone these skills and develop this art.

Meals, Conversations, and Women

The civilizing relationships of the table have been out of the purview of most political studies because women have been in charge of them. They are presumably what women naturally do—take care of others and feed them. They are outside the bounds of the so-called real politics of waging war, nation-building, governmental decision making, interest-group lobbying, and voting. They are private, not public—peripheral to politics. The argument here is that they are constitutive of politics.

To talk about women and the politics of food in this way sounds both old and new. The traditional view of women's "proper place" puts them in the kitchen, pleasing others, and taking orders from a breadwinning husband. In this scenario, generosity and thoughtfulness mean that women should give to others and downplay their own needs. If we want more civility, women should stay home and cook and raise children. Men will do battle in the cruel, competitive world of the marketplace and seek comfort in the civilized home front. My argument is not a "proper place" argument. It is a call to redefine generosity and thoughtfulness based on democracy in the household. My argument sounds new relative to a feminist claim that women should get out of the kitchen and into the workforce. Of course, this claim has been primarily espoused by white, middle- and professional-class women who do not necessarily question the corporate fast-food and convenience-food industries and who can afford to pay others to prepare their food. Most employed women face the double duty of work for pay, and responsibility for food preparation. Generosity and thoughtfulness have to be recast in terms of equitable contemporary household responsibilities.

Significant social and political costs have resulted from fast food and convenience foods, grazing and snacking instead of sitting down for leisurely meals, watching television during mealtimes instead of conversing, viewing food as fuel rather than sustenance, discarding family recipes and foodways, and denying that eating has social and political dimensions. We must be honest about these costs and devise alternatives that neither confine women to the kitchen nor pretend that the quality of our lives is improved when no one is in it.

At first glance, it may seem odd that a scholar of the U.S. women's movement is issuing a call about the importance of meals and food, since many second-wave feminists urged women to get out of the kitchen and into the workplace. Financial independence was the ticket to liberation. There were only so many hours in the day, and the less time spent on food the better. Meals were something to get out of the way, to fuel the body for the workforce, to be purchased and consumed—the faster the better. American women are having second thoughts. And whenever women question their lives, feminist scholars take note. Feminist rumblings always begin with the politics of everyday life. Feminists take women's experiences seriously and see the political ramifications of personal relationships. There are four reasons why women's experiences are at the center of concerns about food, meals, conversation, civility, community, and democracy.

First, many women feel ground between the gears of workplace and family demands on their time. Compared to their husbands, working wives put in more hours a week around the house, get less sleep, and feel run down. Even with convenience foods and reasonably priced restaurants, women need help. Most women work one shift at the workplace and a second shift in their households. Studies show that women do most of the foodwork, the often-invisible tasks of accommodating other peoples food and dietary preferences, securing provisions, looking for bargains, monitoring table behavior, and juggling schedules. Since the 1970s, with their increased labor force participation, women have had less time to devote to meal preparation, the rituals of eating, festive foods, table conversation, and food sharing.

Second, women are still expected to promote the art of conversation at the table. They are the creators and keepers of mealtime rules, stories, and conventions. They encourage direct, interpersonal interactions as an important corrective to the "screen culture" of visual and auditory stimuli on television and computer screens.

Third, food is still psychodynamically and philosophically associated with women. Hunger is terrifying, and the first food is mothers milk. We cannot get everyone to do foodwork as long as it is "what women do." Household food memories are associated with women. Philosophically, we cannot advance our thinking about the centrality of food to civility until we challenge the mind-body dualism that still permeates conventional wisdom about women and food. Eating by its very nature is a simultaneous mind-body experience. We had better know about food's origins and plan carefully in its preparation, or it can kill us. Hunger is a frightening experience, so we had better do our best to plan to sate it. Food is apprehended through the senses of touch, smell, and taste, which rank lower on the hierarchy of senses than sight and hearing, which are typically thought to give rise to knowledge. In much of philosophy, religion, and literature, food is associated with body, animal, female, and appetite—things civilized men have sought to overcome with reason and knowledge.

Fourth, community and ethnic food traditions remain women's responsibility. Immigrant women's foodways forge group identity in the ongoing process of "becoming American." Food is a source of group pride, and "food travel" to a new cuisine is a way to break down barriers of race, ethnicity, and class. Americans connect with others through food at community rituals, ceremonies, and festivities. And women have been instrumental in promoting community gardens and school gardens.

One goal of this book is to draw attention to the social and political costs of the erosion of the civilizing aspects of food and meal rituals, since women have less time and energy to attend to them. A second aim is to make the case that foodwork needs to be redefined as everyone's responsibility. To this end, three major barriers need to be overcome: finding the time for food rituals in America's fast-paced, consumer, workaholic culture; competing with the screen culture; and resuscitating the dying art of conversation.

What Changes Are Needed?

With workplace and family scheduling demands, it is a challenge to arrange for common mealtimes with family and friends. Between the mid-1970s and the late 1990s, the proportion of married Americans who said that their family usually ate dinner together dropped by one-third: from about 50 to 34 percent. There was a percent decline in social visiting: both going out to see friends and having them over to one's home. The number of picnics per capita plummeted nearly 60 percent.[41]

It is very difficult to take time for food in America's fast-paced culture, where people are tethered to cell phones and e-mail 24/7. Food is a commodity and fuel—not a source of pleasure and community. However, there is growing interest in the Slow Food movement, and in the wake of the September 11 attacks, many Americans vowed to spend more time with family and loved ones and to be less obsessed with work. Americans are rethinking the meanings of work, time, and caretaking in household foodwork.

Since the 1970s, Americas rigid workplace norms have become more flexible to accommodate pregnancies, parental responsibilities, disabilities, elder- care, and the like; they can also bend for foodwork and food enjoyment. It is possible to be a prosperous, advanced industrial economy and still make time for meals and leisure. Europeans have the shortest workweeks and the longest holidays in the world. They value leisure, and less income, over working longer hours to acquire more material goods.[42] Until Americans' workplaces become more accommodating, they will have to reexamine how they spend their leisure hours in order to open up time for meals and conversations.

There is also growing popular fascination with the social and political importance of food. People buy more cookbooks than they can possibly use, whether for the assurance of comfort food, the nostalgia of home-cooked meals, or the adventure of learning about other cultures through their cuisines. Corporations sponsor cooking classes for their employees as team- building exercises. In many metropolitan newspapers, food sections have eclipsed society pages. The Slow Food movement is gathering momentum. Farmers markets, along with community, school, and jail gardens, are springing up all across the country. Meanwhile, farmers have dwindled to less than 2 percent of the American workforce. More is involved than nostalgia for a lost way of life or the idealization of childhood meals. Many Americans are beginning to realize that food choices have environmental, political, economic, social, and cultural consequences. But today there is little time for the joys and pleasures of the table: sparkling conversation, spontaneous sharing, sensual enjoyment, and hilarious banter. Conversation is becoming a dying art as the screen culture wins out over face-to-face encounters.

It is hard to pull oneself away from the privatizing and narcotizing screens of the television and the computer. Television is popular with stressed workers, who understandably want to relax after a hard day. It is a low-concentration activity. But it has its costs. As Robert Putnam observes, television competes for scarce time, has psychological effects that inhibit social participation, and contains programmatic content that undermines civic motivations. Average daily household viewing rose from about four and one-half hours a day in 1950 to over seven hours in 1998. Television is the only leisure activity that seems to inhibit participation in other leisure activities. Putnam writes that TV watching comes at the expense of "nearly every social activity outside the home, especially social gatherings and informal conversations." Studies show that it is habit-forming, mildly addictive, encourages lethargy and passivity, and leads to reduced contacts with relatives, friends, and neighbors. The more time viewers spend watching soap operas, game shows, and talk shows, the less active they are in the community.[43]

Computer-mediated communication has its advantages. Research cited by Putnam shows that online discussions tend to be more frank and egalitarian than face-to-face meetings. In the workplace, "computer-mediated communication is less hierarchical, more participatory, more candid, and less biased by status differences. Women, for example, are less likely to be interrupted in cyberspace discussions." Participants in computer-based groups often come up with a wider range of alternatives and a quicker intellectual understanding of their shared problems. On the down side, they find it harder to reach a consensus and generate the trust and reciprocity necessary to implement that understanding. Putnam notes that "experiments that compare face-to-face and computer-mediated communication confirm that the richer the medium of communication, the more sociable, personal, trusting, and friendly the encounter." Face-to-face conversations allow for deeper relationships than cyberspaces anonymity and fluidity. If the interpersonal going gets rough, it is easy to exit from cyberspace.[44]

American women are fighting an uphill battle against the screen culture to revitalize the dying art of conversation. Where better to hone conversational skills than in food preparation and sharing, where there is much to talk about that is pleasurable and has civic import. At the table, we connect with others—family, our cultural forebears, peers—in the making and sharing of food traditions and innovations. Meal preparation involves daily economic choices, whether to support fast-food chains, supermarkets, farmers' markets, organic producers, or new cuisines. And it involves social choices about who is responsible for foodwork, how to act at the table, and when to prepare festive and ceremonial foods. Food is a universal way to feel connected and civilized. It needs to become everyone's responsibility.

One way to degender foodwork would be to get everyone out of household kitchens and reliant on fast-food restaurants, convenience food, home-delivered food, or communal cafeterias. Even though some feminist Utopian writers imagined communities designed with communal eating facilities, for various reasons, this type of architecture has not taken hold in the United States, although it remains a logical possibility. Commercially produced food and home-delivered food are not realistic options for low-income households. Since most fast food is high fat and high salt, it is unethical to propose that low-income people (or anyone) live on such a diet. It is possible that middle- and upper-income households could learn the art of conversation and norms of civility over a table graced with commercially prepared and/or delivered food. Indeed, it could be argued that *more* time would be available to savor the meal leisurely without frantic meal preparation. What would be lost, of course, are the practical applications of thoughtfulness and generosity that accompany meal planning and preparation. And a class-based solution is not a satisfactory solution.

It would be preferable for everyone—men, women, and children—to go back to the kitchen, as in preindustrial days, and for the workplace to lessen its time demands on people. Many other countries have shorter workweeks and more vacation time than is the case in the United States. Over the last one hundred years, the U.S. labor movement has successfully fought to reduce the workday from twelve to ten to eight hours. In more recent years, employers have adopted flexible work schedules. As more women move into supervisory positions, they should continue with this reduction in work hours to enable all workers to spend more time preparing and sharing food.

There must also be a cultural shift in attitudes. Men and women would need to agree that women, too, deserve a nice meal at the end of a workday, and that it is a household responsibility to prepare it. Americans experienced such a seismic cultural shift once before: in the nineteenth century when men left the farms and went to work in the cities, and meal preparation became an exclusively female activity. Everyone would have to be convinced of the benefits of undergoing another change. Harried working women would probably lead this effort. They would most likely see the benefits of a rewarding family life and work life, if the demands of both could be kept to a level that was not superhuman. Children would no doubt prefer to see mothers who were less exhausted and haggard. Husbands would probably want to reduce the pressure on their wives. And the enjoyment of the pleasures of the table could also play a huge role in changing attitudes. To the extent that enjoyment at the table became more valued than additional consumer goods, people would be less motivated to work extra hours. Less income would be needed as people preferred time for food over one more "must have" gadget.

For democracy and civility to thrive, people need frequent, everyday occasions to share pleasures, fears, and opinions with others. The household table provides such a place. Children can learn about thoughtfulness and generosity, hear life stories from generations other than their own, and see how conflict can be managed without coming to blows. At the table, they can learn about their identity and what is expected of informed citizens. By becoming participants in meal preparation, they can learn that people have a responsibility to take the needs of others into account, without becoming martyrs to the needs of others. By pitching in to feed others, they can learn the importance of daily doses of gratitude for healthy social relations, and they can play an active role in creating a greater good, which is the goal of civil society and democratic politics.

The table activities that have been at the center of women's lives in the historical division of labor should now be at the center of all our lives to promote civility and democracy. In a time of widespread alienation from politics, Americans must look carefully for those places where we routinely come together for something important and pleasurable, where we put aside certain differences in order to share something in common with others, and where we afford one another the courtesy of a conversation—in short, where we practice being civil to one another. There is a connection between being cut off from food, meals, conversation, and the table, and being politically alienated, voiceless, and uncivil. Sharing a meal at a table is a temporary, yet frequent, locus of civilizing and democratic practice—people of various backgrounds and opinions agree to speak civilly to one another in order to enjoy the food. Heated arguments can wait, since the attack mode causes indigestion. People take turns, listen, and respond politely. The pleasures of the table include convivial talk about subjects worth discussing. The time has come to take a hard look at the social and political costs of America's fast-paced, convenience Culture. It is important to encourage face-to-face conversations at the table, to understand why meal providers feel so pressed for time, and to examine realistic alternatives, especially in households with single parents or two breadwinners.

The following chapters elaborate on the arguments I have introduced here. To make the case for the importance of the civilizing aspects of food, meals, rituals, and sociability—integral building blocks of civil society—we will take a closer look at household foodwork, table conversations, Western philosophy, the delicious revolution of Alice Waters, and community food.

Notes

1. In addition to the works cited later in this discussion, see, for example, Chambers and Kymlicka, *Alternative Conceptions of Civil Society;* Dionne, *Community Works;* Eberly, *Essential Civil Society Reader;* Edwards, Foley, and Diani, *Beyond Tocqueville;* Ehrenberg, *Civil Society;* Fullinwider, *Civil Society;* Novak, *To Empower People;* O'Connell, *Civil Society;* and Post and Rosenblum, *Civil Society and Government.*
2. Edwards, *Civil Society,* 11, 61.
3. Walzer, "Idea of Civil Society," 124,142.
4. Carter, *Civility,* 58, 292, 62.
5. Cahoone, "Civic Meetings, Cultural Meanings," 42.
6. Ibid.; and Schmidt, "Is Civility a Virtue?" 23, 27, 29.
7. Seligman, *Idea of Civil Society.*
8. Schmidt, "Is Civility a Virtue?" 29-30.
9. Dewey, *Public and Its Problems,* 211, 218-19.
10. Boisvert, "Clock Time/Stomach Time."
11. Habermas, *Structural Transformation;* and Chambers, "Critical Theory of Civil Society."
12. Edwards, *Civil Society,* 38-39.
13. Edwards and Foley, "Civil Society and Social Capital."
14. Bourdieu, "Forms of Capital"; Coleman, "Social Capital in the Creation of Human Capital"; and Robert Putnam, *Bowling Alone.*
15. Bobbio, "Gramsci."
16. Edwards, *Civil Society,* 49; and Carter, *Civility.*
17. Dean, "Including Women," 379.
18. Pateman, *Sexual Contract,* 102.
19. Pateman, "Feminist Critiques," 132.
20. Phillips, "Does Feminism Need a Conception?"
21. Elshtain, "Democracy on Trial," 103.
22. Wolfe, *Whose Keeper?* 20.

23. For examples of the social-capital interpretation, see Baron, Field, and Schuller, *Social Capital*·, Caiazza and Putnam, *Women's Status and Social Capital;* Fine, *Social Capital versus Social Theory;* O'Neill and Gidengil, *Gender and Social Capital;* and Putnam, *Bowling Alone.* For examples of the civic-engagement understanding, see Burns, Schlozman, and Verba, *Private Roots of Public Action;* Macedo et al., *Democracy at Risk;* Milner, *Civic Literacy;* Sirianni and Friedland, *Civic Innovation in America;* Skocpol and Fiorina, *Civic Engagement in American Democracy;* and Verba, Schlozman, and Brady, *Voice and Equality.*
24. Schudson, *Good Citizen.*
25. Ellis, *Coffee-House.*
26. For European manners, see Aresty, *Best Behavior.* For manners in the United States, see Kasson, *Rudeness and Civility.*
27. Kathlene, "Power and Influence."
28. Kathlene, "Alternative Views of Crime."
29. Tannen, *Conversational Style.*
30. Blum-Kulka, *Dinner Talk.*
31. DeVault, *Feeding the Family;* and Fishman, "Interaction."
32. Gamson, *Talking Politics.*
33. Eliasoph, *Avoiding Politics.*
34. Walsh, *Talking about Politics.*
35. Skocpol, "Advocates without Members."
36. Putnam, *Bowling Alone,* 102.
37. Edwards, *Civil Society;* and Newton, "Social Capital and Democracy."
38. Eilperin, *Fight Club Politics.*
39. Visser, *Rituals of Dinner,* 39–40.
40. Dinkin, *Voting in Provincial America.*
41. Putnam, *Bowling Alone,* 98–101.
42. Bennhold, "Love of Leisure."
43. Putnam, *Bowling Alone,* 222, 234–43.
44. Ibid., 173–77·

Points of Engagement—Reading Comprehension

1. In the section titled, "Meals, Conversations and Women" Flammang states: "My argument is not a 'proper place' argument" (123). Look at this quotation in context. What is the "proper place" argument? Be specific. What is Flammang's argument instead? To understand her position, focus on this section, especially on the "four reasons" she offers for women's centrality in discussions about meals, food, and work. What are these four reasons? How do they relate specifically to Flammang's goals for her book?
2. Flammang's Introduction contains a standard "literary review" (or "lit review") that outlines previous research done on the issues she cares about, including civility, politics, politeness, civil society, democracy, conversation, and social bonding, amongst others. She focuses on these in two main sections: "Political Theory…" and

"Empirical Studies..." In small groups, break down these sections in which Flammang references other authors/texts, each small group taking a number of paragraphs within the section. First, make a list of the various theorists Flammang cites in your paragraphs and summarize each of their arguments/ideas. Second, decide which of your theorists are most helpful to Flammang's main point in the paragraphs of your section and why. Prepare a group presentation for the class.

3. Why does Flammang write that "civility is not needed when one is by oneself" (121)? Why does she think that paying more attention to "table activities" will improve civility, and by extension, democracy?

Points of Departure—Assignment Questions

1. Though "food" is the centerpiece of her argument, Flammang is ultimately concerned about the role of women in sustaining and promoting civil society: "The table activities that have been at the center of women's lives in the historical division of labor should now be at the center of all our lives to promote civility and democracy" (128). More broadly, her goal is to change American culture by shifting the role of women, and women's work, within it. For this paper, focus on the roles and status of women in cultural change using essays by Flammang, and either Hochschild or Kristof and WuDunn. What roles have women traditionally taken in these essays? What changes do the authors want for the status and roles of women? What broader cultural changes do they anticipate as a result? Do they have concerns about the shift? Is there cause for optimism?
2. Consider the connection Janet Flammang asserts between civility, democracy, and difference: "Civility in a democracy is not the superficial glossing over of differences. Indeed, it is a virtue that is called into play precisely when there are differences especially among strangers" (113). Now consider Diana Eck's essay on "A New Religious America." How might Flammang's ideas help us to understand the flourishing religious diversity in the U.S., and the challenges to religious pluralism, described by Diana Eck? How do the "rituals" of religious practice or food preparation and consumption, as described by these two authors, help to bring people together in civil society? What are the greatest challenges? Write a paper in which you examine the connections between civility and the rituals that help to sustain American democracy. Use their terms to help you define your position and argument.
3. *Technology, Time, and the Table*: Janet Flammang identifies a sense of loss in social bonding as a result of the decline of "table activities" as she calls them. In particular,

she expresses concern about the challenge of "screen culture" to the "dying art of conversation" (125). Sherry Turkle, Adam Gopnik, and Arlie Russell Hochschild also express concern about a decline in the quality or authenticity of social interactions and family bonding in "America's fast-paced, consumer, workaholic culture" (112). Based on what these authors describe, are you convinced there is a decline in the quality of social interaction? If so, do you think the solutions provided by the authors will help? How? Consider also your own experiences. Do these challenge or confirm the arguments made by Turkle, Hochschild, and Flammang about the relationships between technology, time, and the table?

Small Change: Why the Revolution Will Not Be Tweeted

Malcolm Gladwell

Points of Access—Pre-Reading

1. What is activism? What does it involve? Why do it? Are you an activist? For what cause/s? Why?
2. How many texts do you send and/or receive in a given day? Do you use Twitter? Have a Facebook page? How important to you are these tools for staying connected with people? Are they purely social for you or do they serve other purposes? If so, what are they?
3. Do you feel more connected to people you see in person or those you know mostly online? Does the quality of your relationship shift depending on how you are communicating?

At four-thirty in the afternoon on Monday, February 1, 1960, four college students sat down at the lunch counter at the Woolworth's in downtown Greensboro, North Carolina. They were freshmen at North Carolina A. & T., a black college a mile or so away.

"I'd like a cup of coffee, please," one of the four, Ezell Blair, said to the waitress.

"We don't serve Negroes here," she replied.

The Woolworth's lunch counter was a long L-shaped bar that could seat sixty-six people, with a standup snack bar at one end. The seats were for whites. The snack bar was for blacks. Another employee, a black woman who worked at the steam table, approached the students and tried to warn them away. "You're acting stupid, ignorant!" she said. They didn't move. Around five-thirty, the front doors to the store were locked. The four still didn't move. Finally, they left by a side door. Outside, a small crowd had gathered, including a photographer from the Greensboro *Record*. "I'll be back tomorrow with A. & T. College," one of the students said.

By next morning, the protest had grown to twenty-seven men and four women, most from the same dormitory as the original four. The men were dressed in suits and ties. The students had brought their schoolwork, and studied as they sat at the counter.

On Wednesday, students from Greensboro's "Negro" secondary school, Dudley High, joined in, and the number of protesters swelled to eighty. By Thursday, the protesters numbered three hundred, including three white women, from the Greensboro campus of the University of North Carolina. By Saturday, the sit-in had reached six hundred. People spilled out onto the street. White teenagers waved Confederate flags. Someone threw a firecracker. At noon, the A. & T. football team arrived. "Here comes the wrecking crew," one of the white students shouted.

By the following Monday, sit-ins had spread to Winston-Salem, twenty-five miles away, and Durham, fifty miles away. The day after that, students at Fayetteville State Teachers College and at Johnson C. Smith College, in Charlotte, joined in, followed on Wednesday by students at St. Augustine's College and Shaw University, in Raleigh. On Thursday and Friday, the protest crossed state lines, surfacing in Hampton and Portsmouth, Virginia, in Rock Hill, South Carolina, and in Chattanooga, Tennessee. By the end of the month, there were sit-ins throughout the South, as far west as Texas. "I asked every student I met what the first day of the sitdowns had been like on his campus," the political theorist Michael Walzer wrote in *Dissent*. "The answer was always the same: 'It was like a fever. Everyone wanted to go.' " Some seventy thousand students eventually took part. Thousands were arrested and untold thousands more radicalized. These events in the early sixties became a civil-rights war that engulfed the South for the rest of the decade—and it happened without e-mail, texting, Facebook, or Twitter.

The world, we are told, is in the midst of a revolution. The new tools of social media have reinvented social activism. With Facebook and Twitter and the like, the traditional relationship between political authority and popular will has been upended, making it easier for the powerless to collaborate, coordinate, and give voice to their concerns. When ten thousand protesters took to the streets in Moldova in the spring of 2009 to protest against their country's Communist government, the action was dubbed the Twitter Revolution, because of the means by which the demonstrators had been brought together. A few months after that, when student protests rocked Tehran, the State Department took the unusual step of asking Twitter to suspend scheduled maintenance of its Web site, because the Administration didn't want such a critical organizing tool out of service at the height of the demonstrations. "Without Twitter the people of Iran would not have felt empowered and confident to stand up for freedom and democracy," Mark Pfeifle, a former national- security adviser, later wrote, calling for Twitter to be nominated for the Nobel Peace Prize. Where activists were once defined by their causes, they are now defined by their tools. Facebook warriors go online to push for change. "You are the best hope for us all," James K. Glassman, a former senior State Department official, told a crowd of cyber activists at a recent conference sponsored by Facebook, A. T. & T., Howcast, MTV, and Google. Sites like Facebook, Glassman said, "give the U.S. a significant competitive advantage over terrorists. Some time ago, I said that Al Qaeda was 'eating our lunch on the Internet.' That is no longer the case. Al Qaeda is stuck in Web 1.0. The Internet is now about interactivity and conversation."

These are strong, and puzzling, claims. Why does it matter who is eating whose lunch on the Internet? Are people who log on to their Facebook page really the best hope for us all? As for Moldova's so-called Twitter Revolution, Evgeny Morozov, a scholar at Stanford who has been the most persistent of digital evangelism's critics, points out that Twitter had scant internal significance in Moldova, a country where very few Twitter accounts exist. Nor does it seem to have been a revolution, not least because the protests— as Anne Applebaum suggested in the Washington Post—may well have been a bit of stagecraft cooked up by the government. (In a country paranoid about Romanian revanchism, the protesters flew a Romanian flag over the Parliament building.) In the Iranian case, meanwhile, the people tweeting about the demonstrations were almost all in the West. "It is time to get Twitter's role in the events in Iran right," Golnaz Esfandiari wrote, this past summer, in *Foreign Policy.* "Simply put: There was no Twitter Revolution inside Iran." The cadre of prominent bloggers, like Andrew Sullivan, who championed the role of social media in Iran, Esfandiari continued, misunderstood the situation. "Western journalists who couldn't reach—or didn't bother reaching?—people on the ground in Iran simply scrolled through the English-language tweets post with tag #iranelection," she wrote. "Through it all, no one seemed to wonder why people trying to coordinate protests in Iran would be writing in any language other than Farsi."

Some of this grandiosity is to be expected. Innovators tend to be solipsists. They often want to cram every stray fact and experience into their new model. As the historian Robert Darnton has written, "The marvels of communication technology in the present have produced a false consciousness about the past—even a sense that communication has no history, or had nothing of importance to consider before the days of television and the Internet." But there is something else at work here, in the outsized enthusiasm for social media. Fifty years after one of the most extraordinary episodes of social upheaval in American history, we seem to have forgotten what activism is.

Greensboro in the early nineteen-sixties was the kind of place where racial insubordination was routinely met with violence. The four students who first sat down at the lunch counter were terrified. "I suppose if anyone had come up behind me and yelled 'Boo,' I think I would have fallen off my seat," one of them said later. On the first day, the store manager notified the police chief, who immediately sent two officers to the store. On the third day, a gang of white toughs showed up at the lunch counter and stood ostentatiously behind the protesters, ominously muttering epithets such as "burr-head nigger." A local Ku Klux Klan leader made an appearance. On Saturday, as tensions grew, someone called in a bomb threat, and the entire store had to be evacuated.

The dangers were even clearer in the Mississippi Freedom Summer Project of 1964, another of the sentinel campaigns of the civil-rights movement. The Student Nonviolent Coordinating Committee recruited hundreds of Northern, largely white unpaid volunteers to run Freedom Schools, register black voters, and raise civil-rights awareness in the Deep South. "No one should go *anywhere* alone, but certainly not in an automobile and certainly not at night," they were instructed. Within days of arriving in Mississippi, three volunteers—Michael Schwerner, James Chaney, and Andrew Goodman—were kidnapped and killed, and, during the rest of the summer, thirty-seven black churches were set on fire and dozens of safe houses were bombed; volunteers were beaten, shot at, arrested, and trailed by pickup trucks full of armed men. A quarter of those in the program dropped out. Activism that challenges the status quo—that attacks deeply rooted problems—is not for the faint of heart.

What makes people capable of this kind of activism? The Stanford sociologist Doug McAdam compared the Freedom Summer dropouts with the participants who stayed, and discovered that the key difference wasn't, as might be expected, ideological fervor. "*All* of the applicants—participants and withdrawals alike— emerge as highly committed, articulate supporters of the goals and values of the summer program," he concluded. What mattered more was an applicant's degree of personal connection to the civil-rights movement. All the volunteers were required to provide a list of personal contacts—the people they wanted kept apprised of their activities—and participants were far more likely than dropouts to have close friends who were also going to Mississippi. High-risk activism, McAdam concluded, is a "strong-tie" phenomenon.

This pattern shows up again and again. One study of the Red Brigades, the Italian terrorist group of the nineteen-seventies, found that seventy per cent of recruits had at least one good friend already in the organization. The same is true of the men who joined the mujahideen in Afghanistan. Even revolutionary actions that look spontaneous, like the demonstrations in East Germany that led to the fall of the Berlin Wall, are, at core, strong-tie phenomena. The opposition movement in East Germany consisted of several hundred groups, each with roughly a dozen members. Each group was in limited contact with the others: at the time, only thirteen per cent of East Germans even had a phone. All they knew was that on Monday nights, outside St. Nicholas Church in downtown Leipzig, people gathered to voice their anger at the state. And the primary determinant of who showed up was "critical friends"—the more friends you had who were critical of the regime the more likely you were to join the protest.

So one crucial fact about the four freshmen at the Greensboro lunch counter—David Richmond, Franklin McCain, Ezell Blair, and Joseph McNeil—was their relationship with one another. McNeil was a roommate of Blair's in A. & T.'s Scott Hall dormitory. Richmond roomed with McCain one floor up, and Blair, Richmond, and McCain had all gone to Dudley High School. The four would smuggle beer into the dorm and talk late into the night in Blair and McNeil's room. They would all have remembered the murder of Emmett Till in 1955, the Montgomery bus boycott that same year, and the showdown in Little Rock in 1957. It was McNeil who brought up the idea of a sit-in at Woolworth's. They'd discussed it for nearly a month. Then McNeil came into the dorm room and asked the others if they were ready. There was a pause, and McCain said, in a way that works only with people who talk late into the night with one another, "Are you guys chicken or not?" Ezell Blair worked up the courage the next day to ask for a cup of coffee because he was flanked by his roommate and two good friends from high school.

The kind of activism associated with social media isn't like this at all. The platforms of social media are built around weak ties. Twitter is a way of following (or being followed by) people you may never have met. Facebook is a tool for efficiently managing your acquaintances, for keeping up with the people you would not otherwise be able to stay in touch with. That's why you can have a thousand "friends" on Facebook, as you never could in real life.

This is in many ways a wonderful thing. There is strength in weak ties, as the sociologist Mark Granovetter has observed. Our acquaintances—not our friends—are our greatest source of new ideas and information. The Internet lets us exploit the power of these kinds of distant connections with marvellous efficiency. It's terrific at the diffusion of innovation, interdisciplinary collaboration, seamlessly matching up buyers and sellers, and the logistical functions of the dating world. But weak ties seldom lead to high-risk activism.

In a new book called "The Dragonfly Effect: Quick, Effective, and Powerful Ways to Use Social Media to Drive Social Change," the business consultant Andy Smith and the Stanford Business School professor Jennifer Aaker tell the story of Sameer Bhatia, a young Silicon Valley entrepreneur who came down with acute myelogenous leukemia. It's a perfect illustration of social media's strengths. Bhatia needed a bone- marrow transplant, but he could not find a match among his relatives and friends. The odds were best with a donor of his ethnicity, and there were few South Asians in the national bone-marrow database. So Bhatia's business partner sent out an e-mail explaining Bhatia's plight to more than four hundred of their acquaintances, who forwarded the e-mail to their personal contacts; Facebook pages and YouTube videos were devoted to the Help Sameer campaign. Eventually, nearly twenty-five thousand new people were registered in the bone-marrow database, and Bhatia found a match.

But how did the campaign get so many people to sign up? By not asking too much of them. That's the only way you can get someone you don't really know to do something on your behalf. You can get thousands of people to sign up for a donor registry, because doing so is pretty easy. You have to send in a cheek swab and—in the highly unlikely event that your bone marrow is a good match for someone in need—spend a few hours at the hospital. Donating bone marrow isn't a trivial matter. But it doesn't involve financial or personal risk; it doesn't mean spending a summer being chased by armed men in pickup trucks. It doesn't require that you confront socially entrenched norms and practices. In fact, it's the kind of commitment that will bring only social acknowledgment and praise.

The evangelists of social media don't understand this distinction; they seem to believe that a Facebook friend is the same as a real friend and that signing up for a donor registry in Silicon Valley today is activism in the same sense as sitting at a segregated lunch counter in Greensboro in 1960. "Social networks are particularly effective at increasing motivation," Aaker and Smith write. But that's not true. Social networks are effective at increasing *participation—by* lessening the level of motivation that participation requires. The Facebook page of the Save Darfur Coalition has 1,282,339 members, who have donated an average of nine cents apiece. The next biggest Darfur charity on Facebook has 22,073 members, who have donated an average of thirty-five cents. Help Save Darfur has 2,797 members, who have given, on average, fifteen cents. A spokesperson for the Save Darfur Coalition told *Newsweek,* "We wouldn't necessarily gauge someone's value to the advocacy movement based on what they've given. This is a powerful mechanism to engage this critical population. They inform their community, attend events, volunteer. It's not something you can measure by looking at a ledger." In other words, Facebook activism succeeds not by motivating people to make a real sacrifice but by motivating them to do the things that people do when they are not motivated enough to make a real sacrifice. We are a long way from the lunch counters of Greensboro.

The students who joined the sit-ins across the South during the winter of 1960 described the movement as a "fever." But the civil-rights movement was more like a military campaign than like a contagion. In the late nineteen-fifties, there had been sixteen sit-ins in various cities throughout the South, fifteen of which were formally organized by civil-rights organizations like the N.A.A.C.P. and CORE. Possible locations for activism were scouted. Plans were drawn up. Movement activists held training sessions and retreats for would-be protesters. The Greensboro Four were a product of this groundwork: all were members of the N.A.A.C.P. Youth Council. They had close ties with the head of the local N.A.A.C.P. chapter. They had been briefed on the earlier wave of sit-ins in Durham, and had been part of a series of movement meetings in activist churches. When the sit-in movement spread from Greensboro throughout the South, it did not spread indiscriminately. It spread to those cities which had preexisting "movement centers"—a core of dedicated and trained activists ready to turn the "fever" into action.

The civil-rights movement was high-risk activism. It was also, crucially, strategic activism: a challenge to the establishment mounted with precision and discipline. The N.A.A.C.P. was a centralized organization, run from New York according to highly formalized operating procedures. At the Southern Christian Leadership Conference, Martin Luther King, Jr., was the unquestioned authority. At the center of the movement was the black church, which had, as Aldon D. Morris points out in his superb 1984 study, "The Origins of the Civil Rights Movement," a carefully demarcated division of labor, with various standing committees and disciplined groups. "Each group was task-oriented and coordinated its activities through authority structures," Morris writes. "Individuals were held accountable for their assigned duties, and important conflicts were resolved by the minister, who usually exercised ultimate authority over the congregation."

This is the second crucial distinction between traditional activism and its online variant: social media are not about this kind of hierarchical organization. Facebook and the like are tools for building *networks,* which are the opposite, in structure and character, of hierarchies. Unlike hierarchies, with their rules and procedures, networks aren't controlled by a single central authority. Decisions are made through consensus, and the ties that bind people to the group are loose.

This structure makes networks enormously resilient and adaptable in low-risk situations. Wikipedia is a perfect example. It doesn't have an editor, sitting in New York, who directs and corrects each entry. The effort of putting together each entry is self-organized. If every entry in Wikipedia were to be erased tomorrow, the content would swiftly be restored, because that's what happens when a network of thousands spontaneously devote their time to a task.

There are many things, though, that networks don't do well. Car companies sensibly use a network to organize their hundreds of suppliers, but not to design their cars. No one believes that the articulation of a coherent design philosophy is best handled by a sprawling, leaderless organizational system. Because networks don't have a centralized leadership structure and clear lines of authority, they have real difficulty reaching consensus and setting goals. They can't think strategically; they are chronically prone to conflict and error. How do you make difficult choices about tactics or strategy or philosophical direction when everyone has an equal say?

The Palestine Liberation Organization originated as a network, and the international-relations scholars Mette Eilstrup-Sangiovanni and Calvert Jones argue in a recent essay in *International Security* that this is why it ran into such trouble as it grew: "Structural features typical of networks—the absence of central authority, the unchecked autonomy of rival groups, and the inability to arbitrate quarrels through formal mechanisms —made the P.L.O. excessively vulnerable to outside manipulation and internal strife."

In Germany in the nineteen-seventies, they go on, "the far more unified and successful left-wing terrorists tended to organize hierarchically, with professional management and clear divisions of labor. They were concentrated geographically in universities, where they could establish central leadership, trust, and camaraderie through regular, face-to-face meetings." They seldom betrayed their comrades in arms during police interrogations. Their counterparts on the right were organized as decentralized networks, and had no such discipline. These groups were regularly infiltrated, and members, once arrested, easily gave up their comrades. Similarly, Al Qaeda was most dangerous when it was a unified hierarchy. Now that it has dissipated into a network, it has proved far less effective.

The drawbacks of networks scarcely matter if the network isn't interested in systemic change—if it just wants to frighten or humiliate or make a splash—or if it doesn't need to think strategically. But if you're taking on a powerful and organized establishment you have to be a hierarchy. The Montgomery bus boycott required the participation of tens of thousands of people who depended on public transit to get to and from work each day. It lasted a *year*. In order to persuade those people to stay true to the cause, the boycott's organizers tasked each local black church with maintaining morale, and put together a free alternative private carpool service, with forty-eight dispatchers and forty-two pickup stations. Even the White Citizens Council, King later said, conceded that the carpool system moved with "military precision." By the time King came to Birmingham, for the climactic showdown with Police Commissioner Eugene (Bull) Connor, he had a budget of a million dollars, and a hundred full-time staff members on the ground, divided into operational units. The operation itself was divided into steadily escalating phases, mapped out in advance. Support was maintained through consecutive mass meetings rotating from church to church around the city.

Boycotts and sit-ins and nonviolent confrontations—which were the weapons of choice for the civil-rights movement—are high-risk strategies. They leave little room for conflict and error. The moment even one protester deviates from the script and responds to provocation, the moral legitimacy of the entire protest is compromised. Enthusiasts for social media would no doubt have us believe that King's task in Birmingham would have been made infinitely easier had he been able to communicate with his followers through Facebook, and contented himself with tweets from a Birmingham jail. But networks are messy: think of the ceaseless pattern of correction and revision, amendment and debate, that characterizes Wikipedia. If Martin Luther King, Jr., had tried to do a wiki-boycott in Montgomery, he would have been steamrollered by the white power structure. And of what use would a digital communication tool be in a town where ninety-eight per cent of the black community could be reached every Sunday morning at church? The things that King needed in Birmingham—discipline and strategy—were things that online social media cannot provide.

The bible of the social-media movement is Clay Shirky's "Here Comes Everybody." Shirky, who teaches at New York University, sets out to demonstrate the organizing power of the Internet, and he begins with the story of Evan, who worked on Wall Street, and his friend Ivanna, after she left her smart phone, an expensive Sidekick, on the back seat of a New York City taxicab. The telephone company transferred the data on Ivanna's lost phone to a new phone, whereupon she and Evan discovered that the Sidekick was now in the hands of a teenager from Queens, who was using it to take photographs of herself and her friends.

When Evan e-mailed the teenager, Sasha, asking for the phone back, she replied that his "white ass" didn't deserve to have it back. Miffed, he set up a Web page with her picture and a description of what had happened. He forwarded the link to his friends, and they forwarded it to their friends. Someone found the MySpace page of Sasha's boyfriend, and a link to it found its way onto the site. Someone found her address online and took a video of her home while driving by; Evan posted the video on the site. The story was picked up by the news filter Digg. Evan was now up to ten e-mails a minute. He created a bulletin board for his readers to share their stories, but it crashed under the weight of responses. Evan and Ivanna went to the police, but the police filed the report under "lost," rather than "stolen," which essentially closed the case. "By this point millions of readers were watching," Shirky writes, "and dozens of mainstream news outlets had covered the story." Bowing to the pressure, the N.Y.P.D. reclassified the item as "stolen." Sasha was arrested, and Evan got his friend's Sidekick back.

Shirky's argument is that this is the kind of thing that could never have happened in the pre-Internet age—and he's right. Evan could never have tracked down Sasha. The story of the Sidekick would never have been publicized. An army of people could never have been assembled to wage this fight. The police wouldn't have bowed to the pressure of a lone person who had misplaced something as trivial as a cell phone. The story, to Shirky, illustrates "the ease and speed with which a group can be mobilized for the right kind of cause" in the Internet age.

Shirky considers this model of activism an upgrade. But it is simply a form of organizing which favors the weak-tie connections that give us access to information over the strong-tie connections that help us persevere in the face of danger. It shifts our energies from organizations that promote strategic and disciplined activity and toward those which promote resilience and adaptability. It makes it easier for activists to express themselves, and harder for that expression to have any impact. The instruments of social media are well suited to making the existing social order more efficient. They are not a natural enemy of the status quo. If you are of the opinion that all the world needs is a little buffing around the edges, this should not trouble you. But if you think that there are still lunch counters out there that need integrating it ought to give you pause.

Shirky ends the story of the lost Sidekick by asking, portentously, "What happens next?"—no doubt imagining future waves of digital protesters. But he has already answered the question. What happens next is more of the same. A networked, weak-tie world is good at things like helping Wall Streeters get phones back from teen-age girls. *Viva la revolución.*

Points of Engagement—Reading Comprehension

1. Look at the following quotation in context: "Where activists were once defined by their causes, they are now defined by their tools" (134). What does it mean? Give two examples from the text.
2. What was the Mississippi Freedom Summer Project of 1964? Why is it important to Gladwell? What does it teach us about "what activism is"?
3. In comparing the ways people organize through social networks and in real life, Gladwell uses a number of opposites or "binaries": strong ties vs. weak ties, network vs. hierarchy, high risk activism vs. low risk activism. First define each term in the binaries. Which represents the qualities of social networking? Which represents traditional organizing? Make a grid or some other type of drawing that shows how each term connects to the other terms.
4. Who is Clay Shirky? According to Gladwell, what is Shirky's argument regarding social media and its organizing potential? Does Gladwell agree with Shirky's ideas? Disagree? How do you know? Point to specific sentences that inform your answer.

5. Why is Gladwell's essay entitled, "Small Change"? What is he referring to? Use an example to help you answer. What does the title signal about Gladwell's main argument in this essay?

Points of Departure—Assignment Questions

1. Like Gladwell, Ian Bremmer in "Democracy in Cyberspace" wants us to take a second look at the capacity for social media like Twitter and Facebook to organize like-minded people to achieve some purpose. In both cases each writer argues for a particular way of viewing social media. And in both cases each argues against other ways of viewing social media. Identify what the writers argue *against* first. After you have a sense of what each writer argues against, describe what each writer argues *for*. Identify points of similarity between what Bremmer and Gladwell argue for and against, and then try to find areas where there might be differences. For this paper you will want to describe the advantages and disadvantages of bringing people together through social media to accomplish a common purpose, using both Bremmer's and Gladwell's points for and against ways of viewing social media. Weigh and evaluate which points seem to be the most convincing to you, and explain in your paper why.
2. *The ties that bind.* In "Alone Together," Sherry Turkle asks us to think about "how we are changed as technology offers us substitutes for connecting with each other face-to-face" (274). She is concerned about what we may be losing in our transition to a society that interacts increasingly online through text messages, email, and other digital media. Other authors in this reader—Gladwell, Hochschild, Flammang, Bremmer—also describe the effects of advancing technology on the ties we have to one another. What kinds of ties do we lose as we move from traditional to virtual? What do we gain? What other "substitutes" do these authors suggest are getting in the way of our relationships with one another? Is technology really to blame for the weakening of family and other social ties? Or are we just redefining and revaluing how those ties bind us together? Using the terms and ideas offered by these authors, write a paper describing how the transition to a wired society is transforming our lives, and our ties to one another, for the better and for the worse.
3. If Gladwell seems somewhat pessimistic about the possibilities of using media technology for positive social change, James Fallows in "Win in China!" seems more optimistic. Fallows looks at how a reality television show in China tries to educate the Chinese in the values and behaviors necessary for free-market enterprise. What kinds of changes might media technologies promote? What kinds of change might they be

unable to? In what ways do older media like television, film, and radio resemble the social media like Twitter and Facebook that Gladwell discusses? In what ways are these media and the way they connect people different? Why might certain media be better suited to social change than others? Your project for this paper will be to examine the media, technology, and social change in both essays and to make an argument about how they are connected. Consider advantages and disadvantages of different types of media, and pay particular attention to the ways in which media and technology connect people as well as the ways in which they do not.

In the Forests of Gombe

Jane Goodall

Points of Access—Pre-Reading

1. How would you define the "natural world"? Do you think most people have a relationship to the natural world? Should they? Do you have such a relationship? Explain.
2. What does the word "sacred" mean to you? What in your life would you describe using that word or idea?
3. Have you ever struggled with the conflict between scientific ideas and religious belief? Discuss what prompted the conflict and how, or if, you tried to resolve it.

I was taught, as a scientist, to think logically and empirically, rather than intuitively or spiritually. When I was at Cambridge University in the early 1960s most of the scientists and science students working in the Department of Zoology, so far as I could tell, were agnostic or even atheist. Those who believed in a god kept it hidden from their peers.

Fortunately, by the time I got to Cambridge I was twenty-seven years old and my beliefs had already been molded so that I was not influenced by these opinions. I believed in the spiritual power that, as a Christian, I called God. But as I grew older and learned about different faiths I came to believe that there was, after all, but One God with different names: Allah, Tao, the Creator, and so on. God, for me, was the Great Spirit in Whom "we live and move and have our being." There have been times during my life when this belief wavered, when I questioned—even denied—the existence of God. At such times I felt there can be no underlying meaning to the emergence of life on earth.

Still, for me those periods have been relatively rare, triggered by a variety of circumstances. One was when my second husband died of cancer. I was grieving, suffering, and angry. Angry at God, at fate—the unjustness of it all. For a time I rejected God, and the world seemed a bleak place.

It was in the forests of Gombe that I sought healing after Derek's death. Gradually during my visits, my bruised and battered spirit found solace. In the forest, death is not hidden—or only accidentally, by the fallen leaves. It is all around you all the time, a part of the endless cycle of life. Chimpanzees are born, they grow older, they get sick, and they die. And always there are the young ones to carry on the life of the species. Time spent in the forest, following and watching and simply being with the chimpanzees, has always sustained the inner core of my being. And it did not fail me then.

One day, among all the days, I remember most of all. It was May 1981 and I had finally made it to Gombe after a six-week tour in America—six weeks of fund-raising dinners, conferences, meetings, and lobbying for various chimpanzee issues. I was exhausted and longed for the peace of the forest. I wanted nothing more than to be with the chimpanzees, renewing my acquaintance with my old friends, getting my climbing legs back again, relishing the sights, sounds, and smells of the forest. I was glad to be away from Dar es Salaam, with all its sad associations—the house that Derek and I had shared, the palm trees we had bought and planted together, the rooms we had lived in together, the Indian Ocean in which Derek, handicapped on land, had found freedom swimming among his beloved coral reefs.

Back in Gombe. It was early in the morning and I sat on the steps of my house by the lakeshore. It was very still. Suspended over the horizon, where the mountains of the Congo fringed Lake Tanganyika, was the last quarter of the waning moon and her path danced and sparkled toward me across the gently moving water. After enjoying a banana and a cup of coffee, I was off, climbing up the steep slopes behind my house.

In the faint light from the moon reflected by the dew-laden grass, it was not difficult to find my way up the mountain. It was quiet, utterly peaceful. Five minutes later I heard the rustling of leaves overhead. I looked up and saw the branches moving against the lightening sky. The chimps had awakened. It was Fifi and her offspring, Freud, Frodo, and little Fanni. I followed when they moved off up the slope, Fanni riding on her mother's back like a diminutive jockey. Presently they climbed into a tall fig tree and began to feed. I heard the occasional soft thuds as skins and seeds of figs fell to the ground.

For several hours we moved leisurely from one food tree to the next, gradually climbing higher and higher. On an open grassy ridge the chimps climbed into a massive mbula tree, where Fifi, replete from the morning's feasting, made a large comfortable nest high above me. She dozed through a midday siesta, little Fanni asleep in her arms, Frodo and Freud playing nearby. I felt very much in tune with the chimpanzees, for I was spending time with them not to observe, but simply because I needed their company, undemanding and free of pity. From where I sat I could look out over the Kasakela Valley. Just below me to the west was the peak. From that same vantage point I had learned so much in the early days, sitting and watching while, gradually, the chimpanzees had lost their fear of the strange white ape who had invaded their world. I recaptured some of my long-ago feelings—the excitement of discovering, of seeing things unknown to Western eyes, and the serenity that had come from living, day after day, as a part of the natural world. A world that dwarfs yet somehow enhances human emotions.

As I reflected on these things I had been only partly conscious of the approach of a storm. Suddenly, I realized that it was no longer growling in the distance but was right above. The sky was dark, almost black, and the rain clouds had obliterated the higher peaks. With the growing darkness came the stillness, the hush that so often precedes a tropical downpour. Only the rumbling of the thunder, moving closer and closer, broke this stillness; the thunder and the rustling movements of the chimpanzees. All at once came a blinding flash of lightning, followed, a split second later, by an incredibly loud clap of thunder that seemed almost to shake the solid rock before it rumbled on, bouncing from peak to peak. Then the dark and heavy clouds let loose such torrential rain that sky and earth seemed joined by moving water. I sat under a palm whose fronds, for a while, provided some shelter. Fifi sat hunched over, protecting her infant; Frodo pressed close against them in the nest; Freud sat with rounded back on a nearby branch. As the rain poured endlessly down, my palm fronds no longer provided shelter and I got wetter and wetter. I began to feel first chilly, and then, as a cold wind sprang up, freezing; soon, turned in on myself, I lost all track of time. I and the chimpanzees formed a unit of silent, patient, and uncomplaining endurance.

It must have been an hour or more before the rain began to ease as the heart of the storm swept away to the south. At four-thirty the chimps climbed down, and we moved off through the dripping vegetation, back down the mountainside. Presently we arrived on a grassy ridge overlooking the lake. I heard sounds of greeting as Fifi and her family joined Melissa and hers. They all climbed into a low tree to feed on fresh young leaves. I moved to a place where I could stand and watch as they enjoyed their last meal of the day. Down below, the lake was still dark and angry with white flecks where the waves broke, and rain clouds remained black in the south. To the north the sky was clear with only wisps of gray clouds still lingering. In the soft sunlight, the chimpanzees' black coats were shot with coppery brown, the branches on which they sat were wet and dark as ebony, the young leaves a pale but brilliant green. And behind was the backcloth of the indigo sky where lightning flickered and distant thunder growled and rumbled.

Lost in awe at the beauty around me, I must have slipped into a state of heightened awareness. It is hard—impossible, really—to put into words the moment of truth that suddenly came upon me then. It seemed to me, as I struggled afterward to recall the experience, that *self* was utterly absent: I and the chimpanzees, the earth and trees and air, seemed to merge, to become one with the spirit power of life itself. The air was filled with a feathered symphony, the evensong of birds. I heard new frequencies in their music and also in the singing insects' voices—notes so high and sweet I was amazed. Never had I been so intensely aware of the shape, the color of the individual leaves, the varied patterns of the veins that made each one unique. Scents were clear as well, easily identifiable: fermenting overripe fruit; waterlogged earth; cold, wet bark; the damp odor of chimpanzee hair and, yes, my own too. I sensed a new presence, then saw a bushbuck, quietly browsing upwind, his spiraled horns gleaming and chestnut coat dark with rain.

Suddenly a distant chorus of pant-hoots elicited a reply from Fifi. As though wakening from some vivid dream I was back in the everyday world, cold, yet intensely alive. When the chimpanzees left, I stayed in that place—it seemed a most sacred place—scribbling some notes, trying to describe what, so briefly, I had experienced.

Eventually I wandered back along the forest trail and scrambled down behind my house to the beach. Later, as I sat by my little fire, cooking my dinner of beans, tomatoes and an egg, I was still lost in the wonder of my experience. Yes, I thought, there are many windows through which we humans, searching for meaning, can look out into the world around us. There are those carved out by Western science, their panes polished by a succession of brilliant minds. Through them we can see ever farther, ever more clearly, into areas which until recently were beyond human knowledge. Through such a scientific window I had been taught to observe the chimpanzees. For more than twenty-five years I had sought, through careful recording and critical analysis, to piece together their complex social behavior, to understand the workings of their minds. And this had not only helped us to better understand their place in nature but also helped us to understand a little better some aspects of our own human behavior, our own place in the natural world.

Yet there are other windows through which we humans can look out into the world around us, windows through which the mystics and the holy men of the East, and the founders of the great world religions, have gazed as they searched for the meaning and purpose of our life on earth, not only in the wondrous beauty of the world, but also in its darkness and ugliness. And those Masters contemplated the truths that they saw, not with their minds only but with their hearts and souls also. From those revelations came the spiritual essence of the great scriptures, the holy books, and the most beautiful mystic poems and writings. That afternoon it had been as though an unseen hand had drawn back a curtain and, for the briefest moment, I had seen through such a window.

* * *

How sad that so many people seem to think that science and religion are mutually exclusive. Science has used modern technology and modern techniques to uncover so much about the formation and the development of life-forms on Planet Earth and about the solar system of which our little world is but a minute part. Alas, all of these amazing discoveries have led to a belief that every wonder of the natural world and of the universe—indeed, of infinity and time—can, in the end, be understood through the logic and the reasoning of a finite mind. And so, for many, science has taken the place of religion. It was not some intangible God who created the universe, they argue, it was the Big Bang. Physics, chemistry, and evolutionary biology can explain the start of the universe and the appearance and progress of life on earth, they say. To believe in God, in the human soul, and in life after death is simply a desperate and foolish attempt to give meaning to our lives.

But not all scientists believe thus. There are quantum physicists who have concluded that the concept of God is not, after all, merely wishful thinking. There are those exploring the human brain who feel that no matter how much they discover about this extraordinary structure it will never add up to a complete understanding of the human mind—that the whole is, after all, greater than the sum of its parts. The Big Bang theory is yet another example of the incredible, the awe-inspiring ability of the human mind to learn about seemingly unknowable phenomena in the beginning of time. Time as we know it, or think we know it. But what about before time? And what about beyond space? I remember so well how those questions had driven me to distraction when I was a child.

I lay flat on my back and looked up into the darkening sky. I thought about the young man I had met during the six-week tour I had finished before my return to Gombe. He had a holiday job working as a bellhop in the big hotel where I was staying in Dallas, Texas. It was prom night, and I wandered down to watch the young girls in their beautiful evening gowns, their escorts elegant in their tuxedos. As I stood there, thinking about the future—theirs, mine, the world's—I heard a diffident voice:

"Excuse me, Doctor—aren't you Jane Goodall?" The bellhop was very young, very fresh-faced. But he looked worried—partly because he felt that he should not be disturbing me, but partly, it transpired, because his mind was indeed troubled. He had a question to ask me. So we went and sat on some back stairs, away from the glittering groups and hand-holding couples.

He had watched all my documentaries, read my books. He was fascinated, and he thought that what I did was great. But I talked about evolution. Did I believe in God? If so, how did that square with evolution? Had we really descended from chimpanzees?

And so I tried to answer him as truthfully as I could, to explain my own beliefs. I told him that no one thought humans had descended from chimpanzees. I explained that I did believe in Darwinian evolution and told him of my time at Olduvai, when I had held the remains of extinct creatures in my hands. That I had traced, in the museum, the various stages of the evolution of, say, a horse: from a rabbit-sized creature that gradually, over thousands of years, changed, became better and better adapted to its environment and eventually was transformed into the modern horse. I told him I believed that millions of years ago there had been a primitive, apelike, humanlike creature, one branch of which had gone on to become the chimpanzee, another branch of which had eventually led to us.

"But that doesn't mean I don't believe in God," I said. And I told him something of my beliefs, and those of my family. I told him that I had always thought that the biblical description of God creating the world in seven days might well have been an attempt to explain evolution in a parable. In that case, each of the days would have been several million years.

"And then, perhaps, God saw that a living being had evolved that was suitable for His purpose. *Homo sapiens* had the brain, the mind, the potential. Perhaps," I said, "that was when God breathed the Spirit into the first Man and the first Woman and filled them with the Holy Ghost."

The bellhop was looking considerably less worried. "Yes, I see," he said. "That could be right. That does seem to make sense."

I ended by telling him that it honestly didn't matter how we humans got to be the way we are, whether evolution or special creation was responsible. What mattered and mattered desperately was our future development. How should the mind that can contemplate God relate to our fellow beings, the other life-forms of the world? What is our human responsibility? And what, ultimately, is our human destiny? Were we going to go on destroying God's creation, fighting each other, hurting the other creatures of His planet? Or were we going to find ways to live in greater harmony with each other and with the natural world? That, I told him, was what was important. Not only for the future of the human species, but also for him, personally. When we finally parted his eyes were clear and untroubled, and he was smiling.

* * *

Thinking about that brief encounter, I smiled too, there on the beach at Gombe. A wind sprang up and it grew chilly. I left the bright stars and went inside to bed. I knew that while I would always grieve Derek's passing, I could cope with my grieving. That afternoon, in a flash of "outsight" I had known timelessness and quiet ecstasy, sensed a truth of which mainstream science is merely a small fraction. And I knew that the revelation would be with me for the rest of my life, imperfectly remembered yet always within. A source of strength on which I could draw when life seemed harsh or cruel or desperate. The forest, and the spiritual power that was so real in it, had given me the "peace that passeth understanding."

Points of Engagement—Reading Comprehension

1. Why did Jane Goodall go to the forest? How would you describe her relationship with the chimpanzees? Refer to two passages from her essay in your answers.
2. How does Goodall describe her moment of truth on 147? What do you think she means when she says, "*self* was utterly absent"?
3. Why does Goodall tell us about her encounter with the bellhop? What questions do they discuss? What are Goodall's answers? Do you find them persuasive? Why or why not?

Points of Departure—Assignment Questions

1. Goodall writes, "There are many windows through which we humans, searching for meaning, can look out into the world around us?" (148). What are the different windows she is referring to? Consider another text which addresses ways of seeing the world, modes of perception, and metaphors for how we witness our own place in it, such as Wendell Berry, Susan Blackmore, Diana Eck, or Naomi Klein, and use it to reconsider this idea of different "windows." Which window/s are these authors using? What can you learn about Goodall's idea by examining the ways these authors view their work and the world?
2. Goodall tells the bellhop that she believes in both Darwinian evolution and God, two ideas that are often understood in opposition, or conflict, with each other. Consider first how Goodall reconciles these two disparate beliefs, then how another author, such as Lisa Belkin, Wendell Berry, or Lauren Slater, addresses conflicting ideals. How do these other authors present conflict differently from Goodall? What do you learn about the process of analyzing ideas that complicate one another?
3. Alone Together or Together Alone? Goodall asks how we are "going to find ways to live in greater harmony with each other and the natural world (150). How possible is this when we spend so much time in front of our computers, "connected" through means which are everything but natural? Consider Sherry Turkle's essay, "Alone Together," where people feel the need to be "connected" at all times, but for whom the quality of connection is dubious at best. What does "connectivity" even mean in

the modern world? Is it possible to have a sense of harmony without the magnitude of the nature such as Goodall had in Gombe? Explore the possibility of achieving Goodall's notion of harmony, of connectivity, using another text which addresses the complexity of human relationships with the world around us, such as Alain de Botton's "On Habit" or Sherry Turkle's "Alone Together."

Bumping into Mr. Ravioli

Adam Gopnik

Points of Access—Pre-Reading

1. When you hear the word "busy" what do you think of? Does it, for example, have a negative or positive connotation? Do you consider yourself a busy person? Is that mostly good or bad? Why?
2. Did you have an imaginary playmate when you were a young child? What was he or she like?
3. Describe the character of the place where you grew up. What is daily life like for people who live there?
4. How old were you when you got your first cellphone? How did it change your life?

My daughter, Olivia, who just turned three, has an imaginary friend whose name is Charlie Ravioli. Olivia is growing up in Manhattan, and so Charlie Ravioli has a lot of local traits: he lives in an apartment "on Madison and Lexington," he dines on grilled chicken, fruit, and water, and, having reached the age of seven and a half, he feels, or is thought, "old." But the most peculiarly local thing about Olivia's imaginary playmate is this: he is always too busy to play with her. She holds her toy cell phone up to her ear, and we hear her talk into it: "Ravioli? It's Olivia . . . It's Olivia. Come and play? OK. Call me. Bye." Then she snaps it shut and shakes her head. "I always get his machine," she says. Or she will say, "I spoke to Ravioli today." "Did you have fun?" my wife and I ask. "No. He was busy working. On a television," (leaving it up in the air if he repairs electronic devices or has his own talk show).

On a good day, she "bumps into" her invisible friend and they go to a coffee shop. "I bumped into Charlie Ravioli," she announces at dinner (after a day when, of course, she stayed home, played, had a nap, had lunch, paid a visit to the Central Park Zoo, and then had another nap). "We had coffee, but then he had to run." She sighs, sometimes, at her inability to make their schedules mesh, but she accepts it as inevitable, just the way life is. "I bumped into Charlie Ravioli today," she says. "He was working." Then she adds brightly, "But we hopped into a taxi." What happened then? we ask. "We grabbed lunch," she says.

It seemed obvious that Ravioli was a romantic figure of the big exotic life that went on outside her little limited life of parks and playgrounds—drawn, in particular, from a nearly perfect, mynah bird—like imitation of the words she hears her mother use when she talks about *her* day with *her* friends. ("How was your day?" Sighing: "Oh, you know. I tried to make a date with Meg, but I couldn't find her, so I left a message on her machine. Then I bumped into Emily after that meeting I had in SoHo, and we had coffee and then she had to run, but by then Meg had reached me on my cell and we arranged . . .") I was concerned, though, that Charlie Ravioli might also be the sign of some "trauma," some loneliness in Olivia's life reflected in imaginary form. "It seems odd to have an imaginary playmate who's always too busy to play with you," Martha, my wife, said to me. "Shouldn't your imaginary playmate be someone you tell secrets to and, I don't know, sing songs with? It shouldn't be someone who's always *hopping* into taxis."

We thought, at first, that her older brother, Luke, might be the original of Charlie Ravioli. (For one thing, he is also seven and a half, though we were fairly sure that this age was merely Olivia's marker for As Old as Man Can Be.) He is too busy to play with her much anymore. He has become a true New York child, with the schedule of a cabinet secretary: chess club on Monday, T-ball on Tuesday, tournament on Saturday, play dates and after-school conferences to fill in the gaps. But Olivia, though she counts days, does not yet really have days. She has *a* day, and into this day she has introduced the figure of Charlie Ravioli—in order, it dawned on us, to insist that she does have days, because she is too harried to share them, that she does have an independent social life, by virtue of being too busy to have one.

Yet Charlie Ravioli was becoming so constant and oddly discouraging a companion—"He canceled lunch. Again," Olivia would say—that we thought we ought to look into it. One of my sisters is a developmental psychologist who specializes in close scientific studies of what goes on inside the heads of one- and two- and three-year-olds. Though she grew up in the nervy East, she lives in California now, where she grows basil in her garden and jars her own organic marmalades. I e-mailed this sister for help with the Ravioli issue—how concerned should we be?—and she sent me back an email, along with an attachment, and, after several failed cell-phone connections, we at last spoke on a land line.

It turned out that there is a recent book on this very subject by the psychologist Marjorie Taylor, called *Imaginary Companions and the Children Who Create Them,* and my sister had just written a review of it. She insisted that Charlie Ravioli was nothing to be worried about. Olivia was right on target, in fact. Most under-sevens (sixty-three percent, to be scientific) have an invisible friend, and children create their imaginary playmates not out of trauma but out of a serene sense of the possibilities of fiction—sometimes as figures of pure fantasy, sometimes, as Olivia had done, as observations of grown-up manners, assembled in tranquillity and given a name. I learned about the invisible companions Taylor studied: Baintor, who is invisible because he lives in the light; Station Pheta, who hunts sea anemones on the beach. Charlie Ravioli seemed pavement-bound by comparison.

"An imaginary playmate isn't any kind of trauma marker," my sister said. "It's just the opposite: it's a sign that the child is now confident enough to begin to understand how to organize her experience into stories." The significant thing about imaginary friends, she went on, is that the kids know they're fictional. In an instant message on AOL, she summed it up: "The children with invisible friends often interrupted the interviewer to remind her, with a certain note of concern for her sanity, that these characters were, after all, just pretend."

I also learned that some children, as they get older, turn out to possess what child psychologists call a "paracosm." A paracosm is a society thought up by a child—an invented universe with a distinctive language, geography, and history. (The Brontes invented a couple of paracosms when they were children.) Not all children who have an imaginary friend invent a paracosm, but the two might, I think, be related. Like a lonely ambassador from Alpha Centauri in a fifties sci-fi movie who, misunderstood by paranoid Earth scientists, cannot bring the life-saving news from his planet, perhaps the invisible friend also gets an indifferent or hostile response, and then we never find out about the beautiful paracosm he comes from.

"Don't worry about it," my sister said in a late-night phone call. "Knowing something's made up while thinking that it matters is what all fiction insists on. She's putting a name on a series of manners."

"But he seems so real to her," I objected.

"Of course he is. I mean, who's more real to you, Becky Sharp or Gandalf or the guy down the hall? Giving a manner a name makes it real."

I paused. "I grasp that it's normal for her to have an imaginary friend." I said, "but have you ever heard of an imaginary friend who's too busy to play with you?"

She thought about it "No," she said. "I'm sure that doesn't occur anywhere in the research literature. That sounds *completely* New York." And then she hung up.

* * *

The real question, I saw, was not "Why this friend?" but "Why this fiction?" Why, as Olivia had seen so clearly, are grownups in New York so busy, and so obsessed with the language of busyness that it dominates their conversation? Why are New Yorkers always bumping into Charlie Ravioli and grabbing lunch, instead of sitting down with him and exchanging intimacies, as friends should, as people do in Paris and Rome? Why is busyness the stuff our children make their invisible friends from, as country children make theirs from light and sand?

This seems like an odd question. New Yorkers are busy for obvious reasons: they have husbands and wives and careers and children, they have the Gauguin show to see and their personal trainers and accountants to visit. But the more I think about this, the more I think it is—well, a lot of Ravioli. We are instructed to believe that we are busier because we have to work harder to be more productive, but everybody knows that busyness and productivity have a dubious, arm's-length relationship. Most of our struggle in New York, in fact, is to be less busy in order to do more work.

Constant, exhausting, no-time-to meet-your-friends Charlie Ravioli-style busyness arrived as an affliction in modern life long after the other parts of bourgeois city manners did. Business long predates busyness. In the seventeenth and eighteenth centuries, when bourgeois people were building the institutions of bourgeois life, they seem never to have complained that they were too busy—or, if they did, they left no record of it. Samuel Pepys, who had a navy to refloat and a burned London to rebuild, often uses the word "busy" but never complains of busyness. For him, the word "busy" is a synonym for "happy," not for "stressed." Not once in his diary does Pepys cancel lunch or struggle to fit someone in for coffee at four-thirty. Pepys works, makes love, and goes to bed, but he does not bump and he does not have to run. Ben Franklin, a half century later, boasts of his industriousness, but he, too, never complains about being busy, and always has time to publish a newspaper or come up with a maxim or swim the ocean or invent the lightning rod.

Until sometime in the middle of the nineteenth century, in fact, the normal affliction of the bourgeois was not busyness at all but its apparent opposite: boredom. It has even been argued that the grid of streets and cafés and small engagements in the nineteenth-century city—the whole of social life—was designed self-consciously as an escape from that numbing boredom. (Working people weren't bored, of course, but they were engaged in labor, not work. They were too busy to be busy.) Baudelaire, basically, was so bored that he had to get drunk and run out onto the boulevard in the hope of bumping into somebody.

Turn to the last third of the nineteenth century and the beginning of the twentieth, though, and suddenly everybody is busy, and everybody is complaining about it. Pepys, master of His Majesty's Navy, may never have complained of busyness, but Virginia Woolf, mistress of motionless lull, is continually complaining about how she spends her days racing across London from square to square, just like—well, like Charlie Ravioli. Ronald Firbank is wrung out by his social obligations; Proust is constantly rescheduling rendezvous and apologizing for being overstretched. Henry James, with nothing particular to do save live, complains of being too busy all the time. He could not shake the world of obligation, he said, and he wrote a strange and beautiful story, "The Great Good Place," which begins with an exhausting flood of correspondence, telegrams, and manuscripts that drive the protagonist nearly mad.

What changed? That James story helps supply the key. It was trains and telegrams. The railroads ended isolation, and packed the metropolis with people whose work was defined by a complicated network of social obligations. Pepys's network in 1669 London was, despite his official position, relatively small compared even with that of a minor aesthete like Firbank, two centuries later. Pepys had more time to make love because he had fewer friends to answer.

If the train crowded our streets, the telegram crowded our minds. It introduced something into the world which remains with us today: a whole new class of communications that are defined as incomplete in advance of their delivery. A letter, though it may enjoin a response, is meant to be complete in itself. Neither the Apostle Paul nor Horace Walpole ever ends an epistle with "Give me a call and let's discuss." By contrast, it is in the nature of the telegram to be a skeletal version of another thing—a communication that opens more than it closes. The nineteenth-century telegram came with those busy threatening words "Letter follows."

Every device that has evolved from the telegram shares the same character. E-mails end with a suggestion for a phone call ("Anyway, let's meet and/or talk soon"), faxes with a request for an e-mail, answering-machine messages with a request for a fax. All are devices of perpetually suspended communication. My wife recalls a moment last fall when she got a telephone message from a friend asking her to check her e-mail apropos a phone call she needed to make vis-a-vis a fax they had both received asking for more information about a bed they were thinking of buying from Ireland online and having sent to America by Federal Express—a grand slam of incomplete communication.

In most of the Western world outside New York, the press of trains and of telegraphic communication was alleviated by those other two great transformers: the car and the television. While the train and the telegram (and their love children, subways and commuter trains and e-mail) pushed people together, the car and the television pulled people apart—taking them out to the suburbs and sitting them down in front of a solo spectacle. New York, though, almost uniquely, got hit by a double dose of the first two technologies, and a very limited dose of the second two. Car life—car obsessions, car-defined habits—is more absent here than almost anywhere else in the country, while television, though obviously present, is less fatally prevalent here. New York is still a subject of television, and we compare *Sex and the City* to sex and the city; they are not yet quite the same. Here two grids of business remain dominant: the nineteenth- and early-twentieth-century grid of bump and run, and the late-twentieth- and early-twenty-first-century postmodern grid of virtual call and echo. Busyness is felt so intently here because we are both crowded and overloaded. We exit the apartment into a still dense nineteenth-century grid of street corners and restaurants full of people, and come home to the late-twentieth-century grid of faxes and e-mails and overwhelming incompleteness.

We walk across the Park on a Sunday morning and bump into our friend the baker and our old acquaintance from graduate school (what the hell is she doing now?) and someone we have been avoiding for three weeks. They all invite us for brunch, and we would love to, but we are too . . . busy. We bump into Charlie Ravioli, and grab a coffee with him—and come home to find three e-mails and a message on our cell phone from him, wondering where we are. The crowding of our space has been reinforced by a crowding of our time, and the only way to protect ourselves is to build structures of perpetual deferral: I'll see you next week, let's talk soon. We build rhetorical baffles around our lives to keep the crowding out, only to find that we have let nobody we love in.

Like Charlie Ravioli, we hop into taxis and leave messages on answering machines to avoid our acquaintances, and find that we keep missing our friends. I have one intimate who lives just across the Park from me, whom I e-mail often, and whom I am fortunate to see two or three times a year. We are always . . . busy. He has become my Charlie Ravioli, my invisible friend. I am sure that he misses me—just as Charlie Ravioli, I realized, must tell his other friends that he is sorry he does not see Olivia more often.

* * *

Once I sensed the nature of his predicament, I began to feel more sympathetic toward Charlie Ravioli. I got to know him better, too. We learned more about what Ravioli did in the brief breathing spaces in his busy life when he could sit down with Olivia and dish. "Ravioli read your book," Olivia announced, for instance, one night at dinner. "He didn't like it much." We also found out that Ravioli had joined a gym, that he was going to the beach in the summer, but he was too busy, and that he was working on a "show."

("It isn't a very good show," she added candidly.) Charlie Ravioli, in other words, was just another New Yorker: fit, opinionated, and trying to break into show business.

I think we would have learned to live happily with Charlie Ravioli had it not been for the appearance of Laurie. She threw us badly. At dinner, Olivia had been mentioning a new personage almost as often as she mentioned Ravioli. "I talked to Laurie today," she would begin. "She says Ravioli is busy." Or she would be closeted with her play phone. "Who are you talking to, darling?" I would ask. "Laurie," she would say. "We're talking about Ravioli." We surmised that Laurie was, so to speak, the Linda Tripp of the Ravioli operation—the person you spoke to for consolation when the big creep was ignoring you.

But a little while later a more ominous side of Laurie's role began to appear. "Laurie, tell Ravioli I'm calling," I heard Olivia say. I pressed her about who, exactly, Laurie was. Olivia shook her head. "She works for Ravioli," she said.

And then it came to us, with sickening clarity: Laurie was not the patient friend who consoled you for Charlie's absence. Laurie was the bright-toned person who answered Ravioli's phone and told you that unfortunately Mr. Ravioli was in a meeting. "Laurie says Ravioli is too busy to play," Olivia announced sadly one morning. Things seemed to be deteriorating; now Ravioli was too busy even to say he was too busy.

I got back on the phone with my sister. "Have you ever heard of an imaginary friend with an assistant?" I asked.

She paused. "Imaginary friends don't have assistants," she said. "That's not only not in the literature. That's just . . . I mean—in California they don't have assistants."

"You think we should look into it?"

"I think you should move," she said flatly.

Martha was of the same mind. "An imaginary playmate shouldn't have an assistant," she said miserably. "An imaginary playmate shouldn't have an agent. An imaginary playmate shouldn't have a publicist or a personal trainer or a caterer—an imaginary playmate shouldn't have . . . *people.* An imaginary playmate should just *play.* With the child who imagined it." She started leaving on my pillow real-estate brochures picturing quaint houses in New Jersey and Connecticut, unhaunted by busy invisible friends and their entourages.

* * *

Not long after the appearance of Laurie, though, something remarkable happened. Olivia would begin to tell us tales of her frustrations with Charlie Ravioli, and, after telling us, again, that he was too busy to play, she would tell us what she had done instead. Astounding and paracosmic tall tales poured out of her: she had been to a chess tournament and brought home a trophy; she had gone to a circus and told jokes. Searching for Charlie Ravioli, she had "saved all the animals in the zoo"; heading home in a taxi after a quick coffee with Ravioli, she took over the steering wheel and "got all the moneys." From the stalemate of daily life emerged the fantasy of victory. She had dreamed of a normal life with a few close friends, and had to settle for worldwide fame and the front page of the tabloids. The existence of an imaginary friend had liberated her into a paracosm, but it was a curiously New York paracosm—it was the unobtainable world outside her window. Charlie Ravioli, prince of busyness, was not an end but a means: a way out onto the street in her head, a declaration of potential independence.

Busyness is our art form, our civic ritual, our way of being us. Many friends have said to me that they love New York now in a way they never did before, and their love, I've noticed, takes for its object all the things that used to exasperate them—the curious combination of freedom, self-made fences, and paralyzing preoccupation that the city provides. "How did you spend the day?" Martha and I now ask each other, and then, instead of listing her incidents, she says merely, "Oh, you know . . . just . . . bumping into Charlie Ravioli," meaning, just bouncing from obligation to electronic entreaty, just spotting a friend and snatching a sandwich, just being busy, just living in New York. If everything we've learned in the past year could be summed up in a phrase, it's that we want to go on bumping into Charlie Ravioli for as long as we can.

Olivia still hopes to have him to herself someday. As I work late at night in the "study" (an old hallway, an Aalto screen) I keep near the "nursery" (an ancient pantry, a glass-brick wall), I can hear her shift into pre-sleep, still muttering to herself. She is still trying to reach her closest friend. "Ravioli? Ravioli?" she moans as she turns over into her pillow and clutches her blanket, and then she whispers, almost to herself, "Tell him call me. Tell him call me when he comes home."

Points of Engagement—Reading Comprehension

1. On page 155 Adam Gopnik describes talking with his sister on the phone about his daughter's too-busy imaginary friend. Gopnik's sister responds, "That sounds completely New York." What does she mean? Point to specific passages in Gopnik's essay that help you answer.
2. What does Gopnik mean when he refers to "perpetually suspended communication" (157)? What are the two "grids of busyness [that] remain dominant" in New York? Why are they important to Gopnik?

3. What is a "paracosm"? Describe it in your own words and using quotations from Gopnik's essay. How does this idea help explain Olivia's invention of Mr. Ravioli? How does it help Gopnik to understand his daughter?
4. Why does Gopnik write, "We want to go on bumping into Mr. Ravioli as long as we can" (160)? What kind of human longing is he describing? Do you think it's a healthy or unhealthy longing? Why?

Points of Departure—Assignment Questions

1. In several essays in this reader, technology is a kind of bogeyman, something we are afraid of because of its power over us, and yet irresistibly drawn to. Sherry Turkle describes our internal conflict this way: "If the problem is that too much technology has made us busy and anxious, the solution will be another technology that will organize, amuse, and relax us" (272). For this paper, consider our addiction to technology, the benefits and risks of technology for our human selves, as laid out by Adam Gopnik, Sherry Turkle, Lisa Belkin, Malcolm Gladwell, or Lauren Slater. How much is too much for human nature to cope with, or is technological advancement always progress? If so, where is it taking us? What are the consequences of our addiction to technology? What do these authors think? What do you think?

2. What does Adam Gopnik learn about himself and fellow New Yorkers by observing his 3-year-old daughter so closely? Think about how his perspective changes when viewing his own New York experience through the eyes of his child. Then consider the following question: What can we learn about the world and ourselves by considering both through someone else's eyes? Your project for this paper is to answer this question using Gopnik and insights from essays by Amy Chua, Alain de Botton, Diana Eck, James Fallows, Jane Goodall, Naomi Klein, Gregory Orr, Sherry Turkle, or Kenji Yoshino.
3. Adam Gopnik's essay "Bumping Into Mr. Ravioli" provides a look at a specific modern American lifestyle, the life of the New Yorker. Does the essay reveal anything broader about contemporary American ideals, values, or interests? Consider the kinds of lifestyles described in essays by Ian Bremmer, Amy Chua, James Fallows, Janet Flammang, Arlie Russell Hochschild, or Sherry Turkle. Use Gopnik and one of these texts to explore this notion of contemporary American values—what they are, where they come from, where they take us, how they are perceived—and whether

they are exclusively "American." Keep in mind that Gopnik is writing specifically about New York City as you extend your ideas beyond his.

4. Adam Gopnik refers to the "grids" of "business" and of "busyness" that shape life in New York City. Alain de Botton, in "On Habit," refers to the "grid of interests" he has imposed on his local street, and Sherry Turkle writes about people terrified of being "cut off from the 'grid,'" of losing their cellphones. Why the focus on "grids"? What are they? How do these kinds of grids work? Why do we create them, only to find them restricting? Are they a part of our environment, or a product of thought or perception? Are they fundamentally positive, negative, or benign? Could we use this concept to change the way we live? How? Draw on all three essays as you frame answers for these questions about the grids in which we live.

Possible Worlds: Why Do Children Pretend?

Alison Gopnik

Points of Access—Pre-Reading

1. Think back to the time you were a young child. What games of "pretend" did you play?
2. Adults are often encouraged to stop dreaming and to face reality. Why do you think this is so?
3. What is knowledge? What is imagination? Do you think they are the same or different? How?
4. Who is smarter? A baby or a computer? Why? What are you measuring when you rank them?

Human beings don't live in the real world. The real world is what actually happened in the past, is happening now, and will happen in the future. But we don't just live in this single world. Instead, we live in a universe of many possible worlds, all the ways the world could be in the future and also all the ways the world could have been in the past, or might be in the present. These possible worlds are what we call dreams and plans, fictions and hypotheses. They are the products of hope and imagination. Philosophers, more drily, call them "counterfactuals."

Counterfactuals are the woulda-coulda-shouldas of life, all the things that might happen in the future, but haven't yet, or that could have happened in the past, but didn't quite. Human beings care deeply about those possible worlds—as deeply as they care about the real actual world. On the surface counterfactual thinking seems like a very sophisticated and philosophically puzzling ability. How can we think about things that aren't there? And why should we think this way instead of restricting ourselves to the actual world? It seems obvious that understanding the real world would give us an evolutionary edge, but what good do we get from imaginary worlds?

We can start to answer these questions by looking at young children. Is counterfactual thought present only in sophisticated grown-ups? Or can young children think about possibilities too? The conventional wisdom, echoed in the theories of both Sigmund Freud and Jean Piaget, is that babies and young children are limited to the here and now—their immediate sensations and perceptions and experience. Even when young children pretend or imagine they can't distinguish between reality and fantasy: their fantasies, in this view, are just another kind of immediate experience. Counterfactual thought requires a more demanding ability to understand the relation between reality and all the alternatives to that reality.

Cognitive scientists have discovered that this conventional picture is wrong. We've found out that even very young children can already consider possibilities, distinguish them from reality, and even use them to change the world. They can imagine different ways the world might be in the future and use them to create plans. They can imagine different ways the world might have been in the past, and reflect on past possibilities. And, most dramatically, they can create completely imaginary worlds, wild fictions, and striking pretenses. These crazy imaginary worlds are a familiar part of childhood—every parent of a three-year-old has exclaimed, "What an imagination!" But the new research profoundly changes the way we think about those worlds.

In the past ten years we've not only discovered that children have these imaginative powers—we've actually begun to understand how these powers are possible. We are developing a science of the imagination. How could children's minds and brains be constructed to allow them to imagine this dazzling array of alternate universes?

The answer is surprising. Conventional wisdom suggests that knowledge and imagination, science and fantasy, are deeply different from one another—even opposites. But the new ideas I'll outline show that exactly the same abilities that let children learn so much about the world also allow them to change the world—to bring new worlds into existence—and to imagine alternative worlds that may never exist at all. Children's brains create causal theories of the world, maps of how the world works. And these theories allow children to envisage new possibilities, and to imagine and pretend that the world is different.

The Power of Counterfactuals

Psychologists have found that counterfactual thinking is absolutely pervasive in our everyday life and deeply affects our judgments, our decisions, and our emotions. You would think that what really matters is what actually happens, not what you imagine might have happened in the past or could happen in the future. This is particularly true of counterfactuals about the past—what might have happened but didn't—the woulda-coulda-shouldas of life. Yet the woulda-coulda-shouldas have a deep impact on experience.

In one experiment, the Nobel Prize-winning psychologist Daniel Kahneman and his colleagues asked people to imagine the following sort of scenario. Mr. Tees and Mr. Crane are both in a taxi to the airport, desperate to catch their respective planes, which are both scheduled to take off at 6:00. But traffic is impossibly snarled and the minutes tick by. Finally, at 6:30 they arrive at the airport. It turns out that Mr. Tees's flight left at 6:00 as planned but Mr. Crane's flight was delayed till 6:25 and Mr. Crane sees it take off as he arrives. Who is more upset?

Just about everyone agrees that Mr. Crane, who just missed his flight, will be much more unhappy. But why? They both missed their flights. It seems that what is making Mr. Crane unhappy is not the actual world but the counterfactual worlds, the ones in which the taxi arrived just that much earlier or the plane was delayed just a few minutes more.

You needn't turn to artificial scenarios like this one to see the effects of counterfactuals. Consider the medalists in the Olympics. Who is happier, the bronze medalist or the silver? You'd think that objectively the silver medalist, who, after all, has actually done better, would be happier. But the relevant counterfactuals are very different for the two. For the bronze medalist the relevant alternative was to finish out of the medals altogether—a fate she has just escaped. For the silver medalist, the relevant alternative was to get the gold medal—a fate she has just missed. And, in fact, when psychologists took clips of the medals ceremonies and analyzed the facial expressions of the athletes, it turned out that the bronze medalists really do look happier than the silver medalists. The difference in what might have been outweighs the difference in what is.

Like Mr. Crane at the airport, or the silver medalist, people are most unhappy when a desirable outcome seems to be just out of reach, or to have just been missed. As Neil Young adapted John Greenleaf Whittier: "The saddest words of tongue and pen are these four words, 'it might have been.'"

Why do we humans worry so much about counterfactuals, when, by definition, they are things that didn't actually happen? Why are these imaginary worlds just as important to us as the real ones? Surely "it is, and it's awful" should be sadder words than "it might have been."

The evolutionary answer is that counterfactuals let us change the future. Because we can consider alternative ways the world might be, we can actually act on the world and intervene to turn it into one or the other of these possibilities. Whenever we act, even in a small way, we are changing the course of history, nudging the world down one path rather than another. Of course, making one possibility come true means that all the other alternative possibilities we considered won't come true—they become counterfactuals. But being able to think about those possibilities is crucial to our evolutionary success.

Counterfactual thinking lets us make new plans, invent new tools, and create new environments. Human beings are constantly imagining what would happen if they cracked nuts or wove baskets or made political decisions in a new way, and the sum total of all those visions is a different world.

Counterfactuals about the past, and the characteristically human emotions that go with them, seem to be the price we pay for counterfactuals about the future. Because we are responsible for the future, we can feel guilty about the past; because we can hope, we can also regret; because we can make plans, we can be disappointed. The other side of being able to consider all the possible futures, all the things that could go differently, is that you can't escape considering all the possible pasts, all the things that could have gone differently.

Counterfactuals in Children: Planning the Future

Can children think counterfactually? The most evolutionarily fundamental kind of counterfactual thinking comes when we make plans for the future—when we consider alternative possibilities and pick the one we think will be most desirable. How can we tell if a very young baby can do this? In my lab, we showed the baby the sort of post with stacking rings that is a standard baby toy. But I had taped over the hole in one of the rings. How would the baby respond to this apparently similar but actually recalcitrant ring? When we brought a fifteen-month-old into the lab he would use a kind of trial-and-error method to solve the problem. He would stack some of the rings, look carefully at the taped-over one—and then try it on the post. And then try it on the post again, harder. And try it on the post one more time. Then he would look up puzzled, try one of the other rings again—and then again try the taped-over one. Basically, young babies would keep at this until they gave up.

But as they got older and learned more about how the world worked, babies would behave entirely differently. An eighteen- month-old would stack all the other rings and then hold up the trick ring with a "Who do you think you're kidding?" look and refuse even to try it. Or she would immediately pick the trick ring up and dramatically throw it across the room, and then calmly stack the rest. Or, equally dramatically, she would hold it up to the post and shout "No!" or "Uh-oh!" These babies didn't have to actually see what the ring would do—they could imagine what would happen if you put it on the post, and act accordingly.

In another experiment we saw whether babies could discover a new use for an object—if they could, in a simple way, invent a new tool. I put a desirable toy out of the babies' reach and placed a toy rake beside it. As with the ring, fifteen-month-olds sometimes did pick up the rake, but they couldn't figure out how to use it as a tool. They pushed the toy from side to side or even, frustratingly, farther away from them, till they either accidentally got it or gave up. But older babies looked at the rake and paused thoughtfully. You could almost see the wheels spinning. Then they produced a triumphant smile and often a certain look of smugness.

You could almost see the lightbulb switching on. Then they put the rake in just the right position over the toy and triumphantly used it to bring the toy toward them. Again they seemed able to mentally anticipate—to imagine—all the possible ways the rake could affect the toy and then chose just the right possibility.

Simple trial and error, trying different actions until one succeeds, is actually often a very effective way of getting along in the world. But anticipating future possibilities lets us plan in this other more insightful way—using our heads instead of our hands. The older babies seemed to be anticipating the possible future in which the ring or the rake would fail and avoiding that future. Other studies have shown that this isn't just a difference between fifteen- and eighteen-month-olds. Even younger babies can solve problems insightfully if they have the right kinds of information.

This ability to solve problems insightfully seems to be particularly human. There is a little evidence that chimpanzees, and even some very smart birds like crows, can do this occasionally. But even chimpanzees and crows, and certainly other animals, overwhelmingly rely on either instinct or trial and error to get along in the world. And, in fact, instinct and trial and error are often very effective and intelligent strategies. It is extremely impressive to see a bird putting together the complex set of instinctive behaviors that allows it to build a nest, or a chimpanzee using trial and error to gradually zero in on the right strategy to open a box with elaborate locks. But they are different from the strategies that babies and very young children use. Anthropologists agree that using tools and making plans, both abilities that depend on anticipating future possibilities, played a large role in the evolutionary success of *Homo sapiens*. And we can see these abilities emerging even in babies who can't talk yet.

Reconstructing the Past

In these experiments babies seem to be able to imagine alternative possibilities in the future. Can children also imagine past counterfactuals, different ways the world might have been? We have to infer babies' counterfactual thinking from what they do, but we can explicitly ask older children counterfactual woulda-coulda-shoulda questions. Until recently psychologists claimed that children were quite bad at thinking about possibilities. Children are indeed quite bad at producing counterfactuals about subjects they know little about, but when they understand the subject matter even two- and three-year-olds turn out to be adept at generating alternative worlds.

The English psychologist Paul Harris probably knows more than anyone about young children's imaginative abilities. Harris is tall, thin, reserved, and very English, and worked for many years at Oxford University. His work, like the work of the great Oxford writer Lewis Carroll, is a peculiarly English combination of the strictest logic applied to the wildest fantasy.

Harris told children a familiar English countryside story. Then he asked them about future and past counterfactuals. Naughty Ducky is wearing muddy boots and is about to walk into the kitchen. "What would happen to the floor if Ducky walked through the kitchen? Would it be clean or dirty?" "What would have happened to the floor if Ducky had cleaned his boots first? Would it be clean or dirty?" Even young three-year-olds say that the floor would have been spared if only Ducky had cleaned his boots.

In my lab, David Sobel and I designed a set of storytelling cards—cartoon pictures that told the right story if you put them in order. We showed children a sequence of pictures, say a girl going to a cookie jar, opening the jar, looking inside, finding cookies, and looking happy. But we also had a set of several other pictures, including the girl finding that there were no cookies, and the girl looking sad and hungry. We showed the children the cards in the right sequence and asked them to tell the story. Then we said, "But how about if the girl had been sad at the end instead?" and changed the last card, so that the girl looked sad instead of happy. "What would have had to happen then?" Three-year-olds consistently changed the earlier pictures to fit the hypothetical ending—they replaced the picture of the full cookie jar with the picture of the empty one. These very young children could imagine and reason about an alternative past.

Imagining the Possible

We can also see evidence for counterfactual thinking in children's play. Babies start pretending when they are as young as eighteen months old or even younger. Pretending involves a kind of present counterfactual thinking—imagining the way things might be different. Even babies who can't talk yet, and are barely walking, can still pretend. A one-and-a-half-year-old baby may fastidiously comb her hair with a pencil, or rest her head on a pillow dramatically pretending to be asleep, giggling all the while. A little later babies start to treat objects as if they were something else. Toddlers turn everything from blocks to shoes to bowls of cereal into means of transportation by the simple expedient of saying "brrm-brrm" and pushing them along the floor. Or they may carefully, tenderly, put three little toy sheep to bed.

We take this for granted when we choose toys for these young children. The toddler sections of toy stores are full of toys that encourage children to pretend: the farmhouse, the gas station, the zoo—even the toy ATM and cell phone. But it's not that two-year-olds pretend because we give them dolls; instead we give them dolls because they love to pretend. Even without toys toddlers are just as likely to turn common objects—food, pebbles, grass, you, themselves—into something else. And even in cultures where pretend play is discouraged, rather than cultivated, like Mr. Gradgrind's school in Dickens's *Hard Times,* children continue to do it anyway. ("No child left behind" testing policies seem to be echoing Mr. Gradgrind, replacing dress-up comers and pretend play with reading drills in preschools.)

As soon as babies can talk they immediately talk about the possible as well as the real. As a graduate student at Oxford I recorded all the words that nine babies used when they first began to talk. These babies, who were still just using single words, at the very start of language, would use them to talk about possibilities as well as actualities. There was not only the ubiquitous "brrm-brrm," but "apple" when pretending to eat a ball, or "night-night" when putting a doll to bed. One particularly charming red-haired toddler had a beloved teddy bear, and his mother had knitted two long scarves, like the ones Dr. Who wears in the British TV series, a small one for the bear and a larger one for Jonathan. Jonathan one day put his teddy bear's scarf around his neck and, with enormous grins and giggles, announced his new identity: "Jonathan Bear!"

In fact, learning language gives children a whole powerful new way to imagine. Even young babies who can't talk yet have some ability to anticipate and imagine the future. But being able to talk gives you a particularly powerful way to put old ideas together in new ways, and to talk about things that aren't there. Consider the power of "no," one of the very first words that children learn. When parents think about "no" they immediately think of the terrible two-year-old absolutely refusing to do something. And children do use "no" that way. But they also use "no" to tell themselves not to do something, like the child who said "no" holding the taped-up ring over the post. And they use "no" to say that something isn't true. When Jonathan's equally charming mom teased him by saying that the swimming pool was full of orange juice, he immediately said, "No juice!" Other less obvious words have some of the same power. Take "uh-oh." This hardly counts as a word for grown-ups but it's one of the most common words that young children use. And "uh-oh," like "no," is a word about what could have happened.

Babies use it when they try to do something and fail—"uh-oh" contrasts the ideal with the unfortunate real.

Being able to say "no" and "uh-oh" immediately puts you in the world of the counterfactual and the possible—the road not taken, the possibility that isn't real. And we discovered that, in fact, babies start talking about unreal possibilities at the same time that they start to use tools in an insightful way. Being able to talk about possibilities helps you to imagine them.

By the time they are two or three children quite characteristically spend much of their waking hours in a world of imaginary creatures, possible universes, and assumed identities. Walk into any day-care center and you will be surrounded by small princesses and superheroes in overalls who politely serve you nonexistent tea and warn you away from nonexistent monsters. And these children are adept at playing out the consequences of their counterfactual pretend premises. Paul Harris found that even two-year-olds will tell you that if an imaginary teddy is drinking imaginary tea, then if he spills it the imaginary floor will require imaginary mopping- up. (As with Ducky, toddlers seem particularly taken with the possibilities involved in making a terrible mess.) Children were quite specific about their counterfactuals. If the teddy spills tea you'll need a mop, but if he spills baby powder you'll need a broom.

In the past, this imaginative play has been taken to be evidence of children's cognitive limitations rather than evidence of their cognitive powers. Earlier psychologists, including both Freud and Piaget, claimed that make-believe was a sign that young children are unable to discriminate between fiction and truth, pretense and reality, fantasy and fact. Of course, if you saw an adult doing the same things that preschoolers do—if, for example, someone with wild hair and a sparkly cloak around her shoulders announced to you that she was queen of the fairies—you would probably conclude that she *was* confused about reality and fantasy, and that she should probably make sure she got back on her meds. However, neither Freud nor Piaget investigated this question systematically.

More recently, cognitive scientists have carefully explored what children know about imagination and pretense. It turns out that even two- and three-year-olds are extremely good at distinguishing imagination and pretense from reality. One of the most distinctive things about even the earliest pretend play is the fact that it's accompanied by giggles. It's the giggles, the knowing look, the dramatic exaggeration, that signal that this is not to be taken seriously. In fact, there turns out to be a consistent set of signals—giggles, exaggerated gestures, theatrical and melodramatic facial expressions— that indicate that actions are "just pretend." And, after all, even the youngest children don't actually try to eat the pretend cookies or even try to actually talk to Mom on the pretend cell phone.

Preschool children spend hours pretending, but they *know* that they are pretending. The psychologist Jacqui Woolley did an experiment where children pretended that there was a pencil in one box, and actually saw a pencil in another box. Then the boxes were closed. An assistant came into the room, looking for a pencil, and asked the children which box she should open. Three-year-olds said quite clearly that she should look in the box with the real pencil, not the pretend one. In much the same way three-year-olds say that everyone can see and touch a real dog but not an imaginary one, and that you can turn an imaginary dog, but not a real one, into a cat just by thinking about it.

Children may seem confused because they are such expressive and emotional pretenders. They can have real emotional reactions to entirely imaginary scenarios. Rather than asking children to imagine pencils in the box, Paul Harris asked them to imagine a monster in the box. Children again said very clearly that really there was no monster in the box, and that they would not see one if they opened the box—they were just imagining it. Nevertheless, when the experimenter left the room many children gingerly moved away from the box.

In this respect, however, children don't seem to be that different from adults. The psychologist Paul Rozin asked adults to fill a bottle with water from the tap, write "cyanide" on a label, and affix it to the bottle. Although they knew perfectly well that they were .only pretending that the water was poisonous, they still wouldn't drink it. I am perfectly capable of being scared silly by Hannibal Lecter although I have absolutely no doubt of his fictional status.

Children's emotions are more intense and more difficult to control than adult emotions, whether the causes of those emotions are real or not. To a worried parent, it may seem that the child trembling under the covers must believe that there really is a monster in the closet. But the scientific studies show that this is not because children don't understand the difference between fiction and fact. They are just more moved by both than grown-ups.

Imagination and Causation

We know that even very young children constantly think about future, past, and present possible worlds. And we know that this ability gives us distinctive evolutionary advantages. How do human minds, even the very youngest human minds, manage to produce counterfactuals? How can we think about the possible worlds that might exist in the future or could have existed in the past, when those worlds don't actually exist now? Even more important, our evolutionary advantage comes because we can not only imagine possibilities but also act on them—we can turn them into reality. But how do we know which possibilities will come true in what circumstances? And how do we decide just what we have to do to make them real?

Part of the answer is that our ability to imagine possible worlds is closely tied to our ability to think causally. Causal knowledge is itself an ancient philosophical puzzle. The great Scottish philosopher David Hume thought we could never really know that one event caused another—all we could know was that one event tended to follow another. What makes causal knowledge more than just one damned thing after another? The modern philosopher David Lewis was the first to point out the close link between causal knowledge and counterfactual thinking, and many philosophers have followed this idea up since then.

Once you know how one thing is causally connected to another you can predict what will happen to one thing if you act to change another—you can see what a difference making things different will make. You can also imagine what would have happened if you had acted in a certain way, even though you didn't. Once I know that smoking causes cancer I can imagine possible worlds in which my actions cause people to stop smoking, and conclude that in those worlds they will be less likely to become ill. I can take a wide variety of actions, from advertising to legislation to inventing nicotine patches, to get people to stop smoking, and I can accurately predict just how these actions will change the world. I can make a world with less cancer than the world had before. And I can also look backwards and calculate how many lives would have been saved if the tobacco industry had not resisted those changes in the past.

Causal understanding lets you deliberately do things that will change the world in a particular way. We might simply have had the ability to track the world as it unfolded around us. But, in fact, we have the ability to intervene in the world, as well, to actually make things happen. Intervening deliberately in the world isn't the same as just predicting what will happen next. When we intervene we envision a particular possible future we would like to bring about and our action actually changes the world to make that future real.

Of course, other animals, or people in some situations, may act on the world effectively without necessarily understanding the world in a causal way. Like the fifteen-month-olds and the ring, or like the chimpanzees, you may just hit on the right action to solve a problem through trial and error. Chimpanzees may notice that when you poke a stick in a termite nest, the termites emerge. Fifteen-month-olds may see that when you try the taped-over ring it fails, and doctors may observe that when you prescribe aspirin your patients' headaches go away. Then you can just repeat that action the next time.

But having a causal theory of the world makes it possible to consider alternative solutions to a problem, and their consequences, before you actually implement them, and it lets you make a much wider and more effective range of interventions. If you know that the hole allows the ring to descend on the post, or that the rake causes the toy to move with it, you can design a new strategy to deal with the taped-over ring or the distant toy. If you know that a cascade of electrical impulses on the trigeminal nerve leads the blood vessels to expand, which puts pressure on nerves, which leads to a headache, you can design drugs that influence just the electrical processes or just the blood pressure. When you take a drug like sumatriptan to relieve a migraine headache you are taking advantage of the causal knowledge about migraines that neurologists have discovered, and the possible remedies that it allowed them to design.

Children and Causation

Understanding what causes migraines and cancer, and using this knowledge to change the world, is, of course, the work of science. But are scientists the only people who can think about causation and use it to bring new worlds into being? Ordinary adults also seem to know a lot about the causal structure of the world and they irresistibly think about counterfactuals, even when all they do is lead to guilt and regret.

We saw that children are also extremely good at counterfactual thinking. If counterfactual thinking depends on causal understanding and is a deep, evolved part of human nature, then even very young children should also be able to think causally. In fact, it turns out that they do already know a great deal about the causal structure of the world—about how one thing makes another happen. In fact, this is one of the most important, and most revolutionary, recent discoveries of developmental psychology.

Just as psychologists used to think that children don't understand much about counterfactuals, they also used to think that young children don't understand much about causation. Children's thinking was supposed to be restricted to their immediate perceptual experience—they might know that one event happened after another but not that one event caused another. In particular, psychologists thought that children didn't understand the hidden causal relations that are the stuff of science—the way that something in a seed makes it grow, or germs make you ill, or magnets make iron filings move, or hidden desires make people act. Piaget, for example, claimed that children were "precausal" until they were well into the school-age years.

But over the past twenty years we have discovered that babies and young children do know a lot about how objects and people work, and they learn more as they grow older.

Piaget asked children about causal phenomena that they didn't know much about. He asked preschoolers interesting and hard causal questions like "Why does it get dark at night?" or "Why do the clouds move?" The children either simply got confused or produced answers that were deficient by adult standards though they sometimes had a logic of their own ("It gets dark so we can sleep" or "The clouds move because I want them to").

More recently psychologists decided to try asking children questions about things they know a lot about, like "Why did Johnny open the refrigerator when he was hungry?" or "How does a tricycle work?" Children as young as two gave perfectly good, and sometimes even elaborate, causal explanations. "He thought there was food in there and he wanted food so he opened the fridge so he could get the food." Very young children are consumed with insatiable curiosity about causes, as their unstoppable "why?" questions show.

The psychologist Henry Wellman spent a sabbatical year simply searching through CHILDES, a computer database of recordings of hundreds of children's everyday conversations. (Wellman, who once taught preschool, said that it was odd and touching to simultaneously be in the scholarly adult peace of the computer room at the Center for Advanced Studies in the Behavioral Sciences at Stanford and yet be surrounded once more by these invisible three-year-olds.) He found that two- and three-year-olds both produced and asked for dozens of causal explanations a day. They gave explanations for physical phenomena: "The teddy's arm fell off because you twisted it too far"; "Jenny had my chair because the other chair was brokened." They gave accounts of biological causes: "He needs more to eat because he is growing long arms"; "Mean hawks eat meat because meat is tasty for mean hawks." But most of all they liked psychological explanations: "I didn't spill it last night because I'm a good girl"; "I not gone go up there because I frightened of her." The explanations might not always have been the same ones a grown-up would give but they were perfectly good logical explanations all the same.

Other studies show that young children understand quite abstract and hidden causes. They understand that something in a seed makes it grow or that invisible germs make you ill. The Japanese psychologists Giyoo Hatano and Kayoko Inagaki explored children's everyday biology—their understanding of life and death. They found that when they're around five years old children around the world develop a vitalist causal theory of biology much like the theory in traditional Japanese and Chinese medicine. These children seem to think that there is a single vital force, like the Chinese chi, that keeps us alive. They predict that if you don't eat enough, for example, this force will wane and you'll get sick. They think that death is the irreversible loss of this force, and predict that animals that die won't come back to life. (This new understanding of mortality is a mixed blessing. Younger children think that death is more like a move than an ending; Grandmom has simply temporarily taken up residence in the cemetery or in heaven, and might come back. Many children start to become much more anxious about death once they think of it as the irreversible loss of a vital force.) This theory allows them to make a whole network of predictions, counterfactuals, and explanations—like the child Henry Wellman studied who said that someone "needs more to eat because he is growing long arms."

Causation is what gives fantasy its logic. Think about the children in Paul Harris's studies who could work out precisely what the imaginary consequences would be if Teddy spilled the imaginary tea. A pretend game in which absolutely anything goes would just be a mess. Instead, pretend works by establishing imaginary premises ("I'm the mommy and you're the baby") and then working out the causal consequences of those premises quite strictly. Children can become quite passionate about whether the right causal rules are being followed: "You didn't get me with your ray gun 'cause I was behind the shield!" "You hafta drink your milk 'cause you're the baby!"

Causes and Possibilities

Children develop causal theories of the world from a very early age. If causal knowledge and counterfactual thinking go together, then this might explain how young children have the parallel ability to generate counterfactuals and to explore possible worlds. If children understand the way things work, they should be able to imagine alternative possibilities about them. This might also explain the cases where children don't think counterfactually. Think back to the fifteen-month-old who futilely tries to jam the solid ring over the pole. It could be that she just doesn't understand yet how poles and holes fit together. Children might sometimes fail to think counterfactually because they don't have the right kind of causal knowledge, not because they're unable to imagine possibilities, just as I would have a hard time telling you what could have been done to prevent the space shuttle crash, or what should be done to prevent it in the future.

Henry Wellman showed that children talk about causes in their everyday conversations. Then he took the next step and asked children to say what was possible or impossible, based on their causal knowledge of the physical, biological, and psychological world. He found that children consistently used their knowledge to discriminate possibilities. They said, for example, that Johnny could simply decide to hold up his arm, but he couldn't possibly decide to simply jump in the air and stay there, or decide to grow taller, or decide to walk through a table.

One little boy we tested decided to demonstrate his counterfactual knowledge by actually acting out each of the possibilities after he had made the predictions. "You can't just jump in the air and stay there, look!" he said, jumping as high as he could. And then: "Watch! Table I will walk through you!" at which he dramatically and theatrically bumped against the table and said, "Ow, see, you can't do it."

Even the youngest children already have causal knowledge about the world and use that knowledge to make predictions about the future, to explain the past, and to imagine possible worlds that might or might not exist. But at a deeper level, what would children's minds have to be like in order to do this? One way Wellman, Hatano and Inagaki, and I tried to capture these ideas was by saying that children have everyday theories of the world—everyday ideas about psychology, biology, and physics. These theories are like scientific theories but they are largely unconscious rather than conscious, and they are coded in children's brains, instead of being written down on paper or presented at scientific conferences. But how could something as abstract as a theory be coded in children's brains?

Maps and Blueprints

Children's brains construct a kind of unconscious causal map, an accurate picture of the way the world works. These causal maps are like the more familiar maps we, and even computerized systems such as Mapquest, use to represent space. Many animals, from squirrels to rats to people, construct "cognitive maps" of their spatial world, internal pictures of where things are in space, much like the external pictures of printed maps. Once you represent spatial information in a map you can use that information much more flexibly and productively. We even know something about where and how those spatial maps are encoded in animal brains. They appear to be located in a region called the hippocampus—remove a rat's hippocampus and it will no longer be able to find its way around a maze.

One thing a map does is to let you make blueprints. A blueprint looks like a map, but instead of making the blueprint match the world, we change the world to match the blueprint. Once we know how to make spatial maps, we can also decide to make changes in the spatial layout of objects, including our own bodies, and predict the effects of those changes.

If you are in a strange city without a map, you may find yourself wandering around from the hotel until you hit on the train station or the restaurant, and you may repeat that route once you've found it. Once you have a map, though, you can discover that there were much shorter and more convenient routes you could have taken. The map lets you compare different routes to a place, and lets you discover the most efficient route, without having to actually take each one. You don't need a printed map to do this. Animals with good cognitive maps, like rats, can explore a maze, construct an internal map, and then immediately, without trial and error, find the shortest route from one location in the maze to another.

You might not think of using the map in this way as using the map as a blueprint. After all, the world the map represents stays the same. But you are, in fact, changing the location of one very important object on the map, namely the little red dot that means "you are here." When you imagine the different routes you could take you are imagining, creating really, different cognitive maps with that red dot in different locations. A map is a very efficient device for constructing different cognitive blueprints, pictures of what will happen as you move yourself around through space.

Moreover, with a map you can consider other, more complex, spatial possibilities. When you set out to design a new garden, for example, your first step is to make a map of the existing backyard (noting, for example, the slab of cracked concrete, the broken jungle gym, and the patch of weeds). But the second step is to construct a similar map of the ideal garden that will replace it (sketching in the fountain, the brick pathways, and the flowering trees). The great landscape garden designer Capability Brown once remarked, looking at a particularly sinuous stretch of the river Thames, "Clever!" Brown was thinking of the landscape as the outcome of a blueprint, as a human invention, rather than as a natural phenomenon accurately represented in a map. In a much simpler way, animals such as squirrels can use spatial maps to plan where to hide their nuts and then to recover the nuts later.

Once we have the new ideal map, the blueprint, we can set about acting on objects to realize it. We can move ourselves to a new location by the shortest route. Or we can move the jungle gym away to the dump and haul the fountain in to replace it. Maps also help us to consider all the spatial possibilities before we commit ourselves. We can consider whether it would be faster to take the side streets or stick to the boulevard. We can look at the assorted places that the fountain might be—the ways that it might interact with the brick path or the flowering tree—before we actually decide to go ahead and install it in a particular place.

Causal Maps

Human beings also construct a different kind of map—a map of the complex causal relations among events. The neurologist has a kind of map of migraines—outlining all the causal links between neural activity and pressure and pain. Or think about the children who could make all those predictions about the biological world. Rather than considering each of the causal relationships between life and death and growth and disease and food separately, children seem to have a single coherent vitalist picture of the world. They think that eating causes you to have more energy, while illness drains you of that energy—that growth lets you dial up your causal force while death robs you of it. They can make new predictions, often ones they've never heard about before. They'll say that as long as you keep eating you could just keep growing indefinitely, or that a grown-up who is taller must be older than one who is shorter (my own son insisted that, at five feet two inches, I couldn't really be friends with a young basketball-playing colleague because he was big and I was just little). Or they'll explain that you have to eat because it gives you power. This causal map of biology lets them draw all these consequences—and more.

While other animals clearly make spatial cognitive maps, it is not clear that they make causal maps in the same way. Other animals are able to understand specific kinds of causal relationships. For example, they understand that their own actions cause the events that immediately follow those actions—say, that poking the termite nest makes the termites come out—or they may understand a few particularly important causal links, such as the link between bad food and nausea. However, other animals don't seem to make the kind of maps that we see even in very young children. Other animals seem to rely more on the kind of trial-and-error learning that allows us to notice that aspirin makes our headaches go away, instead of the kind of theory making that lets us design a new drug such as sumatriptan to get rid of migraines.

In the pineries a group of philosophers of science at Carnegie Mellon University led by Clark Glymour started trying to give a mathematical account of how scientific theories might work. At the same time computer scientists at UCLA, led by Judea Pearl, were trying to write programs that would be able to make the same sort of predictions and recommendations that scientific experts make. The two groups hit upon the same set of ideas about causal maps. They worked out how to describe the maps mathematically and how to use them to accurately generate new predictions, interventions, and counterfactuals. The new mathematical descriptions, called "causal graphical models," have taken over artificial intelligence and have inspired new ideas about causation in philosophy.

You can make computer programs that use these causal maps, just the way that Mapquest uses spatial maps. Mapquest uses a single map to automatically produce millions of routes from one place to another. In much the same way the computer programs that use these causal maps can do the same kinds of sophisticated counterfactual reasoning that human scientists—and children—do. These programs can make medical diagnoses and suggest possible treatments, or make suggestions about what might help prevent climate change. NASA has explored using these ideas in the next generation of Mars robots.

The core idea of cognitive science is that our brains are a kind of computer, though far more powerful than any of the actual computers we know about. Psychologists try to find out exactly what kinds of programs, our brains use, and how our brains implement those programs. Since children are so good at understanding causes, we thought that children's brains just might be constructing causal maps and using them in the same way as the computer programs. In fact, collaborating with the philosophers and computer scientists gave me the causal map idea in the first place. (For many years, in many bars, I argued with Glymour about whether my babies were smarter than his computers. The answer, of course, is that they're smarter in some ways but not others—but still, overall, after ten years of experiments, I've got him voting for the babies.)

Detecting Blickets

How could we find out whether children really do make causal maps of the world around them, and use them to imagine new possibilities and to make the world different? How could we discover if they use the same kinds of programs as the expert computers? One thing we could do is actually to introduce three- and four-year-olds to new causal events and see if they could use that knowledge to make predictions, design new interventions, and consider new possibilities. That way we could know for sure that the children were drawing these conclusions based just on the causal information we gave them—the new map—and nothing else.

With the help of the guys in the shop and the graduate students in my lab, I invented a machine we call the "blicket detector." The machine is a square box that lights up and plays music when some blocks, but not others, are placed on top of it. We tell children, "Look, here's my blicket machine! Blickets make the machine go. Can you tell me which things are the blickets?" Children are fascinated by the machine and immediately begin to explore and experiment to find out more about how it works and which things are blickets—trying out blocks on the machine, pressing harder or softer, even scratching on the blocks to find out what might be inside them.

The truth, fortunately unsuspected by any of the children, is what we might call Wizard of Oz causality. There is a little man, or rather an undergraduate research assistant, behind a curtain pressing buttons to make the machine go. My youngest son, Andres, was a pilot subject—aka guinea pig—for the blicket detector experiments. After several months I finally explained to him how it really worked. He reacted pretty much like Neo in *The Matrix* when he wakes up and realizes that the world is just an elaborate deception. (At twenty, he has forgiven me, possibly because he thinks this experience is a precursor to saving the universe, or at least dating Carrie Moss.)

Once the children start to discover which blocks make the machine go, they can use that information to envision new possibilities and make new predictions, including counterfactual predictions. In one of the first tests we did we taught children that a particular block was a blicket that activated the machine, and then combined the blicket with a nonblicket and put both of them on the machine. The machine, of course, still lit up. One of the first four-year-olds we tested immediately came up with a counterfactual any philosopher would be proud of. "But s'pose," he said excitedly, "you didn't put on the blicket that time, s'pose you only put on that one (pointing to the nonblicket) then it wouldn't have gone."

If you ask children to make the machine go they will choose only the blickets. More tellingly, if you ask them to make the machine stop, they will say that you have to remove the blicket, even though they have never seen anyone stop the machine this way before. They can use the new causal information to draw the right kinds of conclusions, including counterfactual conclusions. They can imagine what will happen if you take the blicket off the machine or what might have happened if you had taken it off before.

New causal knowledge can lead to bigger changes, too. Figuring out which block makes the machine go or stop may not seem like a big deal. But my student Laura Schulz and I decided to do the same experiment in a different way. We showed the children a similar machine with a switch attached. The children didn't know how this new machine worked. Then we asked them whether the machine would go on if you flicked the switch, and whether it would go on if you just told it to go. At first, every single one of the children said that the switch could make the machine go, but simply talking to it couldn't. These children have learned that machines work differently than people do.

But then, if we actually demonstrate that talking to the machine causes it to light up, children change their minds. If you ask them to make the machine stop they very politely say, "Machine, please stop," instead of reaching for the switch. And if you ask the children to predict what will make a new machine go, they are much more willing to entertain the "talk to it" possibility than they were before, though they still think the switch is a better bet. Giving the children new causal knowledge changed the way they thought about possibilities, and changed the kinds of actions they would take. Children could imagine a listening machine that had seemed downright impossible before.

In the same way, for adult scientists, new causal knowledge allows us to imagine possibilities that would have seemed unimaginable before. In science fiction films, where imagination should run riot, what strikes you most is that the directors' imaginations are so limited by their current knowledge. In *Blade Runner,* for example, Harrison Ford runs desperately to a pay phone—with a video screen. The screenwriters could imagine a pay phone with a TV, but not that pay phones would disappear altogether. Nothing is more dated than visions of the future, because to imagine the future's possibilities, we need to have the future's knowledge.

Often, people treat knowledge and imagination as if they were different, even as if they were necessarily opposed to each other, but the new work on causal maps suggests just the opposite. Understanding the causal structure of the world and generating counterfactuals go hand in hand. In fact, knowledge is actually what gives imagination its power, what makes creativity possible. It's because we know something about how events are connected in the world that we can imagine altering those connections and creating new ones. It's because we know about this world that we can create possible worlds.

This profoundly human blend of knowledge and imagination isn't just the province of adults. In fact, it underpins even the wildest childhood fantasies. The three-year-old pretending to be a fairy princess isn't just being adorable and creative. She's also demonstrating a uniquely human kind of intelligence. And with these new scientific ideas in hand we can think about many other kinds of imagination in new ways. In the next chapter I'll talk about the distinctive kind of imagination that creates imaginary people, and about the way this is related to the grown-up play of writers and actors.

Points of Engagement—Reading Comprehension

1. What is a "counterfactual"? Describe it in your own words. How does it allow children to interact in the world?
2. According to Alison Gopnik, what is the cognitive relationship between knowledge and imagination? What is surprising or un-conventional about her position? Find three quotations from her chapter that support your answers.

3. On page 169, Gopnik writes that "learning language gives children a whole powerful new way to imagine." What does she mean by that? Would a child who is speech-delayed necessarily have a less-developed imagination? Why or why not?

Points of Departure—Assignment Questions

1. According to Alison Gopnik, "Even very young children constantly think about future, past, and present possible worlds" (171). How does this ability to think about "possible worlds" encourage or discourage religious beliefs? Answer this question using essays by Alison Gopnik, and either Wendell Berry or Jane Goodall.
2. What can we learn about the world and our place in it by looking through the eyes of a child? Consider this question by using Alison Gopnik's "Possible Worlds: Why do Children Pretend?" and one of the following authors: Adam Gopnik, Zadie Smith, Sherry Turkle, Jeanette Winterson, or Kenji Yoshino.
3. According to Alison Gopnik, "people treat knowledge and imagination as if they were different…but the new work…suggests just the opposite" (181). If knowledge and imagination are integrated, as Gopnik suggests, how should this shape the ways children are socialized and educated? Answer this question using Alison Gopnik and one of the following authors: Amy Chua or Nicholas Kristof and Sheryl WuDunn.
4. By examining how children think and learn, Alison Gopnik gives us a very fluid sense of time and the relation between past, present, and future. When we mess with time, we also mess with reality: what was, what is, what could be, what might have been. For this paper, use Gopnik's research into the "possible worlds" she describes as part of human perception, in order to answer the following question: How does the passing of time change the way we view reality? Use Gopnik's ideas to consider the experiences in essays by Gregory Orr, Alain de Botton, Zadie Smith, Sherry Turkle, or the short story by Jeanette Winterson.
5. Several authors in this reader offer descriptions of our brains or our minds as "maps" or "blueprints" or "grids." How does thinking of our brains in these ways help us to understand how we make decisions? How do our emotional responses figure into all the logic of decision-making? In making decisions, are we following a map, or creating one as we go? Answer these questions using essays by Alison Gopnik and either Susan Blackmore, Alain de Botton, or Lauren Slater.

From the Frying Pan into the Fire

Arlie Russell Hochschild

Points of Access—Pre-Reading

1. Do you think that shopping—shopping at the mall, shopping for groceries, etc.—has a closer connection with your leisure time, and the time you spend with friends and family, or with your work life? Are there different kinds of shopping? What makes them different? What aspects of your attitude toward shopping make you associate it with leisure, or with work?
2. In your own words, what is capitalism? What is it for? What does it do? Do you think it affects your life in any direct way? Look up capitalism in your dictionary or online after you've thought about your own ideas concerning what it is, and see how the two match up. Did you see anything unexpected in the definition? What?
3. When you hear the word "busy" what do you think of? Does it have a negative or positive connotation? Do you consider yourself a busy person? Is that mostly good or bad? Why?
4. Unlike many other countries, the United States has very few public holidays, designated by the state as times for work to stop, and time to be given instead to family and community. Thanksgiving and Memorial Day are two of only a few weekday holidays. Consider how you would feel if you had a holiday like Thanksgiving or Memorial Day every couple of months, where every store shut, all services were at their minimal level—in fact, the whole country took the day off. How would that affect you? At all? Why would this kind of regular, state-sanctioned vacation time be a good idea? Why would it be bad, or inconvenient? Think also, about which you look forward to the most: Thanksgiving itself with your family, the long weekend away from work or school, or the shopping day in between?

An advertisement for Quaker Oats cereal in an issue of *Working Mother* magazine provides a small window on the interplay between consumption and the application of the idea of efficiency to private time in modern America.[1] In the ad, a mother,

[1]See Hochschild 1997a.

dressed in a business suit, affectionately hugs her smiling son. Beneath the image, we read: "Instant Quaker Oatmeal, for moms who have a lot of love but not a lot of time."

The ad continues with a short story: "Nicky is a very picky eater. With Instant Quaker Oatmeal, I can give him a terrific hot breakfast in just 90 seconds. And I don't have to spend any time coaxing him to eat it!"

The ad then presents "facts" about mother and child: "Sherry Greenberg, with Nicky, age four and a half, Hometown: New York City, New York, Occupation: Music teacher, Favorite Flavor: Apples and Cinnamon." The designers of this ad, we could imagine, want us to feel we've been let in on an ordinary moment in a middle-class American morning. In this ordinary moment, Sherry Greenberg is living according to a closely scheduled, rapidly paced "adult" time, while Nicky is living according to a more dawdling, slowly paced "child" time. So the mother faces a dilemma. To meet her work deadline, she must get Nicky on "adult" time. But to be a good mother it is desirable to give her child a hot breakfast—"hot" being associated with devotion and love. To cook the hot breakfast, though, Sherry needs *time*. The ad suggests that it is the cereal itself that solves the problem. It conveys love because it is hot, but it permits efficiency because it's quickly made. The cereal would seem to reconcile an image of American motherhood of the 1950s with the female work role of 2000 and beyond.

The cereal also allows Sherry to avoid the unpleasant task of struggling with her child over scarce time. In the ad, Nicky's slow pace is implicitly attributed to his character ("Nicky is a very picky eater") and not to the fact that he is being harnessed to an accelerating pace of adult work time or protesting an adult speed-up by staging a "slowdown." By permitting the mother to avoid a fight with her son over time, the ad brilliantly evokes a common problem and proposes a commodity as a solution.

Attached to the culture of time shown in the ad is a key but hidden social logic. This modern working mother is portrayed as resembling Frederick Taylor, the famed efficiency expert of modern industry. The principle of efficiency is not located, here, at work in the person of the owner, the foreman, or the worker. It is located in the worker-as-mother. We do not see a boss pressing the worker for more efficiency at the office. Instead, we see a mother pressing her son to eat more efficiently at home. This efficiency-seeking is transferred from man to woman, from workplace to home, and from adult to child. Nicky becomes his own task master, quickly gobbling his breakfast himself because it is so delicious. Frederick Taylor has leapt the fence from factory to home, adult to child, and jumped, it seems, into the cereal box itself. Frederick Taylor has become a commodity. *It* provides efficiency. Thus, the market reinforces the idea of efficiency twice—once at a locus of production, where the worker is pressed to work efficiently, and again, as a supplier of consumer goods, where it promises to deliver the very efficiency it also demands.

Quaker Oats cereal may be a paradigm for a growing variety of goods and services—frozen dinners, computer shopping services, cell phones,[2] and the like—that claim to save time for busy working parents. They often save time at home. But the ethic of "saving time" raises the question of what we want to save time for.[3] In the case above, the photo of the happy mother and child suggests that the mother is rushing her son through breakfast, not to race out to an all-absorbing job at a dot-com company, but to teach a few piano lessons. The picture doesn't challenge our idea of the primacy, even sacredness, of Nicky's home. So we don't much notice the sly insinuation of Frederick Taylor into the scene.

Conventional versus Unconventional Wisdom

If, through modern Western eyes, the Greenbergs of this ad were a normal family, we could imagine them feeling that family life superseded all other aspects of life. That is, according to modern conventional wisdom, a happy family life is an end in itself. Earning and spending money are the means for achieving this end. Home and community are primary; workplace and mall are secondary. When we go out to work, it's to put bread on the table for the family. When we shop at the mall, it's often to buy a Christmas, birthday, or house present "for the family." Put in other terms, we often see the home and the community as sacred, and the workplace and the mall as profane. We are who we are at home and in our communities. We do what we do at work and buy what we buy at the mall.

---

[2]Cell phones, home fax machines, car dictating machines, and similar gadgets are marketed, purchased, and used on the premise that these machines, like the cereal, will "save time"so that the consumer can then enjoy more leisure. In practice, though, such technology often becomes a delivery system for pressure to do more paid work. Along with new technology come new norms. Electronic mail, for example, once hailed as a way of "saving time" has escalated expectations shortening the period of time one has before one is considered rude or inattentive not to reply.

[3]Among affluent Americans, time-saving goods and services also force parents to define parenthood less in terms of production and more in terms of consumption. For example, a "good mother" in the American middle class is often seen as one who prepares her child's birthday, bakes the cake, blows up the balloons, invites her child's friends to a party. Increasingly, the busy working mother is tempted to buy the cake; in addition, new birthday services are available in American cities to help organize the party, send out the invitations, buy the gifts, blow up the balloons, and set up the food. The definition of a "good mother" moves from production to consumption. The "good mother" is now one who enjoys the party with the child. The gift is one of derationalized time.

To be sure, we make exceptions for the odd workaholic here or shopaholic there, but, as the terms imply, an overconcern with the profane realms of work and mall are, given this way of seeing things, off moral limits. Sherry Greenberg fits right in. She is in her kitchen feeding her son. She has what one imagines to be a manageable job. It's just that she's wanting to hurry things along a bit.

Implicit in this conventional view of family life is the idea that our use of time is like a language. We speak through it. By either what we say we want to spend time doing or what we actually spend time doing, we say what it is we hold sacred. Maybe we don't think of it just this way, but we assume that each "spending time" or each statement of feeling about time ("I wish I could spend time") is a bow from the waist to what we hold dear. It is a form of worship. Again, Sherry Greenberg is symbolizing the importance of family. It's just that she's slightly on the edge of that conventional picture because she's in a hurry to get out of it. The Quaker Oats ad both appeals to this family-comes-first picture of life and subtly challenges it, by taking sides with her desire to feed Nicky "efficiently."

The subtle challenge of the ad points, I believe, to a larger contradiction underlying stories like that of the Greenbergs. Reflecting on my research on the Fortune 500 company I call Amerco, I'll try to explore it. Increasingly, our belief that family comes first conflicts with the emotional draw of both workplace and mall. Indeed, I would argue that a constellation of pressures is pushing men and women further into the world of workplace and mall. And television—a pipeline, after all, to the mall—is keeping them there. Family and community life have meanwhile become less central as places to talk and relate, and less the object of collective rituals.

Many of us respond to these twin trends, however, not by turning away from family and community, but by actually elevating them in moral importance. Family and community are not a realm in decline, as David Popenoe argues about the family and Robert Putnam argues for the community. To many people, both have become even more important morally. We encapsulate the idea of the cherished family.[4] We separate ideal from practice. We separate the idea of "spending time with X" from the idea of "believing in the importance of X." We don't link what we think with what we do. Or as one Amerco employee put it, using company language, "I don't walk the talk at home." This encapsulation of our family ideal allows us to accommodate to what is both a pragmatic necessity and a competing source of meaning—the religion of capitalism. I say pragmatic necessity, because most Americans, men and women alike, have to work for food and rent.

---

[4]See Gillis 1994; also Popenoe 1989 and Putnam 2000.

At the same time, a new cultural story is unfolding. It is not that capitalism is an unambiguous object of worship. After all, American capitalism is, in reality, a highly complex, internally diverse economic system for making, advertising, and selling things. But, without overstating the case, it seems true that capitalism is a cultural as well as an economic system and that the symbols and rituals of this cultural system compete with, however much they seem to serve, the symbols and rituals of community and family. This means that working long hours and spending a lot of money— instead of spending time together—have increasingly become *how* we say "I love you" at home. As Juliet Schor argues in *The Overspent American*, over the last twenty years, Americans have raised the bar on what feels like enough money to get along. In 1975, according to a Roper poll, 10 percent of people mentioned a second color TV as part of "the good life," and 28 percent did in 1991. A 1995 Merck Family Fund poll showed that 27 percent of people who earned $100,000 or more agreed with the statement, "I cannot afford to buy everything I really need." At the same time, between 1975 and 1991, the role of family in people's idea of "the good life" declined while the importance of having money increased. The importance of having a happy marriage to "the good life" declined from 84 percent in 1975 to 77 percent in 1991. Meanwhile having "a lot of money" went from 38 percent in 1975 to 55 percent in 1991.[5]

How much of a stretch is it, I wonder, to go from the trends Schor points out to Harvey Cox's daring thesis: that capitalism has become a religion? As Cox puts it:

> Just as a truly global market has emerged for the first time in human history, that market is functioning without moral guideposts and restraints, and it has become the most powerful institution of our age. Even nation-states can often do little to restrain or regulate it. More and more, the idea of "the market" is construed, not as a creation of culture ("made by human hands," as the Bible says about idols), but as the "natural" way things happen. For this reason, the "religion" the market generates often escapes criticism and evaluation or even notice. It becomes as invisible to those who live by it as was the religion of the preliterate Australians whom Durkheim studied, who described it as just "the way things are."[6]

Capitalism has, Cox suggests, its myth of origin, its legends of the fall, its doctrine of sin and redemption, its notion of sacrifice (state belt-tightening), and its hope of salvation through the free market system. Indeed, if in the Middle Ages the church provided people with a basic orientation to life, the multinational corporation's workplace,

---

[5]Schor 1998, pp. 16–17

[6]Cox 2001, p. 124.

with its "mission statements," its urgent deadlines, its demands for peak performance and total quality, does so today. Paradoxically, what would seem like the most secular of systems (capitalism), organized around the most profane of activities (making a living, shopping), provides a sense of the sacred. So what began as a *means* to an end—capitalism the means, a good living as the end—has become an *end* itself. It's a case of mission drift writ large. The cathedrals of capitalism dominate our cities. Its ideology dominates our airwaves. It calls for sacrifice, through long hours of work, and offers its blessings, through commodities. When the terrorists struck the twin towers on 9/11, they were, perhaps, aiming at what they conceived of as a more powerful rival temple, another religion. Heartless as they were, they were correct to see capitalism, and the twin towers as its symbol, as a serious rival religion.

Like older religions, capitalism partly creates the anxieties to which it poses itself as a necessary answer. Like the fire-and-brimstone sermon that begins with "Man, the lowly sinner," and ends with "Only this church can redeem you," so the market ethos defines the poor or unemployed as "unworthy slackers" and offers work and a higher standard of living as a form of salvation. Capitalism is not, then, simply a system in the *service of* family and community; it *competes* with the family. When we separate our fantasy of family life, our ideas of being a "good mother and father" from our daily expressions of parenthood, our ideals live timelessly on while we worship at the biggest altar in town, with ten-hour days and long trips to the mall.

A constellation of forces seems to be pressing in the direction of the religion of capitalism. And while no one wants to go back to the "frying pan" of patriarchy, we need to look sharp about the fire of market individualism under capitalism. It is in the spirit of looking at that fire that we can examine several conditions that exacerbate the tendency to apply the principle of efficiency to private life.

The first factor is the inevitable—and on the whole I think beneficial—movement of women into the paid workforce.[7] Exacerbating this squeeze on time is the overall absence of government or workplace policies that foster the use of parental leave or shorter, more flexible hours. Over the last twenty years, workers have also been squeezed by a lengthening workweek. According to a recent International Labor Organization report on working hours, Americans are putting in longer hours than workers of any other industrialized nation. We now work two weeks longer each year than our counterparts

[7]Some commentators blame women's movement into paid work for the strains experienced at home—including the high divorce rate. But I would argue that it is not women's paid work per se, but work in the absence of the necessary social adjustments in the structure of care—male sharing of care at home, family-friendly workplace policies, and social honor associated with care—that make the difference.

in Japan, the vaunted long-work-hour capital of the world.[8] American married couples and single-parent families are also putting in more hours in the day and more weeks in the year than they did thirty years ago. Counting overtime and commuting time, a 1992 national sample of men averaged 48.8 hours of work, and women, 41.7.[9] Work patterns vary by social class, ethnicity, race, and the number and ages of children, of course. But, overall, between 1969 and 1996 the increase in American mothers' paid work combined with a shift toward single-parent families has led to an average decrease of 22 hours a week of parental time available (outside of paid work) to spend with children.[10] And the emotional draw of a work culture is sometimes strong enough to out-compete a weaker family culture (see "Emotional Geography and the Flight Plan of Capitalism," Chapter 15).

The Other Side of the Market Religion: Not Walking the Talk at Home

If capitalism began as a means but became an end in itself, then families and local communities must daily face a competing urgency system and a rival conception of time. Company deadlines compete with school plays. Holiday sales at the mall vie with hanging out at home. The company's schedule and rules have come, for workers, to define those of families. For the managers and production workers at Amerco, the company I studied for the *Time Bind*, the debut of a certain kind of product and its "product life cycle" came to prevail over personal anniversaries and school holidays. When family events did take precedence, they did so on company terms. As one woman explained, "My mother died and I went back to arrange for the funeral and all. I went for four days. The company gives us that for bereavement, and so that's the time I spent." In the early industrial period in Europe, whole workforces disappeared at festival time, or workers put an iron bar in the machinery, stopped the assembly line, and took a break. Company time did not always rule.

---

[8]Doohan 1999. The 600-page ILO report compared hours of work in 240 countries. Useem (2000) cites 751 time-management titles listed on Amazon.com, including *Eating on the Run*, and *Please Hold: 102 Things to Do While You Wait on the Phone.*

[9]Galinsky, Bond, and Friedman 1993, p. 9.

[10] "Families and the Labor Market, 1969-1999: Analyzing the Time Crunch," May 1999, Report by the Council of Economic Advisors, Washington, D.C. Also a 2000 report found that 46 percent of workers work 41 hours or longer, 18 percent of them 51 hours or longer (see Center for Survey Research and Analysis, University of Connecticut, "2000 Report on U.S. Working Time"). Another recent study found that elementary school teachers—those in what is often thought to be a "woman's" job—reported working ten-hour days (see Drago et al. 1999). Less time away from work means less time for children. Nationwide, half of children wish they could see their fathers more, and a third wish they could see their mothers more (Coolsen, Seligson, and Garbino 1985; Hewlett 1991, p. 105). A growing number of commentators draw links, often carelessly, between this decline in family time and a host of problems, including school failure and alcohol and drug abuse (Hewlett 1991).

In response to the challenge of this competing urgency system, I've argued, many families separate their ideal of themselves as "a close family" from a life that in reality is more hurried, fragmented, crowded, and individualized than they would like. They develop the idea of a hypothetical family, the family they would be if only they had time. And then they deal with life in a contrary fashion.

Many Amerco employees came home from a long workday to fit many necessary activities into a limited amount of time. Although there were important exceptions, many workers tried to go through domestic chores rapidly if for no other reason than to clear some space in which to go slowly. They used many strategies to save time—they planned, delegated, did several things simultaneously. They packed one activity close up against the next, eliminating the framing around each event, periods of looking forward to or back upon an event, which might have heightened its emotional impact. A 2:00 to 2:45 play date, 2:45 to 3:15 shopping trip, 3:15 to 4:45 visit to Grandma, and so on. As one mother, a sales manager, said with satisfaction, "What makes me a good employee at work is what makes me able to do all I do at home; I'm a multitasker, but [with a laugh] at work I get paid for it."

With all these activities, family time could be called "hurried" or "crowded." But in fact many working parents took a sporting "have fun" attitude toward their hurried lives: "Let's see how fast we can do this! Come on, kids, let's go!" They brought their image of the family closer to the reality of it by saying, in effect, "We like it this way." They saw hassle as challenge. In other families, parents seemed to encourage children to develop schedules parallel to and as hectic as their own. For example, the average annual vacation time both at Amerco—and in the United States as a whole—is twelve days, while schoolchildren typically have summer holidays of three months. So one Amerco mother placed her eight-year-old son in a nearby summer program and explained to him, in a you're-going-to-love-this way, "You have your job to go to, too." She talked about her schedule as she might have talked about a strenuous hike. She was having fun roughing it with multitasking and chopped-up time.

Another way of resolving the contradiction between ideal and reality was to critique the fun ethic and say, in effect, "Family life isn't supposed to be fun. It's supposed to be a hassle, but we're in the hassle together, and why isn't that okay?" This often carried families over long stretches of time, but it prevented family members from giving full attention to each other. Time was hurried (not enough time allotted for an activity—15-minute baths, 20-minute dinners, for example). Or time was crowded (one or more people were doing more than one thing at a time). Or it was uncoordinated. Only two out of four people could make it to dinner, the ball game, the reunion. If there was not some chronic avoidance of a deep tension, families usually also took another approach. They *deferred* having a good time. Instead of saying, "This hassle is fun," they said, in effect, "This hassle isn't fun. But we'll have fun *later.*" They waited for the weekend, for their vacation, for "quality time."

But the more a family deferred the chance for relaxed communication, the more anxious they sometimes became about it. One man told me: "My wife and I hadn't had time together for a long time, so we decided to take some 'marital quality time' by going out to a restaurant to eat dinner together. We had a nice dinner and afterwards went for a walk. We passed a toy store and my wife wanted to shop for a toy for our child. But I told her, 'No, you have a different quality time with our child. This is *our* quality time.' So we spent the rest of the evening arguing about whose quality time it was we were spending."

Another long-hours Amerco executive seemed to take this strategy of deferral to an extreme. When I asked him whether he wished he'd spent more time with his three daughters when they were growing up, he answered, "Put it this way, I'm pleased with how they turned out." This father loved his daughters, but he loved them as results. Or rather, his feeling was "I want my wife to enjoy the process of raising them. I'll enjoy that vicariously. What I will enjoy directly is the result, the young adults." So he didn't think family life should or shouldn't be fun while the kids were small and adolescent. That was his wife's specialty. He was deferring his real enjoyment until his daughters had grown up. Even Amerco parents who spent far more time with their children occasionally justified this time in terms of future results. They were pleased at how "old for their age" their children were, how "ahead," given a limited expenditure of parental time. Perhaps, most parents held a double perspective on their children—they cared about the child as he or she was growing up and about the child as he or she emerged in adulthood. Most oriented toward the family as a source of intrinsic pleasure were women and workers in the middle or lower ranks of the company; least oriented in this way were upper management or professional men—the congregation and the priests.

From the top to the bottom of the Amerco workforce, workers were forced to answer the challenge of capitalism—not simply as a system that gave them jobs, money, and stuff, but as a system that offered them a sense of purpose and guidance in a confusing time. They had to deal with the religion of capitalism, its grip on honor and sense of worth, its subtraction from—or absorption of—family and community life. We've emerged from an era in which most women had little or no paid work to a era in which most do. Are women jumping from the frying pan of patriarchy into the fire of capitalism? Just as the early industrial workforces took off at festival time, because they were not yet "disciplined" to capitalism, maybe postindustrial ones will work out their own way of living a balanced life. There could be a balance not just between the role of piano teacher, say, and mother, but between the unpaid *world* of home and community and the money *world* of work and mall. That may be the deeper issue underlying the ad for Quaker Oats cereal. For, our cultural soil is surreptitiously prepared for ads, like that for Quaker Oats cereal, that make you spend time buying one more thing that promises to save time—which increasingly we spend earning and buying.

Points of Engagement—Reading Comprehension

1. Consider Hochschild's title, "From the Frying Pan into the Fire." What is the "frying pan" she is talking about? What is the fire? Quote from her text in support of your answer. Why are these two metaphors useful to her? What other significance is there to her using this expression?
2. Hochschild describes a "constellation of pressures [that are] pushing men and women further into the world of workplace and mall" (186).Why does Hochschild group "workplace and mall" together in this context? What pressures does she identify? List them from the text. How does she suggest we might deal with or lessen these pressures? Do you find her suggestions realistic? Why or why not?
3. Why does Hochschild treat capitalism as a religion? Give reasons from the text. What do you think of these reasons? Has Hochschild taken the comparison too far, or do you think she represents American society accurately?

Points of Departure—Assignment Questions

1. All the families in Hochschild's essay seem very busy. Adam Gopnik and Sherry Turkle also observe this aspect of American life. How do these three authors approach the phenomenon of our busy lives as they affect our relationships with other people? What's the main project of each author? Why kinds of critiques are they each offering? Do they take the same position on the causes and effects of "busyness"? Write a paper in which you engage with each author's position on the role of "busyness" in our lives, and offer your own assessment of their observations.
2. According to Hochschild, "the emotional draw of a work culture is sometimes strong enough to out-compete a weaker family structure" (189). In her essay, Hochschild

shows, as it were, a worst-case scenario for the American family. What happens, though, when that "work culture" is focused on the family itself? In "Why Chinese Mothers are Superior," Amy Chua gives us an entirely different picture of the role of "work" in family life. How does each author define "work" and its relationship with family? How does that definition affect the way they observe and approach parenthood and raising children? For example, how is Amy Chua's family similar to the families in Hochschild's essay? How are they different? What are the goals and rewards of "work" in each? Use each essay to examine the argument of the other: How does Chua's critique of Western parenting change the way we read Hochschild's argument about American families and their emphasis on work? How does Hochschild's focus on "American" culture, in particular, influence the way we read Chua's argument regarding Chinese parenting? For this paper you will be thinking, in part, about the differences between the adult world and the child world, but your focus should be on this idea of "work" which bridges both. You might also use Adam Gopnik's essay to enrich your paper.

3. Consider the following quotation from Hochschild's essay: "Family and community life have … become less central as places to talk and relate, and less the object of collective rituals" (186). Janet Flammang also observes a decrease in "food rituals in America's fast-paced, workaholic culture" (112). Why is each author so concerned about the decline in these rituals? What role does food and food preparation have in signaling this decline? What else do the authors hold responsible for the decline in our family ties? What are the broader consequences for each? Assuming the assault on American family structure is real, which set of problems do you find more responsible for the current state of things? Stake out their positions in your paper, and provide your own critique of their arguments. Which author provides more compelling solutions for the problems they identify for American families today?
4. Consider the following quotation from Hochschild's essay: "So what has become a means to an end – capitalism the means, good living as the end – has become an end in itself" (188). Hochschild makes the above observation about the effects of capitalism, mostly directing her attention to middle-class American society. How does the argument about the benefits and drawbacks to capitalism change in a developing nation? In their chapter, Nicholas Kristof and Sheryl WuDunn show a very different side of economic development and capitalism. Do the female workers whom Kristof and WuDunn discuss bear out Hochschild's observation? How, or how not? How are the workers they talk about different from the middle-class

Americans, such as those at Amerco as discussed by Hochschild? How are they the same? Does the pervasiveness of capitalism as an end in itself threaten more than just leisure time? Or does the possibility for "good living" provided by capitalism, and for "transformation" and "emancipation" (Kristof/WuDunn), especially for women, outweigh the risks?

Fences of Enclosure, Windows of Possibility

Naomi Klein

Points of Access—Pre-Reading

1. Have you ever participated in a protest? If so, what was the experience like? Who or what were the memorable moments of the rally? Was the demonstration successful? If you haven't participated in a protest, do you think you ever would? Why or why not? For what cause/s?
2. In your lifetime, what services or programs, that were formally public, became privatized? Conversely, what privatized functions have become free for public use?
3. You may have heard of the term "freedom fighter." What does this mean to you? Where would you draw the line between an activist and a terrorist?
4. How would you feel if you had to pay for access to clean water or primary education? What barriers, either physical or economic, existed in the community where you grew up?

A few months ago, while riffling through my column clippings searching for a lost statistic, I noticed a couple of recurring themes and images. The first was the fence. The image came up again and again: barriers separating people from previously public resources, locking them away from much needed land and water, restricting their ability to move across borders, to express political dissent, to demonstrate on public streets, even keeping politicians from enacting policies that make sense for the people who elected them.

Some of these fences are hard to see, but they exist all the same. A virtual fence goes up around schools in Zambia when an education "user fee" is introduced on the advice of the World Bank, putting classes out of the reach of millions of people. A fence goes up around the family farm in Canada when government policies turn small-scale agriculture into a luxury item, unaffordable in a landscape of tumbling commodity prices and factory farms. There is a real if invisible fence that goes up around clean water in Soweto when prices skyrocket owing to privatization, and residents are forced to turn to contaminated sources. And there is a fence that goes up around the very idea of democracy when Argentina is told it won't get an International Monetary Fund loan unless it further reduces social spending, privatizes more resources and eliminates supports to local industries, all in the midst of an economic crisis deepened by those very policies. These fences, of course, are as old as colonialism. "Such usurious operations put bars around free nations," Eduardo Galeano wrote in *Open Veins of Latin America.* He was referring to the terms of a British loan to Argentina in 1824.

Fences have always been a part of capitalism, the only way to protect property from would-be bandits, but the double standards propping up these fences have, of late, become increasingly blatant. Expropriation of corporate holdings may be the greatest sin any socialist government can commit in the eyes of the international financial markets (just ask Venezuela's Hugo Chavez or Cuba's Fidel Castro). But the asset protection guaranteed to companies under free trade deals did not extend to the Argentine citizens who deposited their life savings in Citibank, Scotiabank and HSBC accounts and now find that most of their money has simply disappeared. Neither did the market's reverence for private wealth embrace the U.S. employees of Enron, who found that they had been "locked out" of their privatized retirement portfolios, unable to sell even as Enron executives were frantically cashing in their own stocks.

Meanwhile, some very necessary fences are under attack: in the rush to privatization, the barriers that once existed between many public and private spaces—keeping advertisements out of schools, for instance, profit-making interests out of health care, or news outlets from acting purely as promotional vehicles for their owners' other holdings—have nearly all been levelled. Every protected public space has been cracked open, only to be re-enclosed by the market.

Another public-interest barrier under serious threat is the one separating genetically modified crops from crops that have not yet been altered. The seed giants have done such a remarkably poor job of preventing their tampered seeds from blowing into neighbouring fields, taking root, and cross-pollinating, that in many parts of the world, eating GMO-free is no longer even an option—the entire food supply has been contaminated. The fences that protect the public interest seem to be fast disappearing, while the ones that restrict our liberties keep multiplying.

When I first noticed that the image of the fence kept coming up in discussion, debates and in my own writing, it seemed significant to me. After all, the past decade of economic integration has been fuelled by promises of barriers coming down, of increased mobility and greater freedom. And yet twelve years after the celebrated collapse of the Berlin Wall, we are surrounded by fences yet again, cut off—from one another, from the earth and from our own ability to imagine that change is possible. The economic process that goes by the benign euphemism "globalization" now reaches into every aspect of life, transforming every activity and natural resource into a measured and owned commodity. As the Hong Kong-based labour researcher Gerard Greenfield points out, the current stage of capitalism is not simply about trade in the traditional sense of selling more products across borders. It is also about feeding the market's insatiable need for growth by redefining as "products" entire sectors that were previously considered part of "the commons" and not for sale. The invading of the public by the private has reached into categories such as health and education, of course, but also ideas, genes, seeds, now purchased, patented and fenced off, as well as traditional aboriginal remedies, plants, water and even human stem cells. With copyright now the U.S.'s single largest export (more than manufactured goods or arms), international trade law must be understood not only as taking down selective barriers to trade but more accurately as a process that systematically puts up new barriers—around knowledge, technology and newly privatized resources. These Trade Related Intellectual Property Rights are what prevent farmers from replanting their Monsanto patented seeds and make it illegal for poor countries to manufacture cheaper generic drugs to get to their needy populations.

Globalization is now on trial because on the other side of all these virtual fences are real people, shut out of schools, hospitals, workplaces, their own farms, homes and communities. Mass privatization and deregulation have bred armies of locked-out people, whose services are no longer needed, whose lifestyles are written off as "backward," whose basic needs go unmet. These fences of social exclusion can discard an entire industry, and they can also write off an entire country, as has happened to Argentina. In the case of Africa, essentially an entire continent can find itself exiled to the global shadow world, off the map and off the news, appearing only during wartime when its citizens are looked on with suspicion as potential militia members, would-be terrorists or anti-American fanatics.

In fact, remarkably few of globalization's fenced-out people turn to violence. Most simply move: from countryside to city, from country to country. And that's when they come face to face with distinctly unvirtual fences, the ones made of chain link and razor wire, reinforced with concrete and guarded with machine guns. Whenever I hear the phrase "free trade," I can't help picturing the caged factories I visited in the Philippines and Indonesia that are all surrounded by gates, watchtowers and soldiers—to keep the highly subsidized products from leaking out and the union organizers from getting in. I think, too, about a recent trip to the South Australian desert where I visited the infamous Woomera detention centre. Located five hundred kilometres from the nearest city, Woomera is a former military base that has been converted into a privatized refugee holding pen, owned by a subsidiary of the U.S. security firm Wackenhut. At Woomera, hundreds of Afghan and Iraqi refugees, fleeing oppression and dictatorship in their own countries, are so desperate for the world to see what is going on behind the fence that they stage hunger strikes, jump off the roofs of their barracks, drink shampoo and sew their mouths shut.

These days, newspapers are filled with gruesome accounts of asylum seekers attempting to make it across national borders by hiding themselves among the products that enjoy so much more mobility than they do. In December 2001, the bodies of eight Romanian refugees, including two children, were discovered in a cargo container filled with office furniture; they had asphyxiated during the long journey at sea. The same year, the dead bodies of two more refugees were discovered in Eau Claire, Wisconsin, in a shipment of bathroom fixtures. The year before, fifty-four Chinese refugees from Fujian province suffocated in the back of a delivery truck in Dover, England.

All these fences are connected: the real ones, made of steel and razor wire, are needed to enforce the virtual ones, the ones that put resources and wealth out of the hands of so many. It simply isn't possible to lock away this much of our collective wealth without an accompanying strategy to control popular unrest and mobility. Security firms do their biggest business in the cities where the gap between rich and poor is greatest—Johannesburg, Sao Paulo, New Delhi—selling iron gates, armoured cars, elaborate alarm systems and renting out armies of private guards. Brazilians, for instance, spend US$4.5 billion a year on private security, and the country's 400,000 armed rent-a-cops outnumber actual police officers by almost four to one. In deeply divided South Africa, annual spending on private security has reached US$1.6 billion, more than three times what the government spends each year on affordable housing. It now seems that these gated compounds protecting the haves from the have-nots are microcosms of what is fast becoming a global security state—not a global village intent on lowering walls and barriers, as we were promised, but a network of fortresses connected by highly militarized trade corridors.

If this picture seems extreme, it may only be because most of us in the West rarely see the fences and the artillery. The gated factories and refugee detention centres remain tucked away in remote places, less able to pose a direct challenge to the seductive rhetoric of the borderless world. But over the past few years, some fences have intruded into full view—often, fittingly, during the summits where this brutal model of globalization is advanced. It is now taken for granted that if world leaders want to get together to discuss a new trade deal, they will need to build a modern-day fortress to protect themselves from public rage, complete with armoured tanks, tear gas, water cannons and attack dogs. When Quebec City hosted the Summit of the Americas in April 2001, the Canadian government took the unprecedented step of building a cage around, not just the conference centre, but the downtown core, forcing residents to show official documentation to get to their homes and workplaces. Another popular strategy is to hold the summits in inaccessible locations: the 2002 G8 meeting was held deep in the Canadian Rocky Mountains, and the 2001 WTO meeting took place in the repressive Gulf State of Qatar, where the emir bans political protests. The "war on terrorism" has become yet another fence to hide behind, used by summit organizers to explain why public shows of dissent just won't be possible this time around or, worse, to draw threatening parallels between legitimate protesters and terrorists bent on destruction.

But what are reported as menacing confrontations are often joyous events, as much experiments in alternative ways of organizing societies as criticisms of existing models. The first time I participated in one of these counter-summits, I remember having the distinct feeling that some sort of political portal was opening up—a gateway, a window, "a crack in history," to use Subcomandante Marcos's beautiful phrase. This opening had little to do with the broken window at the local McDonald's, the image so favoured by television cameras; it was something else: a sense of possibility, a blast of fresh air, oxygen rushing to the brain. These protests—which are actually week-long marathons of intense education on global politics, late-night strategy sessions in six-way simultaneous translation, festivals of music and street theatre—are like stepping into a parallel universe. Overnight, the site is transformed into a kind of alternative global city where urgency replaces resignation, corporate logos need armed guards, people usurp cars, art is everywhere, strangers talk to each other, and the prospect of a radical change in political course does not seem like an odd and anachronistic idea but the most logical thought in the world.

Even the heavy-handed security measures have been co-opted by activists into part of the message: the fences that surround the summits become metaphors for an economic model that exiles billions to poverty and exclusion. Confrontations are staged at the fence—but not only the ones involving sticks and bricks: tear-gas canisters have been flicked back with hockey sticks, water cannons have been irreverently challenged with toy water pistols and buzzing helicopters mocked with swarms of paper airplanes. During the Summit of the Americas in Quebec City, a group of activists built a medieval-style wooden catapult, wheeled it up to the three-metre-high fence that enclosed the downtown and lofted teddy bears over the top. In Prague, during a meeting of the World Bank and the International Monetary Fund, the Italian direct-action group Tute Blanche decided not to confront the black-clad riot police dressed in similarly threatening ski masks and bandanas; instead, they marched to the police line in white jumpsuits stuffed with rubber tires and Styrofoam padding. In a standoff between Darth Vader and an army of Michelin Men, the police couldn't win. Meanwhile, in another part of the city, the steep hillside leading up to the conference centre was scaled by a band of "pink fairies" dressed in burlesque wigs, silver-and-pink evening wear and platform shoes. These activists are quite serious in their desire to disrupt the current economic order, but their tactics reflect a dogged refusal to engage in classic power struggles: their goal, which I began to explore in the final pieces in this book, is not to take power for themselves but to challenge power centralization on principle.

Other kinds of windows are opening as well, quiet conspiracies to reclaim privatized spaces and assets for public use. Maybe it's students kicking ads out of their classrooms, or swapping music on-line, or setting up independent media centres with free software. Maybe it's Thai peasants planting organic vegetables on over-irrigated golf courses, or landless farmers in Brazil cutting down fences around unused lands and turning them into farming co-operatives. Maybe it's Bolivian workers reversing the privatization of their water supply, or South African township residents reconnecting their neighbours' electricity under the slogan Power to the People. And once reclaimed, these spaces are also being remade. In neighbourhood assemblies, at city councils, in independent media centres, in community-run forests and farms, a new culture of vibrant direct democracy is emerging, one that is fuelled and strengthened by direct participation, not dampened and discouraged by passive spectatorship.

Despite all the attempts at privatization, it turns out that there are some things that don't want to be owned. Music, water, seeds, electricity, ideas—they keep bursting out of the confines erected around them. They have a natural resistance to enclosure, a tendency to escape, to cross-pollinate, to flow through fences, and flee out open windows.

As I write this, it's not clear what will emerge from these liberated spaces, or if what emerges will be hardy enough to withstand the mounting attacks from the police and military, as the line between terrorist and activist is deliberately blurred. The question of what comes next preoccupies me, as it does everyone else who has been part of building this international movement. But this book is not an attempt to answer that question. It simply offers a view into the early life of the movement that exploded in Seattle and has evolved through the events of September 11 and its aftermath. I decided not to rewrite these articles, beyond a few very slight changes, usually indicated by square brackets—a reference explained, an argument expanded. They are presented here (more or less in chronological order) for what they are: postcards from dramatic moments in time, a record of the first chapter in a very old and recurring story, the one about people pushing up against the barriers that try to contain them, opening up windows, breathing deeply, tasting freedom.

Points of Engagement—Reading Comprehension

1. Naomi Klein writes, "All these fences are connected: the real ones made of steel and razor wire, are needed to reinforce the virtual ones, the ones that put resources and wealth out of the hands of so many" (198). In Klein's text, find three examples of real, physical fences and three examples of invisible barriers that separate people from each other or resources.
2. On pages 199 and 200, Klein mentions some rather unorthodox approaches used by activists in their struggles with corporations and governments. She writes, "These activists are quite serious in their desire to disrupt the current economic order, but their tactics reflect a dogged refusal to engage in classic power struggles; their goal...is not to take power for themselves but to challenge power centralization on principle." Choose two examples and explore the meaning and efficacy of these strategies. Do activists lose credibility in choosing unconventional methods? Can they gain more membership this way?
3. What is the role of copyright or patent law in maintaining the virtual fences that allow Western corporations to profit while limiting the well-being of developing countries? Klein claims that, "[C]opyright is now the U.S.'s single largest export..." (197). What does she mean? How does this contribute to her idea of fences?

Points of Departure—Assignment Questions

1. Naomi Klein has strong opinions on the power of fences to do both damage and good: "The fences that protect the public interest seem to be fast disappearing, while the ones that restrict our liberties keep multiplying" (196). What fences or barriers are ethical and beneficial to people? Which ones are harmful? How can we tell the difference? Look for examples in Belkin, Gladwell, and Yoshino. Remember, these barriers can be physical, legal, political, medical, economic or cultural.
2. Klein envisions protests as the precipice for change, as "alternative ways of organizing societies as criticisms of existing models" that bring "a sense of possibility, a blast of fresh air" (199). Can all protests lead to social change? When and how does activism produce results? What do those results look like? Review Orr, Gladwell, Kristof and WuDunn, Bremmer or Yoshino for moments when a "sense of possibility" emerged.

Which outcomes are successful and which are not? Find examples of individuals or groups who found themselves at "a crack in history" (199) and examine how events unfolded from there.

3. The idea of "direct democracy" inspires Klein. "In neighbourhood assemblies, at city councils, in independent media centres, in community-run forests and farms, a new culture of vibrant direct democracy is emerging, one that is fuelled and strengthened by direct participation, not dampened and discouraged by passive spectatorship" (200). How would Gladwell, Bremmer, Flammang, or Eck respond to this claim? Can one individual make a difference given the enormity of the interconnected global landscape? What role does technology have in empowering social movements and the activists who work for democracy?
4. Naomi Klein presents a strong argument against globalism and economic expansion. Much of the progress that Nicholas Kristof and Sheryl WuDunn point to in eliminating the oppression of women would be impossible without a global marketplace. Can both authors be right? As you prepare to write your paper, think about the causes of the problems each author identifies, the manifestations of those problems, and their proposed solutions. Where do their ideas on each of these, as they relate to globalism, line up? Where do they diverge?

The Girl Effect

Nicholas D. Kristof and Sheryl WuDunn

Points of Access—Pre-Reading

1. Have you, or a girl or woman you know, been discriminated against because of your or their gender? What happened? What did you, or the woman you know, do about it?
2. How are women treated in the U.S.? How are women treated globally? What opportunities do they have in the U.S. or abroad? Think about these contexts: education, jobs/economy, household, politics.
3. The founder of Doctors Without Borders has stated that "progress is achieved through women." Think about this statement. What do you think he means by "progress"? Does it seem strange, or sensible, or something in between? Why?
4. Consider this idea: empowering girls will dis-empower terrorists. Does this seem plausible? Ridiculous? How might this work? What if members of the U.S. military were the ones suggesting this as a strategy? How might that fact change the way you considered the idea?

What would men be without women? Scarce, sir, mighty scarce.

— MARK TWAIN

Srey Rath is a self-confident Cambodian teenager whose black hair tumbles over a round, light brown face. She is in a crowded street market, standing beside a pushcart and telling her story calmly, with detachment. The only hint of anxiety or trauma is the way she often pushes her hair from in front of her black eyes, perhaps a nervous tic. Then she lowers her hand and her long fingers gesticulate and flutter in the air with incongruous grace as she recounts her odyssey.

Rath is short and small-boned, pretty, vibrant, and bubbly, a wisp of a girl whose negligible stature contrasts with an outsized and outgoing personality. When the skies abruptly release a tropical rain shower that drenches us, she simply laughs and rushes us to cover under a tin roof, and then cheerfully continues her story as the rain drums overhead. But Rath's attractiveness and winning personality are perilous bounties for a rural Cambodian girl, and her trusting nature and optimistic self-assuredness compound the hazard.

When Rath was fifteen, her family ran out of money, so she decided to go work as a dishwasher in Thailand for two months to help pay the bills. Her parents fretted about her safety, but they were reassured when Rath arranged to travel with four friends who had been promised jobs in the same Thai restaurant. The job agent took the girls deep into Thailand and then handed them to gangsters who took them to Kuala Lumpur, the capital of Malaysia. Rath was dazzled by her first glimpses of the city's clean avenues and gleaming high-rises, including at the time the world's tallest twin buildings; it seemed safe and welcoming. But then thugs sequestered Rath and two other girls inside a karaoke lounge that operated as a brothel. One gangster in his late thirties, a man known as "the boss," took charge of the girls and explained that he had paid money for them and that they would now be obliged to repay him. "You must find money to pay off the debt, and then I will send you back home," he said, repeatedly reassuring them that if they cooperated they would eventually be released.

Rath was shattered when what was happening dawned on her. The boss locked her up with a customer, who tried to force her to have sex with him. She fought back, enraging the customer. "So the boss got angry and hit me in the face, first with one hand and then with the other," she remembers, telling her story with simple resignation. "The mark stayed on my face for two weeks." Then the boss and the other gangsters raped her and beat her with their fists.

"You have to serve the customers," the boss told her as he punched her. "If not, we will beat you to death. Do you want that?" Rath stopped protesting, but she sobbed and refused to cooperate actively. The boss forced her to take a pill; the gangsters called it "the happy drug" or "the shake drug." She doesn't know exactly what it was, but it made her head shake and induced lethargy, happiness, and compliance for about an hour. When she wasn't drugged, Rath was teary and insufficiently compliant—she was required to beam happily at all customers—so the boss said he would waste no more time on her: She would agree to do as he ordered or he would kill her. Rath then gave in. The girls were forced to work in the brothel seven days a week, fifteen hours a day. They were kept naked to make it more difficult for them to run away or to keep tips or other money, and they were forbidden to ask customers to use condoms. They were battered until they smiled constantly and simulated joy at the sight of customers, because men would not pay as much for sex with girls with reddened eyes and haggard faces. The girls were never allowed out on the street or paid a penny for their work.

"They just gave us food to eat, but they didn't give us much because the customers didn't like fat girls," Rath says. The girls were bused, under guard, back and forth between the brothel and a tenth-floor apartment where a dozen of them were housed. The door of the apartment was locked from the outside. However, one night, some of the girls went out onto their balcony and pried loose a long, five-inch-wide board from a rack used for drying clothes. They balanced it precariously between their balcony and one on the next building, twelve feet away. The board wobbled badly, but Rath was desperate, so she sat astride the board and gradually inched across.

"There were four of us who did that," she says. "The others were too scared, because it was very rickety. I was scared, too, and I couldn't look down, but I was even more scared to stay. We thought that even if we died, it would be better than staying behind. If we stayed, we would die as well."

Once on the far balcony, the girls pounded on the window and woke the surprised tenant. They could hardly communicate with him because none of them spoke Malay, but the tenant let them into his apartment and then out its front door. The girls took the elevator down and wandered the silent streets until they found a police station and stepped inside. The police first tried to shoo them away, then arrested the girls for illegal immigration. Rath served a year in prison under Malaysia's tough anti-immigrant laws, and then she was supposed to be repatriated. She thought a Malaysian policeman was escorting her home when he drove her to the Thai border—but then he sold her to a trafficker, who peddled her to a Thai brothel.

Rath's saga offers a glimpse of the brutality inflicted routinely on women and girls in much of the world, a malignancy that is slowly gaining recognition as one of the paramount human rights problems of this century.

The issues involved, however, have barely registered on the global agenda. Indeed, when we began reporting about international affairs in the 1980s, we couldn't have imagined writing this book. We assumed that the foreign policy issues that properly furrowed the brow were lofty and complex, like nuclear nonproliferation. It was difficult back then to envision the Council on Foreign Relations fretting about maternal mortality or female genital mutilation. Back then, the oppression of women was a fringe issue, the kind of worthy cause the Girl Scouts might raise money for. We preferred to probe the recondite "serious issues."

So this book is the outgrowth of our own journey of awakening as we worked together as journalists for *The New York Times*. The first milestone in that journey came in China. Sheryl is a Chinese-American who grew up in New York City, and Nicholas is an Oregonian who grew up on a sheep and cherry farm near Yamhill, Oregon. After we married, we moved to China, where seven months later we found ourselves standing on the edge of Tiananmen Square watching troops fire their automatic weapons at prodemocracy protesters. The massacre claimed between four hundred and fight hundred lives and transfixed the world. It was the human rights story of the year, and it seemed just about the most shocking violation imaginable.

Then, the following year, we came across an obscure but meticulous demographic study that outlined a human rights violation that had claimed tens of thousands more lives. This study found that thirty-nine thousand baby girls die annually in China because parents don't give them the same medical care and attention that boys receive—and that is just in the first year of life.[1] One Chinese family-planning official, Li Honggui, explained it this way: "If a boy gets sick, the parents may send him to the hospital at once. But if a girl gets sick, the parents may say to themselves, 'Well, let's see how she is tomorrow.' " The result is that as many infant girls die unnecessarily *every week* in China as protesters died in the one incident at Tiananmen. Those Chinese girls never received a column inch of news coverage, and we began to wonder if our journalistic priorities were skewed.

A similar pattern emerged in other countries, particularly in South Asia and the Muslim world. In India, a "bride burning"—to punish a woman for an inadequate dowry or to eliminate her so a man can remarry—takes place approximately once every two hours, but these rarely constitute news.[2] In the twin cities of Islamabad and Rawalpindi, Pakistan, five thousand women and girls have been doused in kerosene and set alight by family members or in-laws—or, perhaps worse, been seared with acid—for perceived disobedience just in the last nine years. Imagine the outcry if the Pakistani or Indian *governments* were burning women alive at those rates. Yet when the government is not directly involved, people shrug.

When a prominent dissident was arrested in China, we would write a front-page article; when 100,000 girls were routinely kidnapped and trafficked into brothels, we didn't even consider it news. Partly that is because we journalists tend to be good at covering events that happen on a particular day, but we slip at covering events that

1 Sten Johansson and Ola Nygren, "The Missing Girls of China: A New Demographic Account," *Population and Development Review* 17, no. 1 (March 1991): 35-51

2 The dowry system itself may reflect the degree of female empowerment in society. Some anthropologists believe that where women are permitted to work more outside the house they have greater economic value, and thus dowries matter less or are replaced by a bride price, in which money is paid to the bride's family rather than the other way around. An overview of the dowry and bride price, and an explanation for why they often exist side by side, is in Nathan Nunn, "A Model Explaining Simultaneous Payments of a Dowry and Bride-Price," manuscript, March 4, 2005. He examined 186 societies around the world and found a dowry system alone in 11 of these societies, a bride price alone in 98 societies, a combination of both dowry and bride price in 33 societies, and neither dowry nor bride price in 44 societies.

happen every day—such as the quotidian cruelties inflicted on women and girls. We journalists weren't the only ones who dropped the ball on this subject: A tiny portion of U.S. foreign aid is specifically targeted to women and girls.

Amartya Sen, the ebullient Nobel Prize-winning economist, has developed a gauge of gender inequality that is a striking reminder of the stakes involved. "More than 100 million women are missing," Sen wrote in a classic essay in 1990 in *The New York Review of Books*, spurring a new field of research.[3] Sen noted that in normal circumstances women live longer than men, and so there are more females than males in much of the world. Even poor regions like most of Latin America and much of Africa have more females than males. Yet in places where girls have a deeply unequal status, they *vanish*. China has 107 males for every 100 females in its overall population (and an even greater disproportion among newborns), India has 108, and Pakistan has 111. This has nothing to do with biology, and indeed the state of Kerala in the southwest of India, which has championed female education and equality, has the same excess of females that exists in the United States.

The implication of the sex ratios, Professor Sen found, is that about 107 million females are missing from the globe today. Follow-up studies have calculated the number slightly differently, deriving alternative figures for "missing women" of between 60 million and 101 million. Every year, at least another 2 million girls worldwide disappear because of gender discrimination.

The worst of these abuses tend to occur in poor nations, but the United States and other Western countries are not immune. In America, millions of women and girls face beatings or other violence from their husbands or boyfriends, and more than one in six undergoes rape or attempted rape at some point in her life, according to the National Violence Against Women survey. Then there is forced prostitution: Teenage runaways are beaten, threatened, and branded (with tattoos) by pimps in American cities, and thousands of foreign women are trafficked into the United States as well. Still, in poor countries gender discrimination is often lethal in a way that it usually is not in America. In India, for example, mothers are less likely to take their daughters to be vaccinated than their sons—that alone accounts for one fifth of India's missing females—while studies have found that, on average, girls are brought to the hospital only when they are sicker than boys taken to the hospital. All told, girls in India from one to five years of age are

---

3 "More Than 100 Million Women Are Missing," *The New York Review of Books*, December 20,1990. That was followed by Ansley J. Coale, "Excess Female Mortality and the Balance of the Sexes in the Population: An Estimate of the Number of 'Missing Females,' " *Population and Development Review*, September 17, 1991. The third estimate is Stephan Klasen and Claudia Wink, " 'Missing Women': Revisiting the Debate," *Feminist Economics* 9 (January 2003): 263-99.

50 percent more likely to die than boys the same age.[4] The best estimate is that a little Indian girl dies from discrimination every four minutes.

A big, bearded Afghan named Sedanshah once told us that his wife and son were sick. He wanted both to survive, he said, but his priorities were clear: A son is an indispensable treasure, while a wife is replaceable. He had purchased medication for the boy alone. "She's always sick," he gruffly said of his wife, "so it's not worth buying medicine for her."

Modernization and technology can aggravate the discrimination. Since the 1990s, the spread of ultrasound machines has allowed pregnant women to find out the sex of their fetuses—and then get abortions if they are female. In Fujian Province, China, a peasant raved to us about ultrasound: "We don't have to have daughters anymore!"

To prevent sex-selective abortion, China and India now bar doctors and ultrasound technicians from telling a pregnant woman the sex of her fetus. Yet that is a flawed solution. Research shows that when parents are banned from selectively aborting female fetuses, more of their daughters die as infants. Mothers do not deliberately dispatch infant girls they are obligated to give birth to, but they are lackadaisical in caring for them. A development economist at Brown University, Nancy Qian, quantified the wrenching trade-off: On average, the deaths of fifteen infant girls can be avoided by allowing one hundred female fetuses to be selectively aborted.[5]

The global statistics on the abuse of girls are numbing. It appears that more girls have been killed in the last fifty years, precisely because they were girls, than men were killed in all the battles of the twentieth century. More girls are killed in this routine "gendercide" in any one decade than people were slaughtered in all the genocides of the twentieth century.

In the nineteenth century, the central moral challenge was slavery. In the twentieth century, it was the battle against totalitarianism. We believe that in this century the paramount moral challenge will be the struggle for gender equality around the world.

The owners of the Thai brothel to which Rath was sold did not beat her and did not constantly guard her. So two months later, she was able to escape and make her way back to Cambodia.

---

4 That estimate of excess female mortality among Indian infants comes from the United Nations Development Programme but may be an understatement. Professor Oster cites data indicating that between the ages of one and four years, girls in India die at a rate 71 percent higher than if they were treated the same as boys. Emily Oster, "Proximate Sources of Population Sex Imbalance in India," manuscript, October 1,2007. The 71 percent is derived from Oster's figures of 1.4 percent expected mortality for Indian girls between the ages of one and four, compared to actual mortality of 2.4 percent.

5 Nancy Qian, "More Women Missing, Fewer Girls Dying: The Impact of Abortion on Sex Ratios at Birth and Excess Female Mortality in Taiwan," CEPR Discussion Paper No. 6667, January 2008.

Upon her return, Rath met a social worker who put her in touch with an aid group that helps girls who have been trafficked start new lives. The group, American Assistance for Cambodia, used $400 in donated funds to buy a small cart and a starter selection of goods so that Rath could become a street peddler. She found a good spot in the open area between the Thai and Cambodian customs offices in the border town of Poipet. Travelers crossing between Thailand and Cambodia walk along this strip, the size of a football field, and it is lined with peddlers selling drinks, snacks, and souvenirs.

Rath outfitted her cart with shirts and hats, costume jewelry, note-books, pens, and small toys. Now her good looks and outgoing personality began to work in her favor, turning her into an effective saleswoman. She saved and invested in new merchandise, her business thrived, and she was able to support her parents and two younger sisters. She married and had a son, and she began saving for his education.

In 2008, Rath turned her cart into a stall, and then also acquired the stall next door. She also started a "public phone" business by charging people to use her cell phone. So if you ever cross from Thailand into Cambodia at Poipet, look for a shop on your left, halfway down the strip, where a teenage girl will call out to you, smile, and try to sell you a souvenir cap. She'll laugh and claim she's giving you a special price, and she's so bubbly and appealing that she'll probably make the sale.

Rath's eventual triumph is a reminder that if girls get a chance, in the form of an education or a microloan, they can be more than baubles or slaves; many of them can run businesses. Talk to Rath today—after you've purchased that cap—and you find that she exudes confidence as she earns a solid income that will provide a better future for her sisters and for her young son. Many of the stories in this book are wrenching, but keep in mind this central truth: *Women aren't the problem but the solution. The plight of girls is no more a tragedy than an opportunity.*

That was a lesson we absorbed in Sheryl's ancestral village, at the end of a dirt road amid the rice paddies of southern China. For many years we have regularly trod the mud paths of the Taishan region to Shunshui, the hamlet in which Sheryl's paternal grandfather grew up. China traditionally has been one of the more repressive and smothering places for girls, and we could see hints of this in Sheryl's own family history. Indeed, on our first visit, we accidentally uncovered a family secret: a long-lost stepgrandmother. Sheryl's grandfather had traveled to America with his first wife, but she had given birth only to daughters. So Sheryl's grandfather gave up on her and returned her to Shunshui, where he married a younger woman as a second wife and took her to America. This was Sheryl's grandmother, who duly gave birth to a son—Sheryl's dad. The previous wife and daughters were then wiped out of the family memory.

Something bothered us each time we explored Shunshui and the surrounding villages: Where were the young women? Young men were toiling industriously in the paddies or fanning themselves indolently in the shade, but young women and girls were scarce. We finally discovered them when we stepped into the factories that were then spreading throughout Guangdong Province, the epicenter of China's economic eruption. These factories produced the shoes, toys, and shirts that filled America's shopping malls, generating economic growth rates almost unprecedented in the history of the world—and creating the most effective antipoverty program ever recorded. The factories turned out to be cacophonous hives of distaff bees. Eighty percent of the employees on the assembly lines in coastal China are female, and the proportion across the manufacturing belt of East Asia is at least 70 percent. The economic explosion in Asia was, in large part, an outgrowth of the economic empowerment of women. "They have smaller fingers, so they're better at stitching," the manager of a purse factory explained to us. "They're obedient and work harder than men," said the head of a toy factory. "And we can pay them less."

Women are indeed a linchpin of the region's development strategy. Economists who scrutinized East Asia's success noted a common pattern. These countries took young women who previously had contributed negligibly to gross national product (GNP) and injected them into the formal economy, hugely increasing the labor force. The basic formula was to ease repression, educate girls as well as boys, give the girls the freedom to move to the cities and take factory jobs, and then benefit from a demographic dividend as they delayed marriage and reduced childbearing. The women meanwhile financed the education of younger relatives, and saved enough of their pay to boost national savings rates. This pattern has been called "the girl effect." In a nod to the female chromosomes, it could also be called "the double X solution."

Evidence has mounted that helping women can be a successful poverty-fighting strategy anywhere in the world, not just in the booming economies of East Asia. The Self Employed Women's Association was founded in India in 1972 and ever since has supported the poorest women in starting businesses—raising living, standards in ways that have dazzled scholars and foundations. In Bangladesh, Muhammad Yunus developed microfinance at the Grameen Bank and targeted women borrowers—eventually winning a Nobel Peace Prize for the economic and social impact of his work. Another Bangladeshi group, BRAC, the largest antipoverty organization in the world, worked with the poorest women to save lives and raise incomes—and Grameen and BRAC made the aid world increasingly see women not just as potential beneficiaries of their work, but as agents of it.

In the early 1990s, the United Nations and the World Bank began to appreciate the potential resource that women and girls represent. "Investment in girls' education may well be the highest-return investment available in the developing world," Lawrence Summers wrote when he was chief economist of the World Bank. "The question is not whether countries can afford this investment, but whether countries can afford not to educate more girls." In 2001 the World Bank produced an influential study, *Engendering Development Through Gender Equality in Rights, Resources, and Voice,* arguing that promoting gender equality is crucial to combat global poverty.[6] UNICEF issued a major report arguing that gender equality yields a "double dividend" by elevating not only women but also their children and communities. The United Nations Development Programme (UNDP) summed up the mounting research this way: "Women's empowerment helps raise economic productivity and reduce infant mortality.[7] It contributes to improved health and nutrition. It increases the chances of education for the next generation."

More and more, the most influential scholars of development and public health—including Sen and Summers, Joseph Stiglitz, Jeffrey Sachs, and Dr. Paul Farmer—are calling for much greater attention to women in development. Private aid groups and foundations have shifted gears as well. "Women are the key to ending hunger in Africa," declared the Hunger Project.[8] French foreign minister Bernard Kouchner, who founded Doctors Without Borders, bluntly declared of development: "Progress is achieved through women."[9] The Center for Global Development issued a major report explaining "why and how to put girls at the center of development."[10] CARE is taking women and girls as the centerpiece of its antipoverty efforts. The Nike Foundation and the NoVo Foundation are both focusing on building opportunities for girls in the developing world. "Gender inequality hurts economic growth," Goldman Sachs concluded in a 2008 research report that emphasized how much developing countries could improve their economic performance by educating girls.[11] Partly as a result of that research, Goldman

6 *Engendering Development Through Gender , Equality in Rights, Resources, and Voice,* World Bank Policy Research Report (Washington, D.C.: World Bank, 2001); also, *The State of the World's Children 2007: Women and Children, the Double Dividend of Gender Equality* (New York: UNICEF, 2006).

7 *United Nations Development Programme: Global Partnership for Development, United Nations Development Programme Annual Report 2006* (New York: UNDP, 2006), p. 20.

8 Hunger Project, "Call for Nominations for the 2008 Africa Prize," statement, June 3,2008, New York.

9 Bernard Kouchner, speech to International Women's Health Coalition, New York City, January 2008.

10 *Girls Count: A Global Investment & Action Agenda* (Washington, D.C.: Center for Global Development, 2008).

11 Sandra Lawson, "Women Hold Up Half the Sky," *Global Economics Paper No. 164,* Goldman Sachs, March 4,2008, p. 9.

Sachs committed $100 million to a "10,000 Women" campaign meant to give that many women a business education.

Concerns about terrorism after the 9/11 attacks triggered interest in these issues in an unlikely constituency: the military and counterterrorism agencies. Some security experts noted that the countries that nurture terrorists are disproportionally those where women are marginalized. The reason there are so many Muslim terrorists, they argued, has little to do with the Koran but a great deal to do with the lack of robust female participation in Islamic countries. As the Pentagon gained a deeper understanding of counterterrorism, it became increasingly interested in grassroots projects such as girls' education. Empowering girls, some in the military argued, would disempower terrorists. When the Joint Chiefs of Staff hold discussions of girls' education in Pakistan and Afghanistan, you know that gender is a serious topic on the international affairs agenda. That's evident also in the Council on Foreign Relations. The wood-paneled halls that have been used for discussions of MIRV warheads are now employed as well to host well-attended sessions on maternal mortality.

We will try to lay out an agenda for the world's women focusing on three particular abuses: sex trafficking and forced prostitution; gender-based violence, including honor killings and mass rape; and maternal mortality, which still needlessly claims one woman a minute. We will lay out solutions such as girls' education and microfinance, which are working right now. While the most urgent needs are in the developing world, wealthy countries also need to clean up their own neighborhoods. If we are to lead the way, we must show greater resolution in cracking down on domestic violence and sex trafficking in our own neighborhoods rather than just sputter about abuses far away.

It's true that there are many injustices in the world, many worthy causes competing for attention and support, and we all have divided allegiances. We focus on this topic because, to us, this kind of oppression feels transcendent—and so does the opportunity. We have seen that outsiders can truly make a significant difference.

Consider Rath once more. We had been so shaken by her story that we wanted to locate that brothel in Malaysia, interview its owners, and try to free the girls still imprisoned there. Unfortunately, we couldn't determine the brothel's name or address. (Rath didn't know English or even the Roman alphabet, so she hadn't been able to read signs when she was there.) When we asked her if she would be willing to return to Kuala Lumpur and help us find the brothel, she turned ashen. "I don't know," she said. "I don't want to face that again." She wavered, talked it over with her family, and ultimately agreed to go back in the hope of rescuing her girlfriends.

Rath voyaged back to Kuala Lumpur with the protection of an interpreter and a local antitrafficking activist. Nonetheless, she trembled in the red-light districts upon seeing the cheerful neon signs that she associated with so much pain. But since her escape, Malaysia had been embarrassed by public criticism about trafficking, so the police had cracked down on the worst brothels that imprisoned girls against their will. One of those was Rath's. A modest amount of international scolding had led a government to take action, resulting in an observable improvement in the lives of girls at the bottom of the power pyramid. The outcome underscores that this is a hopeful cause, not a bleak one.

Honor killings, sexual slavery, and genital cutting may seem to Western readers to be tragic but inevitable in a world far, far away. In much the same way, slavery was once widely viewed by many decent Europeans and Americans as a regrettable but ineluctable feature of human life. It was just one more horror that had existed for thousands of years. But then in the 1780s a few indignant Britons, led by William Wilberforce, decided that slavery was so offensive that they had to abolish it. And they did. Today we see the seed of something similar: a global movement to emancipate women and girls.

So let us be clear about this up front: We hope to recruit you to join an incipient movement to emancipate women and fight global poverty by unlocking women's power as economic catalysts. That is the process under way—not a drama of victimization but of empowerment, the kind that transforms bubbly teenage girls from brothel slaves into successful businesswomen.

This is a story of transformation. It is change that is already taking place, and change that can accelerate if you'll just open your heart and join in.

Points of Engagement—Reading Comprehension

1. What is Kristof and WuDunn's goal in writing this book? Who do they hope to affect? How do they hope to do it? Have they been successful? How do you know?
2. What is the "girl effect"? Choose 3 quotations from Kristof and WuDunn's chapter that describe it, and for each quotation, explain what it shows.
3. On page 207 Kristof and WuDunn write that the abuses inflicted on women and girls are "quotidian cruelties." What does this phrase mean? Why is the "quotidian" nature of these abuses so important a factor in the attention that they receive? What effect does it have?
4. Kristof and WuDunn cite Amartya Sen's statement that "[m]ore than 100 million women are missing" (207). What does this claim mean? Where are these women missing from? Why are they missing?

5. Why do Kristof and WuDunn tell Srey Rath's story? What does it show? Why is she, and her life, an important supporting example for the authors' main goal in this essay?
6. Give two or three examples where helping women become economically independent is shown to be a "successful anti-poverty strategy"? Why is it so successful?

Points of Departure—Assignment Questions

1. Kristof and WuDunn discuss the difficulties that they faced, as journalists, in finding ways to report on the violence inflicted upon women and girls. They write that journalists are good at reporting events that happen on a particular day, but not very good at reporting on events that happen every day; violence against women and girls happens every day on a huge scale. Other writers have also suggested that people have difficulty knowing how to respond to events that happen to large groups of people, rather than individuals. Why do you think this is? What would it take to begin caring more about the global, rather than just the local, the multiple rather than singular, the collective, rather than the individual? Connect the ideas and examples in Kristof and WuDunn's essay with those in Eck, Klein, Orr, Gladwell, or Adam Gopnik.
2. One of the points that we can take away from Kristof and WuDunn's essay is that improving the status of women does not just benefit women. From issues of health to economics to national security, women are seen to be central in improving living conditions globally. How can women and girls, especially in developing nations, be so important and so vulnerable at the same time? Even in nations like the U.S. where women are less vulnerable, why do they still seem to be caught between using their "power as economic catalysts" (Kristof and WuDunn 213) and the personal sacrifices they must make to do so? In writing your paper with Kristof and WuDunn at the center, consider also the arguments of Klein, Hochschild, or Flammang.
3. How can we change our own and other's lives? What does achieving true change require? What prompts people to make momentous changes? This paper focuses on the question of "agency" and how people become agents of change for themselves and others. Kristof and WuDunn want to change the way you think about the oppression of women. Consider the examples they provide of women making changes in their own lives in order to convince you to care. Now think about other authors in this reader who tell the stories of dramatic changes for themselves or other people: Malcolm Gladwell, Naomi Klein, Kenji Yoshino, or Jeanette Winterson. How, why,

and for whom have these people become agents of change? Has the change occurred naturally over time, or has it taken real effort? Write a paper in which you propose a "theory of agency and change" based the stories these authors tell.

4. Nicholas Kristof and Sheryl WuDunn's discussion of the consequences of sex discrimination, and Naomi Klein's discussion of globalization both suggest that inequality is at the heart of the problems they identify: specifically gender inequality and economic inequality. Using these two essays, please consider why equality is so important for genuine progress. What are the effects of diminishing the equality gap? What are the consequences of letting it stay wide, or become even wider? Are there any downsides to the kinds of economic opportunities described by Kristof and WuDunn? In developing your paper, you might also reference arguments by Hochschild or Flammang who write about gender and economics in America.

Return to Hayneville

Gregory Orr

Points of Access—Pre-Reading

1. What do you know about the Civil Rights Movement of the 1960s? Who are the important national figures? Where were the flashpoints of struggle? What role/s did white people play? Have you heard of the Freedom Riders? Look them up on the Internet.
2. Would you protest on behalf of a group you did not identify with personally? For example, if you are male, would you consider protesting against unequal pay for women? If you are heterosexual, would you attend a rally to support marriage equality for gays and lesbians? Why or why not? Would your answer be the same if you might get hurt by getting involved?
3. What does time do to our memories? Do things become clearer over time? Or more cloudy? Can we trust our recollections? Does it matter what we are trying to remember?
4. What is race? Is it skin color? Ethnicity? Language? Behavior? Beliefs? How we identify? How others identify us? What is racism? Can everyone experience racism? Why or why not?
5. For what cause would you suffer?

I was born and raised in rural, upstate New York, but who I am began with a younger brother's death in a hunting accident when I was twelve and he was eight. I held the gun that killed him. But if my life began at twelve with my brother's sudden, violent death, then my end, determined by the trajectory of that harsh beginning, could easily have taken place a scant six years later, when, in June 1965, I was kidnapped at gunpoint by vigilantes near the small town of Hayneville, Alabama.

When I was sixteen, in my senior year of high school, I became involved in the civil rights movement partly because I hoped I could lose myself in that worthwhile work. I became a member of CORE (Congress of Racial Equality) and canvassed door-to-door in poorer neighborhoods in the nearby city of Kingston. I traveled down to Atlantic

City with a carload of CORE members to picket the Democratic National Convention in August 1964. Earlier that summer, the Mississippi Freedom Democratic Party—another civil rights group—had chosen a slate of racially-integrated delegates to challenge Mississippi's all-white official Democratic Party delegates for seats at the convention. The goal was to put Lyndon Johnson and the whole liberal wing of the party on the spot—testing their commitment to change. I was one of about twenty or so people parading in a small circle on the dilapidated boardwalk outside the convention hall. We carried signs urging on the drama inside: support the freedom delegation and one man, one vote. I felt confused and thrilled and purposeful all at the same time.

Three marchers carried poles, each bearing a huge charcoal portrait of a different young man. Their larger-than-life faces gazed down at us as we walked our repetitious circle. They were renditions of Andrew Goodman, James Chaney, and Michael Schwerner, SNCC (Student Nonviolent Coordinating Committee) volunteers who had been missing for months, whose bodies had only recently been discovered. They had last been seen alive on June 21, driving away from the Neshoba County sheriff's office in Philadelphia, Mississippi. When an informer led investigators to the spot where their tortured bodies had been bulldozed into a clay dam, the mystery of their whereabouts ended abruptly and they began a second life—the life of martyrs to a cause. Those three faces mesmerized us as we circled the boardwalk, singing and trying to ignore the heckling from bystanders. The artist who had drawn them had resolved their faces into a few bold lines that gave them a subtle dignity. They seemed at peace, all their uncertainties and inner complexities over. I longed to be like them, to transcend my confusions and the agonies of my past and be taken up into some noble simplicity beyond change. I longed to sacrifice myself and escape myself—to become a martyr for the movement. If it took death to gain access to the grandeur of meaning, so be it. And thus are young soldiers born.

I was too young, only seventeen, to go to Mississippi that summer, but a year later I was on my way. I drove south, alone, in a '56 Ford my father had bought me for the trip. And so it commenced—my instruction in the grim distance between the myth of the martyr and the intimate reality of violence.

Cut to November 2006—over forty years have passed since my late-adolescent misadventures in the Deep South. I'm a poet and a professor—that's how I've spent my life. One of the happier perquisites of my profession is that I'm sometimes asked to read my poems at various colleges and universities. One such invitation has come my way—a former student of mine, a poet named Chris, is teaching at Auburn University and has invited me down. I'm reading that same week in Atlanta, and as I look over my Rand McNally, I see that I can not only drive from Atlanta to Auburn, I can proceed an hour or so farther and drive straight through time and into my own past. I decide to go back to Hayneville—the tiny town that has been so long lodged like a sliver in my memory.

Chris says he'll take the trip with me, and he brings Brian, a former student of his own. I'm glad of the company. Three poets from three generations: I'll turn sixty within the year, Chris is in his early forties, Brian in his midtwenties. As we leave town in my rented, economy-size Hyundai, pulling onto the interstate in the late-afternoon drizzle, Brian asks where we're headed. For several days, I've felt a quiet tension about this trip, and suddenly it seems I can release some of the tension by telling Brian and Chris the story of that long-ago summer. At first, I try to talk about what happened to me in Hayneville itself, but I quickly see that I'll have to start further back in order to make a coherent story of it.

As we drive down the highway toward Montgomery, I feel like one of those pilgrims in Chaucer, challenged by my travel companions to entertain them on the journey. Brian's in the back seat, and as I begin my story, I occasionally turn my head slightly as if acknowledging I'm aware of him as an audience, but soon I'll become so caught up in the narrative that I'll lose all sense of my companions and of time and distance passing. I'll drive steadily toward Hayneville, as though the story and the highway were a single, fused flowing.

It was late May 1965. After brief training, another volunteer, a man from Pittsburgh named Steve, and I were assigned to work in Bolivar County, Mississippi—the Delta region, where COFO (Council of Federated Organizations) was trying to gain momentum for a strike of field workers. The going wage was $4 a day—dawn to dusk hoeing the cotton by hand, everyone from seven-year-old kids to octogenarians. We'd been in Bolivar only a week or so, helping out at the office. Suddenly, there was a summons from headquarters: everyone who could be mustered and spared from their local work—any new volunteers and all the local residents who could be persuaded—should report to the state capital in Jackson. The governor of Mississippi had called a secret session of the legislature, and the movement was organizing a mass demonstration to draw national attention to what it suspected was serious political skulduggery.

At ten in the morning on June 14, about five hundred of us—men, women, teenagers, old folks—assembled in Jackson. We walked two abreast down the sidewalk toward the capitol building. Our leaders told us we'd be stopped by the police and warned we could not parade without a permit. At that point, we would have to choose to be arrested or to disperse. We were urged to let ourselves be arrested—the plan was to fill the jail to overflowing and apply the steady pressure of media and economics (they'll have to feed and house us at city expense). The powers-that-be had learned to present a sanitized image to the media, so our arrest was very polite—journalists and photographers there watched each of us ushered onto a truck by two city policemen who held us by both arms, firmly but calmly. The trucks themselves were large, enclosed vehicles—the kind you'd use to transport chairs for a rally or municipal lawn-mowers. They packed about thirty of us inside, then closed the doors. And we were off—each truck with its own motorcycle escort gliding through red lights, heading, we presumed, toward the city jail. But the actual destination was our first big surprise. We activists may have had a plan to demonstrate, but the State of Mississippi and the City of Jackson had their own plan. We were taken to the county fairgrounds—twenty or so fenced acres of clear-cut land set with half a dozen long, low, tin-roofed barns. Another thing we didn't know: when each truck entered the fairgrounds, the gate swung shut behind it, and police turned back anyone else who tried to enter.

The truck I was on stopped, backed up, then came to a final halt. When the doors opened and our eyes adjusted to the flood of light, we saw we weren't at the jail at all—but in a narrow alley between two barns. A score of uniformed officers were gathered there, wearing the uniforms of motorcycle cops—tall leather boots, mirrored sunglasses, and blue helmets with the black earflaps pulled down. Each tanned face was almost indistinguishable under its partial disguise—only the nose and mouth showing—some already grinning at the joke of our surprise and what was in store for us. Each of them had his nightstick out—some tapping their clubs rhythmically in the palms of their hands, others just standing there expectantly with the stick held at each end. I didn't notice until I was up close and even then, in my confusion, didn't comprehend that the lower half of each officer's silver badge, where the identifying number should have been displayed, was neatly covered with black tape. An officer ordered us to climb down, and when some of us didn't, two officers climbed up and pushed us to the edge where others pulled us down. And it began. They swung their clubs right and left, randomly but thoroughly, for about ten minutes. It made no difference what you did, whether you screamed or were silent—you were struck again and again and, if you fell to the ground, kicked. It hurts—to be beaten over the head or back or shoulders with a wooden club. It's also terrifying. Then an order came and the clubbing stopped—we were told to get up (one kid couldn't and was dragged away somewhere, his leg too damaged to stand on).

We filed through a door into one of the barns. Inside, there was a calm that felt surreal after the violence outside. In the middle of the empty concrete floor, five card tables had been set up in a row, each with a typewriter and a city policeman seated in a folding chair. The far end of the barn, half hidden in shadow, was a milling cluster of frightened women and girls who, their initial beating and processing over, had been told to assemble there. Our dazed group lined up, and each of us in turn was formally processed and charged. The women from our truck were sent to join the other women at the far end of the barn. I was told to go out one of the side doors to the next barn where the men were being confined. Just as I was about to go through the door, an officer told me to take my straw hat off and carry it in my hands. I emerged into the outdoors and the bright sunlight and saw them—two lines of about fifteen highway patrolmen on either side. I was ordered to walk, not run, between them. Again, I was beaten with nightsticks, but this time more thoroughly as I was the only target. When I covered my head with raised arms to ward off the first blow from the officer on my right, I was jabbed in the ribs with a club from the other side. Instinctively, I pivoted in that direction, only to be left vulnerable in the other. I heard blows and felt sharp pokes or slaps fall flat and hard across my ribs and back from both directions—whether they were simultaneous or alternating, it made no difference; my defense was hopeless. By the time I neared the end of this gantlet, I was cringing from feinted blows—the humiliation of my fear and their laughter far worse than the physical pain.

Inside the other barn, men and boys were assembled in a dense clump surrounded by a loose ring of officers. Later that afternoon we would go through another ritually structured set of beatings. When anyone tried to sit down or move out to the edge of the impacted group to get some air, two or three officers dashed across the small, intervening space and beat him with clubs. This technique was designed to make us prisoners panic and fight one another to get to the safer center of the mass. But it didn't work. We tried to protect ourselves as best we could and keep the most vulnerable, especially the children, safe in the middle. A bearded young man in our group was noticeably defiant, and at a certain point an officer ran in and deftly struck him with a slicing motion of the blunt end of his nightstick in such a way that the taut skin of his forehead split and blood streamed down over the whole of his face. To see an individual human face suddenly turned into a mask of blood is to witness the eradication of the personal, and, if you're standing nearby as I was, to be sickened and unnerved.

The hours went by as more prisoners were processed and our group continued to grow—there were over a hundred and fifty men and boys in the barn. Evening fell. We were ordered to sit in rows on the concrete floor—three feet apart, three feet between the rows. We didn't know it, but we were waiting for mattresses to be delivered. We were told to sit bolt upright and not move; officers walked up and down the rows. If you leaned a hand down to rest or shifted your weight, a shouting patrolman rushed up with his club raised.

A black kid of maybe ten or twelve sat next to me. We'd been there for an hour and things were pretty quiet when a state patrolman stopped in front of the boy. He looked him over for a minute, then ordered him to take off the pin he was wearing—one of those movement buttons that said freedom now or one man, one vote. No safety clasp, just an open pin. The guard told the kid to pull the pin off his shirt. He did. "Put it in your mouth," the guard said. I turned my head to the right and saw the boy place it in his mouth. "Swallow it," the guard said, his voice menacing, but not loud. If the kid tried to swallow it, the pin would choke him or pierce his throat and lodge there until he bled to death in agony.

Watching the scene, I felt murderous rage fill my whole being, geysering up in the single second it took to see what seemed about to happen. I became nothing but the impulse to scramble to my feet, grab the guard's pistol before he knew what was happening, and shoot him as many times as possible. Nothing but that intense impulse and a very small voice inside me that said: "You don't stand a chance. It would take longer than you imagine—long enough for him to turn on you, for his buddies to rush up and grab you. And then what? You would be their sudden and absolute target."

How long did that moment last? How long did the guard loom over the boy with his threats? How long did the boy sit there with the pin in his mouth, tasting its metallic bitterness but refusing to swallow, or unable to swallow? It could have been five minutes; it could have been less. The guard repeated his command several times, along with profanities. And then, other officers were there, urging him to give it up, persuading him to move on, to move away.

The mattresses finally arrived, and each of us dragged one off to his place in a row. We were officially segregated according to the laws of the sovereign state of Mississippi—a vigilantly patrolled lane separated two imaginary cell-blocks, one for blacks and one for whites. We lay down to sleep. The pounding of nightsticks on the concrete floor woke us at dawn, and we realized the highway patrolmen who had abused us with such relish and impunity the previous day were nowhere in sight. They'd been replaced by Fish and Game wardens who looked altogether more rustic and thoughtful (some even had moustaches) and made no effort to conceal their badge numbers and even wore name tags. Later that morning, a plainclothes officer entered our barn and announced that the FBI had arrived and that if anyone had complaints about their treatment, they should step forward to be interviewed. I did so and was ushered out into the same alley where we'd first been greeted and beaten. The narrow lane had been rigged at one end with an awning for shade. Under the awning, four FBI agents sat at small desks. When my turn came, I told my narrative about the beatings, but how could I identify the perpetrators?

The agent asked if I could specify hair or eye color, or badge number? I couldn't. Could I point out now, in person, any of the officers who had beaten me? They weren't there, of course—they'd left in the middle of the night. The agent recorded my story of the previous day's beatings and violence and thanked me for my time. If they had actually wanted to protect us, the FBI could easily have arrived any time the preceding day. Many in the movement already knew what was inconceivable to me at the time—that events like this were stage-managed and that the FBI wasn't a friend or even a neutral ally of the civil rights movement.

For the next ten days, we lay each morning on our mattresses until breakfast—grits and a molasses syrup and powdered milk so watered-down I could see all the way to the bottom of the fifty-gallon pot that held it. After breakfast, we rolled up our mattresses and either sat all day on the concrete floor or paced the imaginary confines of our collective cell. Twice a day, we were lined up for the bathroom—it was then or never as we stood pressed up against one another, waiting for our brief turn in one of the five stinking stalls. No showers, no chance to wash at all, the same, reeking clothes day after day. Hot as hell once the sun heated the tin roof, but chill at night when we huddled, blanket-less, in the dark on our bare mattresses. The mosquito logger sprayed around the outside of the barn each evening, sending its toxic cloud in under the closed doors to set us all coughing. Boredom, stench, heat. Word came from outside—we could, at any time, be released by posting a $50 bond that the movement would provide, but the plan called for as many as possible to stay inside for as long as we could. There was hope we would seriously inconvenience the state by staying, that another demonstration in support of us might take place—there was even talk of Martin Luther King Jr. himself showing up for it. Rumors and hope; and a request to persevere. Most of us stayed, though some of the youngest and oldest chose to leave. The violence mostly gone; if it occurred, it was sporadic and spontaneous and ended quickly without major consequence. Exhausted by lack of substantial food, worn down by boredom and discomfort, I gradually lost heart. I had dreamed of meaningful work and even heroic martyrdom, but here I was merely cannon fodder. I held a place; I counted—but only as an integer in the calculus of a complex political game playing out in rooms far above me. And close up, as close as the arc of a swung billy club, I had discovered that for every martyr whose life was resolved into a meaningful death, there were hundreds of others who were merely beaten, terrorized, humiliated. Even as I sank into depression and brooded in the stifling heat of that jail-barn, I was learning that I wanted to live.

On the tenth day there, my name was called and I was led outside and taken to a pay phone attached to a post near our barn. Picking up the receiver, I heard the voice of my father's lawyer, who was calling from upstate New York. We'd only met once; I hardly knew him. He began by saying he couldn't stand me or any of the causes I believed in, but my father was his dear friend and was frantic with worry. My fine had been paid. I was to leave now and drive back north immediately if I cared a damn about my family. End of story. His tongue-lashing eliminated the last of my resolve. The officer standing beside me took me in a patrol car to where I'd left the Ford ten days ago, as if the whole thing had been prearranged.

I should have called the COFO office and told them I was leaving, was heading north that very day—but I was ashamed. I was deserting—a frightened and confused teenager. The map told me my quickest route north was by state roads from Jackson to Selma, Alabama, and then on to Montgomery, where the interstate began. When I passed through Selma it was early evening and I was starved (we'd been fed nothing but vegetables and grits for ten days), but I was too afraid to stop for dinner.

It was dusk on US 80, past Selma and within fifteen miles of Montgomery, when I heard a siren. A white car pulled up close behind me, flashing its lights. I thought it was a police car and pulled over, but the two men who jumped out, one tall and rather thin, the other shorter and stout, wore no uniforms. They did each wear holsters, and as they approached, one on each side of my car, they drew their pistols. I rolled up my windows and locked my doors. Rap of a pistol barrel on the window two inches from my head: "Get out, you son of a bitch, or I'll blow your head off."

I got out and stood on the road's shoulder, beside my car. They prodded me with their guns and told me they were going to kill me. They searched my car and found SNCC pamphlets in the trunk. They were sure I was an agitator rumored to be coming to their town—my New York license plates had been a strong clue that the pamphlets confirmed. The men made two promises about my immediate future, the first was that they would kill me and dump my body in the swamps. The second, made a few moments later, was that they were going to take me to a jail where I would rot. With those two contradictory threats left floating in the air, they took my wallet and went back to their vehicle, ordering me to follow them in my own car. They pulled onto the highway and zoomed off. I started my car and followed them. We hadn't driven more than a mile when they signaled and turned off to the right, onto a smaller road. I hesitated, uncertain what to do, then made the turn and followed.

I pause in this story I'm telling Chris and Brian when I realize we've reached the green sign marking the turnoff for Hayneville. I'd been so caught up in telling it that I hardly noticed we'd passed through Montgomery and were speeding down Route 80 toward Selma. Suddenly, I realize the old story and my present journey are eerily coinciding at this forlorn intersection. It's as if my ghost Ford from forty years ago is approaching the turnoff from the west, coming from Selma, at the same moment that my shiny, white rental reaches that same turn from the direction of Montgomery. The terrified boy in the ghost Ford drives right into us, and for a moment, we and the story are one and the same. Now, I'm driving slowly down that backroad toward Hayneville, telling Chris and Brian what it felt like the first time I took this road, alone, following the car driven by my would-be killers.

Their car was newer than mine and faster. It sped up. A voice in my head started screaming: "What are you doing? You are obligingly speeding to your own death—driving to your own grave! Turn around and make a run for it!" But how could I? They had my wallet with my license and all my money. It was pitch-dark now. The road was so narrow there was no place to turn around; there were swamps on either side. If I tried to make a getaway, their car could easily overtake mine, and they would surely shoot me. This hysterical dialogue raged in my head for the ten long minutes of that ride, and then we emerged out of the dark into Hayneville. We passed the courthouse, pulled into a narrow street, and stopped in back of a small jail.

Even as I describe that terrifying drive, I see that the wooded swamps are gone. (Or were they imagined in the dark so long ago?) It's mostly fields and pasture with a pond here and there gleaming like oil in the deepening gloom. And now we're arriving in the town itself. Again, as with the first time I was here, it's almost completely dark under the overarching trees, only a glimpse of a gray sky from which all trace of light is gone. I recognize things: there is the courthouse—no wonder it stood out—white and two stories high on its tree-filled lawn in a town of twenty or so tiny houses and bungalows. And there is something completely new in town (the only new thing as far as I can see)—a BP convenience store where I stop for gas. The station is shiny and all lit up, its blue-green signs glowing intensely in the dark like those roadside stores in Edward Hopper paintings, gleaming forlornly against the primeval dark of rural Anywhere, America. I'm trembling with a kind of giddy excitement as I pump the gas. Even here I can see changes—the man behind the counter in the station, whom I take to be the owner, is black, so are most of his customers. Back then, whites owned everything. As I pull my car out of the station across from the courthouse, I see that the sheriff's car, just now parking beside the small police bungalow behind the courthouse, is driven by a black officer.

When we got to the jail forty years ago, I felt relieved. At least the terrifying drive was over. But my torment was only entering another phase. I'd be held there in solitary confinement without charges for eight days. I was kept on the second floor the entire time, separate from all other prisoners and personnel, seeing and talking to no one except the silent trustee who brought me food twice a day and took away my empty tray. Why was I so isolated from the rest of the prisoners? It was possible they didn't want people to know where I was as they waited to find out if anyone was aware that I was "missing." Ever since the murders of Goodman, Schwerner, and Chaney, volunteers were under strict orders to check in with headquarters before traveling any distance, to record their destination and expected arrival time, so that if anything went wrong an alert could be sent out for an immediate search. I hadn't called, so no one knew I was in Hayneville's jail.

Four days into my incarceration, my father's lawyer called the DA in Jackson, Mississippi, to ask if he knew why I hadn't arrived home. The DA didn't know; they'd let me go. Then he tried the state attorney general's office in Montgomery, which was run at the time by Richmond Flowers, a racial moderate. His office made inquiries and learned I was being held in Hayneville, but they couldn't offer any help. They told Dad's lawyer that Lowndes County resisted all outside interference, even from Alabama state authorities. On my fifth day there, my father's lawyer managed to call the jail and was told (by the sheriff himself, slyly posing as a deputy) that indeed a young man named Greg Orr was there and was at that moment playing checkers with the sheriff.

Of course this was a lie. I had no knowledge of the call, no sense that anyone in the world knew where I was. Each day I spent in that cell was an eternity. I was unmoored from structures except food and the alternation of day and night. I didn't know when my spell in solitary would end. If someone had said to me: "You'll be kept alone in a small cell with no one to speak to for eight days," I could have tried to organize the ordeal in my mind—I could have, for starters, kept track of the days and known that each one passing brought me closer to the end. But there was no known end point and so no measurement—it was wholly arbitrary and made me even more aware of my own powerlessness. Already depressed and disoriented by the ten days in "jail" in Jackson, I was even more frightened in Hayneville: I had a better sense of how dangerous my situation was, and my imagination took over from there.

In the middle of my eighth day the sheriff came to my cell, unlocked it, and told me I was free to go. That was it: no apology, no formal charges, no anything. I was taken to my car, told to get out of town. I was set free as abruptly and mysteriously as I had been captured and incarcerated. I got in my car and drove. I drove and drove. I have one memory of stopping in some rest area in South Carolina in the middle of the night and trying to wash and shave, but my hands were shaking too much to control the razor. I slept whenever I couldn't drive any longer, pulling into parking lots and climbing into the back seat. By the time I reached New Jersey, I was hallucinating huge rats running across the highway in front of my headlights. And then I was home, back in the Hudson River Valley town I'd left only a month or so earlier.

I spent July in my hometown, but in early August I took a job in New York with a small film company, synchronizing sound and picture. On my way home from work one August day, I bought a New York Times to read on the subway. When I looked at the front page, I saw a story about a murder that had just taken place in Hayneville. I turned to the inner page to finish the article and was stunned to see a photograph of one of the men who had kidnapped me on the highway. The news article related that he had shotgunned Jonathan Daniels, an Episcopalian seminary student and civil rights volunteer, in broad daylight on the courthouse lawn, in front of half a dozen witnesses. From what I could tell, the victim and the others with him might have been the "outside agitators" whom I had been mistaken for. According to the newspaper, they, like me, had been arbitrarily arrested and held without charges for days in the jail and then suddenly released. But unlike me, they had no car. They spent several hours desperately trying to find someone to drive them to Montgomery, while the murderer, a friend of the sheriff's and a "special unpaid deputy," became more and more agitated. He found the released organizers near the courthouse and aimed his shotgun at a young black woman, Ruby Sales. The seminary student pushed her aside and stood in front just as the gun went off.

Though he was charged with murder, the verdict, given by a local, all-white jury in that very courthouse, was "not guilty" on the basis of self-defense. The same courthouse later saw the trial of the killers of Viola Liuzzo, the Detroit housewife who, three months before my arrival in town, had participated in the Selma to Montgomery march. On the evening of March 25, she was killed by gunfire while ferrying marchers in her car on Route 80. Her slayers, quickly apprehended, were also found not-guilty by another all-white Hayneville jury, even though eye-witness prosecution testimony was given by one of the four Klansmen (a paid FBI informer) present that night in the murder car.

My situation in Hayneville resembled the seminary student's: arbitrary arrest, jail time without arraignment or trial, and then sudden release. But I had a car, and timing mattered: the *New York Times* article stressed that the killer had been upset about the passage of the Voting Rights Act—as if part of his motivation was a kind of crazed act of political protest. When I was apprehended and jailed, the status quo in Hayneville seemed secure—if my presence there was a sign of change, it was the sort of change they felt they could easily contain and control.

Two others died there; a murder in March; another in August—and in between, in late June, my own narrow escape as I slipped through the same violent landscape. "Slipped through" makes me sound like a fish that found a hole in the net, but surely I was trapped in it, surely it was luck that pulled me from its entanglements and casually tossed me back into the sea.

And here I am again, forty-one years later, approaching the jail, that brick edifice in which all my emotions and memories of Hayneville are concentrated. Not the memory or idea of jail, but this dingy incarnation of incarceration—a building full of little cages where people are captive. I've been monologuing until now, spewing out non-stop the whole story that brought me here, but as we travel the last few blocks, I go silent with anticipation. Chris and Brian are also quiet but excited—now that we're in the town itself, certain key nouns connect to real things—there is the courthouse pretty much as I described it. And here, down this little lane a half block past the courthouse, is the jail itself, that brick, L-shaped building I've been talking about. But how different it is from what I remembered and described! It's an empty husk. Boarded up—from the looks of it, abandoned a number of years ago. Deserted, dilapidated, the mortar rotted out between the grimy bricks. The only thing not in utter disrepair is a small exercise yard attached to the back, behind a chain-link fence topped with razor wire.

When I stop in the cinder parking lot and hop out of the car I feel like a kid who has arrived at a playground. I'm surprised by my responses. Here, at a place that was a locus of some of the most intense misery I've ever known, I'm feeling curiously happy. Chris and Brian have also climbed out. I can see they're glad, too—pleased to have found some real, palpable thing at the end of a tunnel of words burrowing from the distant past. Chris has a camera and begins to take pictures, though it's night now and there's no way of knowing if anything will register. The doors to the building are locked, but Brian, exploring the fence's gate, finds it's open, and we're able to enter the yard. We climb some rusty steps to a second-floor landing; from there I can point to the window that was across the corridor from my cell and that I peered out of after shinnying up my cell door's bars and craning my neck. That giddiness I felt when I first set my feet on the parking lot has been growing more intense—I'm laughing now, and when I'm not laughing, I'm unable to stop grinning. Earlier, in the car, telling the stories of my long-ago misadventures, the words had zipped directly from my brain's private memory to my tongue in a kind of nonstop narrative that mostly bypassed my emotions. Now my brain has stopped functioning almost entirely, and I'm taken over by this odd laughter that's bubbling up from some wordless source far down in my body-some deep, cellular place.

Brian and Chris poke around the weed-grown yard, looking for anything interesting, some rusty artifact to point to or pick up and ponder. I'm ordinarily a person who likes souvenirs—a shell from a beach, a rock from a memorable walk in the woods—but I have no wish to take anything physical from this place. Even a pebble would weigh me down, and the truth is I feel weightless right now, as if I'm a happy spirit moving through a scene of desolation.

My beginning was a rifle shot and someone innocent suddenly dead. My end might well have been something eerily similar: perhaps a pistol shot, my own death in this tiny town so far from my home—a beginning and end so close to each other as to render the life cryptic and tragic by way of its brevity. Only, Hayneville wasn't my end. It was a place where my life could have ended but didn't, and now, almost half a century later, I stand beside that closed-down, dilapidated jail, laughing. But laughing at what, at whom? Not at the confused and earnest kid I was all those years ago, the one who blundered through and escaped thanks to blind luck. What is this laughter that's fountaining up through me?

As we're leaving and I pause in the cindery parking lot with one hand on my car-door handle, taking a last look at the old jail, a single word comes to me: joy. It's joy I'm feeling—joy is at the heart of this peculiar laughter. Joy is my body's primal response to the enormity of the gift it has been given—a whole life! A whole life was there waiting for me the day I left this town. A life full of joys I couldn't imagine back then: a long, deeply satisfying marriage to a woman I love, two wonderful daughters, forty years of writing poems and teaching the craft of poetry. Laughing to think that the kid I was had come south seeking the dark blessing of death in a noble cause, but had instead been given the far more complex blessing of life, given his whole existence and all the future struggle to sort it out and make it significant—to himself and, if he was lucky as a writer, to others also. Laughing at how my life went on past this town and blossomed into its possibilities, one of which (shining in the dark) was love.

Points of Engagement—Reading Comprehension

1. Consider the following quote from page 218: "I longed to be like them, to transcend my confusions and the agonies of the past and be taken up into some noble simplicity beyond change. I longed to sacrifice myself and escape myself – to become a martyr for the movement. If it took death to gain access to the grandeur of meaning, so be it. And thus are young soldiers born." Now look at the quote in context. Who is "them" in this quotation? What had they done that got Orr's attention? What are the "confusions and agonies of the past" he is trying to escape? What do you think he means by the "grandeur of meaning"? Why does Orr write "And thus are young soldiers born"? What connection is he making?

2. In his trip to the south in May 1965, Orr is instructed in the "grim distance between the myth of the martyr and the intimate reality of violence" (218). What does this phrase mean? Break down each term and explain what it means in context. In what way does Orr's essay explore this distance between myth and reality? Cite evidence from the text to support your answer.
3. What is the significance of the incident in which Orr witnesses a guard forcing a black boy to swallow a pin? What does this incident reveal about the guard, the boy, and Orr himself?
4. Orr tells the story of his 1965 imprisonment in Hayneville during a road trip back to the town. How is the Hayneville of 2006 different from the Hayneville of 1965? Be specific. Orr describes his return to the jail where he was incarcerated: "I'm laughing now, and when I'm not laughing, I'm unable to stop grinning" (228). What do you think of Orr's emotional response during his return to Hayneville? What might explain his laughter and sense of joy and love? Look for evidence in the text to support your answer.
5. Why do you think Orr starts this article with the accidental killing of his brother? What does that tragic detail add to his narrative? What connection do you see with the rest of his story?
6. Orr's trip to Alabama in 1965 could easily be seen as a failure. Does he see it that way? Do you? What does he learn during his trip in 2006? How do you know? Point to the text.

Points of Departure—Assignment Questions

1. Following his violent ordeal in Mississippi, Orr describes his involvement in the Civil Rights Movement in the following way: "I gradually lost heart . . . I had discovered that for every martyr whose life was resolved into a meaningful death, there were hundreds of others who were merely beaten, terrorized, humiliated" (223). What makes a death meaningful? Are all sacrifices meaningful ones? What are the limits of sacrifice? How much sacrifice is too much? Who gets to decide? Answer these questions using essays by Orr, Klein, Gladwell, Bremmer, or Slater.
2. Gregory Orr describes political protest as something he experienced "close up, as close as the arc of a swinging billy club" (223). His harrowing experience in 1965 confirms Gladwell's assertion that "activism that challenges the status quo—that attacks deeply rooted problems—is not for the faint of heart" (Gladwell 136). How can

one decide when the status quo is no longer acceptable? What are we willing to do today in order to change it? Use Orr's personal account of protest to enrich your reading of Gladwell's comparisons between social activism during the Civil Rights era of the 1960s and in the era of Facebook and Twitter. Think about Orr's chosen "instruction in the grim distance between the myth of the martyr and the intimate reality of violence." (218) If faced with the challenges of the 1960s today—in the era of activism with social media—would Orr, as we know him through his story, pursue the "myth of the martyr"? Does real social change, or revolution, still require the "reality of violence"?

3. *Time and Place.* Orr's essay is written as a memoir, a story about himself when he was younger. What effect does this perspective of looking back have on our understanding of Orr's original experience? What does the passing of time do to Orr's experience of place? His memory of past places? His experience of revisiting them in the present? Use the specific terms offered in essays by Alison Gopnik or Alain de Botton to help explain the story that Orr tells about himself.
4. Gregory Orr is a white man. He tells the story of violent discrimination for his active support of the Civil Rights Movement. What does his story tell us about the history of race and diversity in the U.S.? What does it tell us about discrimination for what we believe? How we behave? Who we become? What does it tell us about assimilation and preserving the status quo? Write a paper in which you propose answers to these questions using essays by Orr and Kenji Yoshino or Diana Eck.

Who Holds the Clicker?

Lauren Slater

Points of Access—Pre-Reading

1. What do you think of when you hear the term "mind control"? If it were actually possible to control someone else's mind, by stimulating their brain, do you think it would be ethical to do so? Under what circumstances?
2. How different is stimulating the brain from stimulating the heart? Is it? Why or why not?
3. Do you think the "brain" and the "mind" are different? How do you think each is affected by the body? Do you think of something called a "soul" as a separate category?
4. Try to think of a discovery or advance in science/technology that has been used for either good or bad. Could the discoverers have predicted which way it would go?
5. Think of times you have been sad, angry, or scared. Are these feelings mild forms of depression, rage, or obsession, or do you believe there is a clear dividing line between normal moods and mental illness?

Mario Della Grotta is 36 years old, with a buzz cut and a tattoo of a rose on his right bicep. He wears a gold chain around a neck that is thick as a thigh. He's the kind of guy you might picture in a bar in a working-class neighborhood, a cigarette wedged in the corner of his lip and a shot glass full of something amber. He seems, on first appearance, like the kind of guy who swaggers his way through the world, but that is not true of Mario. There was a time when rituals to ward off panic consumed 18 hours of his day. He couldn't stop counting and checking. Fearful of dirt, he would shower again and again. He searched for symmetries. His formal diagnosis was obsessive-compulsive disorder, which is just a fancy way of saying scared. Had he remembered to lock the car door? Did he count that up correctly? The French call obsessive-compulsive disorder *folie du doute,* a much more apt title than our clinical OCD; *folie du doute,* a phrase that gets to the existential core of worry, a clenched, demonic doubting that overrides evidence, empiricism, plain common sense. For Mario, his entire life was crammed into a single serrated question mark.

Mario's anxiety was so profound, and so impervious to other treatments, that six years ago his psychiatrists at Butler Hospital in Providence, Rhode Island, suggested psychosurgery, or what—in an effort to avoid the stigmatization associated with lobotomies and cingulotomies—is now being labeled more neutrally: neurosurgery for psychiatric disorders. Medtronic, a Minneapolis-based company, has adapted implants it originally developed to treat movement disorders in Parkinson's patients for use in the most intractable but common psychiatric problems: anxiety and depression. These neural pacemakers, composed of eight bilateral implanted electrodes, four per hemisphere, emit an electrical current that, theoretically, jams pesky brain circuits, the ones that say *you suck you suck you suck* or *oh no oh no oh no.* This idea made sense to Mario. His experience of mental illness was one of a terrible loop de loop. So he said yes to surgery. He said yes in part because he knew that if he didn't like the neural implants, he could simply have them switched off.

And so, Mario became one of the first American psychiatric patients to undergo this highly experimental procedure. Worldwide there have so far been only some 50 implantations for OCD and 15 for depression, but the technology suggests a not-too-distant future when options other than drugs may be available to sufferers of serious mental illness. Industry analysts predict that the entire "neurostimulation market"—already worth $550 million and growing 20 percent a year—could top $5 billion and that the technology will be adapted to combat everything from addiction to obesity.

Such fervor has critics nervous that rather than curing problems antidepressants have been unable to address, the implant industry could repeat the problems that have scandalized the pharmaceutical world.[1] And psycho-surgery, by its very nature, brings with it a thicket of ethical twisters. Whose head is it? By directly manipulating the brain might we turn ourselves into Maytag technicians, programming speed cycles and rinses? Could it be possible to actually control the content of another's thinking, as opposed to merely their affective states? Even setting aside these sci-fi concerns, should doctors wade into apparently healthy brain tissue when they have yet to precisely locate mental pathology?

The first researcher to confirm that brain function, and by extension dysfunction, could be localized was French neurologist Paul Broca, in 1861. Autopsying a patient who could say only one word—"tan"—Broca identified organic damage to what he

1 http://www.motherjones.com/news/feature/2005/11/war_of_wires.html

theorized was the speech center. But it took 75 years, and a Portuguese neurologist by the name of Egas Moniz, to take Broca's theory of speech localization and apply it to madness. Moniz, who would win a Nobel Prize for his invention of lobotomy, used to stride through the hallways of Lisbon's insane asylums looking for patients suitable for the frontal lobe surgery, which Moniz's surgical colleagues performed, first via ether injections, the alcohol essentially burning away the brain, and later with a leucotome, an ice-pick-shaped device with a retractable wire to whisk out gray matter.

In 1936, shortly after the first lobotomies were performed in Lisbon, the procedure came to our side of the sea, where it was adapted with all-American vigor. By the late 1950s, more than 30,000 patients had had lobotomies and the surgery was being used to "cure" everything from mental retardation to homosexuality to criminal insanity. Its most fervent promoter, Dr. Walter Freeman, eventually performed surgeries on multiple patients in an assembly-line fashion. Post-surgery, it was common for a lobotomy recipient to be perpetually placid, a carbon copy of themselves, faint and fuzzy.

While Moniz and his protégés were sawing through skulls, Robert Heath was studying an alternate form of psychosurgery—deep brain stimulation, or DBS—at the Tulane University School of Medicine. Heath took patients culled from the back wards of Louisiana's mental hospitals, slit open their skulls, and dropped electrodes down deep inside them. With the use of a handheld stimulator, Heath discovered that electrodes placed in the hippocampus, the thalamus, or the tegmentum could produce states of rage or fear, while electrodes placed in the brain's septal area and part of the amygdala could produce feelings of pleasure. Heath "treated" a homosexual man (identified as B-19) by firing electrodes in his pleasure center while having him watch movies of heterosexual encounters, and within 17 days B-19 was a newly made man. He proved it to Heath by sleeping with a prostitute Heath himself had hired for this demonstration.

Neural implants dramatically illustrated Broca's notions of localization, and, in so doing, changed the way we thought of the brain. Prior to localists like Broca, people believed thoughts and emotions were carried through the head via hollow tunnels. Now, however, diffuse tunnels were out and in their place, an image of discrete segments, real estate, if you will, some of it swampland, some of it stately, but all of it perhaps subject to human renovation.

And unlike lobotomies, those renovations did not have to be permanent. In a public demonstration at a bullring in Spain, another researcher, Yale's Jose Delgado, provoked an implanted bull with a matador's red cape. The enraged animal raced toward him, head down, stopping only at the very last second, when Delgado, with a push of a button, fired the implant and the bull, its aggression eradicated, trotted away. The potential uses and abuses of neural implants were obvious: You could control prison populations; you could effectively wipe out violence.

By the late 1960s, implants appealed to those in the medical and law enforcement communities who believed that urban riots were born not of poverty or oppression but of "violent tendencies" that could be monitored or altered. The federal Law Enforcement Assistance Administration handed out large sums to researchers studying implants and other behavior-modification techniques. Under one such grant proposal, in 1972 Dr. Louis Jolyon West of UCLA was to form the Center for the Study and Reduction of Violence and conduct research at various California prisons. The plan was to take inmates, implant them, and then monitor their brain activity after discharge. When a Washington Post reporter investigated this scheme, he discovered a precedent: In 1968 officials at California's Vacaville prison performed electrode surgery on three inmates (including a minor) with the assistance of military doctors.

A series of Senate hearings in the mid-1970s brought these and other government forays into behavior modification to the public's attention, and the public, particularly African Americans, were more than a little perturbed at the thought that mind control was seen as a viable solution to social injustice or crime. Meanwhile, the CIA was rumored to be experimenting with implants to break down POWs and discredit rebellious citizens (Heath admitted he'd been approached by the agency), and Michael Crichton's *The Terminal Man*, in which the main character receives implants to control his epilepsy and turns psychotic, became a best-seller.

All this, concomitant with the rise of the antipsychiatry movement, ensured that neural implants fell into disrepute. They were resurrected in 1987 when a French neurosurgeon, Alim-Louis Benabid, operating on a Parkinson's patient, discovered that if he touched the patient's thalamus with an electrical probe, the patient's shaking stopped. A decade later, Medtronic's neural implants were approved by the FDA for treating tremors, and some 30,000 patients worldwide have since been implanted for movement disorders. But something else was observed. Those implanted Parkinson's patients, a few brightened right up. It appeared the circuits controlling physical shaking were somehow connected to mental quaking as well. "It's how a lot of medicine happens," says neurosurgeon Jeff Arle of the Lahey Clinic in Burlington, Massachusetts. "It's by extrapolating backwards. Someone then has to have the chutzpah to say 'Gee, maybe we ought to try this for certain psychiatric problems.' You believe it's worth the risk. You don't know until you try it."

By the mid-1990s a small, international group of psychiatrists, neurologists, and neurosurgeons was considering using the implants for mental illness. One of their primary questions: Where, precisely, in a psychiatric patient, would one put the electrodes? While

Heath and Delgado demonstrated that you can crudely trigger generalized states of affect—like terror and rage—by stimulating areas of the limbic system, no one has so far found those millimeter-sized snarls of circuitry where researchers hope the more nuanced forms of human mental health, or illness, reside. "We want more than anything," says Dr. Helen Mayberg of Emory University, a DBS depression researcher, "to find that sweet spot, and go there." Dr. Ben Greenberg, one of Mario's psychiatrists, notes that it took a long time to hone in on the targets with Parkinson's. "We are several years into that process," he says. "We will find the circuitry involved in psychiatric conditions. I think it's going to happen."

Some scientists question the very premise that despair can be localized. "Psychosurgery is based on a flawed and impoverished vision of the relationship between brain tissue and psychological disorder. It is extremely unlikely that any psychiatric problem can be located in one so-called 'abnormal' brain region," says Dr. Raj Persaud, a consulting psychiatrist at London's Maudsley Hospital. "The notion of abnormality remains deeply problematic given the huge overlap between psychiatric and normal populations in all contemporary measurements of brain structure and function. Instead, dysfunction is much more likely to result from a change in relationships between several areas, and so psychosurgery is based on a flawed attempt to carry over the same physicalist thinking that has been so powerful in bodily medicine, inappropriately to the medicine of the mind."

If finding the exact loci of depression or obsession proves to be problematic, couldn't scientists simply override people's psychic pain by stimulating their pleasure centers? That would be too crude, neuroscientists say, akin to getting patients high. Adds Harold Sackheim of the New York State Psychiatric Institute, "If you can get relief without invasive surgery"—this procedure comes with up to a 5 percent chance of hemorrhage; a 2 to 25 percent chance of infection—"you might want to pursue that other avenue first." Pills. That's the other avenue we should supposedly pursue first. And we have. For all our consumption, though, the risk of suicide associated with antidepressants is now considered dangerous enough to adolescents that the FDA has mandated black-box warnings on labels alerting doctors and patients of the dangers. Equally compelling is data that suggests that antidepressants leave a staggering number of users without any relief at all. "We have searched and searched," says depression researcher Dr. William Burke of the University of Nebraska Medical Center, "for the Holy Grail, and we have never found it." That's true. Thirty percent of people who take an antidepressant are not helped by it. Of the 70 percent who are helped, only 30 percent feel robust relief; the other 40 percent get some symptom relief and limp along. Doctors advise the limpers to switch or combine drugs, but between 10 and 20 percent of patients never improve no matter what pills they take.

Mario, who'd tried some 40 different combinations of medications, knows this all too well. He wanted a shot at the ordinary, a lawn he might mow just once a week. The ability to endure the mess and touch of children. He decided the implants were well worth the risk.

On a Monday in early February 2001, as Mario woke up next to his pregnant wife, neurosurgeons at Rhode Island Hospital were suiting up for his operation. A week or so before, Mario had gone to a tattoo artist and had the Chinese sign for "child" inked into his wrist. "If I didn't make it, if I never got to see my daughter be born, then at least I would have this tattoo," he says. "Child. With it on my skin, I knew I could go to the grave with some meaning."

As it is impossible to use animal testing to gauge whether or not DBS can treat depression and anxiety, the only guinea pigs available are people like Mario. To be eligible for neural implants he had to exhaust every available pharmacological option at either optimal or above-optimal doses and undergo at least 20 hours of behavior therapy. He had to understand the risks and implications of the procedure and provide his consent. His case was reviewed by three review boards. The FDA, which regulates medical devices, gave its blessing to this experiment. "We don't want to repeat the mistakes of the past," says Dr. Greenberg, his psychiatrist. "We want to be sure this therapy is not only not used indiscriminately, but that it is reserved for the group of people who have failed trials of everything else."

Once in the OR, Mario was given a local anesthetic. His head had been shaved, his brain targeted to millimeter precision by MRIs. Attached to his head was a stereotactic frame to provide surgeons with precise coordinates and mapping imagery. He'd undergone extensive neuropsychological testing to determine where to put the implants and to provide a preoperative baseline of functioning. After surgery, a DBS patient will be retested with these core questions in mind: Have the symptoms improved or deteriorated or stayed the same? By implanting these electrodes, how has cognitive functioning changed, if at all?

DBS doctors choose their targets—in Mario's case, the anterior limb of the internal capsule, an area that connects the thalamus with the orbital and medial prefrontal cortex—based on past lobotomies and cingulotomies that were deemed to provide some relief for the symptoms at hand. There is a problem, however, in using past lobotomy lesions as one's DBS guidebook: All sorts of surgical lesions have attenuated anxiety and depression in desperate patients, lesions on the cingulate gyrus or the caudate nucleus, lesions to the left or right, up or down, here or there. Without a single sweet spot, the possibilities are disturbingly numerous.

Doctors are anxious to separate DBS from the psychosurgeries of the past, when ice-pick-like instruments were thrust up under open eyes, blades swished through the brain. While the finer points of brain functionality are still hazy, the surgery itself is conducted with far more precision and technological finesse than Moniz or Heath could have ever hoped for. But some facts remain the same. There is a gruesome quality to any brain surgery. The drill is huge; its twisted bit grinds through bone, making two burr holes on either side of the skull.

The drilling was over in a few minutes; surgeons then took a couple of hours to get the implants in place. As is the practice with brain surgery, Mario remained awake throughout and he was repeatedly questioned: "Are you okay? Are you alert?" His head was in the steel halo screwed to his skull. The operating room was cold, despite the relentless surgical sun. The surgeon threaded two 1.27-millimeter wires through the burr holes, wires on which the tiny platinum/iridium electrodes were strung. Picture it as ice fishing. There is the smooth bald lake, the hole opening up, dark water brimming like blood within the aperture, and then the slow lowering of string, the searching, searching, for where the fish live.

Mario could feel none of this because the brain, the seat of all sensation, itself has no sensory nerves. Next the surgeons implanted two two-inch by three-inch battery packs beneath each of Mario's clavicles and ran wires from the packs (the batteries of which have to be replaced every few months) up under the skin of his neck to the implants. The packs, controlled by a remote programming device, power the electrodes when the doctor flips the switch and adjusts the current. Mario lay there, waiting.

He would have to wait awhile. Psychiatrists do not turn the electrodes on right after surgery. That happens later, when the swelling in the head has gone down, when the bruised brain has had a chance to heal itself and the burr holes have sealed with skin. Then Ben Greenberg would pass a programmer over Mario's chest, and the wires would leap to life.

After three weeks, Mario went back to Greenberg's office. The men sat facing each other, Greenberg with the programmer on his lap. He snapped open the laptoplike device and, using a handheld controller inside, activated the implants. Mario remembers the exact moment they went on. "I felt a strange sadness go all through me," he says. Mario recalls Greenberg's fingers tapping on the keyboard, adjusting the current, the pulse duration, and the frequency. After a few taps, the sadness went away. "With DBS the thing has a certain immediacy to it," says Dr. Steven Rasmussen, Mario's other psychiatrist.

"You can change behavior very, very rapidly. On the flip side of it there's a danger too. This really is a kind of mind control, you know what I mean."

This is the rare admission. For the most part, researchers insist DBS has nothing to do with mind control or social shaping; they are simply psychiatrists targeting symptoms. These doctors have seen severe psychiatric anguish and know its remission is always a blessing. But anytime a psychiatrist tries to tweak a patient's mind, he does so in accordance with social expectations.

Tap tap. Now Mario felt a surge inside of him. Later, outside, Mario peered at the world turned on, turned up, and indeed it did look different, the grass a cheerful lime green, the yellow-throated daffodils. Mario went home. He wanted to talk. He had things to do. Who needed sleep? "You're like the Energizer Bunny," his wife said to him. "I felt revved," Mario says.

Mario is not the only person to become a little too happy on the wire. "That's one of the dangers," says Greenberg. Dr. Don Malone of the Cleveland Clinic says, "We don't want hypomania. Some patients like that state. It can be pleasurable. But this is just like having a drug prescription. We decide how much, when, and how."

But it's not the same as with a drug prescription. A patient can decide to take no drugs, or five drugs. A patient can split his drugs with his spouse, feed them to the dog, or just switch psychopharmacologists.

Despite prescription regulations, there is tremendous freedom in being a pill popper. But not so for those with implants. True, no one any longer is dragged to the operating table in terror. No one is cut without exquisitely careful consideration. Instruments have been honed, imaging devices advanced. And yet, patients do not, cannot, fully understand, or appreciate, the degree to which, after the surgery, they will be under their doctor's control. Once a month OCD patients must visit their psychiatrist for what are called adjustments. (Emory's Dr. Mayberg says that for her depression patients, the rule is "set it and forget it.") Adjustment decisions, altering the "stimulation parameters," reflect how the patient scores on a paper-and-pencil test of symptom intensity, and they take into account the family's and the patient's subjective report, but the final and ultimately complete control lies with the treatment provider. At a 2004 meeting of the President's Council on Bioethics, Massachusetts General neurosurgeon and Harvard professor Dr. G. Rees Cosgrove gave a presentation on the issues surrounding DBS. At the end, another Harvard professor asked: "Who holds the clicker?"

Cosgrove's answer: "The doctor."

Mario's good mood continued. He had obsessions and compulsions, but they were smaller now, overshadowed by the grand energy that saturated his existence. For two weeks, he saw Greenberg every day. Greenberg adjusted the settings, turning the frequency, current, and pulse up or down. Sometimes, as a setting was changed, Mario felt that peculiar wash of sadness. Then he evened out.

Six weeks went by. Mario's daughter, Kaleigh, was born. She was a textbook perfect case of a baby; she screamed, she shat, she drooled, her entire unregulated being a little vortex of chaos. Mario changed her diaper, saw the golden smear of shit, and in his heart he backed way up. Over the next few months, his mood dipped. He had a terrible time feeding the baby. Sometimes it took him so long to give her breakfast that it would be time for lunch and he'd have to start all over again. The baby, strapped in the high chair, screamed, squash all over her mouth. Wipe that up. Right away. He was better, yes, but not nearly enough.

Mario went back to see Greenberg. Over a span of a few months, with Mario reporting the waxing and waning of his symptoms, Greenberg eventually got the setting right. Mario began to pick up dirty things. It was, at last, okay.

When Mario talks about that time now, tears come to his eyes. "It was like a miracle," he says. "I still have some OCD symptoms but way, way less. Dr. Greenberg and Rasmussen saved my life. Sometimes they travel to conferences together on the same plane. I tell them not to do it. It makes me very nervous. Who would adjust me if the plane went down? No one else in this country knows how to do it. It's like the president and the vice president traveling together."

At three research sites in this country (Butler Hospital, the Cleveland Clinic, and the University of Florida, funded to various degrees by Medtronic, the NIMH, and the National Alliance for Research on Schizophrenia and Depression), 15 or so OCD patients have since been implanted. So far, Greenberg and his fellow researchers have seen 50 percent of these patients improve, to varying degrees. Some experience a complete remission, others a more partial relief. In March, Mayberg released the first findings on depression —of her six patients, four experienced complete remission, while the other two derived no benefit at all. "The results for depression are extremely encouraging," says Mayberg. "We are very excited."

This excitement, coupled with our growing awareness of psychopharmacology's limitations, positions psychosurgery for a potential comeback. After all, when you take a drug you are perhaps altering your brain in ways as or more profound than neural implants do. When you take combinations of drugs, as many psychiatrically ill people do, you put yourself at risk for medication-induced Parkinson's and a whole raft of other serious side effects. "There is seemingly an advantage to any treatment that can be reversed. However, in the case of DBS this advantage is somewhat illusory," warns

Elliot Valenstein, professor emeritus of psychology and neuroscience at the University of Michigan. "Stimulation on neural tissue is likely to induce long-lasting, and perhaps permanent, changes in neural circuitry and chemistry." But Dr. Mayberg asks, "How do we know those changes aren't for the better?" Indeed, researchers hope that DBS might allow patients to better engage in behavioral therapy, eventually making artificial stimulation no longer necessary.

The hopes of implant makers like Medtronic are as big as the market they imagine. They forecast a day when neural implants will treat a wide variety of psychiatric problems, from eating disorders to substance abuse to schizophrenia. "How many people eat too much or don't eat enough or have some sort of mental illness?" asks Thomas Gunderson, a health care analyst with Piper Jaffray & Co. "There's a big market out there." Yet as these devices proliferate, so too will the ethical issues that stick to them like barnacles. Beyond questions of whether a severely mentally ill patient can provide informed consent, there continue to hover fears that DBS could fall into the hands of the state, or the overworked prison systems, and be used as a management device. After all, both of these things nearly did happen in the last century. Neurosurgeon Rees Cosgrove, at that bioethics conference, said, in an effort to caution restraint and thereby prove to the public that times have truly changed, "If we do not do this right and carefully, and, you know, properly . . . I do not think we will have another opportunity."

"It's easy for any good neurosurgeon to do this now," Cosgrove added. "That's the dangerous part—it's easy." Even now, no formal regulations prohibit doctors from using Medtronic implants for psychiatric purposes. And whether or not a particular device or usage has received FDA sanction means little anyway. Drugs are used all the time for "off label" purposes; so too could surgery. What will stop neurosurgeons both mercenary and curious from performing these operations on a public clamoring for relief? How long until implants are used to treat milder forms of mental illness? To take this its inevitable step forward, what will stop people from pursuing implants for augmentation purposes? Cosgrove described a patient who, after implantation, became more creative.

But perhaps the simplest conundrum is this: DBS for psychiatric disorders is very experimental. There are no animal models of DBS for anxiety or depression, so these forays into the human brain are largely unguided, despite all the high-tech equipment. At the 2004 meeting Cosgrove, who believes the procedure holds great promise, ticked off other issues: There's no possibility of large-scale, placebo-blind trials. Thus far Medtronic is the only maker of brain implants, and the major funder of the investigational studies. There's a risk of infection, of equipment malfunction. Most importantly, Cosgrove said, "We don't understand how deep brain stimulation works. We are not clear what the optimal targets are. We don't even know what the optimal stimulation parameters are, and we don't know what the long-term effects are . . .it's not as simple as we make it out to be."

But for Mario, it is simple. "I've had a hard life," he says. "My parents got divorced. My father died. I broke my foot. I have OCD." He pauses. "But," he says, "I have been helped."

Back in the 1950s, Rune Elmquist and Ake Senning developed the first implantable cardiac pacemaker, which made some people nervous, suggesting, as it did, an ever-diminishing gap between technology and the soul. Now, pacemakers are as common as grass. Perhaps there will come a time when neural prosthetics will be just as banal, when we will view the brain and its surgical manipulations without awe and handwringing.

And yet in no other place is there the potential for a surgeon to so acutely and immediately make memories evaporate, dreams rise, fingers freeze, hopes sputter. The argument could be made that we are not entirely our kidneys, but that we do live entirely within the circle of our skulls.

For Mario, this is all armchair philosophizing, irrelevant to his situation. "I don't care what it means," he says. "I care that I'm better. I'm not all better, but I'm better." So much better that recently he's let the batteries to his implants run down, though whether this indicates a DBS cure or just an OCD remission, Dr. Greenberg says, it is far too soon to tell.

Either way, Mario is proud of his progress. His wife recently gave birth to a second child. He carries with him pictures of his four-year-old daughter, Kaleigh, who wears tiny gold hoops in her ears. She and Mario play "tent" in the morning, climbing under the quilts, where he shows her shadow puppets. A bird flies. See, a spider. This is the chapel, this is the steeple, open it up, and here are the people. His wife showers; water hits the walls with a sound like static. Outside, cars roar on the roads. Under there, so close to his daughter, Mario can hear her breathe: He is not afraid to hold her hand. Some might say Mario, with his implants, has agreed to a strange sort of bondage, but Mario doesn't think so. He would say he's been freed.

Points of Engagement—Reading Comprehension

1. What is Lauren Slater referring to in the title of her essay, "Who Holds the Clicker?" Explain the title and its implications. Refer to specific places in the text that explain why the answer to this question is so important.

2. Slater writes, "Doctors are anxious to separate DBS [Deep Brain Stimuation] from the psychosurgeries of the past" (239). What were those psychosurgeries of the past? How are they viewed today? Point to several places in the text that illustrate why this separation is so important. Does the text suggest that doctors can successfully make this distinction?
3. In the third paragraph, Slater writes that "psychosurgery, by its very nature, brings with it a thicket of ethical twisters." Explain at least two of these "ethical twisters" in your own words and cite specific parts of the text to support your explanation.
4. What are the differences and similarities between using pills and performing surgery to relieve psychological symptoms? Make sure you consider Slater's entire essay in answering.

Points of Departure—Assignment Questions

1. Slater's essay asks us to consider how much personal control is too much to give up to relieve painful symptoms of OCD or any other illness. Given that Mario Della Grotta *chooses* to share his autonomy with a doctor doesn't make this any less complicated. If someone else "holds the clicker," can we still live with "authenticity" as described by Kenji Yoshino? Does psychosurgery, the reality of its effect on the brain, make the pursuit of a true or authentic self any less compelling? More compelling? Is there such a thing as a "true self"? Use Lauren Slater and Yoshino to work out your position on these questions. Consider as you draft, Slater and Yoshino's positions on the relationship between the control people have, the control they don't have (or give up), and their abilities to carve out and maintain an "authentic" or "true" self.
2. Any time a new protocol is introduced, someone is taking chances. Even the best of intentions may bring unforeseen or undesirable consequences. Surely the goals of Mario and his doctors are benevolent, as are companies creating companion robots for the elderly, or doctors providing contraception in developing nations. When goals like relieving personal misery, alleviating loneliness, or controlling population growth, are so lofty and the need is so urgent, who should make the decisions about when and how to intervene? Using Slater and either Sherry Turkle, Lisa Belkin, or Nicholas Kristof and Sheryl WuDunn formulate your own ideas about when, and how, people should intervene, and what role politics, ethics, social norms, culture, or religion should play in those decisions.
3. Lauren Slater recounts an encouraging story of the relief of Mario Della Grotta's crippling OCD symptoms through Deep Brain Stimulation, but she admits that "DBS

for psychiatric disorders is very experimental" (242). Physicians are painfully well aware of the only marginal understanding that the lobotomists of the last century acted on, yet current treatments have some negative consequences doctors know about and probably many they do not. Sherry Turkle writes about people who struggle with loneliness and are afforded relief, comfort, and companionship through robots. This, too, is very experimental; we have no idea how establishing what we think of as close relationships with robots will influence who we are as human beings. For this paper, answer this question using Slater and Turkle, and provide answers of your own: How much understanding is needed to allow experimental solutions to human needs? What risks are we taking when we do? What benefits result?

4. One consequence of psychosurgery is that it allows Mario Della Grotto to see the world in an entirely new way, a happier way; it changes the shape of his future. Consider other essays where this also happens, but where it does not involve intervention by doctors: Alain de Botton's "On Habit," Alison Gopnik's "Possible Worlds," Gregory Orr's "The Return to Hayneville," or Jeanette Winterson's "The World and Other Places." In the essays you've chosen, what triggers this new way of seeing? Is it permanent? Does it require effort, or is it a natural thing? What do these essays reveal about the potential of our brains to create new ways of perceiving, and living in, the world?
5. Lauren Slater raises questions about what ethicists refer to as a *slippery slope*: "What will stop neurosurgeons both mercenary and curious from performing these operations on a public clamoring for relief?... To take this its inevitable step forward, what will stop people from pursuing implants for augmentation purposes?" (242). Lisa Belkin and Wendell Berry are also concerned with the consequences of stepping onto the slippery slope. Belkin asks, "Is the potential for abuse in some circumstances reason not to pursue research that can be lifesaving under the right circumstances?" Should the "slippery slope" argument scare us away? Work with Slater and Belkin or Berry to form your position on Belkin's question.

Speaking in Tongues

Zadie Smith

Points of Access—Pre-Reading

1. Do you speak differently when you are with certain groups of people? Is the voice you use in the classroom different from the voice you use when you are with friends or family? Does changing this voice also cause you to change your behavior?
2. In the essay you're about to read, Zadie Smith writes about the complicated identity she possesses as the child of white and black parents. She writes, "I love to be black and I love that I had a white father" (254). Do you have a diverse cultural or ethnic heritage, and if so, what challenges or benefits does it bring?
3. Does changing the way we speak to suit the environment a manifestation of phoniness, or part of adaptation to the environment? What informs your answer?
4. Do you think having a bicultural or biracial background might be an asset in an American President? How is it a liability?

1.

Hello. This voice I speak with these days, this English voice with its rounded vowels and consonants in more or less the right place—this is not the voice of my childhood. I picked it up in college, along with the unabridged *Clarissa* and a taste for port. Maybe this fact is only what it seems to be—a case of bald social climbing—but at the time I genuinely thought *this* was the voice of lettered people, and that if I didn't have the voice of lettered people I would never truly be lettered. A braver person, perhaps, would have stood firm, teaching her peers a useful lesson by example: not all lettered people need be of the same class, nor speak identically. I went the other way. Partly out of cowardice and a constitutional eagerness to please, but also because I didn't quite see it as a straight swap, of this voice for that.

My own childhood had been the story of this and that combined, of the synthesis of disparate things. It never occurred to me that I was leaving the London district of Willesden for Cambridge. I thought I was *adding* Cambridge to Willesden, this new way of talking to that old way. Adding a new kind of knowledge to a different kind I already had. And for a while, that's how it was: at home, during the holidays, I spoke with my old voice, and in the old voice seemed to feel and speak things that I couldn't express in college, and vice versa. I felt a sort of wonder at the flexibility of the thing. Like being alive twice.

But flexibility is something that requires work if it is to be maintained. Recently my double voice has deserted me for a single one, reflecting the smaller world into which my work has led me. Willesden was a big, colorful, working-class sea; Cambridge was a smaller, posher pond, and almost univocal; the literary world is a puddle. This voice I picked up along the way is no longer an exotic garment I put on like a college gown whenever I choose—now it is my only voice, whether I want it or not. I regret it; I should have kept both voices alive in my mouth. They were both a part of me. But how the culture warns against it! As George Bernard Shaw delicately put it in his preface to the play *Pygmalion,* "many thousands of [British] men and women . . . have sloughed off their native dialects and acquired a new tongue."

Few, though, will admit to it. Voice adaptation is still the original British sin. Monitoring and exposing such citizens is a national pastime, as popular as sex scandals and libel cases. If you lean toward the Atlantic with your high-rising terminals you're a sell-out; if you pronounce borrowed European words in their original style—even if you try something as innocent as *parmigiano* for "parmesan"—you're a fraud. If you go (metaphorically speaking) down the British class scale, you've gone from Cockney to "mockney," and can expect a public tar and feathering; to go the other way is to perform an unforgivable act of class betrayal. Voices are meant to be unchanging and singular. There's no quicker way to insult an ex-pat Scotsman in London than to tell him he's lost his accent. We feel that our voices are who we are, and that to have more than one, or to use different versions of a voice for different occasions, represents, at best, a Janus-faced duplicity, and at worst, the loss of our very souls.

Whoever changes their voice takes on, in Britain, a queerly tragic dimension. They have betrayed that puzzling dictum "To thine own self be true," so often quoted approvingly as if it represented the wisdom of Shakespeare rather than the hot air of Polonius. *"What's to become of me? What's to become of me?"* wails Eliza Doolittle, realizing her middling dilemma. With a voice too posh for the flower girls and yet too redolent of the gutter for the ladies in Mrs. Higgins's drawing room.

But Eliza—patron saint of the tragically double-voiced—is worthy of closer inspection. The first thing to note is that both Eliza and *Pygmalion* are entirely didactic, as Shaw meant them to be. "I delight," he wrote,

> in throwing [*Pygmalion*] at the heads of the wiseacres who repeat the parrot cry that art should never be didactic. It goes to prove my contention that art should never be anything else.

He was determined to tell the unambiguous tale of a girl who changes her voice and loses her self. And so she arrives like this:

> Don't you be so saucy. You ain't heard what I come for yet. Did you tell him I come in a taxi? . . . Oh, we are proud! He ain't above giving lessons, not him: I heard him say so. Well, I ain't come here to ask for any compliment; and if my moneys not good enough I can go elsewhere. Now you know, don't you? I'm come to have lessons, I am. And to pay for em too: make no mistake. I want to be a lady in a flower shop stead of selling at the corner of Tottenham Court Road. But they won't take me unless I can talk more genteel.

And she leaves like this:

> I can't. I could have done it once; but now I can't go back to it. Last night, when I was wandering about, a girl spoke to me; and I tried to get back into the old way with her; but it was no use. You told me, you know, that when a child is brought to a foreign country, it picks up the language in a few weeks, and forgets its own. Well, I am a child in your country. I have forgotten my own language, and can speak nothing but yours.

By the end of his experiment, Professor Higgins has made his Eliza an awkward, in-between thing, neither flower girl nor lady, with one voice lost and another gained, at the steep price of everything she was, and everything she knows. Almost as afterthought, he sends Eliza's father, Alfred Doolittle, to his doom, too, securing a three-thousand-a-year living for the man on the condition that Doolittle lecture for the Wannafeller Moral Reform World League up to six times a year. This burden brings the philosophical dustman into the close, unwanted embrace of what he disdainfully calls "middle class morality." By the time the curtain goes down, both Doolittles find themselves stuck in the middle, which is, to Shaw, a comi-tragic place to be, with the emphasis on the tragic. What are they fit for? What will become of them?

How persistent this horror of the middling spot is, this dread of the interim place! It extends through the specter of the tragic mulatto, to the plight of the transsexual, to our present anxiety—disguised as genteel concern—for the contemporary immigrant, tragically split, we are sure, between worlds, ideas, cultures, voices—whatever will become of them? Something's got to give—one voice must be sacrificed for the other. What is double must be made singular.

But this, the apparent didactic moral of Eliza's story, is undercut by the fact of the play itself, which is an orchestra of many voices, simultaneously and perfectly rendered, with no shade of color or tone sacrificed. Higgins's Harley Street high-handedness is the equal of Mrs. Pierce's lower-middle-class gentility, Pickering's kindhearted aristocratic imprecision every bit as convincing as Arthur Doolittle's Nietzschean Cockney-by-way-of-Wales. Shaw had a wonderful ear, able to reproduce almost as many quirks of the English language as Shakespeare's. Shaw was in possession of a gift he wouldn't, or couldn't, give Eliza: he spoke in tongues.

It gives me a strange sensation to turn from Shaw's melancholy Pygmalion story to another, infinitely more hopeful version, written by the new president of the United States of America. Of course, his ear isn't half bad either. In *Dreams from My Father,* the new president displays an enviable facility for dialogue, and puts it to good use, animating a cast every bit as various as the one James Baldwin—an obvious influence— conjured for his own many-voiced novel *Another Country*. Obama can do young Jewish male, black old lady from the South Side, white woman from Kansas, Kenyan elders, white Harvard nerds, black Columbia nerds, activist women, churchmen, security guards, bank tellers, and even a British man called Mr. Wilkerson, who on a starry night on safari says credibly British things like: "I believe that's the Milky Way." This new president doesn't just speak *for* his people. He can *speak* them. It is a disorienting talent in a president; we're so unused to it. I have to pinch myself to remember who wrote the following well-observed scene, seemingly plucked from a comic novel:

> "Man, I'm not going to any more of these bullshit Punahou parties."
>
> "Yeah, that's what you said the last time.."
>
> "I mean it this time. These girls are A-1, USDA-certified racists. All of 'em. White girls. Asian girls — shoot, these Asians worse than the whites. Think we got a disease or something."
>
> "Maybe they're looking at that big butt of yours. Man, I thought you were in training."
>
> "Get your hands out of my fries. You ain't my bitch, nigger . . . buy your own damn fries. Now what was I talking about?"
>
> "Just 'cause a girl don't go out with you doesn't make her a racist."

This is the voice of Obama at seventeen, as remembered by Obama. He's still recognizably Obama; he already seeks to unpack and complicate apparently obvious things ("Just 'cause a girl don't go out with you doesn't make her a racist"); he's already gently cynical about the impassioned dogma of other people ("Yeah, that's what you said the last time"). And he has a sense of humor ("Maybe they're looking at that big butt of yours"). Only the voice is different: he has made almost as large a leap as Eliza Doolittle. The conclusions Obama draws from his own Pygmalion experience, however, are subtler than Shaw's. The tale he tells is not the old tragedy of gaining a new, false voice at the expense of a true one. The tale he tells is all about addition. His is the story of a genuinely many-voiced man. If it has a moral it is that each man must be true to his selves, plural.

For Obama, having more than one voice in your ear is not a burden, or not solely a burden—it is also a gift. And the gift is of an interesting kind, not well served by that dull publishing-house title *Dreams from My Father: A Story of Race and Inheritance* with its suggestion of a simple linear inheritance, of paternal dreams and aspirations passed down to a son, and fulfilled. *Dreams from My Father* would have been a fine title for John McCain's book *Faith of My Fathers,* which concerns exactly this kind of linear masculine inheritance, in his case from soldier to soldier. For Obama's book, though, it's wrong, lopsided. He corrects its misperception early on, in the first chapter, while discussing the failure of his parents' relationship, characterized by their only son as the end of a dream. "Even as that spell was broken," he writes, "and the worlds that they thought they'd left behind reclaimed each of them, I *occupied the place* where their dreams had been."

To *occupy* a dream, to exist in a dreamed space (conjured by both father and mother), is surely a quite different thing from simply *inheriting* a dream. It's more interesting. What did Pauline Kael call Cary Grant? *"The Man from Dream City."* When Bristolian Archibald Leach became suave Cary Grant, the transformation happened in his voice, which he subjected to a strange, indefinable manipulation, resulting in that heavenly sui generis accent, neither west country nor posh, American nor English. It came from nowhere, *he* came from nowhere. Grant seemed the product of a collective dream, dreamed up by moviegoers in hard times, as it sometimes feels voters have dreamed up Obama in hard times. Both men have a strange reflective quality, typical of the self-created man—we see in them whatever we want to see. " *Everyone wants to be Cary Grant,"* said Cary Grant. *"Even I want to be Cary Grant."* It's not hard to imagine Obama having that same thought, backstage at Grant Park, hearing his own name chanted by the hopeful multitude. *Everyone wants to be Barack Obama. Even I want to be Barack Obama.*

2.

But I haven't described Dream City. I'll try to. It is a place of many voices, where the unified singular self is an illusion. Naturally, Obama was born there. So was I. When your personal multiplicity is printed on your face, in an almost too obviously thematic manner, in your DNA, in your hair and in the neither this nor that beige of your skin—well, anyone can see you come from Dream City. In Dream City everything is doubled, everything is various. You have no choice but to cross borders and speak in tongues. That's how you get from your mother to your father, from talking to one set of folks who think you're not black enough to another who figure you insufficiently white. It's the kind of town where the wise man says "I" cautiously, because "I" feels like too straight and singular a phoneme to represent the true multiplicity of his experience. Instead, citizens of Dream City prefer to use the collective pronoun "we."

Throughout his campaign Obama was careful always to say we. He was noticeably wary of "I." By speaking so, he wasn't simply avoiding a singularity he didn't feel, he was also drawing us in with him. He had the audacity to suggest that, even if you can't see it stamped on their faces, most people come from Dream City, too. Most of us have complicated back stories, messy histories, multiple narratives.

It was a high-wire strategy, for Obama, this invocation of our collective human messiness. His enemies latched on to its imprecision, emphasizing the exotic, un-American nature of Dream City, this ill-defined place where you could be from Hawaii and Kenya, Kansas and Indonesia all at the same time, where you could jive talk like a street hustler and orate like a senator. What kind of a crazy place is that? But they underestimated how many people come from Dream City, how many Americans, in their daily lives, conjure contrasting voices and seek a synthesis between disparate things.

Turns out, Dream City wasn't so strange to them.

Or did they never actually see it? We now know that Obama spoke of *Main Street* in Iowa and of *sweet potato pie* in Northwest Philly, and it could be argued that he succeeded because he so rarely misspoke, carefully tailoring his intonations to suit the sensibility of his listeners. Sometimes he did this within one speech, within one line: "We worship an *awesome* God in the blue states, and we don't like federal agents poking around our libraries in the red states." *Awesome God* comes to you straight from the pews of a Georgia church; *poking around* feels more at home at a kitchen table in South Bend, Indiana. The balance was perfect, cunningly counterpoised and never accidental. It's only now that it's over that we see him let his guard down a little, on *60 Minutes*, say, dropping in that culturally, casually black construction "Hey, I'm not stupid, *man,* that's why I'm president," something it's hard to imagine him doing even three weeks earlier. To a certain kind of mind, it must have looked like the mask had slipped for a moment.

Which brings us to the single-voiced Obamanation crowd. They rage on in the blogs and on the radio, waiting obsessively for the mask to slip. They have a great fear of what they see as Obama's doubling ways. "He says one thing but he means another"—this is the essence of the fear campaign. He says he's a capitalist, but he'll spread your wealth. He says he's a Christian, but really he's going to empower the Muslims. And so on and so forth. These are fears that have their roots in an anxiety about voice. *Who is he?* people kept asking. *I mean, who is this guy, really?* He says *sweet potato pie* in Philly and *Main Street* in Iowa! When he talks to us, he sure *sounds* like us—but behind our backs he says we're clinging to our religion, to our guns. And when Jesse Jackson heard that Obama had lectured a black church congregation about the epidemic of absent black fathers, he experienced this, too, as a tonal betrayal; Obama was "talking down to black people." In both cases, there was the sense of a double-dealer, of someone who tailors his speech to fit the audience, who is not *of* the people (because he is able to look at them objectively) but always above them.

The Jackson gaffe, with its Oedipal violence ("I want to cut his nuts out"), is especially poignant because it goes to the heart of a generational conflict in the black community, concerning what we will say in public and what we say in private. For it has been a point of honor, among the civil rights generation, that any criticism or negative analysis of our community, expressed, as they often are by white politicians, without context, without real empathy or understanding, should not be repeated by a black politician when the white community is listening, even if (*especially* if) the criticism happens to be true (more than half of all black American children live in single-parent households). Our business is our business. Keep it in the family; don't wash your dirty linen in public; stay unified. (Of course, with his overheard gaffe, Jackson unwittingly broke his own rule.)

Until Obama, black politicians had always adhered to these unwritten rules. In this way, they defended themselves against those two bogeymen of black political life: the Uncle Tom and the House Nigger. The black politician who played up to, or even simply echoed, white fears, desires, and hopes for the black community was in danger of earning these epithets—even Martin Luther King was not free from such suspicions. Then came Obama, and the new world he had supposedly ushered in, the postracial world, in which what mattered most was not blind racial allegiance but factual truth. It was felt that Jesse Jackson was sadly out of step with this new postracial world: even his own son felt moved to publicly repudiate his "ugly rhetoric." But Jackson's anger was not incomprehensible nor his distrust unreasonable. Jackson lived through a bitter struggle, and bitter struggles deform their participants in subtle, complicated ways. The idea that one should speak one's cultural allegiance first and the truth second (and that this is a sign of authenticity) is precisely such a deformation.

Right up to the wire, Obama made many black men and women of Jackson's generation suspicious. How can the man who passes between culturally black and white voices with such flexibility, with such ease, be an honest man? How *will* the man from Dream City keep it real? Why won't he speak with a clear and unified voice? These were genuine questions for people born in real cities at a time when those cities were implacably divided, when the black movement had to yell with a clear and unified voice, or risk not being heard at all. And then he won. Watching Jesse Jackson in tears in Grant Park, pressed up against the varicolored American public, it seemed like he, at least, had received the answer he needed: only a many-voiced man could have spoken to that many people.

A clear and unified voice. In that context, this business of being biracial, of being half black and half white, is awkward. In his memoir, Obama takes care to ridicule a certain black girl called Joyce—a composite figure from his college days who happens also to be part Italian and part French and part Native American and is inordinately fond of mentioning these facts, and who likes to say:

> I'm not black. . . I'm *multiracial*. . . Why should I have to choose between them? . . . It's not white people who are making me choose. . . No—it's *black people* who always have to make everything racial. *They're* the ones making me choose. *They're* the ones who are telling me I can't be who I am. . .

He has her voice down pat and so condemns her out of her own mouth. For she's the third bogeyman of black life, the tragic mulatto, who secretly wishes she "passed," always keen to let you know about her white heritage. It's the fear of being mistaken for Joyce that has always ensured that I ignore the box marked "biracial" and tick the box marked "black" on any questionnaire I fill out, and call myself unequivocally a black writer and roll my eyes at anyone who insists that Obama is not the first black president but the first biracial one. But I also know in my heart that it's an equivocation; I know that Obama has a double consciousness, is black and, at the same time, white, as I am, unless we are suggesting that one side of a person's genetics and cultural heritage cancels out or trumps the other.

But to mention the double is to suggest shame at the singular. Joyce insists on her varied heritage because she fears and is ashamed of the singular black. I suppose it's possible that subconsciously I am also a tragic mulatto, torn between pride and shame. In my conscious life, though, I cannot honestly say I feel proud to be white and ashamed to be black or proud to be black and ashamed to be white. I find it impossible to experience either pride or shame over accidents of genetics in which I had no active part. I understand how those words got into the racial discourse, but I can't sign up to them. I'm not proud to be female either. I am not even proud to be human—I only love to be so. As I love to be female and I love to be black, and I love that I had a white father.

It's telling that Joyce is one of the few voices in *Dreams from My Father* that is truly left out in the cold, outside of the expansive sympathy of Obama's narrative. She is an entirely didactic being, a demon Obama has to raise up, if only for a page, so everyone can watch him slay her. I know the feeling. When I was in college I felt I'd rather run away with the Black Panthers than be associated with the Joyces I occasionally met. It's the Joyces of this world who "talk down to black folks." And so to avoid being Joyce, or being seen to be Joyce, you unify, you speak with one voice.

And the concept of a unified black voice is a potent one. It has filtered down, these past forty years, into the black community at all levels, settling itself in that impossible injunction "keep it real," the original intention of which was unification. We were going to unify the concept of Blackness in order to strengthen it. Instead we confined and restricted it. To me, the instruction "keep it real" is a sort of prison cell, two feet by five. The fact is, it's too narrow. I just can't live comfortably in there. "*Keep it real*" replaced the blessed and solid genetic fact of Blackness with a flimsy imperative. It made Blackness a quality each individual black person was constantly in danger of losing. And almost anything could trigger the loss of one's Blackness: attending certain universities, an impressive variety of jobs, a fondness for opera, a white girlfriend, an interest in golf. And of course, any change in the voice. There was a popular school of thought that maintained the voice was at the very heart of the thing; fail to keep it real there and you'd never see your Blackness again.

How absurd that all seems now. And not because we live in a postracial world—we don't—but because the reality of race has diversified. Black reality has diversified. It's black people who talk like me, and black people who talk like L'il Wayne. It's black conservatives and black liberals, black sportsmen and black lawyers, black computer technicians and black ballet dancers and black truck drivers and black presidents. We're all black, and we all love to be black, and we all sing from our own hymn sheet. We're all surely black people, but we may be finally approaching a point of human history where you can't talk up or down to us anymore, but only *to* us. *He's talking down to white people*—how curious it sounds the other way round! In order to say such a thing one would have to think collectively of white people, as a people of one mind who speak with one voice—a thought experiment in which we have no practice. But it's worth trying. It's only when you play the record backward that you hear the secret message.

3.

For reasons that are obscure to me, those qualities we cherish in our artists we condemn in our politicians. In our artists we look for the many-colored voice, the multiple sensibility. The apogee of this is, of course, Shakespeare: even more than for his wordplay we cherish him for his lack of allegiance. *Our* Shakespeare sees always both sides of a thing, he is black and white, male and female—he is everyman. The giant lacunae in his biography are merely a convenience; if any new facts of religious or political affiliation were ever to arise we would dismiss them in our hearts anyway. Was he, for example, a man of Rome or not? He has appeared, to generations of readers, not of one religion but of both, in truth, beyond both. Born into the middle of Britain's fierce Catholic-Protestant culture war, how could the bloody absurdity of those years not impress upon him a strong sense of cultural contingency?

It was a war of ideas that began for Will—as it began for Barack—in the dreams of his father. For we know that John Shakespeare, a civic officer in Protestant times, oversaw the repainting of medieval frescoes and the destruction of the rood loft and altar in Stratford's own fine Guild Chapel, but we also know that in the rafters of the Shakespeare home John hid a secret Catholic "Spiritual Testament," a signed profession of allegiance to the old faith. A strange experience, to watch one's own father thus divided, professing one thing in public while practicing another in private. John Shakespeare was a kind of equivocator: it's what you do when you're in a corner, when you can't be a Catholic and a loyal Englishman at the same time. When you can't be both black and white. Sometimes in a country ripped apart by dogma, those who wish to keep their heads—in both senses—must learn to split themselves in two.

And this we *still* know, here, at a four-hundred-year distance. No one can hope to be president of these United States without professing a committed and straightforward belief in two things: the existence of God and the principle of American exceptionalism. But how many of them equivocated, and who, in their shoes, would not equivocate, too?

Fortunately, Shakespeare was an artist and so had an outlet his father didn't have—the many-voiced theater. Shakespeare's art, the very medium of it, allowed him to do what civic officers and politicians can't seem to: speak simultaneous truths. (Is it not, for example, experientially true that one can both believe and *not* believe in God?) In his plays he is woman, man, black, white, believer, heretic, Catholic, Protestant, Jew, Muslim. He grew up in an atmosphere of equivocation, but he lived in freedom. And he offers us freedom: to pin him down to a single identity would be an obvious diminishment, both for Shakespeare and for us. Generations of critics have insisted on this irreducible multiplicity, though they have each expressed it different ways, through the glass of their times. Here is Keats's famous attempt, in 1817, to give this quality a name:

> At once it struck me, what quality went to form a Man of Achievement especially in Literature and which Shakespeare possessed so enormously—I mean *Negative Capability*, that is when man is capable of being in uncertainties, Mysteries, doubts, without any irritable reaching after fact and reason.

And here is Stephen Greenblatt doing the same, in 2004:

> There are many forms of heroism in Shakespeare, but ideological heroism— the fierce, self-immolating embrace of an idea or institution—is not one of them.

For Keats, Shakespeare's many voices are quasi-mystical as suited the Romantic thrust of Keats's age. For Greenblatt, Shakespeare's negative capability is sociopolitical at root. Will had seen too many wild-eyed martyrs, too many executed terrorists, too many wars on the Catholic terror. He had watched men rage absurdly at rood screens and write treatises in praise of tables. He had seen men disemboweled while still alive, their entrails burned before their eyes, and all for the preference of a Latin Mass over a common prayer or vice versa. He understood what fierce, singular certainty creates and what it destroys. In response, he made himself a diffuse, uncertain thing, a mass of contradictory, irresolvable voices that speak truth plurally. Through the glass of 2009, "negative capability" looks like the perfect antidote to "ideological heroism."

From our politicians, though, we still look for ideological heroism, despite everything. We consider pragmatists to be weak. We call men of balance naive fools. In England, we once had an insulting name for such people: trimmers. In the mid-1600s, a trimmer was any politician who attempted to straddle the reviled middle ground between Cavalier and Roundhead, Parliament and the Crown; to call a man a trimmer was to accuse him of being insufficiently committed to an ideology. But in telling us of these times, the nineteenth-century English historian Thomas Macaulay draws our attention to Halifax, great statesman of the Privy Council, set up to mediate between Parliament and Crown as London burned. Halifax proudly called himself a trimmer, assuming it, Macaulay explains, as

> a title of honour, and vindicat[ing], with great vivacity, the dignity of the appellation. Everything good, he said, trims between extremes. The temperate zone trims between the climate in which men are roasted and the climate in which they are frozen. The English Church trims between the Anabaptist madness and the Papist lethargy. The English constitution trims between the Turkish despotism and Polish anarchy. Virtue

> is nothing but a just temper between propensities any one of which, if indulged to excess, becomes vice.

Which all sounds eminently reasonable and Aristotelian. And Macaulay's description of Halifax's character is equally attractive:

> His intellect was fertile, subtle, and capacious. His polished, luminous, and animated eloquence...was the delight of the House of Lords.. His political tracts well deserve to be studied for their literary merit.

In fact, Halifax is familiar—he sounds like the man from Dream City. This makes Macaulay's caveat the more striking:

> Yet he was less successful in politics than many who enjoyed smaller advantages. Indeed, those intellectual *peculiarities which make his writings valuable* frequently impeded him in the contests of active life. For he always saw passing events, not in the point of view in which they commonly appear to one who bears a part in them, but in the point of view in which, after the lapse of many years, they appear to the philosophic historian.

To me, this is a doleful conclusion. It is exactly men with such intellectual peculiarities that I have always hoped to see in politics. But maybe Macaulay is correct: maybe the Halifaxes of this world make, in the end, better writers than politicians. A lot rests on how this president turns out—but that's a debate for the future. Here I want instead to hazard a little theory, concerning the evolution of a certain type of voice, typified by Halifax, by Shakespeare, and very possibly the President. For the voice of what Macaulay called "the philosophic historian" is, to my mind, a valuable and particular one, and I think someone should make a proper study of it. It's a voice that develops in a man over time; my little theory sketches four developmental stages.

The first stage in the evolution is contingent and cannot be contrived. In this first stage, the voice, by no fault of its own, finds itself trapped between two poles, two competing belief systems. And so this first stage necessitates the second: the voice learns to be flexible between these two fixed points, even to the point of equivocation. Then the third stage: this native flexibility leads to a sense of being able to "see a thing from both sides." And then the final stage, which I think of as the mark of a certain kind of genius: the voice relinquishes ownership of itself, develops a creative sense of disassociation in which the claims that are particular to it seem no stronger than anyone else's. There it is, my little theory—I'd rather call it a story. It is a story about a wonderful voice, occasionally used by citizens, rarely by men of power. Amidst the din of the 2008 culture wars it proved especially hard to hear.

In this lecture I have been seeking to tentatively suggest that the voice that speaks with such freedom, thus unburdened by dogma and personal bias, thus flooded with empathy, might make a good president. It's only now that I realize that in all this utilitarianism I've left joyfulness out of the account, and thus neglected a key constituency of my own people, the poets! Being many-voiced may be a complicated gift for a president, but in poets it is a pure delight in need of neither defense nor explanation. Plato banished them from his uptight and annoying republic so long ago that they have lost all their anxiety. They are fancy-free.

"I am a Hittite in love with a horse," writes Frank O'Hara.

> *I don't know what blood's*
> *in me I feel like an African prince I am a girl walking downstairs*
> *in a red pleated dress with heels I am a champion taking a fall*
> *I am a jockey with a sprained ass-hole I am the light mist*
> *in which a face appears*
> *and it is another face of blonde I am a baboon eating a banana*
> *I am a dictator looking at his wife I am a doctor eating a child*
> *and the child's mother smiling I am a Chinaman climbing a mountain*
> *I am a child smelling his father's underwear*
> *I am an Indian sleeping on a scalp*
> *and my pony is stamping in*
> *the birches,*
> *and I've just caught sight of the*
> Niña, *the* Pinta *and the* Santa
> Maria.
> *What land is this, so free?*

Frank O'Hara's republic is of the imagination, of course. It is the only land of perfect freedom. Presidents, as a breed, tend to dismiss this land, thinking it has nothing to teach them. If this new president turns out to be different, then writers will count their blessings, but with or without a president on board, writers should always count their blessings. A line of O'Hara's reminds us of this. It's carved on his gravestone. It reads: "Grace to be born and live as variously as possible."

But to live variously cannot simply be a gift, endowed by an accident of birth; it has to be a continual effort, continually renewed. I felt this with force the night of the election. I was at a lovely New York party, full of lovely people, almost all of whom were white, liberal, highly educated, and celebrating with one happy voice as the states turned blue. Just as they called Iowa my phone rang and a strident German voice said: "Zadie! Come to Harlem! It's vild here. I'm in za middle of a crazy Reggae bar—it's so vonderful! Vy not come now!"

I mention he was German only so we don't run away with the idea that flexibility comes only to the beige, or gay, or otherwise marginalized. Flexibility is a choice, always open to all of us. (He was a writer, however. Make of that what you will.)

But wait: all the way uptown? A crazy reggae bar? For a minute I hesitated, because I was at a lovely party having a lovely time. Or was that it? There was something else. In truth I thought: but I'll be ludicrous, in my silly dress, with this silly posh English voice, in a crowded bar of black New Yorkers celebrating. It's amazing how many of our cross-cultural and cross-class encounters are limited not by hate or pride or shame, but by another equally insidious, less-discussed, emotion: embarrassment. A few minutes later, I was in a taxi and heading uptown with my Northern Irish husband and our half-Indian, half-English friend, but that initial hesitation was ominous; the first step on a typical British journey. A hesitation in the face of difference, which leads to caution before difference and ends in fear of it. Before long, the only voice you recognize, the only life you can empathize with, is your own. You will think that a novelist's screwy leap of logic. Well, it's my novelist credo and I believe it. I believe that flexibility of voice leads to a flexibility in all things. My audacious hope in Obama is based, I'm afraid, on precisely such flimsy premises.

It's my audacious hope that a man born and raised between opposing dogmas, between cultures, between voices, could not help but be aware of the extreme contingency of culture. I further audaciously hope that such a man will not mistake the happy accident of his own cultural sensibilities for a set of natural laws, suitable for general application. I even hope that he will find himself in agreement with George Bernard Shaw when he declared, "Patriotism is, fundamentally, a conviction that a particular country is the best in the world because you were born in it." But that may be an audacious hope too far. We'll see if Obama's lifelong vocal flexibility will enable him to say proudly with one voice "I love my country" while saying with another voice "It is a country, like other countries." I hope so. He seems just the man to demonstrate that between those two voices there exists no contradiction and no equivocation but rather a proper and decent human harmony.

Points of Engagement—Reading Comprehension

1. Smith speaks with regret about losing her childhood "voice" and of now speaking in one voice. She writes "I should have kept both voices alive in my mouth" (248). Why did Smith eventually lose her childhood accent, why is she regretful about this loss, and what is the value, according to Smith, of having the ability to speak in different voices or "tongues"? Cite evidence from the text to support your answer.
2. What does the expression "keep it real" mean to Zadie Smith? Why is this important?
3. Smith refers to the idea of Dream City, a "place of many voices, where the unified singular self is an illusion" (251). What are some characteristics of Dream City? In what ways does Barack Obama embody this idea, according to Smith? Why, according to Smith, are some Americans uncomfortable with Dream City, and with Obama's ability to speak in many voices and move between different worlds? Why do some wonder how "the man from Dream City [will] keep it real?" (253).
4. Who is the figure of "Joyce" in Smith's essay? What is her significance to Smith?
5. In the final paragraph, Smith claims "flexibility of voice leads to a flexibility in all things." What does she mean by that? Do you agree with her? Is flexibility always a positive attribute? Why or why not?
6. What is the significance of the anecdote Smith tells at the end of her essay about being invited to the "crazy reggae" bar in Harlem? Why was she hesitant, at first, about accepting the invitation?
7. Consider Zadie Smith's statement that "those qualities we cherish in our artists we condemn in our politicians" (256). Why does Smith make this claim? Develop a discussion of how people might view the same traits in people differently depending on what role they play in society.

Points of Departure—Assignment Questions

1. Zadie Smith gives many examples of people who are trying to get a story out, from Barack Obama to William Shakespeare. Kenji Yoshino, Gregory Orr, and Jeanette Winterson have stories to tell too, and they revolve around coming of age. What might help someone tell a personal story that is accessible to many people? Does being able to speak from more than one perspective make it easier or harder for a person to tell his or her story? Do their multiple perspectives help or do they compromise who they are as they grow up, making it difficult or impossible to "keep it real"? Is

not keeping it real such a bad thing? In this paper, engage with the specific terms and ideas of Smith and Yoshino, Orr or Winterson.

2. Zadie Smith is very conscious of the effect the environment has on the way she both perceives and expresses herself. Using essays by Smith and Adam Gopnik, Jane Goodall, Alain de Botton, or Kenji Yoshino describe how the influence of environment can alter self-perception and/or communication.
3. Zadie Smith describes President Obama as having multiple voices. For Smith this is a positive attribute, "a gift" (251). Is the ability to understand differing viewpoints and communicate in multiple voices more of a burden or a gift? Why? Propose your own answers using Smith and Wendell Berry, Amy Chua, Jane Goodall, Naomi Klein, or Kenji Yoshino.
4. The United States is now part of a globalized world. Can the ability to interact using a "flexible" voice, as Zadie Smith describes, be used to enhance the relationship the United States has with other countries, or would this flexibility compromise American self-interest? Your project is to answer this question and formulate your own thesis using Smith and Ian Bremmer, Diana Eck, or Naomi Klein.

Alone Together

Sherry Turkle

Points of Access—Pre-Reading

1. What would you think about leaving your cellphone off for a day? A week? What would change in your life? How would you feel? Why?
2. Do you have an online identity that is different from your real-life identity? Do you know anyone who does? Even if you "play yourself" online, how does your screen identity compare with your real-life one? Does assuming that identity change the way you interact with people, the nature of your relationships? Is your screen identity more authentic than your real-life one? Less? Why?
3. Do you think of robots as more science fiction or real life? What do they do for us? Can robots be substitutes for people? Is it possible to have empathy for a robot who has no feelings? What if we do? What would that mean about *us*?

Technology proposes itself as the architect of our intimacies. These days, it suggests substitutions that put the real on the run. The advertising for Second Life, a virtual world where you get to build an avatar, a house, a family, and a social life, basically says, "Finally, a place to love your body, love your friends, and love your life."[1] On Second Life, a lot of people, as represented by their avatars, are richer than they are in first life and a lot younger, thinner, and better dressed. And we are smitten with the idea of sociable robots, which most people first meet in the guise of artificial pets. Zhu Zhu pet hamsters, the "it" toy of the 2009–2010 holiday season, are presented as "better" than any real pet could be. We are told they are lovable and responsive, don't require cleanup, and will never die.

Technology is seductive when what it offers meets our human vulnerabilities. And as it turns out, we are very vulnerable indeed. We are lonely but fearful of intimacy. Digital connections and the sociable robot may offer the illusion of companionship without the demands of friendship. Our networked life allows us to hide from each other, even as we are tethered to each other. We'd rather text than talk. A simple story makes this last point, told in her own words by a harried mother in her late forties:

> I needed to find a new nanny. When I interview nannies, I like to go to where they live, so that I can see them in their environment, not just in mine. So, I made an appointment to interview Ronnie, who had applied for the job. I show up at her apartment and her housemate answers the door. She is a young woman, around twenty-one, texting on her BlackBerry. Her thumbs are bandaged. I look at them, pained at the tiny thumb splints, and I try to be sympathetic. "That must hurt." But she just shrugs. She explains that she is still able to text. I tell her I am here to speak with Ronnie; this is her job interview. Could she please knock on Ronnie's bedroom door? The girl with the bandaged thumbs looks surprised. "Oh no," she says, "I would never do that. That would be intrusive. I'll text her." And so she sent a text message to Ronnie, no more than fifteen feet away.

This book, which completes a trilogy on computers and people, asks how we got to this place and whether we are content to be here.

In *The Second Self,* I traced the subjective side of personal computers—not what computers do for us but what they do to us, to our ways of thinking about ourselves, our relationships, our sense of being human. From the start, people used interactive and reactive computers to reflect on the self and think about the difference between machines and people. Were intelligent machines alive? If not, why not? In my studies I found that children were most likely to see this new category of object, the computational object, as "sort of" alive—a story that has continued to evolve. In *Life on the Screen,* my focus shifted from how people see computers to how they forge new identities in online spaces. In *Alone Together,* I show how technology has taken both of these stories to a new level.

Computers no longer wait for humans to project meaning onto them. Now, sociable robots meet our gaze, speak to us, and learn to recognize us. They ask us to take care of them; in response, we imagine that they might care for us in return. Indeed, among the most talked about robotic designs are in the area of care and companionship. In summer 2010, there are enthusiastic reports in the *New York Times* and the *Wall Street Journal* on robotic teachers, companions, and therapists. And Microsoft demonstrates a virtual human, Milo, that recognizes the people it interacts with and whose personality is sculpted by them. Tellingly, in the video that introduces Milo to the public, a young man begins by playing games with Milo in a virtual garden; by the end of the demonstration, things have heated up—he confides in Milo after being told off by his parents.[2]

We are challenged to ask what such things augur. Some people are looking for robots to clean rugs and help with the laundry. Others hope for a mechanical bride. As sociable robots propose themselves as substitutes for people, new networked devices offer us machine-mediated relationships with each other, another kind of substitution.

We romance the robot and become inseparable from our smartphones. As this happens, we remake ourselves and our relationships with each other through our new intimacy with machines. People talk about Web access on their BlackBerries as "the place for hope" in life, the place where loneliness can be defeated. A woman in her late sixties describes her new iPhone: "It's like having a little Times Square in my pocketbook. All lights. All the people I could meet." People are lonely. The network is seductive. But if we are always on, we may deny ourselves the rewards of solitude.

The Robotic Moment

In late November 2005, I took my daughter Rebecca, then fourteen, to the Darwin exhibition at the American Museum of Natural History in New York. From the moment you step into the museum and come face-to-face with a full-size dinosaur, you become part of a celebration of life on Earth, what Darwin called "endless forms most beautiful." Millions upon millions of now lifeless specimens represent nature's invention in every corner of the globe. There could be no better venue for documenting Darwin's life and thought and his theory of evolution by natural selection, the central truth that underpins contemporary biology. The exhibition aimed to please and, a bit defensively in these days of attacks on the theory of evolution, wanted to convince.

At the exhibit's entrance were two giant tortoises from the Galápagos Islands, the best-known inhabitants of the archipelago where Darwin did his most famous investigations. The museum had been advertising these tortoises as wonders, curiosities, and marvels. Here, among the plastic models at the museum, was the life that Darwin saw more than a century and a half ago. One tortoise was hidden from view; the other rested in its cage, utterly still. Rebecca inspected the visible tortoise thoughtfully for a while and then said matter-of-factly, "They could have used a robot." I was taken aback and asked what she meant. She said she thought it was a shame to bring the turtle all this way from its island home in the Pacific, when it was just going to sit there in the museum, motionless, doing nothing. Rebecca was both concerned for the imprisoned turtle and unmoved by its authenticity.

It was Thanksgiving weekend. The line was long, the crowd frozen in place. I began to talk with some of the other parents and children. My question— "Do you care that the turtle is alive?"—was a welcome diversion from the boredom of the wait. A ten-year-old girl told me that she would prefer a robot turtle because aliveness comes with aesthetic inconvenience: "Its water looks dirty. Gross." More usually, votes for the robots echoed my daughters sentiment that in this setting, aliveness didn't seem worth the trouble.

A twelve-year-old girl was adamant: "For what the turtles do, you didn't have to have the live ones." Her father looked at her, mystified: "But the point is that they are real. That's the whole point."

The Darwin exhibition put authenticity front and center: on display were the actual magnifying glass that Darwin used in his travels, the very notebook in which he wrote the famous sentences that first described his theory of evolution. Yet, in the children's reactions to the inert but alive Galápagos tortoise, the idea of the original had no place. What I heard in the museum reminded me of Rebecca's reaction as a seven-year-old during a boat ride in the postcard-blue Mediterranean. Already an expert in the world of simulated fish tanks, she saw something in the water, pointed to it excitedly, and said, "Look, Mommy, a jellyfish! It looks so realistic!" When I told this story to a vice president at the Disney Corporation, he said he was not surprised. When Animal Kingdom opened in Orlando, populated by "real"—that is, biological—animals, its first visitors complained that they were not as "realistic" as the animatronic creatures in other parts of Disneyworld. The robotic crocodiles slapped their tails and rolled their eyes—in sum, they displayed archetypal "crocodile" behavior. The biological crocodiles, like the Galápagos tortoises, pretty much kept to themselves.

I believe that in our culture of simulation, the notion of authenticity is for us what sex was for the Victorians—threat and obsession, taboo and fascination. I have lived with this idea for many years; yet, at the museum, I found the children's position strangely unsettling. For them, in this context, aliveness seemed to have no intrinsic value. Rather, it is useful only if needed for a specific purpose. Darwin's endless forms so beautiful were no longer sufficient unto themselves. I asked the children a further question: "If you put a robot instead of a living turtle in the exhibit, do you think people should be told that the turtle is not alive?" Not really, said many children. Data on aliveness can be shared on a "need-to-know basis"—for a purpose. But what are the purposes of living things?

Only a year later, I was shocked to be confronted with the idea that these purposes were more up for grabs than I had ever dreamed. I received a call from a *Scientific American* reporter to talk about robots and our future. During that conversation, he accused me of harboring sentiments that would put me squarely in the camp of those who have for so long stood in the way of marriage for homosexual couples. I was stunned, first because I harbor no such sentiments, but also because his accusation was prompted not by any objection I had made to the mating or marriage of people. The reporter was bothered because I had objected to the mating and marriage of people to robots.

The call had been prompted by a new book about robots by David Levy, a British-born entrepreneur and computer scientist. In 1968 Levy, an international chess master, famously wagered four artificial intelligence (AI) experts that no computer program would defeat him at the game in the subsequent decade. Levy won his bet. The sum was modest, 1,250 British pounds, but the AI community was chastened. They had overreached in their predictions for their young science. It would be another decade before Levy was bested in chess by a computer program, Deep Thought, an early version of the program that beat Gary Kasparov, the reigning chess champion in the 1990s.[3] These days, Levy is the chief executive officer at a company that develops "smart" toys for children. In 2009, Levy and his team won—and this for the second time—the prestigious Loebner Prize, widely regarded as the world championship for conversational software. In this contest, Levy's "chat bot" program was best at convincing people that they were talking to another person and not to a machine.

Always impressed with Levy's inventiveness, I found myself underwhelmed by the message of this latest book, *Love and Sex with Robots*.[4] No tongue-in- cheek science fiction fantasy, it was reviewed without irony in the *New York Times* by a reporter who had just spent two weeks at the Massachusetts Institute of Technology (MIT) and wrote glowingly about its robotics culture as creating "new forms of life."[5] *Love and Sex* is earnest in its predictions about where people and robots will find themselves by mid-century: "Love with robots will be as normal as love with other humans, while the number of sexual acts and lovemaking positions commonly practiced between humans will be extended, as robots will teach more than is in all of the world's published sex manuals combined."[6] Levy argues that robots will teach us to be better friends and lovers because we will be able to practice on them. Beyond this, they will substitute where people fail. Levy proposes, among other things, the virtues of marriage to robots. He argues that robots are, of course, "other" but, in many ways, better. No cheating. No heartbreak. In Levy's argument, there is one simple criterion for judging the worth of robots in even the most intimate domains: Does being with a robot make you feel better? The master of today's computerspeak judges future robots by the impact of their behavior. And his next bet is that in a very few years, this is all we will care about as well.

I am a psychoanalytically trained psychologist. Both by temperament and profession, I place high value on relationships of intimacy and authenticity. Granting that an AI might develop its own origami of lovemaking positions, I am troubled by the idea of seeking intimacy with a machine that has no feelings, can have no feelings, and is really just a clever collection of "as if" performances, behaving as if it cared, as if it understood us. Authenticity, for me, follows from the ability to put oneself in the place of another, to relate to the other because of a shared store of human experiences: we are born, have families, and know loss and the reality of death.[7] A robot, however sophisticated, is patently out of this loop.

So, I turned the pages of Levy's book with a cool eye. What if a robot is not a "form of life" but a kind of performance art? What if "relating" to robots makes us feel "good" or "better" simply because we feel more in control? Feeling good is no golden rule. One can feel good for bad reasons. What if a robot companion makes us feel good but leaves us somehow diminished? The virtue of Levy's bold position is that it forces reflection: What kinds of relationships with machines are possible, desirable, or ethical? What does it mean to love a robot? As I read *Love and Sex*, my feelings on these matters were clear. A love relationship involves coming to savor the surprises and the rough patches of looking at the world from another's point of view, shaped by history, biology, trauma, and joy. Computers and robots do not have these experiences to share. We look at mass media and worry about our culture being intellectually "dumbed down." *Love and Sex* seems to celebrate an emotional dumbing down, a willful turning away from the complexities of human partnerships—the inauthentic as a new aesthetic.

I was further discomforted as I read *Love and Sex* because Levy had interpreted my findings about the "holding power" of computers to argue his case. Indeed, Levy dedicated his book to Anthony,* an MIT computer hacker I interviewed in the early 1980s. Anthony was nineteen when I met him, a shy young man who found computers reassuring. He felt insecure in the world of people with its emotional risks and shades of gray. The activity and interactivity of computer programming gave Anthony—lonely, yet afraid of intimacy—the feeling that he was not alone.[8] In *Love and Sex*, Levy idealizes Anthony's accommodation and suggests that loving a robot would be a reasonable next step for people like him. I was sent an advance copy of the book, and Levy asked if I could get a copy to Anthony, thinking he would be flattered. I was less sure. I didn't remember Anthony as being at peace with his retreat to what he called "the machine world." I remembered him as wistful, feeling himself a spectator of the human world, like a kid with his nose to the window of a candy store. When we imagine robots as our future companions, we all put our noses to that same window.

I was deep in the irony of my unhappy Anthony as a role model for intimacy with robots when the *Scientific American* reporter called. I was not shy about my lack of enthusiasm for Levy's ideas and suggested that the very fact we were discussing marriage to robots at all was a comment on human disappointments—that in matters of love and

*This name and the names of others I observed and interviewed for this book are pseudonyms. To protect the anonymity of my subjects, I also change identifying details such as location and profession. When I cite the opinions of scientists or public figures, I use their words with permission. And, of course, I cite material on the public record.

sex, we must be failing each other. I did not see marriage to a machine as a welcome evolution in human relationships. And so I was taken aback when the reporter suggested that I was no better than bigots who deny gays and lesbians the right to marry. I tried to explain that just because I didn't think people should marry machines didn't mean that any mix of adult people wasn't fair territory. He accused me of species chauvinism: Wasn't I withholding from robots their right to "realness"? Why was I presuming that a relationship with a robot lacked authenticity? For me, the story of computers and the evocation of life had come to a new place.

At that point, I told the reporter that I, too, was taking notes on our conversation. The reporter's point of view was now data for my own work on our shifting cultural expectations of technology—data, that is, for the book you are reading. His analogizing of robots to gay men and women demonstrated that, for him, future intimacy with machines would not be a second-best substitute for finding a person to love. More than this, the reporter was insisting that machines would bring their own special qualities to an intimate partnership that needed to be honored in its own right. In his eyes, the love, sex, and marriage robot was not merely "better than nothing," a substitute. Rather, a robot had become "better than something." The machine could be preferable—for any number of reasons—to what we currently experience in the sometimes messy, often frustrating, and always complex world of people.

This episode with the *Scientific American* reporter shook me—perhaps in part because the magazine had been for me, since childhood, a gold standard in scientific publication. But the extravagance of the reporter's hopes for robots fell into a pattern I had been observing for nearly a decade. The encounter over *Love and Sex* most reminded me of another time, two years before, when I met a female graduate student at a large psychology conference in New Orleans; she had taken me aside to ask about the current state of research on robots designed to serve as human companions. At the conference, I had given a presentation on *anthropomorphism*—on how we see robots as close to human if they do such things as make eye contact, track our motion, and gesture in a show of friendship. These appear to be "Darwinian buttons" that cause people to imagine that the robot is an "other," that there is, colloquially speaking, "somebody home."

During a session break, the graduate student, Anne, a lovely, raven-haired woman in her mid-twenties, wanted specifics. She confided that she would trade in her boyfriend "for a sophisticated Japanese robot" if the robot would produce what she called "caring behavior." She told me that she relied on a "feeling of civility in the house." She did not want to be alone. She said, "If the robot could provide the environment, I would be happy to help produce the illusion that there is somebody really with me." She was looking for

discuss machine + smth. alien

a "no-risk relationship" that would stave off loneliness. A responsive robot, even one just exhibiting scripted behavior, seemed better to her than a demanding boyfriend. I asked her, gently, if she was joking. She told me she was not. An even more poignant encounter was with Miriam, a seventy-two-year-old woman living in a suburban Boston nursing home, a participant in one of my studies of robots and the elderly.

I meet Miriam in an office that has been set aside for my interviews. She is a slight figure in a teal blue silk blouse and slim black pants, her long gray hair parted down the middle and tied behind her head in a low bun. Although elegant and composed, she is sad. In part, this is because of her circumstances. For someone who was once among Boston's best-known interior designers, the nursing home is a stark and lonely place. But there is also something immediate: Miriam's son has recently broken off his relationship with her. He has a job and family on the West Coast, and when he visits, he and his mother quarrel—he feels she wants more from him than he can give. Now Miriam sits quietly, stroking Paro, a sociable robot in the shape of a baby harp seal. Paro, developed in Japan, has been advertised as the first "therapeutic robot" for its ostensibly positive effects on the ill, elderly, and emotionally troubled. Paro can make eye contact by sensing the direction of a human voice, is sensitive to touch, and has a small working English vocabulary for "understanding" its users (the robot's Japanese vocabulary is larger); most importantly, it has "states of mind" affected by how it is treated. For example, it can sense whether it is being stroked gently or with aggression. Now, with Paro, Miriam is lost in her reverie, patting down the robots soft fur with care. On this day, she is particularly depressed and believes that the robot is depressed as well. She turns to Paro, strokes him again, and says, "Yes, you're sad, aren't you? It's tough out there. Yes, it's hard." Miriam's tender touch triggers a warm response in Paro: it turns its head toward her and purrs approvingly. Encouraged, Miriam shows yet more affection for the little robot. In attempting to provide the comfort she believes it needs, she comforts herself.

Because of my training as a clinician, I believe that this kind of moment, if it happens between people, has profound therapeutic potential. We can heal ourselves by giving others what we most need. But what are we to make of this transaction between a depressed woman and a robot? When I talk to colleagues and friends about such encounters—for Miriam's story is not unusual—their first associations are usually to their pets and the solace they provide. I hear stories of how pets "know" when their owners are unhappy and need comfort. The comparison with pets sharpens the question of what it means to have a relationship with a robot. I do not know whether a pet could sense Miriam's unhappiness, her feelings of loss. I do know that in the moment of apparent connection

between Miriam and her Paro, a moment that comforted her, the robot understood nothing. Miriam experienced an intimacy with another, but she was in fact alone. Her son had left her, and as she looked to the robot, I felt that we had abandoned her as well.

Experiences such as these—with the idea of aliveness on a "need-to-know" basis, with the proposal and defense of marriage to robots, with a young woman dreaming of a robot lover, and with Miriam and her Paro—have caused me to think of our time as the "robotic moment." This does not mean that companionate robots are common among us; it refers to our state of emotional—and I would say philosophical—readiness. I find people willing to seriously consider robots not only as pets but as potential friends, confidants, and even romantic partners. We don't seem to care what these artificial intelligences "know" or "understand" of the human moments we might "share" with them. At the robotic moment, the performance of connection seems connection enough. We are poised to attach to the inanimate without prejudice. The phrase "technological promiscuity" comes to mind.

As I listen for what stands behind this moment, I hear a certain fatigue with the difficulties of life with people. We insert robots into every narrative of human frailty. People make too many demands; robot demands would be of a more manageable sort. People disappoint; robots will not. When people talk about relationships with robots, they talk about cheating husbands, wives who fake orgasms, and children who take drugs. They talk about how hard it is to understand family and friends. I am at first surprised by these comments. Their clear intent is to bring people down a notch. A forty-four-year-old woman says, "After all, we never know how another person really feels. People put on a good face. Robots would be safer." A thirty-year-old man remarks, "I'd rather talk to a robot. Friends can be exhausting. The robot will always be there for me. And whenever I'm done, I can walk away."

The idea of sociable robots suggests that we might navigate intimacy by skirting it. People seem comforted by the belief that if we alienate or fail each other, robots will be there, programmed to provide simulations of love.[9] Our population is aging; there will be robots to take care of us. Our children are neglected; robots will tend to them. We are too exhausted to deal with each other in adversity; robots will have the energy. Robots won't be judgmental. We will be accommodated. An older woman says of her robot dog, "It is better than a real dog . . . It won't do dangerous things, and it won't betray you . . . Also, it won't die suddenly and abandon you and make you very sad."[10]

The elderly are the first to have companionate robots aggressively marketed to them, but young people also see the merits of robotic companionship. These days, teenagers have sexual adulthood thrust upon them before they are ready to deal with the complexities of relationships. They are drawn to the comfort of connection without the demands of intimacy. This may lead them to a hookup—sex without commitment or even caring. Or it may lead to an online romance—companionship that can always be interrupted. Not surprisingly, teenagers are drawn to love stories in which full intimacy cannot occur—here I think of current passions for films and novels about high school vampires who cannot sexually consummate relationships for fear of hurting those they love. And teenagers are drawn to the idea of technological communion. They talk easily, of robots that would be safe and predictable companions.[11]

These young people have grown up with sociable robot pets, the companions of their playrooms, which portrayed emotion, said they cared, and asked to be cared for.[12] We are psychologically programmed not only to nurture what we love but to love what we nurture. So even simple artificial creatures can provoke heartfelt attachment. Many teenagers anticipate that the robot toys of their childhood will give way to full-fledged machine companions. In the psychoanalytic tradition, a symptom addresses a conflict but distracts us from understanding or resolving it; a dream expresses a wish.[13] Sociable robots serve as both symptom and dream: as a symptom, they promise a way to sidestep conflicts about intimacy; as a dream, they express a wish for relationships with limits, a way to be both together and alone.[14]

Some people even talk about robots as providing respite from feeling overwhelmed by technology. In Japan, companionate robots are specifically marketed as a way to seduce people out of cyberspace; robots plant a new flag in the physical real. If the problem is that too much technology has made us busy and anxious, the solution will be another technology that will organize, amuse, and relax us. So, although historically robots provoked anxieties about technology out of control, these days they are more likely to represent the reassuring idea that in a world of problems, science will offer solutions.[15] Robots have become a twenty-first-century deus ex machina. Putting hope in robots expresses an enduring technological optimism, a belief that as other things go wrong, science will go right. In a complicated world, robots seem a simple salvation. It is like calling in the cavalry.

But this is not a book about robots. Rather, it is about how we are changed as technology offers us substitutes for connecting with each other face-to-face. We are offered robots and a whole world of machine-mediated relationships on networked devices. As we instant-message, e-mail, text, and Twitter, technology redraws the boundaries between intimacy and solitude. We talk of getting "rid" of our e-mails, as though these notes are so much excess baggage. Teenagers avoid making telephone calls, fearful that they "reveal too much." They would rather text than talk. Adults,

too, choose keyboards over the human voice. It is more efficient, they say. Things that happen in "real time" take too much time. Tethered to technology, we are shaken when that world "unplugged" does not signify, does not satisfy. After an evening of avatar-to-avatar talk in a networked game, we feel, at one moment, in possession of a full social life and, in the next, curiously isolated, in tenuous complicity with strangers. We build a following on Facebook or MySpace and wonder to what degree our followers are friends. We recreate ourselves as online personae and give ourselves new bodies, homes, jobs, and romances. Yet, suddenly, in the half-light of virtual community, we may feel utterly alone. As we distribute ourselves, we may abandon ourselves. Sometimes people experience no sense of having communicated after hours of connection. And they report feelings of closeness when they are paying little attention. In all of this, there is a nagging question: Does virtual intimacy degrade our experience of the other kind and, indeed, of all encounters, of any kind?

The blurring of intimacy and solitude may reach its starkest expression when a robot is proposed as a romantic partner. But for most people it begins when one creates a profile on a social-networking site or builds a persona or avatar for a game or virtual world.[16] Over time, such performances of identity may feel like identity itself. And this is where robotics and the networked life first intersect. For the performance of caring is all that robots, no matter how sociable, know how to do.

I was enthusiastic about online worlds as "identity workshops" when they first appeared, and all of their possibilities remain.[17] Creating an avatar—perhaps of a different age, a different gender, a different temperament—is a way to explore the self. But if you're spending three, four, or five hours a day in an online game or virtual world (a time commitment that is not unusual), there's got to be someplace you're not. And that someplace you're not is often with your family and friends—sitting around, playing Scrabble face-to-face, taking a walk, watching a movie together in the old-fashioned way. And with performance can come disorientation. You might have begun your online life in a spirit of compensation. If you were lonely and isolated, it seemed better than nothing. But online, you're slim, rich, and buffed up, and you feel you have more opportunities than in the real world. So, here, too, better than nothing can become better than something—or better than anything. Not surprisingly, people report feeling let down when they move from the virtual to the real world. It is not uncommon to see people fidget with their smartphones, looking for virtual places where they might once again be more.

Sociable robots and online life both suggest the possibility of relationships the way we want them. Just as we can program a made-to-measure robot, we can reinvent

ourselves as comely avatars. We can write the Facebook profile that pleases us. We can edit our messages until they project the self we want to be. And we can keep things short and sweet. Our new media are well suited for accomplishing the rudimentary. And because this is what technology serves up, we reduce our expectations of each other. An impatient high school senior says, "If you really need to reach me, just shoot me a text." He sounds just like my colleagues on a consulting job, who tell me they would prefer to communicate with "real-time texts."

Our first embrace of sociable robotics (both the idea of it and its first exemplars) is a window onto what we want from technology and what we are willing to do to accommodate it. From the perspective of our robotic dreams, networked life takes on a new cast. We imagine it as expansive. But we are just as fond of its constraints. We celebrate its "weak ties," the bonds of acquaintance with people we may never meet. But that does not mean we prosper in them.[18] We often find ourselves standing depleted in the hype. When people talk about the pleasures of these weak-tie relationships as "friction free," they are usually referring to the kind of relationships you can have without leaving your desk. Technology ties us up as it promises to free us up. Connectivity technologies once promised to give us more time. But as the cell phone and smartphone eroded the boundaries between work and leisure, all the time in the world was not enough. Even when we are not "at work," we experience ourselves as "on call"; pressed, we want to edit out complexity and "cut to the chase."

Connectivity and Its Discontents

Online connections were first conceived as a substitute for face-to-face contact, when the latter was for some reason impractical: Don't have time to make a phone call? Shoot off a text message. But very quickly, the text message became the connection of choice. We discovered the network—the world of connectivity—to be uniquely suited to the overworked and overscheduled life it makes possible. And now we look to the network to defend us against loneliness even as we use it to control the intensity of our connections. Technology makes it easy to communicate when we wish and to disengage at will.

A few years ago at a dinner party in Paris, I met Ellen, an ambitious, elegant young woman in her early thirties, thrilled to be working at her dream job in advertising. Once a week, she would call her grandmother in Philadelphia using Skype, an Internet service that functions as a telephone with a Web camera. Before Skype, Ellen's calls to her grandmother were costly and brief. With Skype, the calls are free and give the compelling sense that the other person is present—Skype is an almost real-time video link. Ellen could now call more frequently: "Twice a week and I stay on the call for an hour," she told me. It should have been rewarding; instead, when I met her, Ellen was unhappy. She knew that her grandmother was unaware that Skype allows surreptitious multitasking.

Her grandmother could see Ellen's face on the screen but not her hands. Ellen admitted to me, "I do my e-mail during the calls. I'm not really paying attention to our conversation."

Ellen's multitasking removed her to another place. She felt her grandmother was talking to someone who was not really there. During their Skype conversations, Ellen and her grandmother were more connected than they had ever been before, but at the same time, each was alone. Ellen felt guilty and confused: she knew that her grandmother was happy, even if their intimacy was now, for Ellen, another task among multitasks.

I have often observed this distinctive confusion: these days, whether you are online or not, it is easy for people to end up unsure if they are closer together or further apart. I remember my own sense of disorientation the first time I realized that I was "alone together." I had traveled an exhausting thirty-six hours to attend a conference on advanced robotic technology held in central Japan. The packed grand ballroom was Wi-Fi enabled: the speaker was using the Web for his presentation, laptops were open throughout the audience, fingers were flying, and there was a sense of great concentration and intensity. But not many in the audience were attending to the speaker. Most people seemed to be doing their e-mail, downloading files, and surfing the Net. The man next to me was searching for a *New Yorker* cartoon to illustrate his upcoming presentation. Every once in a while, audience members gave the speaker some attention, lowering their laptop screens in a kind of curtsy, a gesture of courtesy.

Outside, in the hallways, the people milling around me were looking past me to virtual others. They were on their laptops and their phones, connecting to colleagues at the conference going on around them and to others around the globe. There but not there. Of course, clusters of people chatted with each other, making dinner plans, "networking" in that old sense of the word, the one that implies having a coffee or sharing a meal. But at this conference, it was clear that what people mostly want from public space is to be alone with their personal networks. It is good to come together physically, but it is more important to stay tethered to our devices. I thought of how Sigmund Freud considered the power of communities both to shape and to subvert us, and a psychoanalytic pun came to mind: "connectivity and its discontents."

The phrase comes back to me months later as I interview management consultants who seem to have lost touch with their best instincts for what makes them competitive. They complain about the BlackBerry revolution, yet accept it as inevitable while decrying it as corrosive. They say they used to talk to each other as they waited to give presentations or took taxis to the airport; now they spend that time doing e-mail. Some tell me they are making better use of their "downtime," but they argue without conviction. The time that they once used to talk as they waited for appointments or drove to the airport was never downtime. It was the time when far-flung global teams solidified relationships and refined ideas.

In corporations, among friends, and within academic departments, people readily admit that they would rather leave a voicemail or send an e-mail than talk face-to-face. Some who say "I live my life on my BlackBerry" are forthright about avoiding the "real-time" commitment of a phone call. The new technologies allow us to "dial down" human contact, to titrate its nature and extent. I recently overheard a conversation in a restaurant between two women. "No one answers the phone in our house anymore," the first woman proclaimed with some consternation. "It used to be that the kids would race to pick up the phone. Now they are up in their rooms, knowing no one is going to call them, and texting and going on Facebook or whatever instead." Parents with teenage children will be nodding at this very familiar story in recognition and perhaps a sense of wonderment that this has happened, and so quickly. And teenagers will simply be saying, "Well, what's your point?"

A thirteen-year-old tells me she "hates the phone and never listens to voicemail." Texting offers just the right amount of access, just the right amount of control. She is a modern Goldilocks: for her, texting puts people not too close, not too far, but at just the right distance. The world is now full of modern Goldilockses, people who take comfort in being in touch with a lot of people whom they also keep at bay. A twenty-one-year-old college student reflects on the new balance: "I don't use my phone for calls any more. I don't have the time to just go on and on. I like texting, Twitter, looking at someone's Facebook wall. I learn what I need to know."

Randy, twenty-seven, has a younger sister—a Goldilocks who got her distances wrong. Randy is an American lawyer now working in California. His family lives in New York, and he flies to the East Coast to see them three or four times a year. When I meet Randy, his sister Nora, twenty-four, had just announced her engagement and wedding date via e-mail to a list of friends and family. "That," Randy says to me bitterly, "is how I got the news." He doesn't know if he is more angry or hurt. "It doesn't feel right that she didn't call," he says. "I was getting ready for a trip home. Couldn't she have told me then? She's my sister, but I didn't have a private moment when she told me in person. Or at least a call, just the two of us. When I told her I was upset, she sort of understood, but laughed and said that she and her fiancé just wanted to do things simply, as simply as possible. I feel very far away from her."

Nora did not mean to offend her brother. She saw e-mail as efficient and did not see beyond. We have long turned to technology to make us more efficient in work; now Nora illustrates how we want it to make us more efficient in our private lives. But when technology engineers intimacy, relationships can be reduced to mere connections. And then, easy connection becomes redefined as intimacy. Put otherwise, cyberintimacies slide into cybersolitudes.

And with constant connection comes new anxieties of disconnection, a kind of panic. Even Randy, who longs for a phone call from Nora on such an important matter as her wedding, is never without his BlackBerry. He holds it in his hands during our entire conversation. Once, he puts it in his pocket. A few moments later, it comes out, fingered like a talisman. In interviews with young and old, I find people genuinely terrified of being cut off from the "grid." People say that the loss of a cell phone can "feel like a death." One television producer in her mid-forties tells me that without her smartphone, "I felt like I had lost my mind." Whether or not our devices are in use, without them we feel disconnected, adrift. A danger even to ourselves, we insist on our right to send text messages while driving our cars and object to rules that would limit the practice.[19]

Only a decade ago, I would have been mystified that fifteen-year-olds in my urban neighborhood, a neighborhood of parks and shopping malls, of front stoops and coffee shops, would feel the need to send and receive close to six thousand messages a month via portable digital devices or that best friends would assume that when they visited, it would usually be on the virtual real estate of Facebook.[20] It might have seemed intrusive, if not illegal, that my mobile phone would tell me the location of all my acquaintances within a ten-mile radius.[21] But these days we are accustomed to all this. Life in a media bubble has come to seem natural. So has the end of a certain public etiquette: on the street, we speak into the invisible microphones on our mobile phones and appear to be talking to ourselves. We share intimacies with the air as though unconcerned about who can hear us or the details of our physical surroundings.

I once described the computer as a second self, a mirror of mind. Now the metaphor no longer goes far enough. Our new devices provide space for the emergence of a new state of the self, itself, split between the screen and the physical real, wired into existence through technology.

Teenagers tell me they sleep with their cell phone, and even when it isn't on their person, when it has been banished to the school locker, for instance, they know when their phone is vibrating. The technology has become like a phantom limb, it is so much a part of them. These young people are among the first to grow up with an expectation of continuous connection: always on, and always on them. And they are among the first to grow up not necessarily thinking of simulation as second best. All of this makes them fluent with technology but brings a set of new insecurities. They nurture friendships on social-networking sites and then wonder if they are among friends. They are connected all day but are not sure if they have communicated. They become confused about companionship. Can they find it in their lives on the screen? Could they find it with a robot? Their digitized friendships—played out with emoticon emotions, so often predicated on rapid response rather than reflection—may prepare them, at times through nothing more than their superficiality, for relationships that could bring superficiality to a higher power, that is, for relationships with the inanimate. They come to accept lower expectations for connection and, finally, the idea that robot friendships could be sufficient unto the day.

Overwhelmed by the volume and velocity of our lives, we turn to technology to help us find time. But technology makes us busier than ever and ever more in search of retreat. Gradually, we come to see our online life as life itself. We come to see what robots offer as relationship. The simplification of relationship is no longer a source of complaint. It becomes what we want. These seem the gathering clouds of a perfect storm.

Technology reshapes the landscape of our emotional lives, but is it offering us the lives we want to lead? Many roboticists are enthusiastic about having robots tend to our children and our aging parents, for instance. Are these psychologically, socially, and ethically acceptable propositions? What are our responsibilities here? And are we comfortable with virtual environments that propose themselves not as places for recreation but as new worlds to live in? What do we have, now that we have what we say we want—now that we have what technology makes easy?[22] This is the time to begin these conversations, together. It is too late to leave the future to the futurists.

NOTES

1. See "What Is Second Life," Second Life, http://secondlife.com/whatis (accessed June 13,2010).
2. Benedict Carey and John Markoff, "Students, Meet Your New Teacher, Mr. Robot," *New York Times,* July 10, 2010, www.nytimes.c0m/2010/07/11/science/11 robots.html (accessed July 10,2010); Anne Tergeson and Miho Inada, "It's Not a Stuffed Animal, It's a $6,000 Medical Device," *Wall Street Journal,* June 21, 2010, http://online .wsj.c0m/article/SB10001424052748704463504575301051844937276.html (accessed August 10, 2010); Jonathan Fildes, '"Virtual Human Milo Comes Out to Play at TED in Oxford," *BBC News,* July 13, 2010, www.bbc.co.uk/news/10623423 (accessed July 13,2010); Amy Harmon, "A Soft Spot for Circuitry: Robot Machines as Companions," *New York Times,* July 4, 2010, www.nytimes.c0m/2010/07/05/science/05r0b0t. html ?pagewanted=all (accessed July 4, 2010); Emily Veach, "A Robot That Helps You Diet," *Wall Street Journal,* July 20, 2010, http://0nline.wsj.c0m/article/SB10001424052 748704682604575369981478383568. html (accessed July 20, 2010).

3. On this, see "The Making of Deep Blue," IBM Research, www.research.ibm .com/deepblue/meet/html/d.3.i.html (accessed June 10, 2010).
4. David L. Levy, *Love and Sex with Robots: The Evolution of Human-Robot Relationships* (New York: Harper Collins, 2007).
5. The book review is Robin Marantz Henig, "Robo Love," *New York Times,* December 2,2007, www.nytimes.com/2007/12/02/books/review/Henig-t.html (accessed July 21,2009). The original article about the MIT robot scene is Robin Marantz Henig, "The Real Transformers," *New York Times,* July 29, 2007, www.nytimes.com/ 2O07/o7/29/magazine/29robots-t.html (accessed July 21, 2009).
6. Levy, *Love and Sex*, 22.
7. On "alterity," the ability to put oneself in the place of another, see Emmanuel Lévinas, *Alterity and Transcendence,* trans. Michael B. Smith (London: Athlone Press, 1999).
8. Sherry Turkle, *The Second Self: Computers and the Human Spirit* (1984; Cambridge, MA: MIT Press, 2005), 183-218.
9. The way here is paved by erotic images of female robots used to sell refrigerators, washing machines, shaving cream, and vodka. See, for example, the campaign for Svedka Vodka (Steve Hall, "Svedka Launches Futuristic, Un-PC Campaign," Andrants.com, September 20, 2005, www.adrants.c0m/2005/09/svedka-launches-futuristic-unpc .php [accessed September 1,2009]) and Phillip's shaving system ("Feel the Erotic Union of Man and Shavebot," AdFreakcom, August 21, 2007, http://adweek.blogs.com/ad freak/2007/08/feel-the-er0tic.html [accessed September 1, 2009]).
10. Sharon Moshavi, "Putting on the Dog in Japan," *Boston Globe,* June 17,1999, Ai.
11. As preteens, the young women of the first Google generation (born roughly from 1987 to 1993) wore clothing widely referred to as "baby harlot"; they listened to songs about explicit sex well before puberty. Their boomer parents had few ideas about where to draw lines, having spent their own adolescences declaring the lines irrelevant. Boomer parents grew up rejecting parental rules, but knowing that there were rules. One might say it is the job of teenagers to complain about constraints and the job of parents to insist on them, even if the rules are not obeyed. Rules, even unheeded, suggest that twelve to fifteen are not good ages to be emotionally and sexually enmeshed.

    Todays teenagers cannot easily articulate any rules about sexual conduct except for those that will keep them "safe." Safety refers to not getting venereal diseases or AIDS. Safety refers to not getting pregnant. And on these matters teenagers are eloquent, unembarrassed, and startlingly well informed. But teenagers are overwhelmed with how unsafe they feel in relationships. A robot to talk to is appealing—even if currently unavailable—as are situations that provide feelings of closeness without emotional demands. I have said that rampant fantasies of vampire lovers (closeness with constraints on sexuality) bear a family resemblance to ideas about robot lovers (sex without intimacy, perfect). And closeness without the possibility of physical intimacy and eroticized encounters that can be switched off in an instant—these are the affordances of online encounters. Online romance expresses the aesthetic of the robotic moment. From a certain perspective, they are a way of preparing for it. On the psychology of adolescents' desire for relationships with constraint, I am indebted to conversations with child and adolescent psychoanalyst Monica Horovitz in August 2009.
12. Commenting on the insatiable desire for robot pets during the 2009 holiday season, a researcher on social trends comments, "A toy trend would be something that reflects the broader society, that tells you where society is going, something society needs." Gerald Celente, founder of the Trends Research Institute, cited in Brad Tuttle, "Toy Craze Explained: A Zhu Zhu Pet Hamster Is Like a 'Viral Infection,'" *Time,* December 9, 2009, http://money.blogs.time.com/2009/12/07/toy-craze-explained-a-zhu- zhu-pet-hamster-is-like-a-viral-infection (accessed December 9, 2009).
13. For classic psychodynamic formulations of the meaning of symptoms, see Sigmund Freud, "The Unconscious," in *The Standard Edition of Sigmund Freud,* ed. and trans. James Strachey et al. (London: Hogarth Press, 1953-1974), 14:159-204; "Introductory Lectures on Psychoanalysis," in *The Standard Edition,* vols. 15 and 16; "From the History of an Infantile Neurosis," in *The Standard Edition,* 17:1-122; "Inhibitions, Symptoms, and Anxiety," in *The Standard Edition,* 20:75-172; and Sigmund Freud and Joseph Breuer, "Studies on Hysteria,"

in *The Standard Edition*, 2:48-106. For Freud on dreams as wishes, see "The Interpretation of Dreams," in *The Standard Edition*, vol. IV.

14. For an argument about the pleasures of limited worlds in another technological realm, see Natasha Schiill's work on gambling, *Addiction by Design: Machine Gambling in Las Vegas* (Princeton, NJ: Princeton University Press, forthcoming).
15. See, for example, Bill Gates, "A Robot in Every Home," *Scientific American*, January 2007, www.scientificamerican.com/article.cfm?id=a-robot-in-every-home (accessed September 2, 2009).
16. See Sherry Turkle, *Life on the Screen: Identity in the Age of the Internet* (New York Simon and Schuster, 1995). On life as performance, the classic work is Erving Goffman, *The Presentation of Self in Everyday Life* (Garden City, NY: Doubleday Anchor, 1959).
17. The apt phrase "identity workshop" was coined by my then student Amy Bruck- man. See "Identity Workshop: Emergent Social and Psychological Phenomena in Text- Based Virtual Reality" (unpublished essay, Media Lab, Massachusetts Institute of Technology, 1992), www.cc.gatech.edu/~asb/papers (accessed September 2, 2009).
18. Sociologists distinguish between strong ties, those of family and close friendship, and weak ties, the bonds of acquaintanceship that make us comfortable at work and in our communities. Facebook and Twitter, friending rather than friendship— these are worlds of weak ties. Today's technology encourages a celebration of these weak ties as the kind we need in the networked life. The classic work on weak ties is Mark S. Granovetter, "The Strength of Weak Ties," *American Journal of Sociology* 78, no. 6 (May 1973): 1360-1380.
19. See, for example, Matt Richtel, "In Study, Texting Lifts Crash Risk by Large Margin," *New York Times*, July 27, 2009, www.nytimes.com/2009/07/28/technology/ 28texting.html (accessed September 1,2009). On the pressure that friends and family members put on drivers who text, see "Driver Texting Now an Issue in Back Seat," *New York Times*, September 9, 2009, www.nytimes.com/20o9/09/09/technol0gy/09distracted.html (accessed September 9,2009). As I complete this book, Oprah Winfrey has made texting while driving a personal crusade, encouraging people across America to sign an online pledge to not text and drive. See "Oprah's No Phone Zone," Oprah.com, www.oprah.com/packages/no-phone-zone.html (accessed May 30,2010).
20. The teenage national average as of January 2010 is closer to thirty-five hundred; my affluent, urban neighborhood has a far higher number. Roger Entner, "Under-aged Texting: Usage and Actual Cost," Nielson.com, January 27, 2010, http://blog.nielsen .com/nielsenwire/online_mobile/under-aged-texting-usage-and-actual-cost (accessed May 30, 2010). On texting's impact on teenage life, see Katie Hafner, "Texting May Be Taking Its Toll," *New York Times*, May 25,2009, www.nytimes.c0m/2009/05/26/health/ 26teen.html?_r=2&8dpc (accessed July 21, 2009).
21. To find friends in the neighborhood, Loopt for the iPhone is a popular "app."
22. A witty experiment suggests that Facebook "friends" won't even show up when you invite them to a party. Hal Niedzviecki, "Facebook in a Crowd," *New York Times*, October 24,2008, www.nytimes.c0m/2008/10/26/magazine/26lives-t.html (accessed July 27, 2010).
23. From Winston Churchill's remarks to the English Architectural Association in 1924, available at the International Centre for Facilities website at www.icf-cebe .com/quotes/quotes.html (accessed August 10, 2010). Churchill's comment is, of course, very similar to the spirit of Marshall McLuhan. See, for example, *Understanding Media: The Extensions of Man* (1964; Cambridge, MA: MIT Press, 1994).

Points of Engagement—Reading Comprehension

1. What is the "robotic moment" according to Turkle? Point to three passages that inform your answer.
2. What does "authentic" mean to Sherry Turkle? To the people she discusses in her essay? Choose one person from Turkle's essay, and describe 1) how that person would define "authentic" and 2) how Turkle's perception of authenticity is similar or different from the perception of the person that you chose.
3. What is Turkle's position on humans' relationships with robots and other "intelligent" machines? Does she think these relationships are more positive than negative, or vice versa? List three things that she worries about or that she sees as beneficial.
4. Turkle writes, "The new technologies allow us to 'dial down' human contact, to titrate its nature and content" (276). What does Turkle mean by this? Use a dictionary if necessary. Do you think this is true? Why? Why not?
5. Turkle mentions, at the beginning and the end of her essay, that humans are in the midst of a "romance" with technology. What does she mean? Do you think this is an accurate description?
6. Is Turkle anti-technology? Why or why not? Point to specific passages in her Introduction that help to explain your response.

Points of Departure—Assignment Questions

1. Why do humans invest so much hope in technology? What will trust in, and reliance on, technology do for us, and to us, either as individuals, or as communities and societies? For this paper, use Turkle, and one of the following: Malcom Gladwell, Alain de Botton, Adam Gopnik, or Lauren Slater.
2. Sherry Turkle asks the following question: "What if relating to robots makes us feel 'good' or 'better' simply because we feel more in control?" (268). With this question in mind, consider what the effect is of being in control of something or someone. What do we lose when we gain control? How much control is too much? When is being in control not best for us, or for others? Use the essays by Turkle, and either Belkin, Chua, Klein, Slater, Adam Gopnik, or Alison Gopnik for your response.
3. In her very first sentence of this book, Sherry Turkle writes, "Technology proposes itself as the architect of our intimacies" (263). We see this idea exemplified quite dramatically in essays by Lisa Belkin, Lauren Slater, and Adam Gopnik. Let's assume for this paper that Turkle's statement is true. Your task is first to show how technology functions as

the "architect of our intimacies" in these essays, and second, to make an argument about whether you think this is a good, inevitable, future for the human race in our relationships with one another, or whether we are heading down a dark path. Be sure to make clear what each author thinks about these difficult questions for the people they describe, and where you stand in relation to authors' positions.

4. Turkle suggests that what she calls "virtual intimacy"—intimacy that is mediated through some kind of technology—"degrade[s] our experience of the other kind [of intimacy] and, indeed, of all encounters of any kind" (273). How does changing the ways in which we connect to others offer us new, positive possibilities? How does it affect us negatively? What do we gain by building virtual intimacy and connections into our lives? What do we lose? Write a paper in which you answer these questions using essays by Turkle and one of the following authors: Flammang, Gladwell, Adam Gopnik, Alison Gopnik, Hochschild, or Winterson. Consider also possible counterarguments to Turkle's claim: for example, how might Alison Gopnik's discussion of counterfactuals challenge Turkle's argument? Do robots allow us to explore what might be, to play out scenarios in real life, specifically because they are not living? Look for other challenges to Turkle's pessimism.

5. What is authenticity? How concerned should we be with the authenticity of our relationships with others? Is dissemblance a natural, inevitable, part of how we relate to one another? Or is a lack of authenticity contributing to less substantial human relationships? Does authenticity even matter? Why or why not? Write a paper in which you answer these questions, using the experiences described by Turkle and either Kenji Yoshino, Zadie Smith, or Winterson. Be sure to rely on the specific terms used by each of these authors as you explore and answer these questions of authenticity.

The World and Other Places

Jeanette Winterson

Points of Access—Pre-Reading

1. Where do you consider "home"? Do you live there now? If not, how do you feel going "home"? Excited, nervous, anxious, ambivalent? What makes you feel the way you do?
2. When you dream at night, or daydream during the day, how do you experience your physical surroundings? Are you more conscious of them? Less? Is the physical world more vivid or does it seem to disappear around you? How are you sitting? Lying down? Do you close your eyes when you daydream, or leave them open? Freewrite for 15 minutes about what happens to you and the world around you when you 'go someplace else' in your mind.
3. When you hear the word "romance" what do you think of? What do you regard as romantic? List as many descriptions of romance as you can. What makes these things romantic? What do these kinds of romances do for you? What do you get from them as a person?
4. Have you ever heard the expressions "I'm going to look for myself" or "I'm going off to find myself"? What do these expressions mean? How do people act on these statements? Do they literally go someplace new? Do they act differently than they normally would? Do you think they find what they're looking for? What do you think that is? What do you think they find?

When I was a boy I made model aeroplanes.

We never had the money to go anywhere, sometimes we didn't have the money to go to the shop. There were six of us at night in the living room, six people and six carpet tiles. Usually the tiles were laid two by three in a dismal rectangle, but on Saturday night, aeroplane night, we took one each and sat cross legged with the expectation of an Arabian prince. We were going to fly away, and we held on to the greasy underside of our mats, waiting for the magic word to lift us.

Bombay, Cairo, Paris, New York. We took it in turns to say the word, and the one whose word it was, took my model aeroplane and spun it where it hung from the ceiling, round and round our blow-up globe. We had saved cereal tokens for the globe and it had been punctured twice. Iceland was held together by Sellotape and Great Britain was only a rubber bicycle patch on the panoply of the world.

* * *

I had memorised the flight times from London Heathrow to anywhere you could guess at in the world. It was my job to announce our flying time, the aircraft data, and to wish the passengers a comfortable trip. I pointed out landmarks on the way and we would lean over the fireplace to take a look at Mont Blanc or crane our necks round the back of the settee to get a glimpse of the Rockies.

Half way through our trip, Mother, who was Chief Steward, swayed down the aisle with cups of tea and toast and Marmite. After that, Dad came forward with next week's jobs around the house scribbled on little bits of paper. We dipped into the pouch, and somebody, the lucky one, would get Duty Free on theirs, and they didn't have to do a thing.

When we reached our destination, we were glad to stand up and stretch our legs. Then my sister gave us each a blindfold. We put it on, and sat quietly, dreaming, imagining, while one of us started talking about the strange place we were visiting.

* * *

How hot it is getting off the plane. Hot and stale like opening the door of a tumble drier. There are no lights to show us where to go. Death will be this way; a rough passage with people we have never met and a hasty run across the tarmac to the terminal building.

Inside, in the day-for-night illumination, a group of Indians were playing cellos. Who are these orchestral refugees? Can it be part of the service? Beyond them, urchins with bare feet are leaping up and down with ragged cardboard signs, each bearing the name of someone more important than ourselves. These are the people who will be whisked away in closed cars to comfortable beds. The rest of us will search for the bus.

Luggage. Heaven or Hell in the hereafter will be luggage or the lack of it. The ones who recognised that love is enough and that possessions are borrowed pastimes, will float free through the exit sign, their arms ready to hug their friends, their toothbrush in their pocket. The ones who stayed up late, gathering and gathering like demented bees, will find that you can take it with you. The joke is that you have to carry it yourself.

* * *

Here comes the bus. It has three wheels, maybe four, and the only part noisier than the engine is the horn. All human life is here. I am travelling between a chicken coop and a fortune teller. The chickens peck at my legs and suddenly the fortune teller grabs my palm. She laughs in my face.

'When you grow up you will learn to fly.'

For the rest of the journey I am bitten by mosquitoes.

* * *

At last we have reached the Hotel Cockroach. Dusty mats cover the mud floor and the Reception Clerk has an open wound in his cheek. He tells me he was stabbed but not to worry. Then he serves me lukewarm tea and shows me my room. It has a view over the incinerator and is farthest from the bathroom. At least I will not learn to think highly of myself.

In the darkness and the silence I can hear, far below, the matter of life continuing without me. The night-shift. What are they doing, these people who come and go, cleaning, bringing food, wanting money, wanting to fight. What will they eat? Where will they sleep? Do they love someone? How many of them will see morning? Will I?

Dreams. The smell of incense and frangipani. The moon sailing on her back makes white passages on the dun floor. The moon and the white clouds at the window. How many times have I seen it? How many times do I stop and look as if I had never seen it before? Perhaps it is true that the world is made new again every day but our minds are not. The clamp that holds me will not let me go.

During the night a mouse gave birth behind the skirting board.

* * *

At the end of my story, my family and I swopped anecdotes and exchanged souvenirs. Later, we retired to bed with the weariness of a traveller's reunion. We had done what the astronauts do, travelled in space that did not belong to us, uncoupled ourselves from time.

That night, I knew I would get away, better myself. Not because I despised who I was, but because I did not know who I was. I was waiting to be invented. I was waiting to invent myself.

* * *

The pilot and I went up in the aeroplane. It was a Cessna, modern and beautiful, off white with a blue stripe right round it and a nose as finely balanced as a pedigree muzzle. I wanted to cup it in both hands and say, 'Well done boy.'

In spite of the air conditioned cockpit, overwarm and muzzy in an unexpected economy class way, the pilot had a battered flying jacket stuffed behind his seat. It was authentic, grubby sheepskin and a steel zip. I asked him why he needed it.

'Romance,' he said, grinning. 'Flying is romantic, even now, even so.'

We were under a 747 at the time, and I thought of the orange seats crammed three abreast on either side, and all the odds and ends of families struggling with their plastic trays and beach gear.

'Is that romantic?' I said, pointing upwards.

He glanced out of the reinforced glass.

'That's not flying. That's following the road.'

For a while we travelled in silence. I watched him; strong jaw with necessary stubble. Brown eyes that never left the sky. He was pretending to be the only man in the air. His dream was the first dream, when men in plus fours and motorcycle goggles pedalled with the single mindedness of a circus chimp to get their wooden frames and canvas wings upwards and upwards and upwards. It was a solo experience even when there were two of you.

What did Amy Johnson say? 'If the whole world were flying beside me I would still be flying alone.' Rhetoric, you think, frontier talk. Then you reach your own frontier and it's not rhetoric anymore.

* * *

My parents were so proud of me when I joined the Air Force. I stood in our cluttered living room in my new uniform and I felt like an angel on a visit. I felt like Gabriel come to tell the shepherds the Good News.

'Soon you'll have your own wings,' said my mother.

My father had bought a bottle of Scotch.

In my bedroom, the model aeroplanes had been carefully dusted. Sopwith Camel. Spitfire. Tiger Moth. I picked them up one by one and turned over their balsa wood frames and rice paper wings. I never used a kit. What hopes they carried. More than the altar at church. More than a good school report. In the secret places, under the fuselage, stuck to the tail-fin, I had hidden my hopes.

My mother came in. 'Will you take them with you?' I shook my head. I'd be laughed at, made fun of. Yet each of us in our bunks at lights-out would be thinking of model aeroplanes and the things from home we couldn't talk about anymore.

She said, 'I gave them a wipe anyway.'

* * *

Bombay. Cairo. Paris. New York. I've been to those places now. The curious thing is that no matter how different they are, the people are all preoccupied with the same things, that is, the same thing; how to live. We have to eat, we want to make money, but in every pause the question returns: How shall I live?

I saw three things that made this clear to me.

* * *

The first was a beggar in New York. He was sitting, feet apart, head in hands, on a low wall beside a garage. As I walked by him, he whispered, 'Do you have two dollars?' I gave him the folded bills, and he said, 'Can you sit with me a minute?'

His name was Tony. He was a compulsive gambler trying to go straight. He thought he might land a job on Monday morning if only he could sleep the weekend in a hostel, get some rest, be clean. For a week he had been sleeping by the steam duct of the garage.

I gave him the hostel money and a little more for food and the clenched fist of his body unfolded. He was talkative, gentle. Already in his mind he had the job, was making a go of it, and had met a sweet woman in a snack bar. Was that the gambler in him or ordinary human hope? Already in his mind he was looking past the job and the apartment into the space that had turned him over the wall.

'Nobody used to look at me,' he said. 'Even when I had money, I was one of those guys who get looked through. It's like being a ghost. If no one can see you you're dead. What's the point of trying to live if you are already dead?'

He shook my hand and thanked me. He was going to the hostel before it closed, or maybe he was going to a dog, I can't know. I don't need to know. There's enough I need to know just for myself.

* * *

I said there were three things. The second was a dress designer living over her studio in Milan. She was rich, she was important. She liked airmen. I used to sit with her in the studio, she never had time for a meal or a trip somewhere, she ate like an urchin, one leg hooked round her stool, palm full of olives. She spat the stones at her models.

We were talking one night and she got angry. She prodded me with the shears she kept on her work table.

'Stop thinking,' she said. 'The more you think, the faster you cut your own throat. What is there to think about? It always ends up the same way. In your mind there is a bolted door. You have to work hard not to go near that door. Parties, lovers, career, charity, babies, who cares what it is, so long as you avoid the door. There are times, when I am on my own, fixing a drink, walking upstairs, when I see the door waiting for me. I have to stop myself pulling the bolt and turning the handle. Why? On the other side of the door is a mirror, and I will have to see myself. I'm not afraid of what I am. I'm afraid I will see what I am not.'

* * *

I said there were three things. The third was a woman in the park with her dog. The dog was young. The woman was old. Every so often she took out a bottle of water and a little bowl and gave the dog a drink.

'Come on Sandy,' she'd say, when he'd finished, and they would both disappear into the bushes, the dog's tail bobbing behind.

She was poor, I could see that. Put us side by side and how do we look? I'm six feet tall in a smart airman's uniform and I have a strong grip and steady eyes. She's about five feet high and threadbare. I could lift her with one hand.

But when she met my gaze one day I dropped my eyes and blushed like a teenager. I was walking past her in the opposite direction and I smiled and said, 'How are you?'

She looked at me with eyes that have long since pierced through the cloud cover and as we talked, I realised she was happy. Happy. The kind of happiness that comes from a steadiness inside. This was genuine. This was not someone who had turned away from the bolted door. It was open. She was on the other side.

* * *

For some years, early in my Air Force days, I did not bother myself with the single simple question that is the hardest in the world. How shall I live? I was living wasn't I? I was adventure, manliness, action. That's how we define ourselves isn't it?

Then one day I awoke with the curious sensation of no longer being myself. I hadn't turned into a beetle or a werewolf and my friends treated me in the same way as before, I put on my favourite well-worn clothes, bought newspapers, took a holiday, went to Milan, walked in the park. At last I called on the doctor. 'Doctor I'm not myself anymore.'

He asked me about my sex life and prescribed a course of antidepressants. I went to the library and borrowed books from the philosophy and psychology sections, terrified in case I should be spotted by someone who knew me. I read Jung who urged me to make myself whole, I read Lacan who wants me to accept that I'm not.

None of it helped me. All the time I thought crazily, 'If this isn't me then I must be somewhere else.'

* * *

That's when I started travelling so much, left the forces, bought my own plane. Mostly I teach flying now, and sometimes I take out families who have won the First Prize in a packet soup competition. It doesn't matter. I have plenty of free time and I do what I need to do, which is to look for myself.

I know that if I fly for long enough, for wide enough, for far enough, I'll catch a signal on the radar that tells me there's another aircraft on my wing. I'll glance out of the reinforced glass, and it won't be a friendly pilot that I'll see, all stubble and brown eyes. It will be me. Me in the cockpit of that other plane.

* * *

I went home to visit my mother and father. I flew over their village, taxied down their road and left the nose of my plane pushed up against the front door. The tail was just on the pavement and I was worried that some traffic warden might issue a ticket for obstruction, so I hung a sign on the back that said 'FLYING DOCTOR.'

I'm always nervous about going home, just as I am nervous about rereading books that have meant a lot to me.

My parents wanted me to tell them about the places I've been and what I've seen, their eyes were eager and full of life.

Bombay. Cairo. Paris. New York. We have invented them so many times that to tell the truth will be a disappointment. The blow-up globe still hangs over the mantelpiece, its plastic crinkly and torn. The countries of the Common Market are held together with red tape.

We went through my postcards one by one. I gave them presents; a sari for my mother and a Stetson for my father. They are the children now.

Time passes through the clock. It's time for me to leave. They come outside to wave me off.

'It's a lovely plane,' says my mother. 'Does it give you much trouble?' I rev the engine and the neighbours stand in astonishment in their doorways as the plane gathers speed down our quiet road. A moment before the muzzle breaks through the apostal window in the church, I take off, rising higher and higher, and disappearing into the end stream of the sun.

Points of Engagement—Reading Comprehension

1. Consider the following quote from page 285: "That night, I knew I would get away, better myself. Not because I despised who I was, but because I did not know who I was. I was waiting to be invented. I was waiting to invent myself." What does the narrator mean by these statements? What happens directly before this passage to influence the narrator's intentions? What happens directly after? How does the structure effect your understanding of the narrator's experiences, intentions and actions?
2. What does Winterson mean when she writes, "Rhetoric, you think, frontier talk. Then you reach your own frontier and it's not rhetoric anymore" (286)? Rewrite this idea in your own words, and expand on it, using examples both from her story and from your own experience.
3. Near the middle of the story, the narrator proclaims that wherever he goes, "people are all preoccupied with the same things, that is, the same thing: how to live" (287). What are the three things that make this clear to the narrator? Look to pages 287-288 for your answers. List them. Then provide 2-3 sentences of explanation for each about why you think these events or observations were so clarifying for the narrator in determining how to live.
4. Consider the following two passages from Winterson: "Then one day I awoke with the curious sensation of no longer being myself . . . All the time I thought crazily, 'If this isn't me then I must be somewhere else'" (289). Why does the narrator no longer feel like himself? Point to specific sentences within this section that help you answer this question.
5. Consider the following refrain in Winterson's essay: "Bombay. Cairo. Paris. New York" (283). Now read this passage in context on page 287, the last place it appears. Why is this refrain important to the narrator? What does it teach us by appearing over and over in the essay? What does it teach the narrator? How do you know?

Points of Departure—Assignment Questions

1. What are dreams and what do they do for us? Can we shape reality through our dreams? How and to what extent? Write a paper in which you answer these questions using essays by Jeanette Winterson and Adam Gopnik, Alison Gopnik, or Zadie Smith.
2. What is true happiness? Do you think it is possible? How do you think it should be defined? What would it look like? Use essays by Winterson and one of the following authors to propose answers to these questions: Alain de Botton, Jane Goodall, Arlie Russell Hochschild, Nichols Kristof and Sheryl WuDunn, Gregory Orr, or Sherry Turkle.
3. Can we invent, and re-invent, ourselves? If so, how do we do it? If not, why not? What does Jeanette Winterson have to say about the possibilities of self-invention, who we are, and who we can be, as human beings? What about Susan Blackmore, James Fallows, Alison Gopnik, Kristof and WuDunn, Lauren Slater, or Kenji Yoshino? Write a paper in which you propose answers to these questions using Winterson and one of these other authors.
4. Consider the following quotation from Winterson's story: "Perhaps it is true that the world is made new again every day but our minds are not. The clamp that holds me will not let me go" (285). What does Winterson mean by this? Does the world around us limit our imaginations, or does the world around us show us the expansiveness of our imaginations? How and in what ways? Your project for this paper is to answer this question using Winterson and one of the following authors: Berry, Blackmore, de Botton, Goodall, Adam Gopnik, Alison Gopnik, Kristof and WuDunn, Orr, Slater, Smith, Turkle, or Yoshino.

Covering: The Hidden Assault on Our Civil Rights

Kenji Yoshino

Points of Access—Pre-Reading

1. Do you sometimes feel like you have to hide parts of who you are to fit in? Do you do it? When? Why? With whom?
2. What would you be willing to change about your appearance or behavior to land a job? Your fashion style? Your hairstyle? The way you talk? Where would you draw the line?
3. What is "assimilation"? Look it up online or in your dictionary. Now define it in your own terms. Does assimilation have more of a positive or a negative connotation? Why?
4. Consider this quote from the essay you're about to read: "It is worth asking when we will live in a society where Americans will feel central without feeling white" (308). What do you think of this question? How does it make you feel? What aspects of your own identity feed your response?

> It is a fact that persons who are ready to admit possession of a stigma (in many cases because it is known about or immediately apparent) may nonetheless make a great effort to keep the stigma from looming large . . . This process will be referred to as *covering*.
>
> —Erving Goffman, ***Stigma: Notes on the Management of Spoiled Identity***

Preface

Everyone covers. To cover is to tone down a disfavored identity to fit into the mainstream. In our increasingly diverse society, all of us are outside the mainstream in some way. Nonetheless, being deemed mainstream is still often a necessity of social life. For this reason, every reader of this book has covered, whether consciously or not, and sometimes at significant personal cost.

Famous examples of covering abound. Ramón Estévez covered his ethnicity when he changed his name to Martin Sheen, as did Krishna Bhanji when he changed his name to Ben Kingsley. Margaret Thatcher covered her status as a woman when she trained with a voice coach to lower the timbre of her voice. Long after they came out as lesbians, Rosie O'Donnell and Mary Cheney still covered, keeping their same-sex partners out of the public eye. Issur Danielovitch Demsky covered his Judaism when he became Kirk Douglas, as did Joseph Levitch when he became Jerry Lewis. Franklin Delano Roosevelt covered his disability by ensuring his wheelchair was always hidden behind a desk before his Cabinet entered.

I doubt any of these people covered willingly. I suspect they were all bowing to an unjust reality that required them to tone down their stigmatized identities to get along in life. Sheen says he needed to "get a name people could pronounce and connect with" if he "wanted to work commercially." Yet he now regrets having done so, and has exhorted his sons—Emilio and Charlie—to use the family name. One of them has not done so, signaling the enduring force of the covering demand.

In a supposedly enlightened age, the persistence of the covering demand presents a puzzle. Today, race, national origin, sex, religion, and disability are all protected by federal civil rights laws. An increasing number of states and localities include sexual orientation in civil rights laws as well. Albeit with varying degrees of conviction, Americans have come to a consensus that people should not be penalized for being different along these dimensions. That consensus, however, does not protect individuals against demands that they mute those differences. We need an explanation for why the civil rights revolution has stalled on covering.

Covering has enjoyed such a robust and stubborn life because it is a form of assimilation. At least since Hector St. John de Crevecoeur's 1782 *Letters from an American Farmer,* this country has touted assimilation as the way Americans of different backgrounds would be "melted into a new race of men." By the time Israel Zangwill's play of that name was performed in 1908, the "melting pot" had acquired the burnish of an American ideal. Only with the civil rights movement of the 1960s was this ideal challenged in any systematic way, with calls to move "beyond the melting pot" and to "celebrate diversity." And notwithstanding that challenge, assimilation has never lost its hold on the American imagination. Indeed, as our country grows more pluralistic, we have seen a renaissance of the melting pot ideal. Fearful that we are spinning apart into balkanized groups, even liberals like Arthur Schlesinger have called for a recommitment to that ethic. In the United States, as in other industrialized democracies, we are seeing the "return of assimilation."

I recognize the value of assimilation, which is often necessary to fluid social interaction, to peaceful coexistence, and even to the dialogue through which difference is valued. For that reason, this is no simple screed against conformity. What I urge here is that we approach the renaissance of assimilation in this country critically. We must be willing to see the dark side of assimilation, and specifically of covering, which is the most widespread form of assimilation required of us today.

Covering is a hidden assault on our civil rights. We have not been able to see it as such because it has swaddled itself in the benign language of assimilation. But if we look closely, we will see that covering is the way many groups are being held back today. The reason racial minorities are pressured to "act white" is because of white supremacy. The reason women are told to downplay their child-care responsibilities in the workplace is because of patriarchy. And the reason gays are asked not to "flaunt" is because of homophobia. So long as such covering demands persist, American civil rights will not have completed its work.

Unfortunately, the law has yet to perceive covering as a threat. Contemporary civil rights law generally only protects traits that individuals cannot change, like their skin color, chromosomes, or innate sexual orientations. This means that current law will not protect us against most covering demands, because such demands direct themselves at the behavioral aspects of our personhood. This is so despite the fact that covering imposes costs on us all.

The universality of the covering demand, however, is also a potential boon for civil rights advocates. I, too, worry about our current practice of fracturing into groups, each clamoring for state and social solicitude. For this reason, I do not think we can move forward by focusing on old-fashioned group-based identity politics. We must instead build a new civil rights paradigm on what draws us together rather than on what drives us apart. Because covering applies to us all, it provides an issue around which we can make common cause. This is the desire for authenticity, our common human wish to express ourselves without being impeded by unreasoning demands for conformity.

I thought I would make this argument in purely political terms. As a law professor, I have become accustomed to the tones of legal impersonality. But I came to see that I could not compose an argument about the importance of human authenticity without risking such authenticity myself. So I have written this book in a more intimate voice, blending memoir with argument. In trying to make the stakes of assimilation vivid, I draw on my attempts to elaborate my identity as a gay man, and, to a lesser extent, my identity as an Asian-American.

Yet this is not a standard "coming out" narrative or racial memoir. I follow the Romantics here in their belief that if a human life is described with enough particularity, the universal will begin to speak through it. What interests me about my story, and the stories of others, is how similar they are in revealing the bones of our common human endeavor, the yearning for human emancipation that stirs within us all.

Racial Covering

No one here can tell why the bells ring in the village temple. The chimes roll in widening circles through the August heat—through the walls of the low-eaved house of my grandparents, through the stiff paper of our handheld fans. I sit with my grandparents at the *kotatsu*—a low table fitted over a square cavity. In the winters, a heater hums in the cavity, and a table quilt traps the heat. Then, my grandparents huddle here for warmth. In the summers, we settle here because, in this chairless house, it is the only place we can sit with legs extended. Even at thirteen, I cannot kneel for long with my legs folded beneath me. Happily, in their seventies, my grandparents have a new appreciation for dangling their feet.

They confront heat with dignity. The paddle-shaped fans scattered throughout the house are blue, splotched with white. As fast as it pulses, my grandmother's fan cannot disturb hair pulled taut as a tatami mat. My grandfather wields his fan more equably. We have cups of hot tea in front of us, which will make us feel cooler if we can bear to drink them. My grandparents drink.

Each chime passes through the house as if it is the last. My grandmother eats silver mints from a stoppered glass bottle. I have tried to acquire a taste for these but have not—they taste as metallic as they look.

Her tongue is made of quicksilver. She speaks of how our neighbor has belied his name of "All Riches," of how his long-lashed daughters grow portly and unmarriageable, coming home like switched cows in the hungering nightfall. She speaks of how her friend's Akita died in the summer floods because the dog knew only one way home and followed it into the floodwaters. Hearing the bells continue, she speaks of how my father spent hours of his youth scaling the roof of the temple. At the slip of his knee, a fish green tile rattled the monks at their brooms.

Someone must be counting the chimes, and carefully. Yet it seems they will never end. My mind begins to swing like the monkey my grandmother says I am, from toll to toll, to the counterfeit last one. The lulls between the chimes begin to ring.

Later that afternoon, my grandmother gives me a calligraphy lesson. I fold a sheet of rice paper into quadrants, a beginner's trick that crafts a trellis on which the characters can hang. I pour water into a trough and rub a new inkstone against its slick downward slope. The edge of the stone squeaks against the trough before surrendering to its surface, what is hard being taken by what is harder. The water darkens to jet. I dip the horsehair brush, and the ink rises into it.

The moment before the brush descends is a long moment. In the centuries of peace that followed the unification of Japan in the seventeenth century, the samurai traded their swords for calligraphy brushes. Now, as then, the character on the page is thought to reveal that of the calligrapher.

My grandmother's script represents her well. When she writes me in Japanese cursive, I find her all but incomprehensible. From what I can make of these cards and the etiquette they follow, these are conventional words of weather, of cherry blossoms. So I have never asked her to untangle that thread. Her characters are artifacts I can see without seeing through—I cherish my ignorance of them as I cherish my ignorance of constellations.

My grandmother tells me to think of rain as I form the character for "rain"; she' tells me to envision the dashes I must make under a line as raindrops leaking through a roof. I get the stroke order right. I am full of information about these characters—how the bottom of the character for "fish" splays out like a fish's tail, how the character for "flight" is difficult to balance. Yet these ideas do not survive their executions. My brush clumps with too much ink, then the hairs separate because they are too dry. The creases that should have guided my characters now rebuke them.

Does my grandmother sigh as she rubs a red stone in a smaller trough? This ink is cinnabar, the color of Shinto gates, the color of the emperor's rescripts. With a smaller brush, she begins each stroke where I began it, to show the path I missed. How can she produce, time after time, these thinning strokes that end in nubs or swishes of fire? She circles particular mistakes. As I watch her brush, it seems to travel over my entire summer—circling the honorifics I have misused, the bows I have failed to make.

I have come to my grandparents' house in the country after two months in a Tokyo junior high school. My parents have been heroic in their quest to preserve the Japaneseness of their two children. In America, a sheaf of mustard yellow paper arrives each month from a correspondence school. It is homework in Japanese, which will teach us the characters we will need to read a newspaper. As a child, I hate these pages for showcasing my inadequacy—my very name is rickety. But resistance to Japanese makes the faces of my parents close like doors.

The capstone of their plan was to bring my older sister and me back to Japan each summer so we could attend school in June and July. We began at a private school called the Family School, whose mission was to assimilate returnee children like ourselves into Japanese society. The place carried an aura of wrongfulness. Japanese children are not meant to leave Japan, as it is believed only children raised in Japan can become true Japanese.

Many of these students were half Caucasian, what the Japanese call *konketsuji,* or "children of confused blood." Over lunch, we debated whether it was better to be *haafu*—half Japanese—or pure. The *haafu* would say it was easier to be pure Japanese, because we could pass. People didn't rake us with their eyes in the subway, children didn't run after us yelling *"Haroo."* We pure Japanese would retort we were expected to be more Japanese than we actually were. The Japanese proverb says "the protruding nail gets hammered," and all Japanese society seemed entitled to do the hammering. A pure girl described a taxi ride. Her driver kept asking her questions, and grew increasingly exasperated by her broken Japanese. Suddenly, he pulled the cab over and slammed open the partition between them. The words came in a mist of spittle—he asked if she wasn't ashamed to be so ignorant. It was when his face softened and he asked if she was retarded that she fled the cab in tears.

When I was in fifth grade, my parents decided the Family School was inadequate. How could we learn to be Japanese from returnee children? They enrolled us in a normal Tokyo public school. I do not know how they convinced the superintendent to let two nonresident children flit into his school for two months of every year. Perhaps the urgency of the case spoke for itself. Where else would I have learned to inhabit a Japanese body—to rise, to straighten, and to bow; to do morning calisthenics on the count of eight; to sit ramrod straight in my high-collared uniform; to pass the handkerchief, tooth, and fingernail tests? Where else would I have read textbooks mandated by the Ministry of Education— a curriculum whose uniformity makes the most conservative American defenders of the Western canon sound recklessly pluralistic? From whom but my Japanese peers would I have learned the "Japlish" lyrics to the latest hit song by the Pink Ladies and to mispronounce these and all other English phrases, so as not to be pummeled for being arrogant? Where else would I have heard a teacher try to thwart suicides around college examinations by describing how students soiled themselves in midair as they jumped off buildings?

Perhaps my allergy to assimilation began at Higashiyama School, in Matsumoto-sensei's fifth-grade classroom. The class had a darling. She could have been the heroine of a *shojo manga,* the ubiquitous comics for preteen girls, with her chestnut eyes set off by double eyelids, and skin so vellum-thin blue deltas shone at her wrists. When she stood to answer a question, the other girls would croon *"Kawaiiiiii,"* elongating the word for "adorable." The class also had a pariah, a stoop-shouldered mumbler. He would elicit the cry *"Kuraiiiii,"* an extension of the word for "gloomy." Matsumoto-sensei smiled benignly at these rituals. It was good to come to consensus.

The Japan scholar Edwin Reischauer once compared the Japanese to a school of fish, darting one way together, then, if startled, darting the other, but always in seamless synchronicity. Over the years, I would conjure other similes for my classmates, who seemed at times like army ants with their single hive mind, or, when bobbing through their calisthenics, like the chuntering pistons of a well-tempered engine. Yet only Reischauer's fish capture their occasional beauty. I have seen these fish in the Boston aquarium, have seen them undulate together as if each fish were a single scale on one larger fish. This is the closest thing to magic fish do, the triangles of their steel heads drawn to an unseen magnet. I have looked to see if there was a single fish out of place in that silent churn, and have realized that if I cannot find that fish, it may be because I am it.

My parents emphasized that the grades on my Japanese report cards were unimportant—this was an education not in social studies or chemistry but in becoming Japanese. I would have wished it to be the opposite. Subjects could be learned from books. Becoming Japanese required an ability to read my social situation. And this I could not do. I clumped indoors with my outdoor shoes, or called a student in the grade above me by her first name. I passed Japanese language but flunked Japanese race.

It is an exacting subject. The Japanese believe they are a race apart, proclaiming their blood more pure than that of other peoples. Over the years, I would repeatedly watch Japanese racism dawn on white Americans. Initially, the American would be charmed, as Japanese would praise his halting Japanese as much as his exoticism. He would tell me he felt an affinity for the culture, that he might be Japanese inside. I would give a noncommittal nod. In a month, or a year, or five years, he would realize he would never be accepted as Japanese. It might come to him when he went to a hospital for the first time, and watched the doctor recoil from his "butter-stinking" torso. Or it might come when he realized only an exceptional Japanese woman would date him seriously, that her family would probably oppose a marriage, and that his children, if he had them, would face discrimination as "children of confused blood." Or it might come, paradoxically, when he had perfected his Japanese. While many Japanese laud foreigners who speak broken Japanese, many find it *kimochiwarui*—nauseating— when foreigners become fluent.

By virtue of my two native parents, I had a chance to assimilate no American of non-Japanese descent possessed. As my sister demonstrated, it was a real chance. Living now in Tokyo, she has gone so native that Japanese compliment her *English.* I used to marvel at how she passed until one day in college I watched her answer the telephone with Japanese manner and mannerism and realized she was no longer passing. She was Japanese.

Today, when Japanese encounter me here, they often ask if I am half Caucasian. My sister never fields this question. This may be due to physical variation between us. But it seems more likely I do not code as Japanese because of a set of behaviors—how I hold my body, how I move through space, how I speak. Japanese who interact with me are assaulted by my difference from them. They make sense of that difference by implanting it in my body.

In Japan, I realized racial identity has a behavioral component. I am not alluding to the postmodern idea that race is entirely a social construct. I am invoking the more modest notion that perceptions of an individual's race do not rest on biology alone. Both my sister and I have the blood and skin of the Japanese majority. Yet while these biological traits were necessary to our status as "true Japanese," they were not sufficient. Our race was also defined by our behaviors.

It would be some time before I would apply that insight to my identity as an Asian-American. I was, of course, aware of the demand to assimilate to American norms. I had spent two days in my Boston nursery school before my mother received a call from my teacher, who complained I was teaching the other children Japanese and asked my mother to stop me before I confused them beyond recall. At dinner, my parents gently impressed on me that while I should be proud to be Japanese, I should also keep it private. That was the first iteration of what would become a mantra in the home: "Be one hundred percent American in America, and one hundred percent Japanese in Japan."

That mantra shaped their lives. My parents fashioned a racial sanctum within their Boston apartment, keeping their Japanese magazines and newspapers in their bedroom. It was on their king- sized bed, beneath a massive maroon and amber scroll I could not read, that I tested my Japanese on newspapers whose vertical print smudged so easily under my laboring index finger. It was here, too, that I leafed through the back issues of *Bungei Shunju* magazine, whose stylized covers depicted *tanabata* bamboo hung with the colorful wishes of children, or snowmen whose features were made of dried seaweed rather than carrots and coal. The public spaces of the apartment, where guests might roam, were filled with other books—books in English—so clearly meant for show I never thought to read them. I once took down *David Copperfield* from an endless row of navy hardcovers embossed with gold. It was abridged. The shelf looked gap-toothed without it, so I quickly slid it back into place.

But even my parents did not keep the injunction to be purely American in America. Every window of their apartment was fitted with sliding rice paper screens. As a child,

I thought this was because my father was a scholar, that even the light had to be read through paper. When I was older, I heard a friend of mine say her Greek mother papered over the windows of her house because she was "tired of looking at America." I thought my parents had arrived at the more elegant solution.

Nonetheless, as a young child, I took the injunction at face value. I was abetted by the lily-whiteness of my school, which meant I was usually the only Asian child in my classes. Surrounded at all times by whites, I could half forget my difference. Recently, a Caucasian friend of mine who is a Japanese literature professor said the object he most abhors while in Japan is a mirror. In the absence of reflection, he can pretend he is Japanese—surrounded by Japanese, speaking Japanese, what else could he be? Listening to him, I saw my own childhood aversion to mirrors in a new light.

Only when I went to boarding school did I encounter Asian-Americans in any numbers. In one of my first calls home, I mentioned to my father there were many Asians here, that they even had a group. My father asked if I was planning to join it, and I said I didn't know. "What can they teach you that you do not already know?" he asked. This sounded familiar—in Japan, he had pulled me from the Family School because only pure Japanese could teach me to be Japanese. Here, I heard him saying only pure Americans could teach me to be American. And pure, in this case, meant white. I did student government instead.

In hindsight, I see my father and I misunderstood the purposes of the Asian-American group, one of which was to resist the notion that American meant white. Yet I still appreciate what my father wished for me. He wanted me to be at the center of any experience—Japanese, American, or otherwise. I will always be grateful to him for teaching me to be bold, to be unafraid of the center.

I suspect other minority students were getting similar advice from their parents. Exeter is a bastion of privilege, self-consciously schooling its students for influence. Many of the racial minorities there had a predilection for assimilating to white norms. Some behaviors were common across groups. Avoiding ethnic organizations was one. Exercising class privilege was another. As if in adherence to the Brazilian proverb "Money whitens," a cadre of minority students outprepped the preps, dressing out of catalogs that featured no racial minorities. And each group followed strategies of its own—Asian-Americans got eyelid surgery, African-Americans straightened their hair, Latinos planed the accents off their names.

The stereotype that plagued me the most was the portrait of the Asian-American as the perpetual foreigner. I came to hate the question "Where are you from, *really*?" that followed my assertion that I had grown up in Boston. I washed away this tincture of foreignness with language. I wish to be careful here, as my pleasure in language feels largely independent of any other identity. Yet my racial identity did spur my will to command English. I could see my parents struggling with a language in which neither of them would ever swim. And my own failure at Japanese gave me direct experience of illiteracy. I collected English words like amulets.

At Exeter, I noticed this mastery whitened me. I liked mathematics too, those rectangles thinning to fit a curve in calculus, "like gold to airy thinness beat." But to excel at mathematics was to collude in a vision of my Asian mind as an abacus, when I experienced it as a blood-warm runnel of ink. And it was in English classes that the teacher's eyes would widen as I talked about a book in a headlong access of speech.

In college, I dated a woman who felt the same way. Janet was Korean-American, a premed English major. We met in a poetry writing seminar. I was drawn to her for many reasons, but one was that I sensed her relationship to language was similar to my own. Her parents were also immigrants—she spoke to them in English, they responded in Korean. We recognized our common desire to write ourselves out of the inscrutability of Asian-American experience—and to do so in the most traditional ways. We disdained classes marked as ethnic, like Asian-American literature. We flew into the heart of the canon: I specialized in Shakespeare, she in Milton.

Our evenings were filled with the happiness of people learning to read, to write. We read to each other from opposite ends of a couch, like a two-headed disputatious literary creature. Much of our pleasure had nothing to do with race. But race was an explicit part of our connection. We confessed our mutual love of the literal color blindness imposed by writing. Our ink was as black, our page as white, as anyone's.

I smile now to see I had the debates with Janet about Asian- American assimilation I would later have with Paul about gay assimilation. In one moment, Janet would rail against a mutual acquaintance, an Asian-American woman, who had gotten eyelid surgery—the "Asian nose job," as she put it. She thought it was self-hating, an attempt to "act white." I wasted my words reminding her that double eyelids were cherished in Japan, and that eyelid surgeries were done there too. She insisted that the spread of the surgery worldwide only proved that white standards of beauty had colonized the world. It was likewise futile to point out she often criticized me for *failing* to assimilate. Whenever I got my hair cut too short, it was Janet who would needle me for looking "fresh off the boat." When I suggested a tension between these two positions, she quoted Whitman. *I am large, I contain multitudes.*

Only in America, my mother would say, shaking her head with bemusement, could a Japanese date a Korean so naturally, quoting American poetry all the while. What had the two countries shared but centuries of racial enmity? When I went to visit Janet's family in Connecticut, my mother told me to get them an "American" gift. I wasn't about to proffer a portrait of the emperor, but I knew what she meant. She wanted me to meet them on the common ground of our assimilation into Asian America.

Yet if dating Janet represented assimilation in one sense, it was also its rejection. To date another Asian was to be raced apart. We would often be the only Asians in a social group, and some would presume we were together from our race alone. Even today, strangers at social functions sometimes assume me to be married to a female Asian colleague. True assimilation would have meant avoiding romantic association with Asians in the way I avoided Asian groups.

Did I yearn to convert to whiteness? As a child, if it had been a matter of pushing a button, there were times when I would have pushed it as idly and insistently as a man waiting for an elevator. Yet the desire to be white never forced me down on my prayer bones as the desire to be straight did. I used to ascribe this difference to the fixity of race until I saw that fixity had not kept peers from aspiring to whiteness. Asian-American friends have described the turmoil they caused in their families when they came home as young children demanding to know when they would become white. And of course I have the indelible image of Arad trying to bleach his skin as a child.

I believe I accepted my race with relative equanimity because of the racial pride my parents gave me. In this regard, their strategy of shuttling their children between the United States and Japan worked brilliantly. They permitted me to access Japanese culture as an affirmative birthright, in moments that shone like mints. Throughout my youth, they also kept steadily visible that my minority status in America was an accident of geography. In Japan, I was part of the majority.

It is a sad truth that one of the most potent psychic antidotes to racism is racism. Every racist belief I encountered in one country had its mirror image in the other, like the Escher in which doves fly into crows. I drew sustenance from that symmetry. After watching an American quiz show in which a white champion dominated the field, my mother turned to me. "Some Americans," she said with wonderment, "actually know quite a lot." I understood then why she assumed I would turn up at the top of any academic class—I was only competing with Americans.

Of course, Americans also expected me to excel academically. During my college years, magazines blared out headlines about "those amazing Asians." Yet the affirmation I got from American culture for being a "model minority" still felt like a patronizing pat. I got more sustenance from Japanese nativism, which toppled the white judge from the dais. I felt like the giant son of Earth in Greek mythology who could draw strength from his mother, so that whenever he was thrown down in combat, he would spring up again, entirely replenished. As alien as Japan felt to me, it was still the earth that renewed me when I touched it.

I started to think rigorously about racial assimilation only when I was deep into my work on gay assimilation. I began to read in Asian-American politics, and recognized covering behaviors in much of what I found. In his memoir, *The Accidental Asian,* Chinese-American Eric Liu follows the statement "Here are some of the ways you could say I am 'white' " with the following catalog:

> *I listen to National Public Radio.*
> *I wear khaki Dockers.*
> *I own brown suede bucks.*
> *I eat gourmet greens.*
> *I have few close friends "of color."*
> *I married a white woman.*
> *I am a child of the suburbs.*
> *I furnish my condo à la Crate & Barrel.*
> *I vacation in charming bed-and-breakfasts.*
> *I have never once been the victim of blatant discrimination.*
> *I am a member of several exclusive institutions.*
> *I have been in the inner sanctums of political power.*
> *I have been there as something other than an attendant.*
> *I have the ambition to return.*
> *I am a producer of the culture.*
> *I expect my voice to be heard.*
> *I speak flawless, unaccented English.*
> *I subscribe to Foreign Affairs.*
> *I do not mind when editorialists write in the first person plural.*
> *I do not mind how white television casts are.*
> *I am not too ethnic.*
> *I am wary of minority militants.*
> *I consider myself neither in exile nor in opposition.*
> *I am considered "a credit to my race."*

Liu stresses his "yellow skin and yellow ancestors"—he has not passed or converted. Yet he believes these covering behaviors have transformed him. Observing that "some are born white, others achieve whiteness, still others have whiteness thrust upon them," he says he has become "white, by acclamation." That metamorphosis is also internal. Liu says that insofar as he has moved "away from the periphery and toward the center of American life," he has "become white inside."

My first reaction to this list is a jolt of Linnaean pleasure. Liu's list includes all four of my covering axes: *appearance* ("I wear khaki Dockers," "I own brown suede bucks"); *affiliation* ("I listen to National Public Radio," "I furnish my condo à la Crate & Barrel," "I speak flawless, unaccented English"); *activism* ("I do not mind how white television casts are," "I am not too ethnic," "I am wary of minority militants"); and *association* ("I have few close friends 'of color,' ""I married a white woman").

But then I become puzzled. I could, with minor revisions, sign my name to this list. This suggests I have covered my own Asian-American identity as much as I have covered my gay one. Yet these two forms of covering feel different. I regret covering my gay identity—refusing Paul's extended hand or abstaining from gay activism. Contemplating my racial covering behaviors incites no such self-recrimination. It strikes me that I, like Liu, am an "accidental Asian"—someone who only "happens to be" Asian.

I believe this country is in the grip of white supremacy as it is in the grip of heteronormativity. So why is it I am so comfortable covering my Asian identity? Is it because Asians are more accepted than gays? Is it because I have always had a place to elaborate my racial self? Is it because racial covering does not feel like a response based on fear?

Like many of my colleagues, I sometimes teach seminars to puzzle through problems. A student once posted a mock course description titled "Law and Me," spoofing the golden thread of narcissism that ravels through our pedagogy. As a student, though, I always welcomed engagements in which the professor was willing to risk transformation. So I teach a seminar to explore the relationship between assimilation and discrimination across race, sex, orientation, and religion.

I give my twelve students Liu's list. Julie, an Asian-American woman, says she is struck by the grammar of the sentences. She points out that each sentence begins with the word "I," that each takes Liu as its subject and not as its object, and that each is declarative and unhedged by qualifiers. This sense of agency, she continues, extends to content—"I am a member of several exclusive institutions," "I expect my voice to be heard." But then she notes this power comes at a price. She says these statements can be paired like contracts—"If you let me into 'the inner sanctums of political power,' I will not be 'too ethnic.'" "If you let me be a 'producer of the culture,' I will 'not mind how white television casts are.'" This, she says, is the deal—if you want to be central, assimilate to the white norm.

I ask the class what they think of this bargain. Jean, also an Asian-American woman, takes Liu to task for being a "banana," an Asian who is yellow on the outside but white on the inside. She thinks Liu is in denial, as she cannot imagine any self-respecting minority could remain untroubled by the whiteness of television. This comment engenders a murmur of disagreement. She retorts that we need not speculate about whether denial is occurring, as Liu says on the list that he has never been a victim of blatant discrimination, but says elsewhere in the book that he grew up being called "chink." She says it bothers her that he thinks any form of English could be "unaccented," and that she thinks of him as an Uncle Tom.

I look at Jean more closely. She has taken a class with me before, in which she said almost nothing, and turned in a perfect exam. What startles me is the passion in her voice. In this class, she will begin a paper, which will later be published. The paper argues that Asian-Americans occupy a kind of closet, in which attributes associated with our culture must be muted in the public sphere. Actors who have made it into the mainstream—such as Keanu Reeves or Dean Cain—closet their racial difference in their very bodies, downplaying their Asian ancestry. Other prominent Asian-Americans, like Liu, cabin their ethnicity in the private spaces of their homes. I read her paper as a primer on Asian covering, and I am startled at how closely it describes my own experience.

Like Robin Shahar, Jean kindles my conscience. I still find many items on Liu's list—the gourmet greens, the suede shoes, the expectation my voice will be heard—unproblematic. Others look more suspect when I revisit them. I realize I accept the whiteness of television casts in part because I dread how Asians will be portrayed if we are included. I also know the absence of Asians from these public portrayals means that Asians—like gays—will be less likely to see ourselves as the protagonists of our lives. I see my students have intuited my long and thoughtless history of not associating with other Asian-Americans—gay students seek me out far more than Asian ones do. I see that my pleasure when I am deemed a "credit to my race" always reinscribes the primacy of an actual or imagined white audience.

Later in the seminar, we read Paul Barrett's *The Good Black.* It breaks our hearts. Barrett, who is white, is a journalist for *The Wall Street Journal.* His subject is his African American law school roommate, Lawrence Mungin. The book describes how Mungin sought all his life to be the "good black," or the black who covered his race. Growing up in poverty in Queens, Mungin was told by his biracial mother: "You are a human being first, . . . an American second, a black third." She favored Martin Luther King Jr. over Malcolm X, punished Mungin for talking "street talk," and told him to "get past" his race. Mungin strove to do so—blazing through high school, Harvard College, and

Harvard Law School with a relentless covering strategy. He laughed along with racially laden comments, avoided African-American groups and the "soul tables" in the dining halls, and never spoke of his experiences with racism. When he arrived at law school, a delegation of the Black Law Students' Association visited Mungin to ask why he hadn't joined and why he was rooming with a white law student. Mungin answered that he was there to get a credential, not to become an activist.

After graduating from Harvard Law School, Mungin worked at three law firms before landing at Katten Muchin & Zavis. At Katten Muchin, Mungin continued to cover along all four axes. With respect to appearance, Barrett's book makes repeated reference to Mungin's sartorial style—he is described as the best-dressed man at the firm. While this might make Mungin seem a fop, Barrett shows that Mungin's attire directly affected perceptions of his race in the middle-class white circles in which he lived and worked. When wearing a suit, Mungin received friendly nods from his neighbors in the suburbs of Alexandria, Virginia. When dressed for the gym, he saw the same neighbors tense up and clutch their purses. Mungin also engaged in affiliation-based covering, stressing his double Harvard pedigree because it sent "another reassuring signal to whites," and speaking with a precision that led him to be described as "very articulate." He avoided anything that might smack of activism, responding to perceived racial slights with exceeding mildness. He also eschewed contact with other African-Americans in the firm and in the broader legal community. As Mungin stated his own credo: "I wanted to show that I was like white people: 'Don't be afraid. I'm one of the *good* blacks.' "

Mungin's relentless covering strategy, however, did not succeed. Isolated in the branch office in which he had chosen to work, Mungin gradually realized he had no chance of making partner. Believing his predicament to be a product of race discrimination, he sued under Title VII of the Civil Rights Act of 1964, a federal law that prohibits race-based employment discrimination. A mostly black jury awarded him $2.5 million, which a mostly white appellate panel reversed as unreasonable.

The tragedy of Mungin's story is not that he lost his lawsuit. After reading Barrett's book and the public documents in the case, I do not think Katten Muchin discriminated against him on the basis of race, by imposing covering demands or otherwise. The tragedy is that Katten Muchin had no occasion to make such covering demands, as Mungin came to the firm covering so assiduously, negating every possible stereotype about African-Americans in his behavior. That negation, of course, was no simple escape from his racial identity. In so carefully reversing every term of the racial stereotype, Mungin was defined by it as surely as a photograph is defined by its negative.

Yet it was only after Mungin left Katten Muchin that he was able to see the costs of this strategy:

> I was going to have to be more publicly honest about the lie I was living. It wasn't that I was around people who were open minded, who thought blacks are terrific. It's that I was bending over backward all the time to avoid making white people uncomfortable. Like my neighbors [in Alexandria]: Now I'm just tired of making them feel comfortable, I don't even talk to them. If they say hello, I'll say hello, but I don't even bother anymore making them feel comfortable late at night. It's too much work.

Sometimes covering comes in the mindless ways we hold ourselves or exchange pleasantries on a bus. At other times, covering is the exhausting burden that Mungin ultimately felt it to be. In either case, however, covering is work.

As I read *The Good Black,* I keep thinking back to Julie's notion of the contract. The book is about a social contract, in which racial minorities are told we will be rewarded for assimilating to white norms. In my view, Mungin sued not for the breach of his employment contract, but for the breach of this broader social contract. For this reason, I believe he should have lost his legal case, but that his challenge to the social contract deserves our sympathy and attention.

I have received the benefit of the social contract of racial covering. Like Liu, I have covered my race and moved to the center of American society. And like Liu, I understand this to be an advance over categorical exclusion: "Times have changed, and I suppose you could call it progress that a Chinaman, too, may now aspire to whiteness." Yet it is worth asking when we will live in a society where Americans will feel central without feeling white.

To measure how far we are from that society, I began to look at racial minorities who breached the social contract of assimilation—individuals who flaunted their racial identities rather than covering them. As in the orientation context, I found the consequences to be grim—an African-American woman was prohibited from wearing cornrows, a Latino was struck from a jury for acknowledging his *capacity* to speak Spanish, a Filipina nurse was barred from speaking Tagalog at work. I felt the old outrage, and looked to the law.

Because the federal Constitution and Title VII of the Civil Rights Act of 1964 both protect race much more robustly than orientation, I expected individuals to fare better against race-based covering demands. This proved overly optimistic. The courts have made the same distinction between being and doing in race cases that they have made in the orientation cases, protecting the immutable but not the mutable aspects of racial identity. A racial minority fired for her ancestry or skin color will win her suit in a hot second. But a racial minority fired for refusing to cover a cultural aspect of her racial identity will generally lose.

Rogers v. American Airlines—decided in 1981 and never overruled—demonstrates this dynamic. Rogers was an African-American woman who worked for American Airlines as an airport operations agent. This job fell under a grooming policy that prevented employees from wearing an all-braided hairstyle. On its face, the policy was race neutral and gender neutral, prohibiting individuals of all races and sexes from wearing all-braided hairstyles. Yet the policy disproportionately burdened African-American women, with whom cornrows are strongly associated. Rogers, who wore cornrows, challenged the policy under Title VII as race and gender discrimination. The district court opinion, which is the final disposition of this case, ruled for the airline on both claims. I focus on her race discrimination claim. Under Title VII, a plaintiff can prevail if an employer enacts a policy that disproportionately burdens racial, minorities and lacks a business justification. The *Rogers* court refused to acknowledge that the no-cornrows policy disproportionately burdened African-Americans. It pointed out that Rogers had not maintained "that an all-braided hair style is worn exclusively or even predominantly by black people." It further noted that the defendants had "alleged without contravention" that Rogers adopted her all- braided hairstyle only after it "had been popularized by a white actress in the film '10.' " We might call this the "Bo Derek" defense. This defense, of course, turns back on itself, because Bo Derek's cornrows were themselves an appropriation of an African-American style.

As if admitting its analysis fell short, the court provided a separate ground for its ruling. It found the cornrow style was not an immutable aspect of race. The court posited that an "Afro/bush" style might be protected under Title VTI "because banning a natural hairstyle would implicate the policies underlying the prohibition of discrimination on the basis of immutable characteristics." The court then maintained that "an all-braided hairstyle is a different matter," insofar as "[i]t is not the product of natural hair growth but of artifice." The court observed that "[a]n all-braided hairstyle is an 'easily changed characteristic,' and, even if socio-culturally associated with a particular race or nationality, is not an impermissible basis for distinctions."

Just as the *Shahar* court distinguished between Shahar's status as a gay person and her same-sex conduct, the *Rogers* court distinguished between Rogers's status as a racial minority and her race-related conduct. The court made clear that if Rogers had been discriminated against on the basis of immutable aspects of her racial identity, like her skin color or a "natural" Afro, she could have prevailed. It made equally clear that Rogers would not receive protection for the mutable aspects of her racial identity, such as cornrows. She was not protected from the demand to cover—to minimize the race-salient traits that distinguished her from the white mainstream.

I can't resist noting that "natural hairstyle" sounds like a contradiction, as the "natural" and the "styled" are generally understood as opposites. To remain purely "natural," the Afro would have had to remain uncut and untended—surely not the style the airline would tolerate or the court would protect. This odd moment in the court's opinion underscores its commitment to the axiom that only immutable traits should be protected. Seized with the desire to protect Afros, the court reclassified that hairstyle as "natural" or "immutable," showing we can gauge the depth of our commitments by how much absurdity we will risk in defending them.

This analysis may not seem shocking for the reason the court gave—hair may seem such a trivial thing. But if hair is trivial, we might ask why American made it grounds for termination. In reading the *Rogers* case, one can hear American Airlines and the court asking Rogers: "Why is this so important to you?" To which Rogers would respond: "Why is this so important to *you*?" It is worth lingering with both questions.

So far as the opinion shows, Rogers gave only a short answer to why wearing cornrows was important to her—she contended that the cornrow style "has been and continues to be part of the cultural and historical essence of Black American women." That answer has been elaborated in an essay on the *Rogers* case written by law professor Paulette Caldwell, herself an African-American woman. Caldwell describes the different reactions she elicits depending on how she wears her hair. When her hair is long and straightened, she is complimented for her "competence, unusual insights, and mastery of subject matter." When she wears an Afro, she is told she looks like a "teenager." When she wears cornrows, she receives questions about the case in which an African-American woman was prohibited from wearing cornrows—namely *Rogers*. Caldwell concludes from these experiences that her hair is a site of racial self-expression, and that "good" hair for African-Americans is "white" hair because "the public equates progress for black women with the imitation of white women." She notes that virtually all novels and autobiographical works by black women writers treat discrimination on the basis of hair, citing instances from Maya Angelou, Gwendolyn Brooks, Alice Walker, and Toni Morrison.

Caldwell's essay shows that a hairstyle can be transformed from a neutral grooming preference into a site of racial contest. Rogers may have been initially indifferent to her hairstyle, as the court suggests through the Bo Derek comment. But that does not weaken her right to resist the airline's demand that she cover it. I have no desire to put a pink triangle button on my bulletin board at work. But it would be perfectly logical for me to fight for such a pin if my dean asked me to take it down. The button would then be freighted with social meanings it did not have before.

To think about what those social meanings might be, we can now ask why it was so important to American that Rogers not wear cornrows, even to the point of suggesting she literally cover them with a hairpiece. As litigation does not provide incentives for employers to be forthright, I looked to grooming manuals written for corporate employees. Republished in 1988, John T. Molloy's perennially popular *New Dress for Success* contains some frank styling advice for racial minorities: "Blacks selling to whites should not wear Afro hair styles." Molloy also tells African-Americans to "wear conservative pinstripe suits, preferably with vests, accompanied by all the establishment symbols, including the Ivy League tie." Similarly, he tells Hispanics to "avoid pencil-line mustaches" and "any hair tonic that tends to give a greasy or shiny look to the hair." He advises them to eschew "any articles of clothing that have Hispanic associations, and anything that is very sharp or precise."

Molloy explains why racial minorities should engage in such appearance-based covering:

> It is an undeniable fact that the typical upper-middle class American looks white, Anglo-Saxon and Protestant. He is of medium build, fair complexion, with almost no pronounced physical characteristics. He is the model of success; that is, if you run a test, most people of all socioeconomic racial and ethnic backgrounds will identify him as such. Like it or not, his appearance will normally elicit a positive response from someone viewing him. Anyone not possessing his characteristics will elicit a negative response to some degree, regardless of whether that response is conscious or subconscious.

Success, it seems, is white and bland. Molloy describes the continuing vitality of white supremacy in American culture, a supremacy that requires racial minorities to bend behavior toward Anglo-conformity. Indeed, Molloy says racial minorities must go "somewhat overboard" to compensate for immutable differences from the white mainstream. After conducting research on African- American corporate grooming, Molloy reports that "blacks had not only to dress more conservatively, but also more expensively than their white counterparts if they wanted to have an equal impact."

Molloy's statement—that racial covering soothes fears of racial difference—is historically well supported. If we travel back to more racist times, we see racial minorities escaping discrimination through covering. Law professor Ariela Gross describes how "acting white" could save a black from a life of slavery in the antebellum South. In so-called race-determination trials, individuals who would have been classified as black under a "one-drop-of-black- blood" rule were often deemed white by judges and juries so long as they behaved in ways associated with whiteness: "Doing the things a white man or woman did became the law's working definition of what it meant to be white." Some of the conduct the courts found salient has a chilling contemporary resonance—individuals were deemed white for their association with and acceptance by whites, for the gentility of their demeanor, and for the straightness of their hair. For these individuals seeking to escape slavery, no less than for Mungin or Rogers, covering was rewarded.

We cannot assume American wanted Rogers to cover in the name of white supremacy. We would need to ask American for the reason behind its covering demand, and to evaluate the credibility of its answer. What's frustrating about the *Rogers* opinion, and what's flawed about the Title VII jurisprudence generally, is that it does not force American to answer that question. Instead, the court only looked at Rogers's capacity to conform. Once the court determined she could assimilate, it assumed she should do so, without regard to the legitimacy of the demand for assimilation.

A reader attentive to dates could fairly ask if I am making too much of a case decided in 1981 and a grooming manual written in 1988. Today, it may seem racial covering demands are no longer made. Black style, Asian cuisine, and Latin music are all staples of American culture. If the application essays to Yale Law School are any indication, applicants feel pressure to flaunt rather than to cover their ethnic diversity. Such pressure to "reverse cover" may be problematic in its own right. But pressure to "act white" may seem a thing of the past.

As in the gay context, however, we should not confuse selective appropriation of minority cultures with general acceptance. The fact that cases like *Rogers* are still on the books means employers can still make such demands for racial assimilation with impunity. And they do: the Molloy book came to my attention because an employee sued his employer in 2003 for assigning the manual to him. Social science data also show that racial minorities perceived to be Haunters continue to encounter discrimination. Economics professors Marianne Bertrand and Sendhil Mullainathan conducted a study in 2002 in which they sent out résumés that were identical except for the names at the top. Half the names were distinctly "white-sounding" names like Emily Walsh or Greg Baker, while the other half were distinctly "African-American-sounding" names like Lakisha Washington or Jamal Jones. The "white" résumés received 50 percent more callbacks from employers than the "African-American" ones. It may be that employers were discriminating against all supposed African-Americans rather than only African-

Americans who flaunted. But this just means passing and covering blur into each other here as well.

This bias toward assimilation also surfaces in Title VII claims based on language. An increasing number of employers have English-only rules that require employees to speak English in the workplace. These policies have been challenged as discrimination on the basis of national origin. Predictably, monolinguals sometimes win their cases, while bilinguals almost invariably lose. As one court put it, "To a person who speaks only one tongue . . . language might well be an immutable characteristic like skin color, sex or place of birth. However, the language a person who is multilingual elects to speak at a particular time is by definition a matter of choice." Because bilingual employees can choose to speak English, they must.

When I teach these language cases, my students generally feel the stakes are higher on both sides than in the grooming cases.

Language is widely recognized as an important aspect of ethnic identity. As sociolinguist Joshua Fishman observes, "since language is the prime symbol system to begin with and since it is commonly relied upon . . . to enact, celebrate and 'call forth' all ethnic activity, the likelihood that it will be recognized and singled out as symbolic of ethnicity is great indeed." From the employer's perspective, however, the reasons to force employees to speak English—such as promoting better service to customers or workplace harmony—also seem plausible.

Again, I am not saying employees should always win these cases. The ultimate determination should balance the interests of the individual against the interests of the employer. Frequently, however, the courts scrutinize only the employee, asking whether the burdened trait is mutable. An affirmative answer often formally or practically ends the inquiry. But stopping there transforms the descriptive claim that the employee *can* assimilate into the normative claim that she *must,* without any exploration of why the employer is demanding assimilation.

When the employer's reasons are examined, they often fall short. In 1988, a federal appellate court considered a challenge to an English-only workplace rule enacted by a state court in Los Angeles. The defendants justified the provision by observing that the employees' use of Spanish threatened to transform the workplace into a Tower of Babel. Yet when the court examined the facts, it found the employees' capacity to speak Spanish was essential in serving non-English-speaking clients. Far from being a liability, the employees' bilingualism was an asset—an unsurprising revelation given that bilingualism is not a lack of knowledge (such as the inability to speak English) but a surfeit of knowledge. English-only statutes punish individuals not for knowing too little, but for knowing too much.

Dissenting from the court's decision denying a rehearing of that case, federal judge Alex Kozinski supported the English-only rule by observing that the United States has been able to avoid the controversies that language difference has evoked in countries such as Canada because, as "[a] nation of immigrants, we have been willing to embrace English as our public language, preserving native tongues and dialects for private and family occasions." This vision goes far beyond requiring that people be able to speak English. It forbids people to speak any language *but* English in the public sphere, requiring us to closet our difference in the ethnic enclave or the family.

When not justified by a reason that stands up to close contextual scrutiny, that ethic unnecessarily pushes national origin minorities into second-class citizenship. It prevents our lives and our culture from making a mark on the common semantic stock. When that cost is considered, Canada starts to look less like a cautionary landscape and more like a Utopian one. Where the United States has embraced the metaphor of the melting pot of assimilation, Canada has espoused the countermetaphor of the mosaic of persisting diversity. It may be time to mix those metaphors.

First performed in 1908, Israel Zangwill's *The Melting Pot* follows the fortunes of David Quixano, a Russian Jewish immigrant who lives in penury as a musician and composer in New York with his uncle and his grandmother. The three generations play out the usual pattern of assimilation. The grandmother speaks little English, and weeps over how her son and grandson must break the Sabbath to earn their livings. Fluent in English, David's uncle Mendel navigates American culture more adroitly, but still turns on David when David declares his love for a gentile, Vera Revendal. A "*pogrom* orphan" whose parents were killed by an anti-Semitic mob, David is a poster child for assimilation. He aspires to compose an "American symphony," inspired by the idea that "America is God's Crucible, the great Melting-Pot where all the races of Europe are melting and re-forming."

This vision leads Vera, also an immigrant from Russia, to overcome her anti-Semitism, and the couple gets engaged. Then David's own commitment to relinquishing old "blood hatreds and rivalries" is tested when he learns the massacre of his parents in Russia was superintended by Vera's father. Traumatized, David breaks off the engagement. The couple, however, is reunited at the first performance of his American symphony. Sitting on a roof garden, they look at a sunset, which David likens to "the fires of God round His Crucible." The play ends with David's paean to the "great Melting-Pot" that will absorb "Celt and Latin, Slav and Teuton, Greek and Syrian, black and yellow" so that. "the great Alchemist" can "melt[ ] and fuse[ ] them with his purging flame."

The Melting Pot is overwrought—it is no accident the title has had a longer run than the play. Yet when I first read it in college, my sympathy for its ideals checked my critical faculties. My reaction was akin to that of Theodore Roosevelt, who allegedly called out, "That's a great play," from his box when it was performed in Washington, D.C., and to whom the published version is dedicated. I shared Roosevelt's vision of a nation peopled by citizens who would cut their ethnic ties—an "America for Americans" in which the hyphenation of identity was a "moral treason." This, after all, was the ideal I had absorbed at home—Roosevelt, too, spoke of the "one hundred percent American." Even now, I am moved by the American ethic of inclusion, which contrasts so sharply with the Japanese ethic of exclusion. I question only the price of admission.

The Melting Pot captures a great sociological truth about assimilation—that older generations cannot assimilate and that younger generations cannot help *but* assimilate. I can read the three generations of Zangwill's play against my own family history—my grandparents, who died Japanese; my parents, who toggle between the two countries; and I, who am now inexorably American. And yet one of the reasons I cannot embrace Zangwill's play is that the fit is not entirely true.

I think of my name, which is more Japanese than my father's American name. When my father came to the States, no one could pronounce his first name. So he asked a friend to rechristen him. He has used his "American" name for his entire professional career. If Zangwill's narrative of the melting pot were truly my own, my parents should have given me an American name—the Mendels of his generation should have ceded to the Davids of mine. Yet they did not.

Even as a child, I found this curious, especially given that there were names that worked in both languages—Ken and Dan and Eugene for boys, Naomi and Amy and Kay for girls—that odd concatenation of Jewish and Irish lexicons. If my parents had truly wanted me to be "one hundred percent American in America, one hundred percent Japanese in Japan," they could have chosen one of these names.

For many years, I felt my name misrepresented me. The character for *Ken* is that for "health," the character for *ji* means "leadership." Neither noun seemed to describe the quiet child I was. Yet now I see my parents encoded a wish in my name—a wish that I could live in an America that would not force me to surrender my ethnicity. They must have intuited that people with white-sounding names fare better than individuals with ethnic ones. But they flaunted a little, on my behalf.

Points of Engagement—Reading Comprehension

1. Yoshino claims that "perceptions of one's race do not rest on biology alone" (300). Look at the quote in context. What else determines one's race? Cite two examples from Yoshino's text that support your answer. How do your selections complicate what an identity means in a social and cultural context?
2. Yoshino and his sister spent two months of every year when they were growing up in Japan. Describe the differences between Kenji's experiences in Japan and his sister's. Why are these differences important to Yoshino? What do they mean to him in terms of identity?
3. In Yoshino's essay, what is *The Melting Pot*? Why is it significant for him? How has the metaphor of the "melting pot" changed for him over time? Be specific.
4. Consider the following quote: "Be one hundred percent American in America, and one hundred percent Japanese in Japan" (300). Who says this? What does it mean? Why is it so important? What are the consequences for it in Yoshino's family and life growing up?
5. What do the Japanese words "konketsuji" and "haafu" mean? Look on page 298 for an answer. Why are these troubling words for Yoshino growing up? What did they say about his connection to the Japanese culture of his parents?
6. Yoshino observes that racist beliefs in one country have what he calls "their mirror image in the other" (303). Look at this quotation in context. How does this observation suggest that "covering" is not a unique response to American culture, but rather a universal trait that humans engage in? What might account for this reaction? Is the need for "agency" something inherent in all cultures? Why?
7. At the end of his essay, Yoshino looks at names and how they convey a type of representation about a person. Look at the names he discusses, and also his own name. What do these names convey in terms of an identity? How might a name become an act of "covering?"
8. Yoshino is a law professor. Choose one case that he discusses and explain why it is important.

Points of Departure—Assignment Questions

1. *Social Contract.* Yoshino introduces the idea of a "social contract" in which members of a society make a deal: "if you want to be central, assimilate to the white norm." He is cynical about the possibility of success for "individuals who flaunted their racial

identities rather than covering them" (308). The stories of Amy Chua, Gregory Orr, and Zadie Smith—in all their complexity—appear to challenge Yoshino's cynicism. For this paper, I want you to sort out the decisions that these authors have made in managing their racial identities in the contexts they describe in their essays. How did they see their social contract? Did they flaunt their racial identities? Did they cover? When and why? Your paper should begin with a specific claim, which you will then support with examples, about what kind of "social contract" these individuals signed on to, whether they kept their end of the deal or whether they breached it, and finally, what they gained and lost from their decisions.

2. *Emancipation.* "What interests me about my story, and the stories of others, is how similar they are in revealing the bones of our common human endeavor, the yearning for human emancipation that stirs within us all" (Yoshino 296). Many essays in this reader describe people who are caught between circumstances that confine them and the idea of freedom. What is holding them back? What ultimately emancipates them? Write a paper focusing on Yoshino and either Goodall, Kristof and WuDunn, Slater, or Winterson. Think about the longings described in these texts, the struggles towards emancipation, and the outcomes. Note the differences in circumstance. Look for experiential connections between Yoshino and the people identified the essay you've chosen. What does "emancipation" look like?
3. *Success and Conformity.* According to Yoshino, "Success, it seems, is white and bland" (311). To what extent does success in life require conformity? To what extent does success require resistance? Using the stories told by Zadie Smith, James Fallows and Amy Chua, propose your own answers to these questions. Choose two or three specific examples in each of these essays that enrich your understanding of the balance between conformity and resistance in the pursuit of success. Examples might include the story of Lawrence Mungin in Yoshino, Barack Obama in Smith, a contestant on *Win in China*, Chua's struggles with Lulu, or many others in each of these texts.
4. *What's in a name?* In Yoshino's essay, there is a naming process that he explores in his examination on identity. We have our personal name, and then the name/s that we give to the group/s we belong to in society. How we name ourselves often becomes relative to what we name ourselves and why. Just as important is why we name others. Yoshino calls himself "Asian-American," Zadie Smith is a "lettered person," Eck is a "Christian lesbian," Chua, a "Chinese mother." Clearly, each of them is more than this name, but they fix on the name to describe a core part of themselves. For this essay, using Yoshino and one other author cited above, explore

how understanding the use of naming becomes a way to "uncover" what happens when one attempts to "cover" an identity. What truths are revealed in naming? In hiding our names? How do the choices of naming by Yoshino and in the other essay you've chosen complicate what it means for one to claim an identity in society? Is "naming" ourselves a way to cover or uncover who we are?

5. *Authenticity and Assimilation.* For Yoshino, the act of "covering" is basically a struggle between authenticity and assimilation. But is this really an either/or proposition? Is it possible to pursue an authentic self and to assimilate to the surrounding culture? Why or why not? When does a performance of identity become identity itself? What is gained or lost in the process? In writing this paper, think about the roles of behavior, biology, culture, and, most importantly, choice, in shaping who we are. Use essays by Yoshino, Blackmore, Chua, Adam Gopnik, Eck, Smith, or Turkle.
6. *Diversity and Assimilation.* Diana Eck describes America as the most religiously diverse nation on earth. We are also a diverse nation of people ethnically, culturally, racially, economically, educationally, and much more. What does all of this diversity say about Yoshino's argument that "everyone covers"? Can it really be true that we are all assimilating with so much difference represented everywhere? Does Diana Eck's goal of super-pluralism demand the kind of assimilation that Yoshino critiques, or is it the first step towards Yoshino's goal of a "new civil rights paradigm"? Think about the challenges that pluralism and diversity bring to Yoshino's argument, and write a paper in which you carve your own position in relation to both author's arguments regarding diversity and assimilation.

Contributors

Since 1995 **Lisa Belkin** has been a contributing writer, specializing in medical and social issues, for *The New York Times Magazine,* where "The Made-to-Order Savior" first appeared in 2001. Her books include *First Do No Harm,* about a hospital's ethics committee, *Show Me A Hero,* about the impact of desegregation, and *Life's Work: Confessions of an Unbalanced Mom.* She currently covers parenting and family for the *New York Times* through her blog and monthly column, "Motherlode." She lives in Westchester County, New York.

Wendell Berry is a prolific American philosopher, activist, poet, novelist, and essayist. His predominant vocation, however, is as a fifth generation farmer in Kentucky. A life-long Christian Baptist and environmental activist, Berry is known as a "man of place" whose spirituality and environmental consciousness are mutually informing. He is a former professor of English at the University of Kentucky, a past fellow of the Guggenheim Foundation and the Rockefeller Foundation, and an elected member of the Fellowship of Southern Writers. He contributes to many important journals and magazines including *Harper's, The Atlantic, Shenandoah,* and *The Sewanee Review* in which "God, Science, and Imagination" appeared in 2010. Berry is actually the author of the famous claim that we do not inherit the earth from our fathers but rather borrow it from our children, even though the quote is often misattributed to John James Audubon. Berry lives and works with his wife, Tanya Berry, on their farm in Port Royal, Kentucky. http://www.wendellberrybooks.com/

Susan Blackmore's *The Meme Machine* has been translated into 15 languages. Dr. Blackmore is a psychologist and writer researching consciousness, memes, and anomalous experiences, and a Visiting Professor at the University of Plymouth. She blogs for the *Guardian* and *Psychology Today,* and often appears on radio and television. Her most recent books include *Conversations on Consciousness* (2005), *Ten Zen Questions* (2009), and a textbook *Consciousness: An Introduction* (new edition 2010). http://www.susanblackmore.co.uk

Ian Bremmer is an American political scientist and the founder and president of Eurasia Group, a firm providing corporate and government clients with research and consulting on how political developments will affect markets. He is a leading expert on global political risk, and the economic threats faced by businesses, individuals, and governments due to non-economic political events. The author of a number of books, including *The End of the Free Market: Who Wins the War Between States and Corporations,* he is a contributor to the *Wall Street Journal, Foreign Affairs,* the *New York Times,* and other publications. He currently teaches at Columbia University.

Amy Chua is a law professor at Yale Law School. She has taught at Duke Law School and worked previously as an attorney in corporate law specializing in international transactions. Her first two books, *World on Fire: How Exporting Free Market Democracy Breeds Ethnic Hatred and Global Instability* (2003) and *Day of Empire: How Hyperpowers Rise to Global Dominance – and Why They* Fall (2007), examine global economic, cultural, and political struggles, both within and between countries. Her third book, *Battle Hymn of the Tiger Mother* (2011), is a memoir of her experience raising two daughters in the U.S. as a Chinese-American. The book became a national media phenomenon after the excerpt reprinted in this reader first appeared in the *Wall Street Journal* and prompted considerable public debate on different parenting styles.

Alain de Botton's work has been described as "philosophy of everyday life." In *The Art of Travel,* from which "On Habit" is selected, he explores the psychology of travel. de Botton's other books include O*n Love, How Proust Can Change your Life, The Consolations of Philosophy, Status Anxiety, The Architecture of Happiness,* and *The Pleasures and Sorrows of Work.* His books have been bestsellers in 30 countries. He lives in London where he is founder and chairman of *The School of Life,* an educational enterprise dedicated to a new vision for living and learning. http://www.alaindebotton.com/

Diana Eck, currently professor of Religion and Indian Studies at Harvard, founded the Pluralism Project in 1991 to study the new face of faith in modern urban American communities. She has authored several books on Hinduism and *A New Religious America: How a "Christian Country" Became the World's Most Diverse Nation* (2001) from which this selection is excerpted. She has served on the US State Department's Advisory Center for Religious Freedom Abroad (1996) and was awarded a National Endowment for the Humanities grant by President Clinton for her work on religious pluralism (1998). Eck identifies herself a "pluralist Methodist." She and her wife, The Reverent Dorothy Austin, are the first same sex couple to serve as co-masters of Harvard's Lowell House.

James Fallows is an American journalist and national correspondent for *The Atlantic Monthly,* and his work has appeared in numerous periodicals. He was Jimmy Carter's chief White House speechwriter for two years, he has been an editor at *U.S. News & World Report* and a software designer for Microsoft, and he has been a frequent contributor to National Public Radio. He is best known for his writings on politics, the military, Asia, and technology. A five-time finalist for the National Magazine Award and one-time winner in 2003, he also received the National Book Award for non-fiction in 1983. The essay in this reader, "Win in China!," first appeared in *The Atlantic Monthly* and was republished in Fallows' most recent book, *Postcards from Tomorrow Square: Reports from China* (2009).

Janet A. Flammang is a professor and chair of political science at Santa Clara University where she teaches courses in U.S. politics with an emphasis on women and politics. Her current research explores the relationship between meals, conversation, community and democracy, and is the subject of her most recent book, *The Taste for Civilization: Food, Politics, and Civil Society*, the Introduction of which appears in this reader. She is also author of *Women's Political Voice: How Women Are Transforming the Practice and Study of Politics*. Flammang has been a member of the Committee on the Status of Women in both the American Political Science Association and the Western Political Science Association. She has received a Phi Beta Kappa award for teaching excellence.

A staff writer for *The New Yorker* since 1996, **Malcolm Gladwell** is author of three number one *New York Times* bestsellers: *The Tipping Point: How Little Things Can Make a Big Difference* (2000), *Blink: The Power of Thinking without Thinking* (2005), *Outliers: The Story of Success* (2008). His most recent book *What the Dog Saw*, is a compilation of stories published in *The New Yorker*, where the essay in this reader, "Small Change: Why the Revolution Will Not Be Tweeted" also appeared. Malcolm Gladwell was born in England, grew up in Canada, and now lives in New York City.

Jane Goodall is in her fifth decade of studying and researching primate behavior in Gombe. She founded the Gombe Stream Research Center in Tanzania and the Jane Goodall Institute for Wildlife Research and Conservation in Silver Spring, MD. Her books include *In the Shadow of Man*, *Reason for Hope*, and two volumes of autobiographical letters. The essay in this reader first appeared in *Orion Magazine* which is devoted to creating a stronger bond between humans and nature. As an ambassador for conservation, Goodall travels the world more than 300 days a year, speaking with students, government officials, holding public lectures and giving interviews. According to the website for the Jane Goodall Institute, http://www.janegoodall.org/, she returns to Gombe at least two times a year to "'recharge her batteries' and see what her now-famous chimpanzees are up to."

A contributing writer to *The New Yorker* since 1986, **Adam Gopnik**'s writing has won the National Magazine Award for Essay and for Criticism and the George Polk Award for Magazine Reporting. He is also frequently broadcast by the Canadian Broadcasting Corporation. His book *Paris to the Moon* chronicles his family's life in Paris from 1995-2000. His most recent book, *Angels and Ages: A Short Book about Darwin, Lincoln, and Modern Life*, looks at the birth of the modern era through these two historical figures born within hours of one another 200 years ago. Despite his sister's advice in "Bumping Into Mr. Ravioli," Adam Gopnik currently lives in New York City with his family.

Alison Gopnik is a developmental psychologist whose research focuses on how babies learn how things happen – what causes what, and how. She holds the positions of Professor of Psychology and affiliate Professor of Philosophy at the University of California-Berkeley. During her interview on the Colbert Report, Gopnik stated that one of the agendas of her current research program – figuring out how babies understand how they and others think – is to put the "make my baby smarter" industry out of business: babies, she says, are already as smart as they're going to be, and all they need to do is play. Watch out, Baby Einstein.

Arlie Russell Hochschild is professor of Sociology at the University of California, Berkeley. The essay in this reader, "From the Frying Pan Into the Fire," is a chapter from her most recent book, *The Commercialization of Intimate Life: Notes from Home and Work*, which explores work, family life, the changing roles of men and women, and how our every day lives are shaped by modern capitalism. She is also the author of *The Managed Heart* and *The Time Bind*. Her work has appeared in *Harper's*, *Mother Jones*, and *Psychology Today*. She lives in San Francisco with her husband, Adam Hochschild, and their two kids.

Naomi Klein is a Canadian author and activist whose work is known for its trenchant criticism of globalization and capitalism. Her recent and best known book *The Shock Doctrine* (2007) examines the role of capitalism and free-market ideology in geopolitical crises as disparate as the Iraq War and the aftermath of Hurricane Katrina. This reader contains an excerpt from the Preface to her second book, *Fences and Windows: Dispatches from the Front Lines of the Globalization Debate* (2002). She is a frequent contributor to *Harper's Magazine, Rolling Stone, The Nation*, the *New York Times*, and many other periodicals. She wrote and co-produced with her husband Avi Lewis the film *The Take* (2004), a documentary about a worker takeover of an automobile manufacturing plant in Argentina which was awarded Best Documentary Jury Prize at the American Film Institute's Los Angeles Film Festival.

Nicholas D. Kristof is an author and Op-Ed columnist at the *New York Times*. **Sheryl WuDunn** is a banker who formerly reported on the global economy, and global industry for the *Times*. These co-authors of *Half The Sky* won a Pulitzer Prize together for their coverage of China, and continue to write about that country, and about human rights issues. They are also co-founders of the *Half The Sky* movement, a global project dedicated to changing the status of women globally by empowering them economically. Kristof and WuDunn live in Scarsdale, NY with their three children.

Gregory Orr is an American poet, author of ten volumes of poetry in addition to essays and a personal memoir. He was born in Albany, New York and earned his MFA from Columbia University. Since 1975, he has taught creative writing at the University of Virginia and has been poetry editor of the *Virginia Quarterly Review,* the journal in which "Return to Hayneville" first appeared in 2008. Orr's short lyric poems as well as his prose often examine pivotal moments in life, most notably the harrowing experience in the Civil Rights struggle retold here as well as the day when he was twelve years old and accidentally shot and killed his brother. Orr said in an interview with National Public Radio, "I believe in poetry as a way of surviving the emotional chaos, spiritual confusions, and traumatic events that come with being alive" (poetryfoundation.org/bio/gregory-orr).

Lauren Slater is a psychologist and author of six books whose work has been included in the *Best American Essays (*1994, 1997). She was Guest Editor of the *Best American Essays* series in 2006. She is a frequent contributor to periodicals from *The New York Times* to *Elle* to *Mother Jones,* where "Who Holds the Clicker" was first published. According to her website, http://laurenslater.com, "She often writes about psychology, mental illness and women's health." Her creative fiction has earned her many awards including the New Letters Literary Award and the Missouri Review Award. Slater lives and works in Massachusetts.

Zadie Smith is a novelist, short story writer, and essayist. She was born in a working class neighborhood north of London to a British father and a Jamaican mother and found her way to Cambridge University where she finished her first novel, the highly acclaimed *White Teeth,* during her senior year. Her second novel, *The Autograph Man,* appeared in 2002 when Smith was a fellow at Harvard University. She then moved on to teach at Columbia and since September of 2010, she has been professor of fiction at NYU. Her third novel, *On Beauty,* appeared in 2005. Her recurrent themes are global ethnic mythologies and the politics of race and gender. She has received many prestigious awards including the Whitbread, the Orange, and the shortlist for the Man Booker. She frequently contributes to *The Guardian, The New Republic, The New Yorker,* and the *New York Review of Books* in which "Speaking in Tongues" was published in 2009.

Sherry Turkle writes about the psychology of how we relate to technology. A professor of Social Studies of Science and Technology at the Massachusetts Institute of Technology and founder and director of its Initiative on Technology and the Self, she is known for her series of books on how what we do with computers and other digital technologies shapes us and the way we view and interact with the world and each other, what she describes as the "subjective side" of technology. Her books include *The Second Self; Computers and the Human Spirit* (1984), *Life on the Screen: Identity and the Age of the Internet* (1995), *Simulation and Its Discontents* (2009), and *Alone Together: Why We Expect More from Technology and Less from Each Other* (2011). She is a frequent contributor in broadcast and in print media on the social and psychological dimensions of technology, and she is also a licensed clinical psychologist.

Growing up in the North of England with Pentecostal parents who wanted her to be a missionary, **Jeanette Winterson** came to attention in the British literary world in 1985 with her first novel *Oranges Are Not The Only Fruit*. Winterson is perhaps best known for her novels, but also has written in various other modes, including the anthology of short stories to which the essay in this collection, "The World And Other Places," gives its name. She is a regular contributor to several major English newspapers, and continues to write novels, the most recent of which is *The Stone Gods*. She has received international recognition for her fiction and adaptations, including the Whitbread Prize and the Prix d'argent. Winterson now divides her time between Gloucestershire and London, with excursions to Paris.

Kenji Yoshino is a professor of constitutional law at NYU School of Law. He was educated at Harvard, Oxford, and Yale and taught at Yale Law School from 1998 to 2008, where he also served for one year as Deputy Dean. His fields are constitutional law, anti-discrimination law, and law and literature. The pieces in this reader are excerpted from Yoshino's first book, *Covering: The Hidden Assault on Our Civil Rights*. His second book is called *A Thousand Times More Fair: What Shakespeare's Plays Teach Us About Justice*. He is currently at work on a third book about the shift from group-based civil rights to universal human rights in the U.S. Supreme Court's jurisprudence. Yoshino has published in major academic journals, and has also written for more popular forums, including *The Los Angeles Times*, *The New York Times*, and *The Washington Post*. He makes regular appearances on various radio and television programs, such as NPR's *The Takeaway* and PBS's *Charlie Rose*. http://www.kenjiyoshino.com

Michelle J. Brazier is an English Department faculty member at Raritan Valley Community College in New Jersey where she teaches literature and composition. Dr. Brazier completed her Ph.D. in English at Rutgers University, and her B.A. at Yale University where she studied English and music. Her research interests include the writings of Gertrude Stein, the history of women's education and composition studies in the U.S., and Basic Writing. Prior to joining the faculty at Raritan Valley, Dr. Brazier served as Executive Assistant to the Vice President for Undergraduate Education at Rutgers. *Points of Departure* was conceived during her five years as an Assistant Director in the Rutgers Writing Program.

How might Sherry Turkley

concept of "autnetay" help

explane problems raised by

Zadie Smith, and how might

Smith's argunet problematiz

the conecept of an "autentic" self?

Accorang to Jay-z and anoTr actro

listed above, to what extnt are

we limited, structurell, and/or freed

by expnace.